Working Life and Gender Inequality

CW01496832

In the modern globalized world of work, society's capitalist and patriarchal norms perpetuate old and create new differences based on gender, class, ethnicity, age, and other social categorizations.

This book proposes a novel conceptual framework offering theoretical and methodological insights for thinking through the present and future inequality challenges in the globalized world of work and working life issues in the context of spatio-temporal relations. Bringing together global feminist studies of intersectionality and transnationalism, work-life research, and studies of space, place, and identity, this edited collection responds to the growing interest in peripheries, rurality, and other spaces beyond the urban and business market centres. In crossing the theoretical boundaries between intersectionality and peripherality, this volume brings these concepts together to identify how racism, capitalism and heteropatriarchy operate on bodies in the name of work, particularly as expressed in precarious labour conditions. It also advocates for transnational solidarity as part of feminist ethics, while providing an opportunity to reflect on ways forward for feminist intersectional studies of work and working life, drawing on embodied relationality and a feminist ethics of care.

Working Life and Gender Inequality explores the intersectional nature of gender, class, race and other inequalities from a global and spatial perspective. It will be of value to researchers, academics, students, managers, consultants, and policy makers in the fields of organizational studies, leadership, feminist and gender studies, working life, intersectionality and transnational feminism.

Angelika Sjöstedt is Associate Professor in Gender Studies at Mid Sweden University, Sweden.

Katarina Giritli Nygren is Professor of Sociology and Director of the Forum for Gender Studies at Mid Sweden University, Sweden.

Marianna Fotaki is Professor of business ethics at the University of Warwick Business School, United Kingdom.

Routledge Studies in Gender and Organizations
Series Editor: Elisabeth K. Kelan

Although still a fairly young field, the study of gender and organizations is increasingly popular and relevant. There are few areas of academic research that are as vibrant and dynamic as the study of gender and organizations. While much earlier research has focused on documenting the imbalances of women and men in organizations, more recently, research on gender and organizations has departed from counting men and women. Instead research in this area sees gender as a process: something that is done rather than something that people are. This perspective is important and meaningful as it takes researchers away from essentialist notions of gender and opens the possibility of analysing the process of how individuals become women and men. This is called 'gendering', 'practising gender', 'doing gender' or 'performing gender' and draws on rich philosophical traditions.

Whilst Routledge Studies in Gender and Organizations has a broad remit, it will be thematically and theoretically committed to exploring gender and organizations from a constructivist perspective. Rather than focusing on specific areas of organizations, the series is to be kept deliberately broad to showcase the most innovative research in this field. It is anticipated that the books in this series will make a theoretical contribution to the field of gender and organization based on rigorous empirical explorations.

Working Life and Gender Inequality

Intersectional Perspectives and the Spatial Practices of Peripheralization

Angelika Sjöstedt, Katarina Giritli Nygren, and Marianna Fotaki

LONDON AND NEW YORK

First published 2021
by Routledge
52 Vanderbilt Avenue, New York, NY 10017

and by Routledge
2 Park Square, Milton Park, Abingdon, Oxon, OX14 4RN

Routledge is an imprint of the Taylor & Francis Group, an informa business

Library of Congress Cataloging-in-Publication Data
Names: Sjöstedt, Angelika, 1979- editor. | Giritli Nygren, Katarina, 1971- editor. | Fotaki, Marianna, editor.
Title: Working life and gender inequality : intersectional perspectives and the spatial practices of peripheralization / edited by Angelika Sjöstedt, Katarina Giritli Nygren and Marianna Fotaki.
Description: New York, NY : Routledge, 2021. | Series: Routledge studies in gender and organizations ; 7 | Includes bibliographical references and index.
Identifiers: LCCN 2020046097 (print) | LCCN 2020046098 (ebook) | ISBN 9780367370176 (hardback) | ISBN 9780429356629 (ebook)
Subjects: LCSH: Sex discrimination in employment--Cross-cultural studies. | Sex role in the work environment--Cross-cultural studies. | Quality of work life--Cross-cultural studies. | Pay equity--Cross-cultural studies. | Labor and globalization. | Feminist ethics. | Intersectionality (Sociology) | Transnationalism.
Classification: LCC HD6060 .W67 2021 (print) | LCC HD6060 (ebook) | DDC 331.4/133--dc23
LC record available at https://lccn.loc.gov/2020046097
LC ebook record available at https://lccn.loc.gov/2020046098

ISBN: 978-0-367-37017-6 (hbk)
ISBN: 978-0-367-74746-6 (pbk)
ISBN: 978-0-429-35662-9 (ebk)

Typeset in Sabon
by MPS Limited, Dehradun

Contents

1 Intersectionality and Peripheralization

Introduction to the Edited Collection

Angelika Sjöstedt, Katarina Giritli Nygren, and Marianna Fotaki

The idea of this book emerged from a workshop held at Mid Sweden University in October 2016, where gender and feminist scholars from different parts of the country gathered together with the editors to debate inequalities through the prism of intersectionality. While the discussions during the workshop were concerned mainly with geographical inequalities in Sweden, most of the presentations referred to work organizations. The group of scholars attending the workshop came together around their interest in gender relations at work, but the discussions did not focus exclusively on questions of gender. The concept of intersectionality was instead used effectively as a tool to explain economic disparities, the collapse of the marketized health and social care system and various forms of exploitation at work, some of which result from unequal relations between the Swedish centre and periphery (Giritli Nygren and Nyhlén, 2017; Sjöstedt Landén, Ljuslinder and Lundgren 2017; Sjöstedt Landén 2012). However, there are much more pronounced inequalities between countries, regions and continents, relating to the ways in which global political-economic processes marginalize and disempower these areas and their capacity to exercise national sovereignty (United Nations 2020), while creating new categories of dispossessed (Sassen 2014). The reference to 'gender inequality' in the title of this volume should therefore be understood as defined by plurality and multiplicity, which will also become obvious in the readings of the various chapters. Our approach to gender inequalities implies an ambition to move beyond understandings of gender equality as an idea, a policy, and a cultural practice emanating exclusively from the Global North. Policies that, on the one hand, have had a positive impact on the lives of some women, and on the other hand, simultaneously served to legitimise capitalist labour market relations and to normalise heteronormative family forms, re-establish differences between groups, and recreate urban, Eurocentric, colonial, and nationalistic stories and orders (see for example Martinsson, Mulinari and Giritli Nygren 2018).

The concept of intersectionality captures 'The interconnected nature of social categorizations such as race, class, and gender, regarded as creating overlapping and interdependent systems of discrimination or disadvantage; a theoretical approach based on such a premise' (https://www.lexico.com/definition/intersectionality). This idea was born out of struggles for racial equality in the US (see e.g. Combahee River Collective 1983). Kimberlé Crenshaw (1989), a legal scholar generally credited with mainstreaming the term, strove to highlight the invisibility of black women under anti-discrimination laws that addressed them either as women or black, or omitted them from both categories. Presumptions of the homogeneity of women's experiences are now regarded as naïve and politically dangerous: '*It is known that the multiple disadvantages experienced by those positioned at the intersections of various markers of difference* are far from being straightforward sums of the component parts forming subjects' identities' (Fotaki and Harding, 2018: 101, citing Harding et al. 2013, with reference to hooks 1987; Acker 2006; italics in the original).

Rooted in Black feminism and critical race theory, intersectionality is now not only a category of analysis in feminist and gender studies (Brah and Phoenix, 2004; Yuval-Davis, 2006; Valentine 2007), but also an interdisciplinary concept inspiring global engagement with the idea as a means to promote social equality. It is a method and a disposition, a heuristic and an analytical tool, which has moved across time, disciplines, issues, and geographic and national boundaries, while retaining its theoretical capacity (Carbado et al. 2013) to offer novel insights into these and other issues, such as work and health (Larson et al. 2016). It is thus well suited to enabling understanding of how new forms of dispossession have emerged on top of old inequalities between centres and peripheries following globalization. This is because the process of globalization has wide-ranging consequences for embedding the old as well as establishing new political, economic and cultural power relations.

Tariff-free globalized trade, reliance on transnational supply chains and unrestrained flows of capital are the tools of neoliberal governance, along with privatization of the commons and increased power and centralization of financial capital at both national and international levels (Boden 2011). In the context of globalization, significant transformations are affecting various parts of the world, as well as particular regions, nations and cities, some of which are considered to be at the core, while others are becoming ever more peripheral (Peeren et al. 2016: 2). Peeren, Stuit and Van Weyenberg's collection entitled *Peripheral visions in the globalizing present: Space, mobility, aesthetics* provides important insights into many aspects of knowledge arising in and from the peripheries. Indeed, peripheral visions 'enable a thinking "otherwise"', which 'takes the shape of a complex relation to a troubled past that, rather than closing it off, seeks to recognize it and to mobilize it for the present and the future' (Jansen 2016: 25). Although Peeren et al. (2016) do not focus on the concept of work *per se*, they show that work and labour play important roles in the materialization of peripherality, and in how it intersects with gender, sexuality, race, ethnicity and class (see, for example, Jansen 2016 in a South African context).

In his frequently cited review of peripherialization research, Kühn (2015: 372) concludes that 'in sociological inequality studies "marginalization" or "peripheralization" are clearly a social relation with spatial implications'. Kühn (2015: 369) also highlights that 'apart from spatial inequalities, centres and peripheries are also determined by temporal inequalities'. The pace of development changes over time, as does what is deemed to be peripheral. However, research strands dedicated to inequality and the production of marginality, such as feminist, postcolonial and intersectional studies, are also curiously marginalized in this review. Yet, although intersectional studies may be marginalized in peripheralization research, peripherality appears to capture intersections of inequalities materialized in labour and work practices. Therefore, we believe that there is much to be gained from developing the concept of peripheralization by placing it in dialogue with intersectionality. For instance, recognizing how wider political and economic transformations affect modes of work and production in organizations, we argue, can help us understand how these shape identities, bodies and subjectivities. Another core argument for attempting to bring these concepts into conversation with each other is to illuminate the issue of labour in terms of transnational dependency and the need for actions of solidarity. As feminist researchers, we have a responsibility to examine the various forms of exploitation in the world of work (e.g. Sjöstedt Landén 2016; Mulinari and Selberg 2013). Moreover, work and labour have been at the core of intersectional analyses in black feminist thinking (see e.g. Crenshaw 1989; Hooks 1987; Hill Collins 2000; Truth 1851), which have been pivotal basis for analytical resources in the field of intersectional research.

Specifically, our edited collection aims to develop critical discourses on inequalities in the context of labour and working lives, through analytical pairing of *intersectionality* and *peripheralization*. To this end, this volume presents a conceptual framework offering theoretical and methodological insights to think through present and future inequality challenges in the globalized world of work. First, in crossing the theoretical boundaries between intersectionality and peripherality, we are interested in determining how thinking through these concepts might enable us to identify how racism, capitalism and heteropatriarchy operate on bodies in the name of work, particularly as expressed in precarious labour conditions. Second, we make a case for combining intersectional analysis with transnationalism to think productively about multiple forms of inequality in different geographical locales, and accounting for how these may have further developed with globalized movements of capital, goods and people. This also allows us to develop transnational solidarity as part of feminist ethics, while providing an opportunity to reflect on ways forward for feminist intersectional studies of work and working life, drawing on embodied relationality and a feminist ethics of care (see also Fotaki and Harding, 2018). Third, the foregoing two-pronged approach contributes to decentralizing hegemonic discourses by unearthing ways in which inequalities are organized; that is, how the 'local' and/or peripheral intersects with and is often discursively and materially co-constituted by the 'global' and/or the centre. Finally, we also see that the concept of intersectionality benefits from spatial and temporal insights that enable discussions of solidarity across geographical, organizational and temporal divides.

Taken together, the contributions of this collection illustrate how power structures, organizational forms and regulatory regimes speak directly to capitalist and patriarchal social norms from intersectional and translocal, regional and national perspectives. This chapter aims to outline a conceptual 'landscape' that connects research fields often articulated as separate, and to explore what they can do when put in conversation with each other. It also foregrounds the concepts we address in specific chapters, which are divided into themes, while emphasizing their processual character and connections with one another. The concepts contribute different histories and theoretical resources that we believe to be fruitful for better understanding and critically engaging with current issues relating to the exploitation of labour across different social and geographical contexts. We hope that this will encourage cross-disciplinary and cross-boundary approaches to construct transnational solidarity, decentralize hegemonic discourses, and deconstruct the organizing of inequalities.

Crossing Boundaries: Intersectionality and Peripherality at Work

Several researchers have argued for a need to cut across disciplinary divides in order to conduct relevant research on work and inequalities in today's globalized economies (McBride et al. 2015; Mulinari and Selberg 2013; Rodriguez et al. 2016) by adopting the concept of intersectionality. McBride et al. (2015: 331) suggest that such research would benefit from 'an intersectional approach to both the design and interpretation of research'. Labour and working life are at the core of some classic texts that conceptualize intersectionality. For example, Kimberlé Crenshaw (1989) uses intersectionality to signify the various ways in which race and gender interact to 'shape the multiple dimensions of Black women's employment experiences', while Patricia Hill Collins (2000) foregrounds work–family relations as a core theme. An important contribution of formulations of work and labour in black feminist thought is that, whether paid or unpaid, 'work is life' and is thus of concern for relations of many kinds, not least care (Hill Collins 2000: 51).

However, 'understandings of work, like understandings of family, vary greatly depending on who controls the definitions' (Hill Collins 2000: 54). Black feminist thought teaches us that oppression intersects in a matrix of relational and context-sensitive domination, as well as allowing us to understand work in terms of organizational, labour market and educational positioning, and families as intertwined and intersecting with power relations based on gender, race, ethnicity and class. Further, in emphasizing spatial dimensions of class, race, gender and work in the US context, Hill Collins implicitly connects intersectionality with processes of peripherialization, for example as a spatial means of producing enslavement, and the transition to 'free' labour intertwined with processes of urbanization. Moreover, how different circumstances operate to form oppression in a particular time and space has always been deconstructed as intersectional in this line of research. The concept of intersectionality is thus attached to multiple struggles for human rights and wellbeing, and is therefore also connected with the construction of a discourse that offers a language of change.

However, theorizing intersectionality and its productive use in other disciplines or politics is not tension-free. One tension has to do with emphasis on the stability of categories (a necessary precondition for recognition) and fluidity between them (to acknowledge change) (see Harding et al. 2013). Thus, while Crenshaw (1991) 'argued that political and structural inequalities are not reducible to each other', Lugones (2007) 'advocated the inseparability of various identities into their sub-component parts and instead proposed an intersectionality frame in which new merging categories can only be understood as "curdled", because they retain their various constitutive aspects when a new hybrid identity is created' (Fotaki and Harding, 2018: 101–102, citing Garry 2011). The other source of contention is whether the salience of Black women's experiences inspiring the intersectionality movement in the US, which is still far from being exhausted both domestically and internationally, has been lost in a generalizable theory about power and marginalization (Carbado et al. 2013). Thus, Jennifer Nash (2019) urges the development of black feminist theory that '*includes* but also *exceeds* intersectionality' and thereby refuses to do service to white women's studies. She discusses how so-called intersectionality wars have taken up far too much energy, losing sight of the concept's true possibilities. Thereby, intersectionality should not be used simply to protect current articulations of the concept itself; rather, its radical potential to imagine freedom must be nourished (Nash 2019). Our understanding of feminist labour research is strongly informed by this notion of intersectionality as a way of listening to what matters for people's lives and wellbeing within and outside current moments and places. This also points to the openness of the concept as a work in progress by considering what it performs already and imagining its potential future uses (Carbado et al. 2013). This collection deploys this aspect to explore peripherality, understood as marginalization in the context of precarious work.

The related concepts of precarity and precarization are closely connected with labour research. Although currently taken up in many disciplines and strands of research, they are still largely taken for granted by Western European and North American positions viewed as 'centres' of capitalist society, whereas Global South and non-urban economies are seen as 'peripheral'. Moreover, debate on precarious work has focused predominantly on waged work, whereas the extremely common and important role of informal work has not been sufficiently taken into account (Betti 2018: 275). Nevertheless, we see potential in the concept of precarious work for exploring how processes of making people exploitable as a labour force take form, and we seek to draw attention to ongoing processes of both precarization and peripheralization.

This suggests that combining the concepts of intersectionality, peripherality and precarization might be a fruitful way forward, allowing us to account for how labour exploitation is expressed in different contexts. For example, the concept of precarization might contribute to the relevance of critiques of types of capitalism and 'different trajectories of precarity/stability across time and space' that 'have rarely been taken into account' (Betti 2018: 275). Kühn (2015: 368) states that widening gaps between rich and poor neighbourhoods in cities, as well as between highly urbanized and rural areas, have sparked increasing use of concepts like 'peripheralization' and 'marginalization'.

Many feminist writers have sought to expand our understanding of work beyond simple distinctions between productive and reproductive or paid and unpaid work (see e.g. Glucksmann 1995, 2012; Hill Collins 2000). However, as previously mentioned, feminist perspectives occupy a marginal position in current peripherality research. Nevertheless peripheralization is stated to be about 'the social' and 'social justice' (Kühn 2015; Fischer-Tahir and Naumann 2013: 12–13) and the concept of peripheralization is usually examined in the context of human geography and social anthropology and concerns the production of peripheries and its social consequences. Through the lens of the concepts suggested in this chapter (intersectionality, peripherality and precarization), we might make these necessary links and connections, which might then lead to mobilization and solidarity building across types of work, spaces and bodies.

Transnational Solidarity and Feminist Ethics

As intersectionality emphasizes the embodiment of work, we see that the concept of peripheralization contributes to the spatiality and temporality of work, acknowledging how spaces become separated or connected.

Butler and Athanasiou (2013) discuss how feminism can depict the neoliberal expropriation of labour and livelihood, constituting the performative condition of injustice. They conclude by asking 'how are we to struggle for a desire to exist and to be free, when this desire is not exactly "ours", in fact can never be exclusively "ours"?' Athanasiou's answer is that solidarity is marked by the 'injurious yet enabling mode of "concerted action" in conditions of dispossession' (Butler and Athanasiou 2013: 184). Here, the concepts of intersectionality and peripherality can be used to decentralize knowledge regimes that are also located within ourselves. We believe that transborder scholarly cooperation must build alliances to counteract inequality regimes. The struggle for a more just, equal and democratic world continues, and there is a need for alternative visions, as well as alliances through which such visions can be developed and practised. Locally-based struggles are important, but may be limited in their ability to challenge the extra-local processes that shape them (see Grewal and Kaplan 2001). As feminist scholars, we have a responsibility to promote a just and equal society beyond our own national and institutional contexts (Fotaki and Harding, 2018) and other forms of situatedness. Therefore, we also think it necessary to unsettle binary conceptions of politics as either global or local, central or peripheral, and instead determine how to create chains of equivalence of knowledge in multiple struggles. Geographically and organizationally separated modes of exploitation and work do not take place in totally different worlds, but actually concern us all because the 'centre' always depends on the 'periphery'.

In Chapter 2, Ayşe Serdar presents one example of empirical research disrupting the illusory nature of such division in her investigation of protests against working conditions on the building site for the New Istanbul airport in Turkey. Serdar demonstrates how everyday organizing of the airport project was performed through intersecting dominations and oppressions under a mode of neoliberal authoritarian governance. Disciplinary practices oppressed workers and exploited readily available discourses and technologies derived from securitization of the Kurdish conflict and racialization of the peripheralized Kurdish population. An intersectional lens reveals that although workers' precarity and disposability is ever-increasing under authoritarian neoliberalist regimes, a class-only or ethnicity-only approach fails to grasp the complexity of social divisions, and thereby blunts their critique. In examining the process of the airport workers' detention, arrest and trial, the chapter demonstrates how multiple dominations and oppressions were played out in this precarious context. An important aspect of making workers disposable was rendering their ethnicity more salient by stripping them of their class identity. This, Serdar argues, was possible owing to the availability of discourses and technologies of securitization, criminalization and penalization of ethnicity-coded dissent, and delegitimization of the workers' protest.

In Chapter 3, Hara Kouki explore solidarity initiatives in Athens since the last economic crisis (2010–2018). She asks how initiatives have been transformed from political protest movements into solidarity networks, arguing that changes to work practices may also change women's positions in such movements. Drawing on research on the role of gender and social reproduction in movement cultures (Daskalaki and Fotaki 2017; Daskalaki et al. 2020; Kouki and Chatzidakis forthcoming), and on extended ethnographic fieldwork on solidarity initiatives in Athens, Kouki explores how solidarity mobilizations have evolved. She shows how the labour invested in the solidarity movements of the crisis disrupted the boundaries between productive and reproductive labour. Kouki also argues that when women and reproductive labour move from the periphery to the centre of social movements, the work performed moves from conflictual demonstrations in the streets to the low-key spaces of social reproduction across urban neighbourhoods defined by the logic of freely and voluntarily given care. Knowledge of multiple struggles also includes correctly naming activities not commonly seen as 'work' and showing the complexities of work contexts, as exemplified in several chapters of this book.

In Chapter 4 of this volume, Nandi Vanqa-Mgijima reflects on the tension between paid and unpaid labour done predominantly by black women in post-apartheid South Africa, and the continued existence of multiple types of discrimination. The chapter builds on knowledge produced through political education workshops, interviews and focus group discussions with women activists involved in paid and unpaid domestic labour, home-based care work and waste picking. Traditionally, these workers have not been well organized because of their geographical isolation and migration status, and because the burden of care work falls heavily on their shoulders. For domestic workers, their workplace is a private sphere, with high levels of insecurity, intimidation and collusion between employers and unions. The courage and persistence needed to organize resistance and rise against these entrenched modes of discrimination are well illustrated in this chapter.

There are also illuminating examples of how organizational settings might work as exclusionary boundaries. These provide insights into specific aspects of work and how it relates to political, societal and economic regimes. In Chapter 5, Manar Faraj and Ambreen Ben-Shmuel write about the everyday organizational practices of grassroots organizations working for Palestinian and Israeli peace. Beyond the obvious boundaries of Palestine and Israel, this research points to ways in which other organizations operating in bi-national or other complex intersectional environments, especially conflict zones, might critically examine their organizational choices, despite political and societal constraints. In such contexts, people are already struggling with numerous challenges arising from fear, discrimination and oppression, and peace organizations play an important role in trying to address these issues. Faraj and Ben-Shmuel argue that it is essential to apply an intersectional perspective to broaden the study of power relations and inequality in this field. The authors seek to move beyond existing research focusing exclusively on national groups, to investigate intersections between gender, ethnicity, nationality and religion, and how they are organized hierarchically in space and time. They build on a solid body of ethnographic data. The workers they interviewed often had longstanding experience of various organizations, and were therefore able to reflect on how their work had changed over time. This chapter provides a good example of the importance of in-depth qualitative studies and longstanding commitment to reveal how intersections of power affect everyday experiences as well as politics. This has implications for everyone involved in peace organizing, including staff and participants, donors who can encourage organizations to address intersectional challenges and needs, and researchers in conflict areas. The field of peace organizing is committed to social justice and creating a better future. In order to achieve this, it is important to understand, name and address injustice, particularly where it is expressed in organizational logic and practice, in order to mitigate intersectional marginalization.

Decentralizing Hegemonic Discourse

As previously mentioned, the radical potential of intersectionality lies in its attachment to struggles for human rights and the possibility of constructing discourses that offer a language of change and freedom. By decentring the hegemonic discourses of whiteness, heterosexism, patriarchy and ableism, intersectional thinking takes us beyond merely observing inequalities, and pushes us to try constantly to disrupt, dislocate and imagine the future differently. Equally, peripheralization decentralizes hegemonic understandings of categorizations in space and time, including those of sexuality (Mizielińska and Kulpa 2011) and disability. In the book *Crip times* McRuer (2018:19) argue that 'given that disabled people themselves have done the labor of resignifying crip, crip is not opposed to disability' and put forward a range of uses of crip as a reformative concept to critique neoliberalism as ableist and expose austerity as crip times. Here, 'to crip', similarly like, 'to queer' is a way to unsettle or 'make strange or twisted' what has become the status quo (Ibid: 23). Following McRuer (2018:23), this could include exposing 'the way in which able-bodiedness and able-mindedness gets naturailzed and the ways that bodies, minds, and impairments that should be at the *absolute center of a space or issue* [our italics] or discussion gets purged from that space or issue or discussion'. We read this as a way of decentralizing hegemonic discourse and exposing how peripherlizations of materiality, identity and politics come into being. These concepts are fruitful for connecting inequalities and struggles posed as disparate in hegemonic discourses, and for considering how these are actually interlinked. While capitalist exploitation works globally, some intellectual traditions and systems of thought thrive on the separation of struggles, as in the constant division between for example urban and rural, centre and periphery. In organizational studies, the widely referenced frameworks of 'inequality regimes' (Acker 2006) and TSOL (Glucksmann 2000) taking inspiration from intersectional analysis have been important in revealing how various 'work activities' are interconnected, even though they tend to be separated analytically (Mulinari and Selberg, 2011: 23). The concept of intersectionality thus draws on a wide range of theoretical and methodological resources devoted to critique and change. Here, the concept of peripheralization contributes by emphasizing the 'territorialization of injustice in terms of access to material and symbolic resources on local, national and transnational scales' (Fischer-Tahir and Naumann 2013: 9).

In Chapter 6, Camila Esguerra Muelle draws on the life stories of care-work migrants to create a testimony of what it means to be part of (trans)national care. The testimony constitutes a collective narrative that shows how care is entangled in the transnational conflict faced by people across Colombia and Spain, and is a form of dispossession of the work of women and feminized individuals. This dispossession is geared to the political and economic apparatus, such as the hegemonic and colonial sex-gender system, and to a racist apparatus of (trans)nationalization of care. This shows how the bodies and knowledge of women and feminized individuals are expropriated through migration, displacement, exile, trafficking, banishment and deportation. The chapter illuminates how intersecting oppression systems of gender, age, class, race, ableism, ethnicity, and sexuality are produced within the framework of global care chains.

In exposing how the legacies of the past perpetuate institutionalized racism and sexism in Malta, in Chapter 7 JosAnn Cutajar uses postcolonial theory in conjunction with intersectional insights to illuminate how people are kept in place. She explores how a gendered division of the labour market results in a distinction between a core of skilled, mainly EU and Maltese male workers, and a marginalized Maltese female and non-EU male workforce. Cutajar stresses the centre and periphery tensions, illustrated in Malta's treatment as an internal colony of Europe whilst being a way into Europe for African migrants. Multiple hierarchies divide the Maltese labour market in particular ways, with women and men, colonized and colonizers occupying different positions.

Although the authors examine a variety of contexts, we see that the different chapters provide important insights into specificities of the precarization of labour as well as the strategies of resistance against such hierarchisation of people and places. Lisa Ridzén focuses not on a particular phenomenon of the labour market, but on how men living in rural countryside villages in the Swedish north narrate their work and lives. In Chapter 8, she describes how they problematize the burden of wage work and their work identities from a life narrative perspective, and how they distance from these ideologically and geographically. Although they try to live up to certain aspects of workfare society and white, urban, middle-class career masculinity that in many ways resonate with traditional hegemonic masculinity, they also use characteristics of the peripheral location to go against some of these stereotypical images.

A core feature that enables the (re-)theorization we advance in this edited collection is that it starts from embodied experiences of work. The various chapters show that this is a way of connecting with the struggles, difficulties and pains of people in different contexts. It is also a 'portal' connecting economic structures with identity struggles and constructions. In each chapter, we gain glimpses of how globalized phenomena both create problems and bring joy to people's lives. In Chapter 9, Emelie Larsson describes the closing of a maternity ward in a small town in the thinly populated Swedish north. The region's peripheral position vis-à-vis the centre motivated this reduction in care services. The author shows how midwives' work practices in the small ward were constructed as exterior/marginal and therefore risky, as a way to justify the ward's closure and the centralization of care to bigger towns. Here, peripheralization worked to veil the economic and New Public Management motivations for the closure. The case presented by Larsson shows the importance of the community coming together with the midwives and nurses, which allowed the protest against the ward closure to endure over time.

The Organizing of Inequalities

As stated earlier, the concept of peripheralization describes 'the production of peripheries through social relations and their spatial implications' (Kühn 2015: 367). Such processes often take place in organizational settings, as exemplified in several chapters of this book. While current uses of the concept of peripheralization stress its preoccupation with social justice (Fischer-Tahir and Naumann 2013: 22), we argue that it might greatly benefit from deeper engagement with research fields dealing with social justice, such as the feminist theory of intesectionality. We therefore seek to deepen knowledge of the inequalities embedded in processes of peripheralization, as well as how intersections of power relations are marked by spatial and temporal specificities.

In Chapter 10, Kristina Johansson and Lisa Ringblom apply intersectional analysis to the conflicted space of the Swedish mining industry. Mining plays a central role in conflicts characterizing the region concerned, especially in relation to environmental and land-use issues. An ongoing cause of conflict is the fact that most mines are located in Sápmi, the land of the indigenous Sami people. This chapter emphasizes the different ways in which work is peripheralized within the organization on grounds of gender and class, and how organizational hierarchies correspond with geographical marginalization. The mining industry wants to change its gender composition and attract women. However, from a critical feminist perspective, this arguably maintains the colonialist status quo in the industry.

An intersectional perspective is important because it shifts the focus away from social categorizations *per se*, to concentrate instead on how these categorizations relate to each other, how they create and reinforce each other, and how they are reproduced in institutional and historical contexts (De los Reyes and Mulinari 2005; Hill Collins 2000; Acker 2006; McCall 2005). Intersectional analysis may therefore decentralize certain aspects of work and labour that have become overly centred in hegemonic discourses, in order to break with current inequalities. Here, a transnational perspective helps us understand what it is to be a mobile and precarious worker in translocal late capitalism (Fotaki and Harding, 2018). This means that we must recognize how individual, socially situated practices are caught up in sequences of actions by people on occasions and in places other than those that are taken for granted (Smith 2005: 94). The concept of transnationalism draw attention to power relations and patterns of inequality that go across different modes of peripheralization, including geographical and organizational, and even tasks that are considered peripheral in relation to central activities. Transnational feminist scholarship (Mohanty 1998; Grewal and Kaplan 2001; Fernandes 2013) visibilizes the excluded 'others' in different geographical locales in relation to the organization of work, identity and emancipation and resist the disposessions connected with such positions.

Taken together, this volume emphasizes that intersections between categorizations and power relations are context-sensitive. The various chapters reveal both struggles to change these relations, and discursive acts of stigmatization and other instances of holding on to the status quo, or the 'non-performance' of equality, as noted in Chapter 11 by Ulrika Schmauch, Björn Ahlström and Britt-Inger Keisu. Intersectional analyses are well suited to detecting how inequality regimes (Acker 2006) are held together, legitimized and normalized in organizational and other settings. Schmauch et al. address the problem that claiming commitment to equality and justice does not necessarily mean that equal rights is a dominant practice. In a Swedish school setting, they also show that different dimensions of power, such as gender, race and class, must be studied in relation to each other, as they are in many ways constitutive of each other. The authors detect a gap between the importance given to the work of equality in policy documents, and what actually happens in the school. The political possibilities of social objectives are down-played, or 'non-performed' (Ahmed 2012), allowing the organization not to prioritize equality work.

Thus, in Chapter 12, Annette Thörnquist explores the equality objectives implied in the Swedish Freedom of Choice Act (LOV). Bringing an intersectional approach into conversation with a centre–periphery approach and the notion of precarious work, she clarifies the problems of implementing gender equality aims through the introduction of new market solutions, and of defining 'diversity' in terms of the market. She relates the effects of the Act to the reality of work and an emphasis on entrepreneurship in home-based elderly care. The reform was expected to promote female entrepreneurship in the tax-financed (quasi-)market for health and social services, which had previously been difficult for small entrepreneurs to enter. A greater diversity of providers competing for labour was also expected to improve the working conditions of workers employed in these strongly female-dominated sectors, but ultimately seems to have had precisely the opposite effect. Indeed, onetalk about how solidarity is of the big discussions for decades in Sweden are the high sick-leave rates for women, especially in the public sector (see also Sjöstedt Landén, Olofsdotter and Bolin 2016). How to push the feminist discussion on this issue further was also one of the themes at the workshop in 2016 that eventually resulted in this book project. In their work on *Sick woman theory*,[1] Johanna Hedva emphasise that 'the body and mind are sensitive and reactive to regimes of oppression – particularly our current regime of neoliberal, white-supremacist, imperial-capitalist, cis-hetero-patriarchy. It is that all of our bodies and minds carry the historical trauma of this, that it is *the world itself* that is making and keeping us sick'.

Fischer-Tahir and Naumann (2013: 9) argue that peripheralization is fostered by 'discursive acts of stigmatization'. This points to the importance of how people's stories are told in spatial terms, and how this grants a certain social status and complexity. The workings of racialization for control and precarization are addressed in Chapter 13, where Paula Mulinari explores how unemployment politics in a Swedish urban municipality makes racialized women a specific group within the labour force. In this way, 'unemployed foreign-born women' are positioned at the periphery of the labour market. Mulinari draws on intersectional analyses of labour that bridge macroeconomic, political and social relations and race and nation classification systems. The chapter explores dominant discourses around the figure of the 'foreign-born unemployed woman' through analysis of governmental and municipal documents. In a second stage of analysis, the author supplements her research with interview data, showing how this dominant representation shapes a labour force that is trained to be flexible, patient and disposable through various forms of temporal regulation. This legitimizes a gendered, classed and racialized labour market, in which working-class women's care work is underpaid, understaffed and precarious. They thus become the periphery of the labour force in the sector and more generally of the labour market in Sweden, from which, as the political and organizational analytical framing suggests, they are seeking to move away.

Care work plays a core role in the figuration of the foreign-born women in Mulinari's chapter, producing a racialized and feminized underclass in the Swedish context. Workers become associated with (and disassociated from) certain occupations, work tasks and spaces of work through various stereotyping practices (Harvey 2001; McDowell 2009). This also speaks to Kristina Zampoukos' suggestion in Chapter 14 that more attention should be directed toward individual workers' agency. She presents a review of current research on intersectionality and peripherality within the discipline of human geography, and suggests that more attention should be paid to the agency of individual workers and how they create their own progressive biographies. This confirms previous deconstructions of peripheralization research (see Fischer-Tahir and Naumann 2013) in an empirical context. People both embody and are embedded in diverse social and spatial relations, and these locations are far from static, but are produced in and through context, including social space and time.

Illuminating Temporal and Spatial Inequalities: A Call for Relationality and for Academics to Speak Out against Injustice

This book illuminates spatial and temporal aspects of intersectional disparities in the context of centre and periphery in industrialized economies, as well as between global North and South. The various chapters bring new insights into what combining intersectional analysis with the concept of peripheralization might provide in analyses of work and labour. Together, the chapters reflect on and contribute to the development of theoretical and methodological research in this field. What has become clearer to us while working on this edited collection is that fluctuations between change and stasis are at the heart of the labour relations researched here. These complexities are detectable precisely as a result of the intersectional and peripheral perspectives adopted.

This shows the importance of looking beyond national contexts and exploring connections at the peripheries of globalized working life in order to understand relations between precarization, dispossession and potential resistance to such processes of capitalist and patriarchal societies. Let us not get stuck in urban/rural divides and talk about how solidarity is constructed between what are usually deemed to be peripheries. As explored in the following chapters, this is always relational. As the chapters will show, temporal and spatial analysis of social relations can be invaluable for charting relationships that link one place with another, both in and around an organization. We thus need to explain and thoroughlyGlobal identities: theorizing explore the many geographical, ideological, ethical and organizational forms that peripheralization takes, to enable us to think relationally and transcend specific locations or situations. The spatiality and temporality of injustices must also be acknowledged and examined to transcend them through solidarity building. Transnational solidarity building is essential, as it enables us to better understand what it is to be a mobile and precarious worker in translocal late capitalism, where none can feel safe, insulated or disconnected from global networks of power and culture (Daskalaki and Fotaki 2017).

Of course, intersectionality may not be the only concept through which to conduct these kinds of readings, but as we are using it, let us remember what it is for. Imaginative concepts have the power to connect times, places and people that have been divided and broken by practices of capitalism and colonization. We therefore still find intersectionality energizing because it has the power to disturb singular readings of power relations. Through the pluralistic lenses of the different chapters, we can also see that intersectionality is doing the work. Divides of gender, race and class have not been solved, and we need to be able to see that they are constructions and can be changed, and that people are indeed changing them from below every day in their practices of resistance while exploitation persists and take new forms. Thus, exploitation and the peripheralization of labour also change, as we believe that the knowledge conveyed in the various chapters of this book show. The underlying motivation is that researchers need to intervene and try to change discourses (Harding et al. 2013), rather than merely 'observing' inequalities. To achieve this, we invest in research to enable academics to speak out against various forms of injustice, and in doing so, to resist them; otherwise, we implicitly participate in smoothing over and giving legitimacy to regimes of exploitation on the grounds of categorization.

Note

1 http://www.maskmagazine.com/not-again/struggle/sick-woman-theory

References

Acker, Joan. 2006. "Inequality regimes: gender, class, and race in organizations." *Gender and Society* 20(4), 441–464.

Ahmed, Sara. 2012. *On being included: racism and diversity in institutional life.* Durham, NC: Duke University Press.

Betti, Eloisa. 2018. "Historicizing precarious work: forty years of research in the social sciences and humanities." *International Review of Social History* 63(2), 273–319.

Boden, Michael. 2011. "Neoliberalism and counter-hegemony in the Global South: reimagining the state." In *Social movements in the Global South: dispossession, development and resistance*, eds. Sara C. Motta and Alf G. Nilsen, 83–103. Basingstoke: Palgrave Macmillan.

Brah, Avtar and Ann Phoenix. 2004. "Ain't I a woman? revisiting intersectionality." *Journal of International Women's Studies* 5(3), 75–86.

Butler, Judith and Athena Athanasiou. 2013. *Dispossession: the performative in the political*. Cambridge: Polity Press.

Carbado, Devon W., Kimberlé W. Crenshaw, Vickie M. Mays and Barbara Tomlinson. 2013. "Intersectionality: mapping the movements of a theory." *Du Bois Review* 10(2), 303–312.

Combahee River Collective. 1983. "The Combahee River Collective statement." In *Home girls: a black feminist anthology*, ed. Barbara Smith, 264–274. New York, NY: Kitchen Table – Women of Color Press.

Crenshaw, Kimberlé. 1989. "Demarginalizing the intersection of race and sex: a black feminist critique of antidiscrimination doctrine, feminist theory, and antiracist politics." *University of Chicago Legal Forum* 1989(1), 139–167.

Crenshaw, Kimberlé. 1991. "Mapping the margins: Intersectionality, identity politics, and violence against women of color." *Stanford Law Review* 43(6), 1241–1299.

Daskalaki, Maria and Marianna Fotaki. 2017. "The neoliberal crisis: alternative organizing and spaces of/for feminist solidarity." In *Feminists and queer theorists debate the future of critical management studies*, Dialogues in Critical Management Studies, Vol. 3, eds. Alison Pullen, Nancy Harding and Mary Phillips, 129–153. Bingley: Emerald Publishing.

Daskalaki, Maria, Marianna Fotaki and Maria Simosi. 2020. "The gendered impact of the crisis: struggles over social reproduction in Greece." *Environment and Planning A*, online first, https://doi.org/10.1177/0308518X20922857.

De los Reyes, Paulina and Diana Mulinari. 2005. *Intersektionalitet: kritiska reflektioner över (o)jämlikhetens landskap* [Intersectionality: critical reflections on the landscape of (in)equality]. Malmö, Sweden: Liber.

Fernandes, Leela. 2013. *Transnational feminism in the United States: knowledge, ethics, power*. New York, NY: New York University Press.

Fischer-Tahir, Andrea and Matthias Naumann, eds. 2013. *Peripheralization: the making of spatial dependencies and social injustice*. Wiesbaden, Germany: Springer.

Fotaki, Marianna and Nancy Harding. 2018. *Gender and the organization: women at work in the 21st century*. Abingdon: Routledge.

Garry, Ann. 2011. "Intersectionality, metaphors, and the multiplicity of gender." *Hypatia* 26(4), 826–850.

Giritli Nygren, Katarina and Sara Nyhlén. 2017. "Mapping the ruling relations of work in rural eldercare intersections of gender, digitalization and the centre–periphery divide." *Journal of Rural Studies*, doi:10.1016/j.jrurstud.2017.07.002.

Glucksmann, Miriam. 1995. "Why 'work'? gender and the 'total social organization of labour'." *Gender, Work and Organization* 2(2), 63–75.

Glucksmann, Miriam. 2000. *Cottons and casuals: the gendered organisation of labour in time and space*. Abingdon: Routledge.

Glucksmann, Miriam. 2012. "Reflecting on women on the line: continuities and change in women's work." *International Labor and Working-Class History* *81*(1), 168–173.

Grewal, Inderpal and Caren Kaplan. 2001. "Global identities: theorizing transnational studies of sexuality." *GLQ* 7(4), 663–679.

Harding, Nancy, Jackie Ford and Marianna Fotaki. 2013. "Is the 'F'-word still dirty? a past, present and future of/for feminist and gender studies in organization." *Organization 20*(1), 51–65.

Harvey, David. 2001. *Spaces of capital: towards a critical geography.* Edinburgh: Edinburgh University Press.

Hill Collins, Patricia. 2000. *Black feminist thought.* London: Hyman.

Holvino, Evangelina. 2010. "Intersections: the simultaneity of race, gender and class in organization studies." *Gender, Work and Organization 17*(3), 248–277.

hooks, bell. 1987. *Ain't I a woman: black women and feminism.* London: Pluto Press.

Jansen, Ena. 2016. "The South African backyard as a very local peripheral space." In *Peripheral visions in the globalizing present: space, mobility, aesthetics*, eds. Esther Peeren, Hanneke Stuit and Astrid Van Weyenberg, 126–139. Leiden, Netherlands: Brill.

Kouki, Hara and Andreas Chatzidakis. Forthcoming. "Implicit feminist solidarity(ies)? the role of gender in the social movements of the Greek crisis." *Gender, Work and Organization.*

Kühn, Manfred. 2015. "Peripheralization: theoretical concepts explaining sociospatial inequalities." *European Planning Studies 23*(2), 367–378.

Larson, Elizabeth, Asha George, Rosemary Morgan and Tonia Poteat. 2016. "10 best resources on… intersectionality with an emphasis on low- and middle-income countries." *Health Policy and Planning 31*(8), 964–969.

Lugones, Maria. 2007. "Heterosexualism and the colonial/modern gender system." *Hypatia 22*(1), 186–209.

Martinsson Lena, Diana Mulinari and Katarina Giritli Nygren. 2018. "Gender equality and beyond: At the crossroads of neoliberalism, anti-gender movements, 'European' values, and normative reiterations in the Nordic model." *Social Inclusion* 6(4).

Massey, Doreen. 1994. *Space, place and gender.* Oxford: Polity Press.

Massey, Doreen. 2005. *For space.* Thousand Oaks, CA: Sage.

McBride, Anne, Gail Hebson and Jane Holgate. 2015. "Intersectionality: are we taking enough notice in the field of work and employment relations?" *Work, Employment and Society 29*(2), 331–341.

McCall, Leslie. 2005. "The complexity of intersectionality." *Signs 30*(3), 1771–1800.

McDowell, Linda. 2009. *Working bodies: interactive service employment and workplace identities.* Hoboken, NJ: John Wiley and Sons.

McRuer, Robert. 2018. *Crip times: disability, globalization and resistance.* New York, NY: New York University Press.

Mizielińska, Joanna and Robert Kulpa. 2011. "Contemporary peripheries: queer studies, circulation of knowledge and East/West divide." In *De-centering*

Western sexualities: Central and Eastern European perspectives, eds. Robert Kulpa and Joanna Mizielińska, 11–26. London: Routledge.

Mohanty, Chandra T. 1998. "Crafting feminist genealogy: on the geography and politics of home, nation, and community." In *Talking visions: multicultural feminism in a transnational age*, ed. Ella Shotat, 485–500. Cambridge, MA: The MIT Press.

Mulinari, P. and R. Selberg. 2011. "What a way to make a living." In *Arbete: intersektionella perspektiv. [Work: intersectional perspectives]*, eds. Mulinari Paula and Selberg Rebecca Malmö: Gleerups.

Mulinari, Paula and Rebecca Selberg. 2013. "Intersectional directions in working life research: a proposal." *Nordic Journal of Working Life Studies* 3(3), 81–98.

Nash, Jennifer C. 2019. *Black feminism reimagined after intersectionality*. Durham, NC: Duke University Press.

Orzeck, R. 2007. "What does not kill you: historical materialism and the body." *Environment and Planning D: Society and Space*, 25(3), 496–514.

Peeren, Esther, Hanneke Stuit and Astrid Van Weyenberg. 2016. *Peripheral visions in the globalizing present: space, mobility, aesthetics*. Leiden, Netherlands: Brill.

Rodriguez, Jenny K., Evangelina Holvino, Joyce K. Fletcher and Stella M. Nkomo. 2016. "The theory and praxis of intersectionality in work and organisations: where do we go from here?" *Gender, Work and Organization* 23(3), 201–222.

Sassen, Saskia. 2014. *Expulsions: brutality and complexity in the global economy*. Cambridge, MA: Belknap Press.

Sjöstedt Landén, Angelika. 2012. "Moving central knowledge to a northern peripher: exploring logics of public sector job relocation in Sweden." *Geografiska Annaler, Series B, Human Geography* 94B(4), 333–350.

Sjöstedt Landén, Angelika, Karin Ljuslinder and Anna Sofia Lundgren. 2017. "The moral geographies of public sector job relocation: discourses of compensation and competence in the Swedish news press." *Social and Cultural Geography* 18(5), 632–644.

Sjöstedt Landén, Angelika. 2016. Nyliberal styrning och ideologi i offentlig verksamhet: teman för feministisk arbetslivsforskning. [Neoliberal governance and ideology in public institutions: themes for feminist work life research]. In *Ambivalenser och maktordningar: Feministiska läsningar av nyliberalism*, [Ambivalences and orders of power: Feminist readings of neoliberalism] eds. Siv Fahlgren, Diana Mulinari and Angelika Sjöstedt Landén, 30–56. Stockholm: Makadam Förlag.

Sjöstedt Landén, Angelika, Olofsdotter, Gunilla and Bolin, Malin eds. 2016. *Sprickor, öppningar och krackeleringar: nya perspektiv på arbetsmiljö*. [Cracks, openings and crackles: new perspectives on work environment issues]. Forum for Gender Studies Working Papers. Sundsvall/Östersund: Mid Sweden University.

Smith, Dorothy. 2005. *Institutional ethnography: a sociology of people*. Lanham, MD: Rowman Altamira.

Truth, Sojourner. 1851. *Ain't I a woman*. Speech delivered at the National Women's Rights Convention, Akron, OH.

United Nations. 2020. *World social report 2020: inequality in a rapid changing world.* New York, NY: United Nations. https://www.un.org/development/desa/dspd/wp-content/uploads/sites/22/2020/01/World-Social-Report-2020-FullReport.pdf.

Valentine, Gill. 2007. "Theorizing and researching intersectionality: a challenge for feminist geography." *The Professional Geographer* 59(1), 10–21.

Yuval-Davis, Nira. 2006. "Intersectionality and feminist politics." *European Journal of Women's Studies* 13(3), 193–209.

2 #WeAreNotSlaves! An Intersectional Analysis of Class and Ethnicity in the Istanbul Airport Resistance

Ayşe Serdar

Introduction

On 29 May 2017, at the building site of Istanbul Airport, planned to be the biggest in the world, 1,453 trucks paraded to commemorate the 1453 conquest of Istanbul. Yusuf Akçayoğlu, then CEO of Istanbul Grand Airport (IGA), the consortium undertaking the public–private partnership project, drew parallels between the conquest of Istanbul and the building of the new airport:

> akin to the conquest spirit which *marked the end of an era and initiated a new one*, we have always been a nation that demonstrated what we can achieve as long as we stand as one. Holding on to the same spirit, we are exerting a full-fledged effort in order to put into life the Istanbul New Airport, a project that the *whole world is watching closely…* We are proud to prove the world our power by crowning the name of our country thanks to the *loyalty and sacrifice* of our employees in this project. When completed, Istanbul New Airport will surely *close an era* in the aviation history and *kick off a whole new period* (IGA n.d.a, emphasis added).

The parade was presented as an allegory of the airport project's ideological and political end, rooted in sacrifice and loyalty with a nationally unifying mission. The parade symbolized a 're-conquest' of the city, a territorial expansion, a victory, a battle won against the enemies. At the ground-breaking ceremony in 2014, Justice and Development Party (AKP) leader and then-prime minister (now president), Recep Tayyip Erdoğan had already described the project not only as an airport, but also as a 'monument of triumph' that would boost 'the nation's self-confidence', which had been lost under previous governments (IGA n.d.b). It was described as a national source of glory of which every Turkish citizen should be proud.

The airport project aspired to make Istanbul a centre, a global hub at the 'meeting point of five continents, at the crossroads of East and West'

(IGA n.d.b). This new global hub is in Istanbul's north-western forest lands. In one respect, the project expands the territorial reaches of the mega-city. To transform Istanbul into a global centre, its rural, green hinterland had to be cleared. The project was criticized by environmentalists, urban planners and citizens for its inappropriate location, as it hosts a special nature reserve, and expert opinion is that the characteristics of the ground and the local climate are hazardous for aviation safety. It was argued that the project would displace and irreversibly destroy the local ecosystem, peasant communities, forest land, water basins, seashores, endemic species, wild animals and migrating birds.[1]

In stark contrast to the imagery of progress, development and global centredness creating national pride, following the launch of the construction in 2014, the building site became infamous for a lack of safety and gruelling working conditions. The frenzied pace of construction caused a disputed number of work-related deaths. This culminated in September 2018 in a spontaneous walkout and protest by thousands of construction workers on the site. They shouted 'we are not slaves', which soon became a slogan identified with the airport resistance. The narratives built around the meaning of the airport and the resistance clashed with each other. After midnight on the day following the protest, according to official numbers, 401 construction workers were detained, and in subsequent days 61 workers were sued, 31 of whom spent up to 78 days in jail prior to their trials. The resistance was brought under control through mass detention, securitization and criminalization of workers' mobilization.

In this study, I argue that the everyday organizing of the airport project was performed through intersecting domination and oppression under a neoliberal authoritarian mode of governance. Criminalizing the workers' resistance was a crystallization of these intersecting acts of domination and oppression. Securitization and criminalization of the resistance was enabled by intersecting means of oppression, particularly, but not exclusively, embedded in the context of the Kurdish question in Turkey, since the majority of construction workers were Kurds, an unofficial ethnic minority group in Turkey. Therefore, I suggest that the dynamics of racialized neoliberal exploitation cannot be fully grasped unless intersecting aspects of the workers' subordination are examined, and particularly the politically-driven ethnic dimension. By using an intersectional framework, it is possible to avoid class-only or race/ethnicity-only explanations (McCall 2005), and to better investigate the mechanisms of global capitalism in temporally- and spatially-specific configurations that deploy context-specific technologies to control, discipline and police intersecting social divisions.

This study draws on both primary and secondary resources, with an extensive examination of all news posted about the Istanbul Airport project on the digital websites of independent Turkish newspapers and news websites since the beginning of the project in 2011. I drew particularly on the *Evrensel*, *Cumhuriyet* and *Birgün* newspapers' digital editions, and *Bianet*'s online news website. I conducted seven in-depth semi-structured interviews in February and March 2020 with interviewees who were all defendants in the ongoing criminal case concerning the airport resistance. Six had spent more than two months in jail under pre-trial arrest, and one had been released on probation. Three were construction trade unionists (from *Dev-Yapı-İş* and *İnşaat-İş* unions), and the other four were young labourers who had worked on the airport's building site before the resistance. All interviewees were male.

In the remainder of this paper, I explain why an intersectional approach is methodologically and ethically more suited to understanding multiple oppressions. I then identify the basic characteristics of Turkey's neoliberal authoritarianism and construction-based growth model, and present an intersectionally framed analysis of Istanbul Airport. This includes the background to the project, the work site as a securitized space and working life as a racialized and precarious experience, and some aspects of racialized Kurdish labour. I also present a chronology of the resistance, and analyze intersecting dominations deployed during the detentions and criminal investigation, and intersectional oppressions of workers as racialized Kurdish migrant labourers.

Intersectionality as an Analytical Framework for Understanding Complex Inequalities

Intersectionality can be used as an analytical tool or framework for understanding the complexity of intertwined inequality and social divisions (Anthias 2012a; Collins and Bilge 2016; Hancock 2016; May 2015). The roots of intersectionality are characterized by a radical agenda to both comprehend and challenge multiple inequalities. Black feminist scholars Patricia Hill Collins (1990) and Kimberlé Crenshaw (1991), who are credited with laying the foundations of intersectional analysis, were informed by black women's feminist struggles and interlocking oppressions and subordinations (Hancock 2016; May 2015). Intersectionality has since travelled across disciplines and has been applied to a variety of contexts.

This study was designed in light of the social justice ethos of intersectionality's capacity to travel, and explores the intersecting oppressions of racialized working-class men. While travelling through disciplines and cases, an intersectional analysis preserves a particular 'way of thinking about the problem of sameness and difference and its relation to power' and treats categories as fluid and changing (Cho, Crenshaw and McCall 2013). An intersectional framework of analysis takes account of broader social landscape and power differentials (Anthias 2012a). Neoliberalism, nationalism, sexism, racism and/or capitalism are intersecting systems of oppression through which matrices of domination are organized. These catalyze complex social formations of spatially- and temporally-specific social inequalities (Collins 1990, 2015; Collins and Bilge 2016). Such inequalities are materialized through a process of peripheralization, which is the production of peripherality through social relations and their spatial implications, determined by unequal power relations (Kühn 2015).

As the analysis of the case will demonstrate, while producing a global centre in the form of 'the world's largest airport', peripheries are concurrently produced, such as loss of the local ecosystem and displaced and dispossessed peasants, while benefiting from other processes of peripheralization at the national level. The simultaneous production of centre and periphery is propagated by precarization. I use precarisation as defined by Butler and Athanasiou (2013: 19) as a "condition of politically induced inequality" integral to the neoliberal regime. Precarious people are exposed to socially and differentially assigned disposability, through injury, violence, poverty, indebtedness and death. In designing research with an intersectional framework, scholars caution against losing sight of the link among state, nationalism and the effects of neoliberalism (Farris 2015; Salem 2018). Farris (2015) suggests that intersecting oppressions can be better examined through the lens of the nation state, which mediates the ideological justification and reproduction of complex inequalities. A central concern of this study is to explore the organization of the state–capital relationship in a neoliberal regime of governance with criminalization and securitization of politicized ethnicities.

Intersectional analysis must also be designed with normative content and a social justice ethos (May 2015; Collins and Bilge 2016; Collins 2015). Intersectionality, as an orientation and disposition, entails intellectual and political commitment to anti-subordination, anti-racism, and eradication of injustice and exploitation, questioning dominant discourses that legitimize such inequalities (May 2015; Bilge 2013). In drawing on these insights concerning the critical lens of intersectionality, I seek to disentangle the intersecting constructions of class and ethnicity in a context of authoritarian neoliberalism. I draw attention to interwoven relations of power between state and capital in their deployment of intersecting oppressions to generate consent and control dissent. Spatially- and temporally-specific power constellations must be taken into account, such as denial of the Kurdish problem as an ethno-political issue (Yeğen 2007) and its criminalization and penalization (Bayır 2014;

O'Connor and Baser 2018), as well as forms of racism against and racialization of Kurdish rural migrants (Ergin 2014; Gönen 2012; Yarkın 2020), the state dependency of the capitalist class and capitalist development (Buğra and Savaşkan 2014; Keyder 1987), the weakening of working-class militancy and labour unions (Bozkurt-Güngen 2018; Ercan and Oğuz 2015), and certainly the rise of Islamist politics as a powerful hegemony-building project in recent decades. AKP governments since 2002 have increasingly evolved toward a neoliberal security state (Kaygusuz 2018) of authoritarian neoliberalism (Tansel 2018) or competitive authoritarianism (Esen and Gumuscu 2016; Özbudun 2015). These factors, among others, have shaped the context in which a specific matrix of power is able to securitize and criminalize mobilization, dissent and protest. These structural factors are integral to the extent to which social institutions are controlled by the dominant group in the matrix of domination (Collins 1990). Collins (1990) states that the matrix of domination, as an interlocking axis of oppression, operates not only at the level of individuals and communities, but also at the level of social institutions.

Construction-Based Growth under Neoliberal Authoritarianism

Under a progressively deepening global neoliberal order, authoritarian neoliberalism assembles various contextually-embedded technologies, rationalities and mechanisms that seek to marginalize, discipline and control dissident social groups and democratic opposition, causing crisis-ridden, contradictory practices (Brenner, Peck and Theodore 2010; Bruff and Tansel 2019; Tansel 2018). In Turkey, the use of technologies of ethnic governance to divide and discipline the working class is a dominant characteristic of the neoliberal regime of governmentality. Under AKP rule, a series of judicial and administrative restructurings and executive centralizations enabled both a dramatic state-led commodification of urban land (see Cengiz, Atmiş and Görmüş 2019) and the selective deployment of state coercion to control social protest and mobilization against these measures. The executive power obtained extraordinary expropriation powers, by-passing the influence of auditing and regulatory authorities (Tansel 2018, 2019). The state of emergency declared after the attempted coup d'etat of 2016 further centralized authority, intensified securitization (Kaygusuz 2018), restrained labour mobilization and enabled a de facto ban on workers' strikes (Bozkurt-Güngen 2018). Governmental decrees under the state of emergency were also used to override legal mechanisms such as environmental impact assessments, and this has become the rule (Adaman, Arsel and Akbulut 2019). Against this backdrop, the construction sector has been the backbone of the AKP's hegemonic model for the production of consent, promotion of economic growth, and redistribution of its surplus, so as to avoid public dissent and create a politically loyal capitalist faction (Balaban 2012; Çavuşoğlu and Strutz 2014; Yeşilbağ 2016).

A fetish for developmentalism and economic growth has been integral to republican modernism and instrumental in generating consent among an internally fragmented population (Akbulut and Adaman 2013; Çavuşoğlu and Strutz 2014). In recent decades, AKP governments have blended this deep-seated fetish with nationalist and Islamic discourses of grandeur and nostalgia, and have structurally reorganized it (Çavuşoğlu and Strutz 2014; Paker 2017). The AKP's neoliberal model of developmentalism relies heavily on the extraction and construction sectors, which attract a precarious labour force of semi-proletarianized workers who remain partially connected and dependent on their rural livelihoods while working as urban labourers. The dramatic transformation of agriculture has pushed peasants out of their rural livelihoods (Adaman et al. 2019; İslamoğlu 2017). The AKP governments inherited an authoritarian legacy in labour relations arising from neoliberalization of the economy since the 1980s. Since 2002, they have further weakened the labouring classes through successive market reforms leading to greater labour flexibility, declining unionization rates and restricted labour militancy. A disciplined, flexible, low-cost, precarious and disposable labour force has been integral to the model of neoliberal developmentalism (Bozkurt-Güngen 2018). Against this backdrop, self-proclaimed 'crazy' mega-projects, such as the new Istanbul Airport, are used as tools for hegemony building, framed as services for the people against which any societal opposition is delegitimized (Paker 2017).

An Intersectional Analysis of the Istanbul Airport Project

Istanbul Airport was among three urban mega-projects planned by the AKP as part of its strategic 'Vision 2023' programme announced before the 2011 national elections, the others being a third bridge across the Bosporus, and a waterway connecting the Sea of Marmara and the Black Sea (Dogan and Stupar 2017). In 2012, the location selected for the airport was in the northwest of the city along the Black Sea shores. A 2009 Environmental Order Plan (EOP), developed by the AKP-controlled Istanbul Metropolitan Municipality had schemed a west–east axis for urban development. Nevertheless, all three mega-projects planned in 'Vision 2023' ignored the 2009 EOP, and moved the proposed urban development to the north of the city, cutting across previously protected natural zones. In 2012, a joint venture of Turkish companies (Kalyon, Kolin, Cengiz, Mapa and Limak) renamed itself Istanbul Grand Airport (IGA), and won the tender for the construction of Istanbul's new airport and its operating rights for 25 years. These contractors were all firms that had previously won major bids for state investments, including privatizations, and were active in the media, energy, resource extraction and construction sectors.[2] The investors won the tender with a bid worth €22,152 billion plus VAT (IGA n.d.b). The project, built over 76.5 million square metres, was the largest ever public–private partnership using a 'build-operate-transfer' model. Later in 2015, six banks, three of them public banks, delivered credit worth €4.5 billion to complete the first phase of the project. The three public banks provided 70% of the loan (Radikal 2015), while the total construction cost was estimated at €10.2 billion (Megaprojeleristanbul n.d). From the start, Istanbul Airport was controversial owing to its ecological impact, alleged corruption and exorbitant building costs. Civil society platforms, organizations, professional chambers and environmentalists drew attention to the ecological damage it would cause, particularly because of its location, as 72% of the designated area was composed of forest, greenery and water resources (see Northern Forests Defense 2015). The total land allocated for the airport project exceeded the airport's own infrastructural requirements. The airport was planned as a part of a commercial 'airport city', a zone for urban development. Despite several lawsuits filed against the project and against land appropriations through 'urgent confiscation', construction of Istanbul Airport continued. The first phase, consisting of two runways and a terminal to accommodate 90 million passengers per year, was completed in October 2018. With the completion of two further phases, it is expected to become the world's largest airport, with six runways and capacity for 200 million passengers annually.

Securitization of Racialized Labour

Studies of the everyday organizing of globally connected construction businesses draw attention to the deployment of diverse forms of intersecting oppressions, from the segregation of precarious migrant workers (Buckley 2014) to racialization and sexualization of the labour force (Paap 2006; Thiel 2012). Urban built environments are sites where intersectional inequalities are embedded into gendered, heteronormative, class and ethnicity-coded practices of oppression (McDowell 2008). In such global contexts enmeshed with local variations, workers experience precarity differently. The Istanbul Airport building site spatially and temporally illustrates complex dominations and subordinations. Both politically and economically, the airport project was a vital investment for the AKP government. In 2018, more than 36,000 workers of more than 15 nationalities were actively employed on this project, the biggest in the country's history. From the beginning, the building site was a high-security zone under strict surveillance. Access to the site by trade unionists, journalists and NGOs was virtually impossible. Several mobile gendarmerie stations were active on the site. Workers were subjected to careful security checks and surveillance by security cameras. They were not permitted to give media interviews on work-related issues. According to the general coordinator of the Assembly of Workers Health and Work Safety (ISIG), the work site 'is like a prison', where workers were afraid of reporting what was going on inside (Yalvaç 2016).

As in other urban mega-projects, the airport construction work employed predominantly Kurdish migrant labour. Thus, understanding the formation and particularities of Kurdish labour is critical to grasp the nature of the intersecting oppressions. The Kurdish question is rooted in denial of the Kurdish identity and forced assimilationist policies (Yeğen 2007; Zeydanlıoğlu 2008). It has escalated into armed conflict and remains unresolved.[3] The Kurdish region, which has faced a 'de-development' policy (Yadırgı 2017) and has been periodically governed under states of emergency and various forms of 'states of exception', can be characterized as a 'peripheralized geography'. Since the 1990s, Kurdish peasants have experienced economically and politically instigated dispossession (Ercan and Oğuz 2015). In addition to being affected by the neoliberal dissolution of agriculture and the increasing trend toward proletarianization,[4] the Kurdish peasantry has been subject to additional disadvantages. They faced further dispossession owing to the forced evacuation of their villages as part of counter-insurgency measures (Ercan and Oğuz 2015; Yükseker 2009). Most internally displaced and effectively dispossessed Kurdish peasants migrated to urban areas, where they faced discrimination. In recent decades, the progress of pro-Kurdish political parties and recognition of some collective rights, such as speaking Kurdish in public, have also increased Kurds' visibility and mobilization. A combination of increasing visibility and a resulting backlash have caused a process of racialization of Kurdish ethnicity (see Ergin 2014; Saraçoğlu 2011; Yarkın 2020). Young, lower-class Kurdish men have particularly suffered from policing and criminalization practices (Gönen 2012). Thus, Kurds as an ethnic group have been subjected to a racialization process and find themselves on the fringes of the urban labour market. Despite the presence of a middle-class Kurdishness, most occupy lower paid, temporary, seasonal and precarious jobs. Several ethnographic studies have documented the racialization and intersectional oppression of Kurdish seasonal workers (Küçükkırca 2012; Uzun 2015).

As a precarious and irregular form of employment, the construction sector employs mainly male Kurdish labourers. Since birth rates are higher among the Kurdish population, young male Kurds commonly drop out of school and start working as child labourers to support their siblings, parents or other family members. Work is normatively entrenched in the reproduction of masculinity, which also pushes young male Kurdish workers to seek employment in construction work. A trade union interviewee noted that 'every Kurd works in construction at some point in his life'. Though perhaps exaggerated, this emphasizes the ethnicization of construction labour in Turkey. Kurdish migrants are extensively employed through sub-contracting networks. Increasingly, Kurdish labourers are employed in urban construction work, but do not move permanently to the western Turkish cities, thereby creating a new type of 'gurbetçi' (temporary migrant) Kurdish worker. They are hired through ethnic kinship networks. Kurdish *dayıbaşı* (head uncles) typically work as foremen to recruit young Kurdish men from their hometowns or villages for sub-contracting firms. These men are accommodated in camps at the work sites. According to the accounts of construction union members, *dayıbaşı* often promise temporary migrant workers higher wages than they are ultimately paid, or force them to pay a commission for arranging jobs. Temporary migrant labourers are preferred by employers because, according to a construction union interviewee, if workers 'have roots in the city' they may be 'more demanding'. Thus, in the current model, sub-contracted construction work operates through ethnicized social capital, which is a source of both networking and patrimonial subordination. Unequal power relations leading to the production of peripheries (Kühn 2015) are integral to the reproduction of sub-contracting networks, which is the underlying organizational scheme for construction-based accumulation. Peripheralization of Kurdish migrants' hometowns through various socioeconomic and political processes is essential to creating a new centre and organizing the authoritarian neoliberal regime of accumulation.

Similarly, Istanbul Airport's construction project employed predominantly Kurdish migrant labourers, who were accommodated on-site. Turnover was high, and most were working on a temporary basis. The numerical domination of Kurdish workers provided them with a safety net. According to one interviewee, 'speaking Kurdish was not so much a problem at the site, because most of the workers were Kurdish'. Another interviewee recounted that 'there were some fascists, who stared at us when we spoke in Kurdish, but it did not matter much because we had power at the building site. We were more than 70% of the workforce on the building site.' A trade union interviewee noted that Kurdish workers are the most dynamic segment in construction work, regardless of union membership. They are politicized for being Kurdish in the first place. For example, when national elections are held, thousands of construction workers empty from the building sites to go back to their homelands to vote, typically for the pro-Kurdish HDP (Peoples' Democratic Party). When the co-chair of the HDP was arrested in 2016, there were walkouts from three large construction sites in Istanbul, and the workers risked being fired or detained (Evrensel 2016).

Precarity and Disposability of Labour

The construction work was organized through chains of sub-contracting networks. According to the president of the Work Health and Safety Employees Union, at the time of the protest, 247 sub-contracting firms were working for IGA. With an obligation to deliver the first phase of the airport on 29 October 2018 (Republic Day), some labourers were working up to 15 or 16 hours a day (Öztürk 2018). The inauguration ceremony had initially been scheduled for the birthday of President Erdoğan in February 2018. Since the official unveiling had already been postponed, the workers were under an enormous time pressure. The construction workers described sub-contracting labour as a system of *'hadi hadi'* (hurry up). IGA was pleased to complete the first phase of the project within 42 months, although, as the firm confessed, 'it could have been finished within 12 years *under normal conditions*' (IGA n.d.a: 7, emphasis added). The extraordinary speed of the work, of which the firm was proud, was considered to be the major cause of work-related accidents on the building site. The rush to deliver the construction in a short time, and with a sub-contracting system, caused systematic violations of work safety. Most work accidents occurred because of the speed of the work and a lack of necessary physical safeguards (see e.g. Evrensel 2019). In addition, most work safety inspectors working on the site were legally precarious employees hired by the firms themselves. The safety inspectors were expected to report their employer for violations and irregularities, who might then fire them (Duram 2018). A trade union interviewee noted that the lack of work safety was not simply a problem of lacking helmets; rather, it was a systematic problem arising from the pressure to deliver the work as fast as possible.

According to workers' accounts, sub-contracting often takes the form of 'sub-contracting for another sub-contractor', bringing further flexibilization and delegation of responsibilities by the principle employer. Sub-contracting has become a regular and permanent characteristic of the neoliberal regime in Turkey. Various legislation has extended its use in the public sector. Under these sub-contracting arrangements, principle employers are protected against accusations for work-related accidents, as documented in several occupational homicide lawsuits (see Lordoğlu and Koçak 2015; Saymaz 2016). Hence, the sub-contracting system functions as a process of peripheralization, producing particular bodies as disposable. Organizational peripheralization through sub-contracting weakens the rights and safety of sub-contracting workers, while simultaneously strengthening the principal employers. The periphery is produced spatially and temporally in the making of the centre.

The number of fatal work accidents remains disputed. Numerous anecdotal accounts of workers refute the official figures. Workers insist that many of the deadly accidents they witnessed were never recounted in the media. On 12 February 2018, a correspondent of the *Cumhuriyet* newspaper published a report based on an interview with an anonymous truck driver working on the site (Kızmaz 2018a). The informant noted that the official figure for deadly accidents did not tell the truth: 'it is said that so far 400 workers must have died in the building of the airport', but the families of the deceased workers have been silenced by being paid 'blood money'. The informant's portrayal of the site as a 'graveyard' drew attention to the gruelling working conditions. Next day, the Ministry of Family, Labour and Social Security was quick to release an official figure for deaths. According to its statement, at the construction site from the beginning of May 2015 till 13 February 2018, '27 workers passed away including traffic accidents and health-related problems' (Hürriyet 2018). IGA quickly filed a lawsuit against the *Cumhuriyet* correspondent, and the court ruling found him guilty of damaging the company's reputation.[5] Ten months later, in December 2018, in response to an opposition MP's official inquiry, the local branch of social security declared that 'between 2013–2018, 52 deadly work accidents' occurred (Bianet 2018a). This figure is still refuted by many workers. According to the interviewees in this study, a figure of 400 deaths would be no exaggeration.

Deadly work accidents, the most dreadful human cost of the intersecting oppressions, are called 'occupational homicides' to draw attention to the fact that most of these accidents arise from preventable factors. Graphic descriptions of occupational homicides illustrate the disposability of workers' bodies and lives in this regime of accumulation. Construction workers died by falling into ponds with their dump trucks, being crushed by cement mixers, dump trucks and other vehicles, steel paddles, moulds and stones, and falling into holes in the dark (Yalvaç 2016). Workers' dead bodies were found accidentally, in one case by their co-workers in a storm drain (Cumhuriyet 2018).[6] According to Butler and Athanasiou (2013), differential exposure to precarity, workplace injury and various forms of violence is generated by socially assigned disposabilities, which are fundamental to a neoliberal regime. Butler's question of 'under what conditions do numbers count and under what conditions are numbers accountable?' (Butler and Athanasiou 2013: 100) is very relevant to this case, since figures for the number of vehicles or amounts of earth moved were so meticulously counted, in contrast to the figures for work-related accidents. Bodies that remain uncounted are disposable bodies, subjected to practices of dehumanization and the violent rhythms of precarity (Butler and Athanasiou 2013: 147–148).

Lack of work safety was not the only problem faced by the workers on the building site. Before the resistance examined in this case, there had been several firm-based protests and walkouts protesting against delays in payments, arbitrary dismissals, long hours wasted in queues for meals, showers or shuttle services, and poor-quality accommodation and food (Birgün 2018a). During the summer of 2018, workers complained repeatedly of bed bugs in the dormitories, which made it practically impossible to rest in their beds. The culmination of all these problems persistently ignored by their employers was a spontaneous protest in the workers' dormitories six weeks before the scheduled inauguration ceremony.

Analysis of the Istanbul Airport Resistance

On 14 September 2018, the airport workers staged a spontaneous walkout, which turned into a massive protest. A couple of days before the protest, two shuttle buses had crashed, leaving at least 17 workers hospitalized. In the early morning of the day of the resistance, workers waited for delayed shuttle services in heavy rain at bus stops with no roof protection. Such events served as catalysts for the walkout. Feeling exhausted, frustrated and ignored for so long, some workers said 'we are not going to work today'. The walkout and the march rapidly grew bigger. Human Rights Watch sources recounted gendarmerie reports of seeing a crowd of 2,000 workers which quickly rose to 10,000 (Human Rights Watch 2018). Protesting workers set garbage containers on fire, and closed off the exit from the accommodation camp to the building site. While the camp authorities announced over speakers that protestors would face 'criminal procedures', the workers' response was to cut the speakers' wires (Birgün 2018b). The workers shouted 'we are not slaves!' in protest against their horrific working conditions. Soon, thousands of citizens in solidarity with the airport resistance shared posts on social media tagged with #koledegiliz (#WeAreNotSlaves). Proliferation of this slogan through social media helped to draw attention to the working conditions, which were framed by the protestors as being worse than those defined by modern capitalism.

A few hours later, the construction site was placed under siege and turned into a military zone. The gendarmerie and riot police attacked the workers with pepper gas and water cannons. Having failed to stop the protest, IGA's management called for a meeting with the workers' representatives who were selected on that day to represent workers from different sub-contracting firms, and with a number of unionists who entered the campus after the incident started. The sequence of events illustrates that the protest was spontaneous. In a handwritten note, the airport construction workers presented a list of 15 demands to IGA (Yalvaç 2018), including solutions to the problems of occupational homicides, overdue wages, partial payments of wages in cash to avoid full social security contributions, lack of hygiene in the accommodation facilities, poor shuttle services, arbitrary dismissals, humiliating treatment by supervisors and white-collar staff, and segregation between workers and foremen, all of which amounted to precarious working conditions and labour law violations by their employers.

Although IGA authorities admitted some of the on-site problems at that meeting, they refused to sign a written protocol. The workers' representatives were told that if they did not terminate the protest, 'necessary measures' would be taken, yet the workers decided to continue the strike the next day. However, at dawn the next morning, police and gendarmerie units raided the workers' dormitories, breaking down the doors (Gazete Karınca 2018) and, according to the official statement, taking 401 workers into custody, more than 250 of whom were quickly released.[7] In the following days, 26 workers and five unionists were arrested and would spend up to 78 days under pre-trial arrest.[8]

Detention and Arrest: Intersecting Authorities

In this section, I explore the complexity of power relations exercised against the workers. Their testimonies reflect the intertwined power relations exercised over them by representatives of state and capital to the extent of violating legal and criminal procedures. On the day of the protest, the commander of the Istanbul Gendarmerie and two local district governors were present at the meeting that is supposed to have been held between the workers and their employer. The unionists who attended that meeting recounted that the district governors behaved as if IGA's CEO, Kadri Samsunlu, were their superior. Furthermore, the presence of top-level civil and military officials restricted the workers' freedom to negotiate with their employer (Kızmaz 2018b). According to workers' testimonies, during their detention several IGA officials were involved in the criminal investigation process. Some workers stated that they had been taken into custody by IGA's security staff (Evrensel 2018b). Photographs taken by the lawyers illustrate that the workers were transported from the site to the gendarmerie stations by IGA's shuttle buses rather than state security force vehicles (Bianet 2018b). An interviewee also recounted that the poor-quality food delivered during their detention was from the same catering company as they were protesting against at the building site: 'The food we got was sent by IGA. I am sure of it. We would recognize that food wherever we see it ... I would recognize that old bread, stinky cheese, even the package was the same.'

Furthermore, during their detention, the workers were first interrogated at the IGA security office, where they were beaten, threatened and insulted by both gendarmerie and IGA officials (Adal 2018; Evrensel 2018b). According to a worker's statement at the hearing, IGA officers 'got this permission from the gendarmerie' (Evrensel 2018b). The physical and symbolic violence to which they were exposed was traumatic for the workers. An interviewee's description of the first moments of the detention reveals a feeling of dehumanization:

> You know, (it was) like animal markets. Before putting in a staple after being brought from a farmer, animals were assigned numbers or marked. Just like that, they got us off the buses, taking our names and last names, they handcuffed us, and lined us up one by one.

> They photographed us. Then they amassed us in a corner. And then they started calling our names one by one.

After leaving the IGA security building, they were held in three separate gendarmerie stations under gruelling conditions, but their families were not informed of their specific locations. They were again beaten, threatened and interrogated to disclose the names and identify workers whose photos were taken during the protest. The lawyers were allowed to speak to only some of the workers on the third day of their detention. They told the lawyers that the workers had been beaten and interrogated to establish whether they had links with 'terrorist organizations', and had been forced to answer questions such as 'are you a traitor?', 'why did you meet up with HDP and CHP MPs?', 'are you a member of PKK?' and 'why did you stone the gendarmerie?' (Evrensel 2018a). After being interrogated day and night, the detained workers were forced to sign written statements without their lawyers being present. They were taken to a room to sign the papers in a rush, after midnight when they were sleepy and careless. According to an interviewee, an IGA official was still around while they were in custody:

> There was also this guy from IGA holding a heavy dossier in his hand, hitting a friend's head with it, saying that 'because of you, I have not slept for three days'. He was an IGA security officer. He was not a gendarme. He had an IGA vest.

The Istanbul Bar Association (2018) released a declaration on the third day of the detention, stating that the workers' detention was the biggest ever mass detention in Turkey, and that Article 149/3 of the Turkish Criminal Procedure Law had been violated at every stage of the investigation and prosecution, since the detained workers had been forced to give statements without their lawyers being present.

After four days of detention, 24 of the detained workers were arrested, followed by seven more workers and unionists in subsequent days. The Terrorism, Smuggling, Economic and Organized Crimes Investigations Bureau of the Gaziosmanpaşa District (Istanbul) Chief Public Prosecutor's Office filed an indictment against the workers, which was conveyed to the Gaziosmanpaşa 14th Penal Court of First Instance. This indictment pressed charges against the 61 workers (31 of whom were under arrest) for 'resisting the fulfilment of duty', 'violating the freedom to work and labour', 'damaging public property' and 'violating the law on meetings and marches by attending with weapons or instruments prohibited by article no. 23'. It claimed that 'a group of about 2,000 people gathered in Akpınar campus, using working conditions as an excuse to protest by slowing down the work, staging a walkout and preventing workers from going on duty'. The indictment presented the protest against the horrific working conditions as unlawful. It cited a workers' WhatsApp group formed for communications on the day of the protest as evidence of the crime (Bianet 2018c, 2018d).

Yuval-Davis (2015) suggests that power relations involving the exclusion and/or exploitation of social divisions deploy different onto-logical discourses and technologies of inferiorization, intimidation or even violence. In the governance of the airport resistance, we observe an effort to shift the debate from work safety or labour rights to 'threat' and 'betrayal'. Following the workers' detention, discourses and instruments of criminalization and securitization were deployed to frame the incident and the protestors. In particular, the Kurdish poor on the urban per-iphery had already been stigmatized by several policing practices inter-linked with the socio-political dynamics of the Kurdish conflict and neoliberalism (Gönen 2012). Furthermore, widespread and ambiguous use of anti-terror laws had criminalized oppositional politics, and espe-cially historically stigmatized groups such as Alevis, minorities, Kurds and socialists (Yonucu 2018). The criminalization of the workers' protest also capitalized on the recent intensification of securitization discourses following the Gezi Park protests in 2013, and the state of emergency implemented between July 2016 and 2018 after the failed coup attempt (Gökarıksel and Türem 2019; Kaygusuz 2018). States of emergency and extraordinary measures had regularly been implemented in the governance of the Kurdish conflict. Such practices were instru-mental in both criminalizing dissent and claiming citizens' consent to such measures through active participation in containing the designated national threats (Gambetti 2013).

Against this backdrop, the instruments necessary to criminalize the airport workers' protest were readily available. On the day of the protest, a narrative of the criminalization of the protest was first man-ufactured by pro-government media sources and Twitter accounts. Here, they deployed a narrative of blaming the workers for intentionally hin-dering the construction work in collaboration with anti-national forces – a treacherous plot proved by photographs of the workers with opposi-tion party MPs who visited the protest. For instance, according to a pro-government newspaper report, none of those in detention were actually workers: they had all entered the work site with fake IDs copied in preceding days, and they had affiliations with terrorist organizations (Sabah 2018b). On the other hand, soon after the incident the IGA authorities adopted a more nuanced strategy that rhetorically separated workers with rightful demands from others who had exploited the workers' problems to halt the construction for their anti-national poli-tical purposes. Days after the protest, IGA's CEO, Kadri Samsunlu stated in an interview with a journalist that 'the workers were right. I apol-ogized to them. There were *some problems* being accumulated *which were not conveyed to me*' (Altaylı 2018, emphasis added). Nevertheless, the firm would not take any action to compensate for the workers' unjust treatment during their detention and afterwards. IGA's subsequent request to take part in the lawsuit against the workers as an 'injured party' was hardly surprising.

Detention, Arrest, Trial and Beyond: Intersecting Oppressions

Historically and spatially constituted forms of intersection may allow one category to be more salient than others, but this saliency is not an onto-logical status in and of itself, as categories become salient in relation to concrete intersections (Anthias 2012b). In this incident, the saliency of the Kurdish workers' ethnicity was produced by stripping them of their class identity. In contrast, in their defence at the hearings, the first of which was held on 5 December 2018, the Kurdish workers sought to establish a po-sition of exploitation as labourers and the problems they suffered as la-bourers. They repeated their complaints about bed bugs, how they had tried to sleep with the lights on, or had spent the night outside the dorms with no rest at all, how they had been overworking, and their friends had been hospitalized from injuries in work accidents. A defendant worker summarized his motivation for attending the protest as follows: 'I attended the protest so as not to wait for hours for a shuttle in the rain, not to queue for an hour every day for lunch, not to sleep on a bed with bed bugs. I was not resisting the police or soldiers' (Mezopotamya Ajansı 2018). At the courthouse, the workers tried to reclaim their rightful class identity and prove the legitimacy of their protest. Their defence lawyers also empha-sized that the workers' protest was legal and defined as a constitutional right. The workers and their lawyers clearly stated that the workers in detention had been beaten, threatened and insulted by both the gen-darmerie and IGA officials, and had been forced to sign statements without their lawyers present. All these factors were completely ignored in the in-dictment (Amnesty International Turkey 2019). The defendants' ethnicity-coded characteristic was not openly spoken of either in the indictment or in their defence.[9] Nevertheless, workers' statements outside the courthouse indicate that most of those taken into custody were Kurdish. Almost all of the workers either arrested or charged were Kurdish. An interviewee re-counted that although there were Turkish workers in the protest, those detained were almost exclusively Kurdish, and at the gendarmerie station in detention, 'everyone was speaking Kurdish'. He regretted that he had been unable to state this fact loudly in the courthouse:

> Being Kurdish was obviously a factor. Always. But unfortunately I did not have the courage to tell this truth to the judge's face. Turkish nationalist workers from Osmaniye to Trabzon,[10] they all knew that we were not working under humane conditions. I saw with my own eyes that there were Turkish nationalist workers among the

protesters; I saw a grey wolf sign – ultra Turkish nationalists' special high sign – next to a victory sign at the protest … The actual factor behind our arrest was that we are Kurdish. Of course, in the indictment it does not say so.

Another interviewee related their ethnic identity as making them a target in the operation. For him, 'it was an operation against the Kurdish youths'. He believed that being Kurdish was more critical than political party sympathies:

> Among us there were supporters of CHP, AKP and HDP. They did not spare us according to the parties we support. At that moment, being Kurd was enough. You are already considered as a terrorist. They already said that the terrorists organized this protest, and (in their eyes) we are familiar with terrorism, causing trouble, starting a quarrel. So it was an attack on the Kurdish youths. Of the 600 detained co-workers, 98% were Kurds.

An interviewee who was an ethnic Arab from a predominantly Kurdish province in Turkey concluded that 'being from the East was equal to being Kurd':

> I am of Arab origin. Honestly, they do not look at whether you are Arab or Kurd, as long as you are from the East, from Batman, or from Şırnak, Van, Diyarbakır. It is done. In their eyes, you are a Kurd. They do not spare you if you are Arab.

His experience illustrates the construction of subjectivity relationally and situationally. He had been photographed with HDP MPs, drinking tea and listening to them. He noted: 'They put this as criminal evidence in my file.' In his own words, he was treated like a Kurd despite not being one. Because he was from 'the East', a geography produced as a periphery, with a history of racialization and stigmatization, his subjectivity was spatially and temporally reconstructed as a Kurd. For him, this violence had been a transformative experience at the time of the arrest:

> I had songs in six different languages on my mobile phone. After the release, it was given back to me. I checked it and realized that they had deleted the songs in Kurdish; among all those languages, only Kurdish songs were deleted. At that moment I realized how the state and the military discriminate against Kurds … In the protest I was standing next to the soldiers. Had there been a stone thrown against them, I would have been the first to protect them. But later I realized that the military and the state try to exploit us and govern us in certain way. I have come to this maturity. I have become disenchanted.

This disenchantment was a result of realizing intersecting oppressions: it was about seeing how he was treated as a worker and how Kurds are treated as citizens by those who hold and exercise authority. For the young worker, the disillusionment resulting from being beaten by the gendarmerie was intense. He said that while waiting in the queue under detention, he had still been clueless about what was going to happen: 'the bad treatment that I would soon face at the hands of the soldiers did not come to my mind at all'. In the end, the worker's consent was broken down.

Kurdish workers' Kurdishness is not only constructed by themselves, but is played out in their interactions with various constellations of power. The workers whose photos were taken while talking or listening to the HDP MPs who came to visit the camp on the day of the protest were specifically interrogated about the photos, and according to the workers' accounts, most were among the arrested workers. Pro-Kurdish parties and the Kurdish political opposition have been systematically criminalized and penalized in the judicial system by accusations of 'Kurdism' or 'separatism' (Bayır 2014). The political representatives of these pro-Kurdish parties are situated at the margins of political legitimacy and are systematically exposed to various forms of criminalization and communal violence (O'Connor and Baser 2018). Hence, talking or listening to HDP MPs was a moment where racialized workers were stripped of their class identity and ascribed to a criminalized (racialized) identity. For the workers, talking or listening to the MPs was a type of contagious contact through which they lost their legitimacy as workers, and what was left afterwards was their naked racialized identity. Thus, intersectional oppression made one form of social division more visible and delegitimized another. According to McCall (2005), people identify and dis-identify with other groups through context-specific alignment. Thus, particular identities may be foregrounded at particular moments. As she suggests, we may need to ask 'what identities are being "done", and when and by whom'. This was crucial in this case because, in order to delegitimize the resistance, power holders sought to deprive the workers of their class status and attribute a stigmatized, securitized and racialized identity to them. On the other hand, in their defence the workers sought to demonstrate their righteousness by reclaiming their class identity. This specific configuration of technologies and discourses of governance must be contextualized in the spatial and temporal alignments of neoliberal authoritarianism and the securitization of the Kurdish question.

Disposability of workers and denigration of their rights and dignities are manifested in the inappropriateness of the physical environment. During their detention at the gendarmerie stations, they were kept in inhumane conditions, with 20 people squeezed into '5–6 square metre cells' where they could not lie down. In a large prison complex outside

Istanbul, the arrested workers were allocated to separate prison buildings along with criminal convicts. According to one interviewee, a cell designed for seven or eight people was allocated to 44 people. The workers were bullied, threatened and accused of treason by other inmates. One of the arrested trade unionists (Dev-Yapı-İş) was separated from everyone else in the prison and put into a cell, a measure otherwise only used for heavy sentences. Denigrating workers through physical inappropriateness continued to be instanced in the hearings. The first and second hearings were held in a cafeteria turned into a makeshift courtroom, where the physical conditions were inappropriate and the testimonies of defendants and lawyers were barely audible to the audience. Despite the regulations stated in the Law of Criminal Procedures, the defendant workers were brought in handcuffs into this makeshift room, and the cuffs were only taken off on their lawyers' request to the judge. Several gendarmes were present in the courtroom with their weapons (Amnesty International Turkey 2019). The third and fourth hearings were held in in small courtrooms, with a 27-seat room being allocated to a case with 67 defendants. The physical and performative aspects of the trial seem comparable to Yonucu's (2018) observations of hearings under anti-terrorism law, where legal ambiguity is expressed in the simultaneous absence and presence of the lawmakers and their performances in courtrooms. She argues that this is not simply 'lawlessness', but also a presence of the law that enables ever-increasing control over lives through legal tools.

Even workers released after the first hearing were subjected to judicial control, meaning that twice a week they had to sign in at a police station in their official town of residence. This judicial control lasted until their second hearing three months later, during which time they could not find jobs because of the de facto constraint on their physical mobility. An interviewee noted the ongoing impact of the resistance on his life: 'Before the airport I was not fired from any work. After the airport incident and having got involved with union organizing, I have been fired from so many jobs.' In a way, they continued to feel the presence of the criminal process in their lives, in the form of uncertainty, stigmatization and risks. At the same time, this episode turned out to be a politically, economically and emotionally transformative experience for many of the young workers.

Conclusion

Several days after the airport workers' arrests, an unnamed worker's dead body was accidently found in a storm drain by Nepalese migrant workers. The worker's nationality and name could not be determined, but it was estimated that the worker must have fallen into the drain three days previously (Kuray 2018). This occupational homicide occurred days after the authorities had reported that 'everything was back to normal' at the building site. 'The accidently found dead body of an unnamed worker' is a spectre in a system of intersecting dominations operating through the production of labourers' precarity and disposability. The workers' slogan, 'we are not slaves', reflects this collective sense of injustice and outcry against intersecting dominations and oppressions that seek to normalize and reproduce their disposability.

The Istanbul Airport project is a microcosm of the AKP's model of accumulation and hegemony building. As a record-breaking mega-project, the airport was meant to transform Istanbul into a 'global centre' or 'a global stage of centredness' by 'occupying' and 're-conquering' otherwise 'useless' forest land and non-urbanized rural hinterland, despite the critical voices of those framed as actors for anti-national forces. I suggest that prior to the mega-projects of the third bridge and Istanbul Airport, the north-western territory of Istanbul was not a periphery in the sense of being 'powerless' (see Kühn 2015), but it became peripheralized by the power-laden spaces of the mega-projects. The creation of a global centre capitalized on the deployment of intersecting oppressions and multiple processes of peripheralization, such as the peripheralization of Istanbul's rural hinterland, exploiting labour from peripheralized geographies and subject to organizational peripheralization through sub-contracting arrangements. The neoliberal authoritarian regime and its production of consent depend on the reproduction of precarity. The sub-contracting system is integral to the construction-based growth and resource allocation of the current regime in Turkey. Sub-contracting is also a type of patrimonial and disciplinary control mechanism applied through specific recruitment practices to deploy and exploit the ethnic capital of migrant Kurdish labourers. The system of sub-contracting, which rests on cut-throat competition and relentless flexibilization, is responsible for the peripheralization, disposability and precarity of workers. Kurdish labourers who form the majority of the construction workforce are exposed to these intersecting dominations.

Given the extraordinary symbolic and material gains expected from the airport's completion, the spontaneous outbreak of a huge workers' protest against disposability and precarity, weeks before the inauguration, was a crisis that had to be contained. The workers' protest was quickly framed as an act of betrayal. I argue that disciplinary practices operated through intersecting oppressions of workers and exploited readily-available discourses and technologies derived from the securitization of the Kurdish conflict and racialization of the peripheralized Kurdish population. In examining the process of the airport workers' detention, arrest and trial, I have sought to demonstrate how multiple dominations and oppressions played out in this specific case. I have argued that the workers' ethnicity was rendered more salient by stripping them of their class identity, which was enabled by the availability of discourses and technologies of securitization, criminalization and pena-lization of ethnicity-coded dissent, in an attempt to de-legitimize the workers' protest.

In this study, viewed through a critical, anti-racist and anti-subordination lens and informed by the travelling capacity of inter-sectionality, I have explored the intersecting oppressions of the workers at Istanbul Airport, which were produced through forms of precarization and peripheralization. The intersectional lens has helped reveal a matrix of domination: the construction workers were oppressed as both workers and racialized citizens, and the containment and criminalization of the resistance capitalized on discourses and technologies entrenched in the governance of the Kurdish question. The intersectional lens de-monstrates that although workers' precarity and disposability are ever-increasing under authoritarian neoliberal regimes, a class-only or ethnicity-only approach would fail to grasp the complexity of social divisions. Intersecting oppressions at the Istanbul Airport building site are part of global capitalism, which creates temporally- and spatially-specific configurations that assemble context-specific technologies to control, discipline and police intersectional social divisions.

Notes

1 For a critique of the Istanbul Airport project, see Northern Forests Defense (2015).
2 A Turkish website, 'Networks of Dispossession' (http://mulksuzlestirme.org/about/) shares 'collective data compiling and mapping the relations of capital and power in Turkey', illustrating the power networks of Istanbul Airport and the Third Bridge (see https://graphcommons.com/graphs/3b103264-92dc-4c54-b9c9-a85a3003ac79).
3 Following failed Kurdish insurrections in the 1920s and 1930s, the Kurdistan Workers Party (Partiya Karkerên Kurdistan, PKK) launched an armed struggle against the Turkish state in 1984.
4 In Turkey, the neoliberalization and globalization of agricultural production under the directives of the World Bank and IMF have led to the removal of price subsidies on products and inputs, and privatization of state marketing and credit cooperatives (İslamoğlu 2017).
5 Because of this ruling, the report was removed from *Cumhuriyet*'s website but accounts are still available on other news websites (see https://www.birgun.net/haber/3-havalimani-insaatinda-400-iscinin-olumu-gizlendi-iddiasi-203998).
6 See Adal (2018) and Garner-Purkis (2019) for other anecdotal witnesses to the unreported deaths.
7 The governor of Istanbul declared that 'in order to prevent this issue being exploited, our security forces took the necessary measures. They carried out identification (ID) checks, whereabouts of workers. 401 people were taken into custody, either who did not have the work ID cards or tried to take provocative actions … Those not involved in the crime will be released. The employer has swiftly started to take action to solve the problems. Now

concerning work peace, there are no more problems there. As of yesterday morning, our workers have been back at work' (Sabah 2018a).
8 On 15 September, trade unionists and citizens tried to organize a demonstration in the Kadıköy district of Istanbul to protest against the airport workers' detention, but they were also tear gassed and attacked by riot police. Twenty-six people were detained and released two days later on probation. After the detentions, security on the construction site was intensified. Trade unionists and MPs from the main opposition CHP (People's Republican Party) were not allowed to visit the site in the following days (Vurgun 2018).
9 At the third hearing in June 2019, a defendant's lawyer asked a gendarmerie officer attending the hearing as a witness 'on what criteria they had detained the workers'. His response might be interpreted as evidence of securitization of the work site prior to the incident in question: 'we identified the workers whom we detained according to our intelligence work that we had been actively pursuing' (Gazete Alınteri 2019).
10 Two provinces that are usually believed to be strongholds of Turkish nationalist ideologies.

References

Adal, Hikmet. 2018. "3. Havalimanı işçisi tutukluk günlerini anlattı" [3rd Airport worker tells about days of detention]. *Bianet*, 7 December. Available at: https://m.bianet.org/bianet/insan-haklari/203320-3-havalimani-iscisi-tutukluluk-gunlerini-anlatti.

Adaman, Fikret, Murat Arsel and Bengi Akbulut. 2019. "Neoliberal developmentalism, authoritarian populism, and extractivism in the countryside: the Soma mining disaster in Turkey." *The Journal of Peasant Studies* 46(3), 514–536.

Akbulut, Bengi and Fikret Adaman. 2013. "The unbearable appeal of modernization: the fetish of growth." *Perspectives: Political Analysis and Commentary from Turkey 5*, 14–17.

Altaylı, Fatih. 2018. "İşçilerden özür diledim, haklıydılar" [I apologized to the workers, they were right]. *Habertürk*, 12 October. Available at: https://www.haberturk.com/yazarlar/fatih-altayli-1001/2177176-ceo-samsunlu-iscilerden-ozur-diledim-hakliydilar.

Amnesty International Turkey. 2019. "3. Havalimanı işçileri davası: İlk duruşmanın ardından" [3rd Airport workers' trial: After the first hearing]. *Amnesty International Turkey* [blog], 3 January. Available at: https://www.amnesty.org.tr/icerik/3-havalimani-iscileri-davasi-ilk-durusmanin-ardindan.

Anthias, Floya. 2012a. "Intersectional what? social divisions, intersectionality and levels of analysis." *Ethnicities 13*(1), 3–19.

Anthias, Floya. 2012b. "Hierarchies of social location, class and intersectionality: towards a translocation frame." *International Sociology 28*(1), 121–138.

Balaban, Osman. 2012. "İnşaat sektörü neyin lokomotifi?" [Whose engine is the construction sector?]. In *İnşaat Ya Resulullah*, ed. Tanıl Bora, 17–32. Istanbul: Birikim Yayınları.

Bayır, Derya. 2014. "The role of the judicial system in the politicide of the Kurdish opposition." In *The Kurdish question in Turkey: new perspectives on violence, representation and reconciliation*, eds. C. Günes and W. Zeydanlıoğlu, 21–46. London: Routledge.

Bianet. 2018a. "CİMER: 3. Havalimanı İnşaatında 52 Ölümlü İş Kazası Gerçekleşti" [CİMER: 52 mortal accidents occurred at the 3rd Airport construction]. *Bianet*, 3 December. Available at: https://m.bianet.org/bianet/insan-haklari/203148-cimer-3-havalimani-insaatinda-52-olumlu-is-kazasi-gerceklesti.

Bianet. 2018b. "3. Havalimanı işçileri üç ayrı karakolda tutuluyor" [3rd Airport workers held in three separate gendarme stations]. *Bianet*, 15 September. Available at: http://bianet.org/bianet/emek/200852-3-havalimani-iscileri-3-ayri-karakolda-tutuluyor.

Bianet. 2018c. "Indictment of 3rd Airport workers accepted." *Bianet*, 7 November. Available at: https://bianet.org/english/law/202420-indictment-of-3rd-airport-workers-accepted.

Bianet. 2018d. "3. Havalimanı işçilerinin iddianamesi kabul edildi" [3rd Airport workers' indictment accepted]. *Bianet*, 7 November. Available at: https://bianet.org/bianet/hukuk/202412-3-havalimani-iscilerinin-iddianamesi-kabul-edildi.

Bilge, Sirma. 2013. "Intersectionality undone: saving intersectionality from feminist intersectional studies." *Du Bois Review 10*(2), 405–424.

Birgün. 2018a. "Üçüncü Havalimanında yüzlerce işçi isyan etti" [Hundreds of workers revolt at the Third Airport]. *Birgün*, 2 February. Available at: https://www.birgun.net/haber/ucuncu-havalimani-nda-yuzlerce-isci-isyan-etti-202727.

Birgün. 2018b. "3. Havalimanında işçiler iş bıraktı" [Workers stopped working at the 3rd Airport]. *Birgün*, 14 September. Available at: https://www.birgun.net/haber/3-havalimani-nda-isciler-is-birakti-230431.

Bozkurt-Güngen, Sümercan. 2018. "Labour and authoritarian neoliberalism: changes and continuities under the AKP governments in Turkey." *South European Society and Politics 23*(2), 219–238.

Brenner, Neil, Jamie Peck and Nik Theodore. 2010. "Variegated neoliberalization: geographies." *Modalities, Pathways, Global Networks 10*(2), 182–222.

Bruff, Ian and Cemal Burak Tansel. 2019. "Authoritarian neoliberalism: trajectories of knowledge production and praxis." *Globalizations 16*(3), 233–244.

Buckley, Michelle. 2014. "On the work of urbanization: migration, construction labor, and the commodity moment." *Annals of the Association of American Geographers 104*(2), 338–347.

Buğra, Ayşe and Osman Savaşkan. 2014. *New capitalism in Turkey: the relationship between politics, religion and business*. Cheltenham: Edward Elgar.

Butler, Judith and Athena Athanasiou. 2013. *Dispossession: the performative in the political*. Cambridge: Polity Press.

Çavuşoğlu, Erbatur and Julia Strutz. 2014. "Producing force and consent: urban transformation and corporatism in Turkey." *City 18*(2), 134–148.

Cengiz, Serhat, Erdoğan Atmiş and Sevgi Görmüş. 2019. "The impact of economic growth oriented development policies on landscape changes in Istanbul Province in Turkey." *Land Use Policy 87*, art. 104086. Available at: https://doi.org/10.1016/j.landusepol.2019.104086.

Cho, Sumi, Kimberlé Williams Crenshaw and Leslie McCall. 2013. "Toward a field of intersectionality studies: theory, applications, and praxis." *Signs: Journal of Women in Culture and Society 38*(4), 785–810.

Collins, Patricia Hill. 1990. *Black feminist thought: knowledge, consciousness, and the politics of empowerment.* London: Harper Collins.

Collins, Patricia Hill. 2015. "Intersectionality's definitional dilemmas." *Annual Review of Sociology 41,* 1–20.

Collins, Patricia Hill and Sirma Bilge. 2016. *Intersectionality.* Cambridge: Polity.

Crenshaw, Kimberlé. 1991. "Mapping the margins: intersectionality, identity politics, and violence against women of color." *Stanfard Law Review 43*(6), 1241–1299.

Cumhuriyet. 2018. "Havalimanı inşaatında korkunç iddia: 3 gün sonra cesedi bulundu" [Terrible claim in airport construction: 3 days later, body found]. *Cumhuriyet,* 21 October. Available at: http://www.cumhuriyet.com.tr/haber/havalimani-insaatinda-korkunc-iddia-3-gun-sonra-cesedi-bulundu-1117411.

Dogan, Evinc and Aleksandra Stupar. 2017. "The limits of growth: a case study of three mega-projects in Istanbul." *Cities 60,* 281–288.

Duram, Aram Ekin. 2018. "Türkiye'de işçi ölümlerinde tablo kararıyor" [Picture darkens in workers' deaths in Turkey]. *DW Türkçe,* 24 January. Available at: https://www.dw.com/tr/türkiyede-işçi-ölümlerinde-tablo-kararıyor/a-42286578.

Ercan, Fuat and Şebnem Oğuz. 2015. "From Gezi resistance to Soma massacre: capital accumulation and class struggle in Turkey." *Socialist Register 51,* 114–135.

Ergin, Murat. 2014. "The racialization of Kurdish identity." *Ethnic and Racial Studies 37*(2), 322–341.

Esen, Berk and Sebnem Gumuscu. 2016. "Rising competitive authoritarianism in Turkey." *Third World Quarterly 37*(9), 1581–1606.

Evrensel. 2016. "İnşaat işçileri HDPlilerin tutuklanmasını protesto etti" [Construction workers protest HDP arrests]. *Evrensel,* 6 November. Available at: https://www.evrensel.net/haber/294988/insaat-iscileri-hdplilerin-tutuklanmasini-protesto-etti.

Evrensel. 2018a. "Havalimanı işçilerine işkence iddiası" [Airport workers alleged torture]. *Evrensel,* 18 September. Available at: https://www.evrensel.net/haber/361623/havalimani-iscilerine-iskence-iddiasi.

Evrensel. 2018b. "3. Havalimanı işçileri için tahliye kararı" [Release decision for 3rd Airport workers]. *Evrensel,* 5 December. Available at: https://www.evrensel.net/haber/367594/3-havalimani-iscileri-icin-tahliye-karari.

Evrensel. 2019. "İş bırakan İstanbul Havalimanı işçileri: Mermer kadar değerimiz yok" [Istanbul Airport workers on work stoppage: We don't have as much value as marble]. *Evrensel,* 4 November. Available at: https://www.evrensel.net/haber/390242/is-birakan-istanbul-havalimani-iscileri-mermer-kadar-degerimiz-yok.

Farris, Sara R. 2015. "The intersectional conundrum and the nation-state." *Viewpoint Magazine,* 4 May. Available at: https://www.viewpointmag.com/2015/05/04/the-intersectional-conundrum-and-the-nation-state/.

Gambetti, Zeynep. 2013. "'I'm no terrorist, I'm a Kurd': societal violence, the state, and the neoliberal order." In *Rhetorics of insecurity: Belonging and violence in the neoliberal era,* eds. Zeynep Gambetti and Marcial Godoy-Anativia, 125–152. New York, NY: NYU Press.

Garner-Purkis, Zak. 2019. "Life in 'the cemetery': uncovering Istanbul Airport's dirty secrets." *Construction News,* 10 October. Available at: https://www.constructionnews.co.uk/agenda/investigations/life-cemetery-uncovering-istanbul-airports-dirty-secrets-10-10-2019/.

Gazete Alınteri. 2019. "3. Havalimanı işçilerinin 3. duruşması görüldü" [3rd Airport workers' third hearing held]. *Gazete Alınteri*, 26 June. Available at: https://gazete.alinteri1.org/3-havalimani-iscilerinin-3-durusmasi-goruldu.

Gazete Karınca. 2018. "3. Havalimanına şafak baskını: İşçi koğuşlarının kapıları kırıldı, 543 gözaltı var" [Dawn raid on the 3rd Airport: Workers' wards broken, 543 detentions]. *Gazete Karınca*, 15 September. Available at: https://gazetekarinca.com/2018/09/3-havalimanina-safak-baskini-isci-koguslarinin-kapilari-kirildi-543-gozalti-var/.

Gökarıksel, Saygun and Z. Umut Türem. 2019. "Banality of exception? law and politics in 'post-coup' Turkey." *The South Atlantic Quarterly* 118(1), 175–187.

Gönen, Zeynep. 2012. "Yoksulluğun suçlulaştırılması, suçun ırksallaştırılması: Kapitalizmin tarihsel mirası ve Türkiye örneği" [Criminalization of poverty, racialization of crime: Capitalism's historical legacy and the example of Turkey]. *Praksis 28*, 57–80.

Hancock, Ange-Marie. 2016. *Intersectionality: an intellectual history*. New York, NY: Oxford University Press.

Human Rights Watch. 2018. "Turkey: Workers behind bars as airport opens." *Human Rights Watch*, 29 October. Available at: https://www.hrw.org/news/2018/10/29/turkey-workers-behind-bars-airport-opens.

Hürriyet. 2018. "Bakanlık, 3. Havalimanı inşaatında hayatını kaybeden işçi sayısını açıkladı" [Ministry announces number of workers lost in 3rd Airport construction]. *Hürriyet*, 13 February. Available at: https://www.hurriyet.com.tr/gundem/3-havalimani-insaatinda-kac-isci-oldu-bakanlik-acikladi-40740951.

IGA. n.d.a "The new airport salutes Istanbul with 1453 trucks." *IGA* [website]. Available at: https://www.igairport.com/en/press-releases/the-new-airport-salutes-istanbul-with-1453-trucks.

IGA. n.d.b "Hayaldi gerçek oldu" [A dream that came true]. *IGA* [website]. Available at: https://www.igairport.com/hayaldi-gercek-oldu-e-kitap.

İslamoğlu, Huri. 2017. "The politics of agricultural production in Turkey." In *Neoliberal Turkey and its discontents: economic policy and the environment under Erdoğan*, eds. F. Adaman, B. Akbulut and M. Arsel, 75–102. London: I.B. Tauris.

Istanbul Bar Association. 2018. "Havalanı işçileri için sürdürülen soruşturmada yasa hükmü uygulanmamaktadır" [Law provision is not applied in progress of investigation for airport workers]. *Istanbul Barosu*, 17 September. Available at: https://www.istanbulbarosu.org.tr/HaberDetay.aspx?ID=13694&Desc=Havaalan%C4%B1-%C4%B0%C5%9F%C3%A7ileri-%C4%B0%C3%A7in-S%C3%BCrd%C3%BCr%C3%BClen-Soru%C5%9Fturmada-Yasa-H%C3%BCkm%C3%BC-Uygulanmamaktad%C4%B1r.

Kaygusuz, Özlem. 2018. "Authoritarian neoliberalism and regime security in Turkey: moving to an 'exceptional state' under AKP." *South European Society and Politics* 23(2), 281–302.

Keyder, Çağlar. 1987. *State and classes in Turkey: a study in capitalist development*. London: Verso.

Kızmaz, Mehmet. 2018a. "3. havalimanı inşaatında 400 işçinin ölümü gizlendi' iddiası" [400 3rd Airport workers 'death hidden in airport construction' claim]. *Cumhuriyet*, 12 February. Available at: https://www.birgun.net/haber/3-havalimani-insaatinda-400-iscinin-olumu-gizlendi-iddiasi-203998.

Kızmaz, Mehmet. 2018b. "Devletten alacaklıyız" [The state is indebted to us]. *Cumhuriyet*, 10 December. Available at: http://www.cumhuriyet.com.tr/haber/turkiye/1166106/devletten-alacakliyiz.html

Küçükkırca, İclal Ayşe. 2012. "Etnisite, toplumsal cinsiyet ve sınıf ekseninde mevsimlik Kürt tarım işçileri" [Seasonal Kurdish agricultural workers in ethnicity, gender and class axis]. *Toplum ve Kuram* 6–7, 197–218.

Kühn, Manfred. 2015. "Peripheralization: theoretical concepts explaining socio-spatial inequalities." *European Planning Studies* 23(2), 367–378.

Kuray, Zeynep. 2018. "İş cinayetinin örtbas edilmesine izin vermeyeceğiz" [We will not allow the occupational homicide to be covered up]. *Birgün*, 23 October. Available at: https://www.birgun.net/haber/is-cinayetinin-ortbas-edilmesine-izin-vermeyecegiz-234523.

Lordoğlu, Kuvvet and M. Hakan Koçak. 2015. "AKP döneminde istihdam, işgücü ve işsizlik" [Employment, labour force and unemployment in the AKP period]. In *Himmet, fıtrat, piyasa: AKP döneminde sosyal politika*, eds. Meryem Koray and Aziz Çelik, 99–123. İstanbul: İletişim.

May, Vivian M. 2015. *Pursuing intersectionality: unsettling dominant imaginaries*. New York, NY: Routledge.

McCall, Leslie. 2005. "The complexity of intersectionality." *Signs: Journal of Women in Culture and Society* 30(3), 1771–1800.

McDowell, Linda. 2008. "Thinking through work: complex inequalities, constructions of difference and trans-national migrants." *Progress in Human Geography* 32(4), 491–507.

Megaprojeleristanbul. n.d. "3. Havalimanı" [3rd Airport]. *Mega Istanbul* [website]. Available at: https://megaprojeleristanbul.com/print/3-havalimani.

Mezopotamya Ajansı. 2018. "Havalimanı işçileri davasında 30 tahliye" [30 releases in airport workers case]. *Mezopotamya Ajansı*, 5 December. Available at: https://mezopotamyaajansi.com/GUNCEL/content/view/41428.

Northern Forests Defense. 2015. *The Third Airport project vis-a-vis life nature, environment, people and law*. Istanbul, Turkey: Northern Forests Defense. Available at: https://kuzeyormanlari.org//wp-content/uploads/2015/05/3rd_airport_project.pdf.

O'Connor, Francis and Bahar Baser. 2018. "Communal violence and ethnic polarization before and after the 2015 elections in Turkey: attacks against the HDP and the Kurdish population." *Southeast European and Black Sea Studies* 18(1), 53–72.

Özbudun, Ergun. 2015. "Turkey's judiciary and the drift toward competitive authoritarianism." *The International Spectator* 50(2), 42–55.

Öztürk, Fundanur. 2018. "İstanbul Yeni Havalimanı eylemleri: İşçiler ne talep ediyor, ana firma İGA taleplere ne diyor?" [Istanbul New Airport actions: What do the workers demand, what does the parent company say about the demands?]. *BBC Türkçe*, 20 September. Available at: https://www.bbc.com/turkce/haberler-turkiye-45559105.

Paap, Kris. 2006. *Working construction: why working class men put themselves and the labor movement in harm's way*. London: ILR Press.

Paker, Hande. 2017. "'Politics of serving' and neoliberal developmentalism: the megaprojects of the AKP as tools of hegemony building." In *Neoliberal Turkey and its discontents: Economic policy and the environment under Erdogan*, eds. F. Adaman, B. Akbulut and M. Arsel, 103–119. London: I. B. Tauris.

Radikal. 2015. "3. Havalimanının finasmanına kamu garantisi" [3rd Airport public guarantee for financing]. *Radikal*, 19 October. Available at: http://www.radikal. com.tr/turkiye/3-havalimaninin-finansmanina-kamu-garantisi-1454724/.

Sabah. 2018a. "İstanbul Valisi'nden üçüncü havalimanı'ndaki olaylar ile ilgili flaş açıklama" [Flash statement from Istanbul Governor on events at Third Airport]. *Sabah*, 16 September. Available at: https://www.sabah.com.tr/gundem/2018/09/16/ istanbul-valisinden-ucuncu-havalimanindaki-olaylar-ile-ilgili-flas-aciklama.

Sabah. 2018b. "2. Gezi provokasyonu" [2nd Gezi provocation]. *Sabah*, 16 September. Available at: https://www.sabah.com.tr/ekonomi/2018/09/16/2-gezi-provokasyonu.

Salem, Sara. 2018. "Intersectionality and its discontents: intersectionality as traveling theory." *European Journal of Women's Studies* 25(4), 403–418.

Saraçoğlu, Cenk. 2011. *Kurds of modern Turkey: migration, neoliberalism and exclusion in Turkey*. London: I. B. Tauris.

Saymaz, İsmail. 2016. *Fıtrat: iş kazası değil cinayet Destiny: Murder, not work accident*. İstanbul: İletişim.

Tansel, Cemal Burak. 2019. "Reproducing authoritarian neoliberalism in Turkey: urban governance and state restructuring in the shadow of executive centralization." *Globalizations* 16(3), 320–335.

Tansel, Cemal Burak. 2018. "Authoritarian neoliberalism and democratic backsliding in Turkey: beyond the narratives of progress." *South European Society and Politics* 23(2), 197–217.

Thiel, Darren. 2012. *Builders: class, gender and ethnicity in the construction industry*. New York, NY: Routledge.

Uzun, Emel. 2015. "Kürt fındık işçileri: bir etnik karşılaşma mekanı olarak Akçakoca" [Kurdish hazelnut workers: Akçakoca as a space of ethnic encounter]. *Moment Dergi* 2(1), 100–132.

Vurgun, Fatma. 2018. "Havalimanına dışarıdan işçi formülü" [Workers from outside formula at airport]. *Sözcü*, 17 September. Available at: https://www.sozcu.com.tr/ 2018/gundem/havalimanindaki-eyleme-disaridan-isci-formulu-2630794/.

Yadırgı, Veli. 2017. *The political economy of the Kurds of Turkey: from the Ottoman Empire to the Turkish Republic*. Cambridge: Cambridge University Press.

Yalvaç, Vedat. 2016. "3. Havalimanı ölüm pistine döndü" [3rd Airport turned into a death track]. *Evrensel*, 27 October. Available at: https://www.evrensel. net/haber/293894/3-havalimani-olum-pistine-dondu.

Yalvaç, Vedat. 2018. "3. Havalimanı işçileri kötü çalışma koşullarına isyan etti" [3rd Airport workers revolt against poor working conditions]. *Evrensel*, 14 September. Available at: https://www.evrensel.net/haber/361434/3-havalimani-iscileri-kotu-calisma-kosullarina-isyan-etti.

Yarkın, Güllistan. 2020. "Fighting racism in Turkey: Kurdish homeownership as an anti-racist practice." *Ethnic and Racial Studies* 43(15):2706–2723. https:// doi.org/10.1080/01419870.2019.1685116

Yeğen, Mesut. 2007. "Turkish nationalism and the Kurdish question." *Ethnic and Racial Studies* 30(1), 119–151.

Yeşilbağ, Melih. 2016. "Hegemonyanın harcı: AKP döneminde inşaata dayalı birikim rejimi" [The mortar of hegemony: Construction-based accumulation regime in the AKP period]. *Ankara Üniversitesi SBF Dergisi* 71(2), 599–626.

Yonucu, Deniz. 2018. "The absent present law: an ethnographic study of legal violence in Turkey." *Social and Legal Studies* 27(6), 716–733.

Yükseker, Deniz. 2009. "Neoliberal restructuring and social exclusion in Turkey." In *Turkey and the global economy*, eds. Ziya Öniş and Fikret Şenses, 262–280. New York, NY: Routledge.

Yuval-Davis, Nira. 2015. "Situated intersectionality and social inequality." *Raisons Politiques* 58, 91–100.

Zeydanlıoğlu, Welat. 2008. "'The white Turkish man's burden': orientalism, Kemalism and the Kurds in Turkey." In *Neo-colonial mentalities in contemporary Europe? language and discourse in the construction of identities*, eds. Guido Rings and Anne Ife, 155–175. London: Cambridge Scholars Publishing.

3 From the Periphery to the Centre of Resistance

Women and/in Anti-Austerity Mobilizations in Crisis-Ridden Athens

Hara Kouki

Introduction[1]

Greece has attracted mass media and research attention over the last decade owing to a multifaceted crisis that has radically disrupted daily lives. The harsh austerity measures imposed on the population since 2010 by international institutions and local governments have generated mass unemployment, homelessness, poverty and social exclusion, provoking what has been described as a full-blown humanitarian crisis. People reacted promptly with a massive anti-austerity movement that dominated most cities, as the majority of the population took to the streets. Soon afterwards, protests were replaced by a broad, grassroots movement of solidarity for those in need of food, medical care, shelter or social support, which was reactivated in 2015 due to an influx of migrant groups. The emergence and spectacular growth of solidarity initiatives has brought about a reconfiguration of social movements in a country that continues to face unending and multifaceted crises.

At the outset of the crisis, anti-austerity actions were criticized and even criminalized for impeding Greece's alignment with its European counterparts. However, a few years later, journalists, researchers and politicians alike were celebrating politics of anti-austerity mobilizations, as by 2015 the solidarity movement had attracted mass appeal with its positive aim, reflecting people's resilience, creativity and collaboration beyond the market or the state. Protest moved from conflictual demonstrations in the streets to spaces of care and social reproduction across urban neighbourhoods, where people supported and related with each other across gender divisions in order to deal with and resist austerity. But what brought about this radical shift in repertoires of action and movement organization? How did people turn from street protests to practices of social reproduction, and what sustained this alternative way of resisting austerity?

The chapter stresses the importance of mundane and methodical forms of reproductive labour for bringing about this transformation. It shows how widespread feelings of vulnerability and dispossession led thousands of people to engage in collective action, triggering acts and spaces of solidarity and belonging, and how such work was largely performed by women. While gender has been typically missing from or deemed irrelevant to analysis of anti-austerity mobilizations, we argue that it was exactly because both women and reproductive labour came to the fore that collective action evolved in different ways and managed to sustain life in a city in disarray. Without explicitly drawing on identity politics or aiming at feminist goals, women, with their knowledge, skills and experience, moved from the periphery to the centre, radically transforming understandings of work and organization within social movements.

This chapter draws on recent research on the role of gender and social reproduction in movement cultures (Daskalaki et al. 2020; Kouki and Chatzidakis forthcoming), and on extended ethnographic data on self-help initiatives in crisis-hit Athens (2010-2018), to look at solidarity mobilizations in crisis-ridden Greece. First, the paper positions the case study in its sociopolitical context and briefly refers to scholarly literature on the impact of gender on social movements and the methodological approach adopted. The main part presents the personal stories of three people actively engaged in solidarity initiatives that reflect how movement practices were transformed to embrace a diversity of experiences that challenged gender norms in activist culture. The concluding section provides a brief reflection on how intersectionality allows us to critically engage with inequalities produced by austerity, as well as within social movements, and thus to develop better understandings of working lives.

Social Movements in Greece in Crisis

Greece has a rich history of social movements and bottom-up mobilizations, commonly organized around trade unions, left-wing parties, radical left-wing organizations, anti-authoritarian/anarchist groups and student disputation. Repertoires of action include strikes, demonstrations, sit-ins, school occupations and road blockades. This contentious political culture has traditionally understood the state as the main opponent and 'other', and has defined itself against state power, revolving around grand narratives and showing little appreciation for particularistic struggles or single-issue demands. Although gender-, sexuality- and ethnicity- related identity issues have surfaced in social movements in post-1974 Greece, feminist activists have failed to radically subvert the patriarchal and hierarchical character of the basis of which (contentious) politics is performed and experienced (e.g. Simiti 2002).

Building on this rich tradition of contention, the country immediately became a laboratory of resistance when the first austerity measures were adopted in 2010. Throughout the first two years of the crisis, urban public life was paralyzed by 24-hour general strikes, conflictual demonstrations, riots and occupations, complemented by the 2011 *indignados* assemblies in town and city squares (Della Porta et al. 2017; Serdedakis and Koufidi 2018). Protests were not constrained to the capital, nor to those usually engaged in protest, but spread throughout most cities and expanded across age, social and professional groups. The radicalization and intensification of social movements went hand in hand with the detrimental effects of an austerity drive that had already deeply penetrated the everyday lives of most Greek households. By 2015, the country had lost more than 30 per cent of its GDP, general unemployment had more than tripled, from 7.7 per cent in 2008 to about 25 per cent in 2015, and youth unemployment had skyrocketed to over 50 per cent (ELSTAT 2015). This was the most severe recession experienced by any established democracy in the post-war era.

Faced with their failure to impact on state politics, the street protests gradually faded, while self-organized, local solidarity initiatives started to mushroom and become more and more vital across the country (Della Porta et al. 2017). Informal neighbourhood groups and initiatives were set up to address needs for food, education, primary healthcare, housing and social support. Emerging from the street protests, solidarity became an act of resistance to austerity at the local level. Although the exact number of such spaces cannot be established owing to their informal character, a 2015 report refers to approximately 40 self-organized solidarity clinics and pharmacies operating throughout the country, 47 self-managed food banks and 21 solidarity kitchens distributing hundreds of food parcels per week, 45 networks without middlemen distributing more than 5,000 tonnes of products, and around 30 solidarity education structures, all of which were enabled by the engagement of thousands of volunteers (S4A 2015). At the same time, solidarity economy initiatives grew considerably to deal with mass unemployment, giving rise to numerous workers' cooperatives (Temple et al. 2017). In addition, the 2015 'refugee crisis' led to the emergence of self-organized hosting initiatives and community groups providing social support to migrant populations (Oikonomakis 2018). These often built on the pre-existing infrastructure developed during the first five years of savage austerity in Greek society following the outbreak of the Eurozone debt crisis.

Social movement researchers have read this mobilization as a 'distinct cycle of protest' (Psimitis 2011; Kousis 2013). Anthropologists and geographers have relaunched solidarity as an analytical category (Rakopoulos 2016; Arampatzi 2018), while the social solidarity economy has been reinvigorated as a concept (Gritzas and Kavoulakos 2015), along with the commons (Kioupkiolis 2014; Stavrides 2016), in an effort to talk about this new creative resistance. Solidarity has gradually become celebrated, if not romanticized, for saving the country from collapse. Yet this approach often runs the risk of exoticizing survival strategies at the periphery of Europe (Kouki 2019), and recasting austerity as a platform for moral prosperity (Mattern 2018). Despite its unquestionably positive aim, presenting solidarity in this way seems to be 'delivering a confirming affective surplus in advance of the lifeworld it's also seeking' (Berlant 2016: 395), and fails to read anti-austerity movements beyond the contingencies of the crisis.

In countering the detrimental impact of austerity, social movements in Greece underwent a radical reconfiguration, moving from protest and militant demonstrations in the streets, to decentralized spaces and everyday acts of social reproduction. Yet the shift from conflictual activism toward everyday, mundane practices of care and social reproduction remains unexplored, as is the role of women in solidarity spaces. Gender is deemed largely irrelevant and is generally overlooked in analyses of social movements in Greece, including in relation to anti-austerity mobilizations. However, women have not only disproportionately experienced the effects of the crisis (Karamessini 2013; Vaiou 2016; Kosyfologou 2018), but have also often been the majority participants in these bottom-up solidarity initiatives (Papageorgiou and Petousi 2018).

Gender and Social Movements in Literature

Although scholarly attention only started to turn toward the intersection of gender and social movements in the 1990s (e.g. Taylor and Whittier 1998), interest has recently been growing in ongoing feminist mobilizations and how these are being reconfigured to address contemporary challenges (Mendes 2015; Larsen 2018). The focus has been on gender-related movements, and especially women's movements and the collective identities formed to resist gender injustices (e.g. Moghadam 2000; Lotz 2003). Importantly, scholars have drawn attention to the fact that in their attempts to fight patriarchy, feminist solidarities have historically emerged from the intersections of race, class and sexuality (e.g. hooks 1986; Mohanty 2003). In exploring the role of gender in social movements, research has also highlighted the structural barriers that have obstructed women's participation in contentious action (Fraser 1992). Studies show how, in their daily lives, women perform work that remains under-appreciated and is not thought of as activist (Brown and Pickerill 2009), while men's labour is more visible and appreciated as more important (Bobel 2007).

Over the last few years, feminist scholars have also touched on neoliberal adjustment programmes that have enforced austerity around the globe. A growing number of studies document the dramatic consequences of the ongoing financial crisis for women's lives, both within and outside their homes (Karamessini and Rubery 2013). Extensive literature on how capitalist crises are played out over social reproduction and women's bodies (Motta and Seppälä 2016; Federici 2019) foreground austerity as a gendered process that builds on pre-existing inequalities in structures of production and reproduction (Baines and McBride 2015; Hall 2020). Research also suggests that the very governance of the financial crisis, and particularly the various measures, institutions and ideologies that craft its everyday implementation, are gendered in ignoring feminist concerns while reproducing a masculine understanding of privilege and power (Griffin 2015). In this context, few studies explore new forms of feminist organization that have emerged during austerity (Daskalaki and Fotaki 2017; Durbin et al. 2017).

Despite these strands of feminist literature, little attention has been paid to the role of gender in mobilizations that do not build on pre-configured gender concerns (Taylor 1999). The impact of women's knowledge and experiences of inequality on collective action seems to remain unexplored and unacknowledged when it is not articulated as feminist. This is because it is difficult to recognize feminism or gender in movements that are not built on a narrow definition of solidarity by women, for women (Cullen and Murphy 2017). As a result, the role of gender remains peripheral and little understood in studies of collective action, including in relation to anti-austerity activism (Cullen and Murphy 2017; Fotaki and Daskalaki 2020; Kouki and Chatzidakis forthcoming).

In order to understand what has taken place in Athens during austerity, we draw on recent literature that challenges assumptions about resistance, who is or can be thought as activists, and how resistance is experienced and felt (Kennelly 2014; Craddock 2017, 2019). In recognizing gender as a constitutive factor in the emergence, nature and outcomes of all social movements, we pose the following questions. What role have women played in anti-austerity mobilizations and bringing about the shift toward social reproduction practices? How can we read mobilizations that are not gender-related but allow for the development of feminist principles? Is there a way to acknowledge (gender) inequalities in austerity governance, while also recognizing (gender) inequalities in anti-austerity movements?

Methodology

From 2010 to 2018 we conducted two stages of extensive fieldwork at various movement sites across Athens. The first stage, from April 2010 to March 2015, was exploratory and allowed us to map the broader anti-austerity movement in Athens as it evolved through trade unions, ultra-left and anti-authoritarian groups, squats, student and neighbourhood assemblies, solidarity initiatives and ad hoc mobilizations. Based on our observations and conversations, we decided to conduct detailed exploration of the shift in activist practices that had flourished organically across the city by focusing on five key solidarity initiatives reflecting major tendencies in the emergent movement (see Table 3.1). Our second

Table 3.1 Solidarity initiatives

Name	Fieldwork dates	Details
Urban Social Clinic	September 2016–June 2018	Established in a middle-class neighbourhood, staffed with more than 200 volunteers in total, including doctors, dentists, pharmacists and support staff. Since 2011 it has provided free medical assistance and medicines to those excluded from the public health system – the unemployed, the uninsured, the poor.
Babylon Solidarity School	November 2016–December 2018	Located in a residential district of Athens, since 2013 it has provided additional tuition, including foreign-language and music lessons, to more than 150 pupils per year.
Mazi Food Cooperative	January 2016–June 2018	Located in a residential neighbourhood in the north of Athens, this is run by over 30 volunteers linking urban consumers and local producers directly. It emerged from a market 'without middlemen' organized locally from 2011 to 2014, distributing products in an unmediated and non-profit-making way with no extra in-between costs.
Limani Solidarity	August 2015–January 2018	A broad 'social support' network established in a working-class district in 2011. Run by 250 volunteers, it started as a collective kitchen and fosod bank, and grew to include additional classes for students, a clothes bank and a refugee support group.
Urban House	January – September 2017	A self-organized squat for refugee populatiors, established in 2016 by a group of migrant solidarity activists in a downtcwn neighbourhood in the centre of Athens. Run on the basis of activists and refugee assemblies, it hosted between 100 and 400 refugees for three years.

phase of fieldwork (April 2015 – March 2018), which informs this chapter, included informal conversations, fieldnotes, and 73 interviews of one to two hours' duration with key members of these initiatives. With regard to sampling, our informants varied by socio-demographic profile and level of involvement in social movement activism. Both they and the chosen solidarity initiatives are anonymised here.

Although this research did not aim at exploring gender in social movements or commit to a feminist framework, everyday life in solidarity initiatives proved to be all about care and social reproduction (e.g. Fraser 1992; Federici 2004): for example, purchasing, exchanging and delivering goods, preparing and serving food, mending clothes, caring for the ill, the young and the elderly, and providing care and emotional support for their kin. In practice, these activities were not differentiated from other forms of anti-austerity mobilizations, such as strikes and demonstrations and the establishment of grassroots unions and workers' collectives. Lived experience and activist labour in social movements arising from the crisis disrupted the boundaries between productive and reproductive labour, echoing recent studies in social reproduction theory revisited during the global financial crisis (e.g. Bhattacharya 2017; Daskalaki et al. 2020). This re-articulates the need to understand working and non-working lives as an integrated work process by revealing interactions between paid and unpaid labour.

While undertaking this research, we realized that many participants in solidarity spaces were women, which had gone unnoticed both by the researchers and very often by the activists themselves. Reflecting the demographics of the solidarity spaces more broadly, 48 out of 73 interviewees in our sample were women. They ranged in age from 23 to 74 years old, with the majority aged between 50 and 65. Most were pensioners, precariously employed or even unemployed. All these aspects made us reconsider intersections between age, gender and class within our spaces of resistance. Austerity measures were not targeted against a specific population, but had detrimental consequences for the lives of millions of people across social categories and groupings. For instance, it was no longer only the migrants, the unemployed or those with disabilities who had to struggle to be heard, become visible and demand equality; more and more people at the intersection of gender, class, ethnicity, age, education or geography found themselves unexpectedly in the category of 'those in need'. This group grew larger and larger, mobilizing radically different social movements in its defence. As a result, intersectionality emerged as a vantage point from which to observe and conceptualize ongoing radical transformations in the movement field. Drawing from people's lived experience, intersectionality served as an analytical tool that objects to the separability of social categories, and proposes instead that these are mutually constituted in the same way as oppression is inflicted simultaneously on them (Crenshaw 1990; McCall 2005).

Overall, our fieldwork led us to turn to critical feminist understandings of work and social reproduction theory and the explanatory framework of intersectionality, in order to figure out ways in which social movements evolved into new forms in Greece. This would not have happened if we had not initially committed to a broadly understood feminist approach to ethnography. When entering these spaces of solidarity, we had no preconfigured aims nor specific questions to ask; rather, our fieldwork spanned over time and was guided by the participants themselves and an interest in their lived experience. Our open-ended questions were built on a concern for ordinary routines and relationships, gestures and feelings; for how inequalities unravel and become normalized in the movement field through decision-making processes, organizational tools and everyday tasks; and for local particularities and sociocultural contexts and their role in shaping people's worldviews and resistance. In doing so, we allowed personal histories and everyday praxis to guide us through the movement field, bringing to the fore themes and ideas that ran implicitly throughout our observations but had been left unexplored. In what follows we focus on three such personal histories: those of Aris, Panagiota and Kalliopi.

Findings

Aris: Shifting to Social Reproduction as a Form of Protest

From the age of 18, Aris (37) had been an active member of a leftist youth organization, and was thus used to participating in assemblies, speaking in front of people, drafting manifestos criticizing state power and repressive policies, demanding workers' or prisoners' rights, and persuading others to take part in demonstrations and become members of the organization. It was natural for him to argue using an ideological, polemical discourse, to disagree with opponents, and to defend his group's position even when he was not very sure that it was the right one. During the first years of the crisis, he became even more active in social movements, which had grown hugely and were flourishing across the city, mobilizing everyone to take to the streets. It was not just the 'usual suspects of protest' (Della Porta et al. 2017) who participated in strikes and demonstrations, but people from every strand of life, who felt angry about being dispossessed and thrown to the margins and wanted to resist what they felt to be structurally unjust. As state politics became ever more authoritative in implementing austerity measures that generated poverty and marginalization, events took on a life of their own as people started to create spaces of solidarity to deal with hardship themselves: 'Sometimes there is no "street" for protesting, since what is needed is precisely streets' (Butler and Athanasiou 2013: 153). After much thought and planning, Aris and a group of friends and comrades decided to squat in an abandoned hotel in the centre of Athens, in order to host hundreds of migrants living on the streets awaiting relocation or processing of their asylum requests. Both migrants and people from Athens moved into this large grey building, with the aim of creating a horizontal participatory space where people created their own terms of coexistence by living together. The noisy life in the squat was managed through endless rounds of assemblies that often proved complicated and exhausting. When asked what had changed in his life during the previous year and a half of living in the squat, Aris, who had in the meanwhile also withdrawn from the leftist organization in which he had been in-volved, replied:

> What has been exhausting is that everyday tasks, like cooking, going to the supermarket, mopping the stairs, become political. We have to decide who will prepare food, at what time, for how many, what we will be eating ... In the past, I would argue during an assembly or a political meeting, I would get mad, I would even see my cause defeated, but then I would go home to watch a movie with friends or my girlfriend, you know ... Now it is completely different; I cannot set apart my personal time from what is thought as political, I cannot take a rest, not even when we hang around chatting!
>
> (Aris, 32, March 2018)

Social movements in Greece traditionally rely on mobilizations em-bedded at the street level, with a view to enhancing visibility, and thus disrupting and challenging the normativity of everyday life to achieve their demands. Action revolves around organizations and is mostly state-centred and conflictual. Over the years, the protest culture gradually shifted from loud, visible and confrontational claim-based mobilization, toward decentralized, prefigurative initiatives to create change in the 'here and now' (Maeckelbergh 2011). This entailed practices to support people in need at the local level, through collective kitchens and food banks that provided prepared meals or baskets of products; markets without middlemen that directly connected producers with consumers; social pharmacies and solidarity clinics set up by volunteers to provide primary healthcare to those excluded from the public health system; schools that taught students who could not afford foreign-language courses or additional help; and workers' collectives and local assemblies that provided social support to the neighbourhood by taking care of households in need of vegetables, oil, bread, cans, milk, clothes, blan-kets, shoes, heating devices, pencils and school books, medical ex-aminations and drugs. This world of solidarity revolved around materials and people receiving, offering, participating, and mobilizing around issues of survival in these small, ordinary places in unnoticed sites in the city (Kouki 2019).

Solidarity was about taking care of the community's food, education, health and survival needs; it was about maintaining life (Mattern 2018), which during the crisis became an act of resistance and a question of social reproduction. This shift toward everyday, routine, mundane activities by both men and women participating in the movement transformed care and social reproduction from a part of private lives and domesticity into a political, visible and common task. Street politics and ideology-driven political confrontation have normalized a male-dominated understanding of resisting power, as it is usually men who engage in what is typically considered to be 'political work: decision-making, public actions, speaking' (Motta and Seppälä 2016: 10). By becoming crucial actors in this newly formed solidarity movement (Papageorgiou and Petousi 2018; Loukidou 2019), women shattered the ideal image of the heroic masculine activist defying police power and persuading his opponents (Craddock 2017). It is hard to fully challenge, let alone subvert, dominant (gender) dynamics, yet the shift at that time in social movements' repertoires of action broadened the terrain of political participation, activating and revaluing skills, values, individuals and groups that had previously been invisible and peripheral. This shift was much more than an increase in women's numbers, as it signified a move toward a different way of resisting power through reproductive politics (Briggs 2018; Hall 2020), unsettling the dividing lines between private/public, valuable/non-valuable work, and visibility/invisibility.

Ari's personal experience reflects this shift from symbolic, angry protest actions staged against the authorities, toward trivial, unheroic work addressing local needs. But it also illustrates the transformative effects that this has had on how care and reproductive labour is experienced, understood and narrated in relation to resistance, and how the self is reconfigured within such social movement struggles.

Panagiota: Using Vulnerability as a Source of Resistance through Social Reproduction

Panagiota (47), an unemployed, single mother, had never engaged in politics or collective action. The crisis ripped her life to pieces, as her small but profitable hotel on a small island went bankrupt. She had to return to Athens to take care of her 89-year-old mother who had fallen severely ill, and to minimize her living costs by avoiding paying rent on two different households. Within only a few years, her middle-class status and lifelong certainties had been totally dismantled, leaving her unable to move on. Seriously indebted and with no health insurance or income, she was advised by a friend to visit her neighbourhood food bank to find clothes for her son, which she could not afford to buy. The place was set up by a group of friends and comrades and gradually attracted more volunteers who originally gathered food and other items to distribute to families in need around the neighbourhood. They subsequently organized a regular market to help link rural producers with urban consumers with no middlemen costs, distributing products to consumers in the area in an unmediated and not-for-profit way. They also offered practical information to indebted households with regard to electricity cut-offs and evictions, unpaid rents and bills, and legal actions against employers' abuse. Those who needed help, like Panagiota, were normal people whose lives had also been shattered overnight, and 'not those whom we had been used to recognize as poor or marginalized' (Gogo, 58, Limani Solidarity). When Panagiota arrived at this small basement location, which she had never noticed before despite it being only five minutes from her house, a volunteer encouraged her to pick whatever she needed, apologizing for the mess. After some days she returned to help tidy up the space. As the weeks passed, she spent more and more time there, calling rural producers, cleaning the space, stacking products on the shelves and talking for hours with passers-by seeking advice. She eventually became a core member.

> I have never been part of anything political before; there are so many people around who know so much more than I do. I have nothing to say really, and if I do, I speak in the wrong way [laughter]! But I gained confidence in here, I feel useful to others, I'm in charge of so many things, and I have met many people. I became sociable again – in the years before that I was so alone, blaming everyone and feeling hopeless … The truth is that a person who has been hungry can better understand and help those who are hungry. I may no longer need help myself, but I do not want to leave this place; it is my home, it is a home for so many people from the neighbourhood. And, you know, at the end of the day, it is not just need; it is joy that brings us here.

Hundreds of people have engaged voluntarily in the management and cleaning of these spaces of solidarity for years, in order to support people who are ill, homeless or cannot afford to eat, buy clothes, pay for the bills, rent and children's education, and who have been left alone to deal with hardships that exceed their skills and energy. Before the crisis, social movements had been built around ideology and political affiliation, and had revolved around relatively informal organizations and groups. A more pragmatist ideological turn (e.g. Chatzidakis 2020) brought radical changes to the membership of social movements. The volunteers were initially people in need, and in many cases had no prior activist or militant education, like Panagiota and other similarly 'apolitical women' (Hanisch 1970). These women had previously been on the periphery of social movements, and had joined these conflicting spaces of solidarity to engage regularly in informal networks organized horizontally through assemblies and time banks, working teams and rotas.

Nevertheless, far from idealizing the function of these initiatives, our informants described their everyday mundane operations as usually painstaking, tedious, and rife with internal conflict and disappointment. In an effort to explore how this infrastructure of solidarity was sustained against all the odds, we asked Panagiota, and indeed most of our informants, 'what keeps you here, after all these years?' or 'have you ever thought of leaving this place?' The majority, like Panagiota, were surprised at the question, to which they retorted 'why should I leave?' This made us challenge our point of departure: solidarity was not a surplus of morality or empathy available to those who had already reached a certain level of personal or social well-being and wanted to support others; on the contrary, 'it was something to hold on to, something collective and socially different that we all needed in order to survive' (Kalliopi, 54, Urban Solidarity Clinic). For many, these spaces were their 'home' (a term repeated 32 times throughout our interviews), conferring central meaning on their lives. Austerity measures had brought about a precarization of everyday life, depriving people of decent living conditions; but it was the same people, those stripped of everything who felt the need to act, offer to and relate with others to resist austerity. 'Life is not only about working and having a family and so on; everyone wants to do something more, something bigger, beyond everyday things' (Nikos, 42, Urban Solidarity Clinic). Thus, vulnerability was not a passive, victimizing condition, nor an obstacle to collective action; rather, it led people to come together and constitute a form of resistance against systemic injustice, in a way that was vehement, spontaneous and different from before (Butler and Athanasiou 2013). It challenged the boundaries between those capable of offering and others in need of receiving, the expert and the average person (e.g. Rai 2018).

Panagiota's experience stands for all these women who did not identify themselves as feminist or as participating in a feminist struggle, but who nonetheless performed care and social reproductive work as a quintessential act of resistance. This solidarity practice created new belongings that were not rooted in ideologies or identity politics, but emerged as interdependent, intersectional and embedded in places.

Kalliopi and Care in Social Movements

Kalliopi, a 58-year-old psychiatrist and mother of two, had engaged in politics for years, as a member of extra-parliamentary leftist organizations struggling against state power, and of grassroots initiatives concerned with migrants' rights and environmental issues. However, over the previous decade or so, family and work obligations and general disappointment with (contentious) politics had made her dissociate from the streets of protest. When the crisis erupted, she received an email invitation to join an emerging Solidarity Clinic being organized in a residential neighbourhood south of the city centre. She was initially hesitant, as she did not know the people setting up this initiative; yet her anger at the aggressive austerity measures and policies impoverishing so many people she knew and the Greek populace more generally, as well as her urgent desire to do something about it, made her visit the space. Kalliopi ended up working as a volunteer doctor there for four years. To begin with, she agreed with the values defining the function of the clinic: self-organization, direct democracy, horizontality and inclusiveness. These were similar to those of other movement initiatives of which she had previously been part. But what really attracted Kalliopi to become active was that this bottom-up initiative was somewhat different:

> We were doing something practical, tangible, action-based, something unprecedented in the sense that we replaced the state in an organic and spontaneous way. Fifty solidarity clinics around the country provided healthcare to thousands of people with no supervising ministry, structure, leadership, top-down organization or financial support. It was through assemblies and networking among us that we did what we did… it was magical and it was different, we offered a social approach to healthcare, an alternative way of being together, a point of reference for thousands of people.

Everyday praxis challenged conventional healthcare in these clinics. Doctors could not treat patients in just 20-minute slots, make as many appointments as possible or act as they normally would. Members of the clinic would listen and talk to the patients, learn about their living conditions and spend time with them. The doctors (in some cases) became secretaries and engaged in the everyday functioning of the clinic, and the patients participated in the tasks and became volunteers. Roles were blurred in these solidarity spaces, and they proved 'therapeutic to both volunteers and visitors' because they offered a place to meet, and not be in a hurry or alone. These were spaces of collective coexistence and relationality at a time when austerity was isolating people and breaking social bonds, making everyone vulnerable and uncertain about their own identity.

As was evident in the field of healthcare, these solidarity spaces did not invent anything new based on expertise or technical knowledge. Rather, their innovative character lay in the fact that they used existing resources and activated previously under-appreciated practices of maintenance and care (Mattern 2018), so as to create urban infrastructures that prevented the city life from collapse. The personal was politicized, shifting the emphasis to mundane and banal activities and people's bodies, whether in the context of families, leftist organizations, trade unions or grassroots mobilizations. Such care work is usually not thought of as important and is assumed to be women's responsibility (Mason-Deese 2016). Talking, asking, touching and relating with individuals and families from the community was a way of learning about their needs and dealing with the shame of not having enough, of losing everything. What was needed and was indeed revalued was to connect, spend time, listen and care; and because it was the main requirement, that caring labour was performed by both men and women.

Thus, care was not a paid task to be performed by professionals, but a broader emancipatory ethics running through everyday functions in solidarity spaces. This was brought about by allowing emotions to come to the fore and occupy a constitutive role in the life of social movements. Contradictory feelings, such as anger, shame, care, rage, empathy, joy, vulnerability and exhaustion, were embraced to create a form of affective solidarity (Hemmings 2012) that became transformative and enabled the formation of broad alliances of people to resist what was felt to be unjust and outrageous. Kalliopi's narrative showcases how the practice of solidarity transformed caring into a universal right (Tronto 2013) and a community endeavour.

Discussion

In this chapter, we suggest that although gender may appear irrelevant in some accounts of anti-austerity mobilizations in Athens, the opposite is actually the case. Extended ethnography and numerous interviews with people who had participated for years in solidarity initiatives across Athens revealed aspects of lived experience that tell a more nuanced story. Social movements underwent a profound reconfiguration in their repertoires of action and membership, with many 'ordinary' people entering the movement field, including women unfamiliar with activist praxis.

In order to make sense of how this changing world came into being to produce solidarity, we have presented the personal stories of three people engaged in anti-austerity mobilization. Aris's story allows us to trace the shift from traditional forms of protest politics and oppositional activism into the realm of social reproduction in the form of clothes and food banks, migrant squats and social clinics. In Panagiota's trajectory, we recognize that those active in social movements were not volunteers who could afford to offer their surplus to others in need; rather, solidarity practices and ideas emerged from those vulnerable and dispossessed by austerity, as a form of coming together, resisting and belonging. Finally, Kalliopi's narrative enables us to observe the extent to which this shift challenged organizational structures and traditional divisions of labour in movements, while embracing affects and emotions in the form of radical care.

Nevertheless, our ethnographic account is not based on explicitly feminist movements or mobilizations that aimed to challenge gender norms – there were only few such feminist mobilizations that took place during the crisis (e.g. Athanasiou 2014; Daskalaki and Fotaki 2017). Likewise, the stories narrated by our participants do not allude to any explicitly articulated feminist demand or concern. Indeed, most of our informants had not necessarily noticed the overwhelming presence of women in the spaces where they spent most of their time. Perhaps not surprisingly, then, the few studies that do deal with increased women's presence in solidarity initiatives refer to the risk of essentializing women's participation in social reproduction initiatives (Loukidou 2019), or even to a potential reification of traditional gendered divisions of labour (Kosyfologou 2018).

Yet this approach does not recognize gender in movements that are not strictly defined as feminist. More importantly, it fails to empirically attune to all those women who were not previously part of contentious politics and who left their homes to inundate solidarity spaces, bringing along their skills and knowledge as well as experiences of inequality so as to relate with unknown people. Their invisible but massive presence shattered what is traditionally understood to be a man's world. The ideal type of activist identity and praxis was challenged by what had hitherto been thought of as personal, intimate, banal, domestic, emotional, unpaid and under-appreciated. Everyday tasks of care and social reproduction that had traditionally been peripheral became a collective and integral part of the urban landscape. Litsa, a 53-year-old woman with a migrant background who did morning shifts in the collective kitchen at Limani Solidarity, was one among the many who drew attention to the role of care in everyday activism:

> You have to arrange things on the shelves nicely and neatly, everything has to be clean, and people should be treated in a way that lifts their dignity. So many come in here crying and repeating how ashamed they are. You have to make them feel proud and have respect for themselves, and then they will let you know what they need and perhaps accept help. This is the most important thing, to make people feel nice about themselves, which requires talking and talking and talking, and it takes time, and more time, but this is the only thing you can do.

Ethnographic observation revealed that care in our movements was performed by both men and women participating and working in these spaces. This brought the personal and the political together. It challenged normative assumptions that defined social movements' ideas and practices as heroic and masculine, primarily performed by men; binary thinking about who and what are valued as important was also dissolved in praxis. Although this remained unarticulated, somewhat invisible and certainly incomplete, it still had an emancipatory potential that challenged gender norms in the movement field, at least for a while.

Thus, we argue that both austerity and anti-austerity mobilizations have been gendered, and that adopting an intersectionality approach might reveal transformative aspects of social movements that have not previously been explored. To begin with, according to recent research, austerity is a feminist issue owing to its disproportionate impact on women (Karamessini 2013). At the same time, governance of the crisis in Greece has been gendered (e.g. Griffin 2015): on the one hand it has transformed Greek people into scapegoats at the EU level, while on the other, it has imposed austerity in aggressive, punitive and exclusionary ways, stigmatizing various socioeconomic groups, such as public employees, pensioners and undocumented migrants (Kouki and Liakos 2015). Meanwhile, spending cuts, new taxes and privatizations have brought about unemployment and bankruptcy, and have impoverished a large part of the populace. Within the space of just a few years, deprivation and precarity became the norm for many Greek households previously self-identified as middle-class and thus perceived as invulnerable to marginalization. The vicious attack of austerity challenged the structural foundations of power, transforming the majority of the population into 'the other', and thus invisibilizing, marginalizing and depriving them. A wide range of groups and individuals at the intersections of gender, age, geography, class and ability, among many others, suddenly experienced the simultaneity of oppression and the utter collapse of class and sociocultural categories.

This, in turn, foregrounded the common experiences of invisibility, lack of agency and injustice. People from various strands of life came together to respond to this (gendered) aggression, and in doing so, social movements against austerity were radically reconfigured, moving from streets politics to care and reproductive labour. Masculine, heroic, verbal and conflictual activist patterns, as well as the devaluation of everyday, reproductive tasks of care and maintenance, were challenged. Women, with their knowledge, skills and experience, moved from the periphery to the centre of social movements and brought forward alternative membership, repertoires of action, organizational patterns and collective identities.

The intersectionality perspective that this study adopted, allows us to critically engage both with inequalities produced by austerity and with power relations in the movement field and to more broadly reflect upon inequalities, exclusions and invisibilities in the world of social movements. It also permits us to explore what was different about the identities and practices that emerged within the solidarity movement, thus allowing those carrying the care burden to become visible and heard. It was these people and practices that enabled this radical but smooth shift toward the practices of care and social reproduction. Grassroots movements and critical feminist thinking in both Latin America and Spain call this process the 'feminization of politics' (Roth and Baird 2017; Perez 2018; Vega Solis et al. 2019). In line with this, Greek anti-austerity mobilizations introduced an ethics of care into movement politics, disrupting what was thought of as 'masculine' and 'feminine', and calling both men and women to feel and act beyond binaries.

In this chapter, we have attempted to navigate through this process by highlighting three themes emerging in five different spaces of solidarity in Athens: practices of social reproduction as the main repertoire of action during austerity; feelings of vulnerability and dispossession that triggered acts of solidarity and belonging; and an ethics of care embedded within the daily function of solidarity initiatives. These together reveal the emergence of different ideas about what it means to be an activist, to participate in social movements, and to resist inequality and oppression. Such ideas seem to be getting more and more traction, as we delve deeper into a world that is in a deep, multi-faceted crisis.

Note

1 The author would like to thank Professor Andreas Chatzidakis for his feedback and Christos Giovanopoulos for his feedback and contribution in data collection.

References

Arampatzi, Athina. 2018. "Constructing solidarity as resistive and creative agency in austerity Greece." *Comparative European Politics* 16(1), 50–66.

Athanasiou, Athena. 2014. "Precarious intensities: gendered bodies in the streets and squares of Greece." *Signs: Journal of Women in Culture and Society* 40(1), 1–9.

Baines, Donna and Stephen McBride. 2015. *Orchestrating austerity: impacts and resistance*. Halifax, NS: Fernwood.

Berlant, Lauren. 2016. "The commons: infrastructures for troubling times." *Environment and Planning D: Society and Space* 34(3), 393–419.

Bhattacharya, Tithi, ed. 2017. *Social reproduction theory: remapping class, recentering oppression*. London: Pluto Press.

Bobel, Chris. 2007. "'I'm not an activist, per se, though I've done a lot of it': doing activism, being activist and the perfect standard in a contemporary movement." *Social Movement Studies* 6(2), 147–159.

Briggs, Laura. 2018. *How all politics became reproductive politics: from welfare reform to foreclosure to Trump*. Oakland, CA: University of California Press.

Brown, Gavin and Jenny Pickerill. 2009. "Space for emotion in the spaces of activism." *Emotion, Space and Society* 2(1), 24–35.

Butler, Judith and Athena Athanasiou. 2013. *Dispossession: the performative in the political.* New York, NY: John Wiley and Sons.

Chatzidakis, Andreas. 2020. "Chronotopic dilemmas: space–time in consumer movements of the Greek crisis." *Environment and Planning D: Society and Space 38*(2), 325–344.

Craddock, Emma. 2017. "Caring about and for the cuts: a case study of the gendered dimension of austerity and anti-austerity activism." *Gender, Work and Organization 24*(1), 69–82.

Craddock, Emma. 2019. "Doing 'enough' of the 'right' thing: the gendered dimension of the 'ideal activist' identity and its negative emotional consequences." *Social Movement Studies 18*(2), 137–153.

Crenshaw, Kimberlé. 1990. "Mapping the margins: intersectionality, identity politics, and violence against women of color." *Stanford Law Review 43*(6), 1241–1299.

Cullen, Pauline and Mary P. Murphy. 2017. "Gendered mobilizations against austerity in Ireland." *Gender, Work and Organization 24*(1), 83–97.

Daskalaki, Maria and Marianna Fotaki. 2017. "The neoliberal crisis: alternative organizing and spaces of/for feminist solidarity." In *Feminists and queer theorists debate the future of critical management studies*, eds. Alison Pullen, Nancy Harding and Mary Phillips, 129–153. Bingley: Emerald.

Daskalaki, Maria, Marianna Fotaki and Maria Simosi. 2020. "The gendered impact of the crisis: struggles over social reproduction in Greece." *Environment and Planning A*, https://doi.org/10.1177/0308518X20922857.

Della Porta, Donatella, Joseba Fernández, Hara Kouki and Lorenzo Mosca. 2017. *Movement parties against austerity.* Malden, MA: Polity.

Durbin, Sue, Margaret Page and Sylvia Walby. 2017. "Gender equality and 'austerity': vulnerabilities, resistance and change." *Gender, Work and Organization 24*(1), 1–6.

ELSTAT. 2015. *Greece in figures, 2015.* Hellenic Statistical Authority [website]. Retrieved from https://www.statistics.gr/en/greece-in-figures#tab-2015.

Federici, Silvia. 2004. *Caliban and the witch.* Brooklyn, NY: Autonomedia.

Federici, Silvia. 2019. "Social reproduction theory." *Radical Philosophy 2*(4), 55–57.

Fotaki, Marianna and Maria Daskalaki. 2020. "Politicizing the body in the anti-mining protest in Greece." *Organization Studies*, https://doi.org/10.1177/0170840619882955.

Fraser, Nancy. 1992. "Rethinking the public sphere: a contribution to the critique of actually existing democracy." In *Habermas and the public sphere*, ed. Craig Calhoun, 109–141. Cambridge, MA: MIT Press.

Griffin, Penny. 2015. "Crisis, austerity and gendered governance: a feminist perspective." *Feminist Review 109*(1), 49–72.

Gritzas, Giorgos and Karolos Iosif Kavoulakos. 2015. "Diverse economies and alternative spaces: an overview of approaches and practices." *European Urban and Regional Studies 23*(4), 917–934.

Hall, Sarah Marie. 2020. "The personal is political: feminist geographies of/in austerity." *Geoforum 110*, 242–251.

Hanisch, Carol. 1970. "The personal is political." In *Notes from the second year. Women's liberation: major writings of the radical feminists*, eds. Shulamith Firestone and Anne Koedt, 76–78. New York, NY: Radical Feminism.

Hemmings, Clare. 2012. "Affective solidarity: feminist reflexivity and political transformation." *Feminist Theory* 13(2), 147–161.

hooks, bell. 1986. "Sisterhood: political solidarity between women." *Feminist Review 23* (Summer), 125–138.

Karamessini, Maria. 2013. "Structural crisis and adjustment in Greece: social regression and the challenge for gender equality." In *Women and austerity: the economic crisis and the future for gender equality*, eds. Maria Karamessini and Jill Rubery, 165–185. London: Routledge.

Karamessini, Maria and Jill Rubery, eds. 2013. *Women and austerity: the economic crisis and the future for gender equality*. London: Routledge.

Kennelly, Jacqueline. 2014. "'It's this pain in my heart that won't let me stop': gendered affect, webs of relations, and young women's activism." *Feminist Theory* 15(3), 241–260.

Kioupkiolis, Alexandros. 2014. *For the commons of freedom*. Athens, Greece: Exarcheia (in Greek).

Kosyfologou, Aliki. 2018. *Austerity, gender, inequality and feminism after the crisis*. Athens, Greece: Rosa Luxemburg Foundation.

Kouki, Hara. 2019. "From claims-based protests to solidarity initiatives: tracing transformations of collective action in Athens, 2010–2017." In *Sharing society: the impact of collaborative collective actions in the transformation of contemporary societies*, eds. Benjamín Tejerina, Cristina Miranda de Almeida and Ignacia Perugorría, 603–612. Bilbao, Spain: Universidad del País Vasco/ Euskal Herriko Unibertsitatea.

Kouki, Hara and Andreas Chatzidakis. 2020. "Implicit feminist solidarity(ies)? the role of gender in the social movements of the Greek crisis." *Gender, Work and Organization*.

Kouki, Hara and Antonis Liakos. 2015. "Narrating the story of a failed national transition: discourses on the Greek crisis, 2010–2014." *Historein* 15(1), 49–61.

Kousis, Maria. 2013. "The nationwide (all-Greek) campaign against memoranda and austerity policies." *Sociological Review 1*, 33–41.

Larsen, C. 2018. "#MeToo in South Korea: a comparative analysis of feminist perspectives in a cultural context." *International Journal of Foreign Studies* 11(2): 39–59. https://doi.org/10.18327/ijfs.2018.12.11.39.

Lotz, Amanda D. 2003. "Communicating third-wave feminism and new social movements: challenges for the next century of feminist endeavor." *Women and Language* 26(1), 2–9.

Loukidou, Katerina. 2019. *Gender aspects of civil society, 2010–2014*. Paper presented at the Symposium for Civil Society and Social Solidarity Economy, National Center of Social Research and Aristotle University of Thessaloniki, Athens, Greece, 13–14 March (in Greek).

Maeckelbergh, Marianne. 2011. "Doing is believing: prefiguration as strategic practice in the alterglobalization movement." *Social Movement Studies* 10(1), 1–20.

Mason-Deese, Liz. 2016. "Unemployed workers' movements and the territory of social reproduction." *Journal of Resistance Studies* 2(2), 65–99.

Mattern, Shannon. 2018. "Maintenance and care." *Places*, November, https://placesjournal.org/article/maintenance-and-care/.

McCall, Leslie. 2005. "The complexity of intersectionality." *Signs 30*(3), 1771–1800.

Mendes, Kaitlynn. 2015. *SlutWalk: feminism, activism and media.* Basingstoke: Palgrave Macmillan.

Moghadam, Valentine M. 2000. "Transnational feminist networks: collective action in an era of globalization." *International Sociology* 15(1), 57–85.

Mohanty, Chandra T. 2003. *Feminism without borders: decolonizing theory, practicing solidarity.* Durham, NC: Duke University Press.

Motta, Sara C. and Tiina Seppälä. 2016. "Feminized resistances." *Journal of Resistance Studies* 2(2), 5–32.

Oikonomakis, Leonidas. 2018. "Solidarity in transition: the case of Greece." In *Solidarity mobilizations in the "refugee crisis": Contentious moves*, ed. Donatella della Porta, 65–98. Basingstoke: Palgrave Macmillan.

Papageorgiou, Yota and Vasiliki Petousi. 2018. "Gender resilience in times of economic crisis: findings from Greece." *Partecipazione e Conflitto* 11(1), 145–174.

Perez, Laura. 2018. "Feminizar la política a través del municipalismo." In *Ciudades sin miedo: guía del movimiento municipalista global*, ed. Ada Colau, 33–38. Barcelona, Spain: Icaria.

Psimitis, Michalis. 2011. "The protest cycle of spring 2010 in Greece." *Social Movement Studies* 10(2), 191–197.

Rai, Shirin M. 2018. "The good life and the bad: dialectics of solidarity." *Social Politics: International Studies in Gender, State and Society* 25(1), 1–19.

Rakopoulos, Theodoros. 2016. "Solidarity: the egalitarian tensions of a bridge concept." *Social Anthropology* 24(2), 142–151.

Roth, Laura and Kate S. Baird. 2017. "Municipalism and the feminization of politics." *Roar Magazine*, 6, https://roarmag.org/magazine/municipalism-feminization-urban-politics/.

S4A. 2015. *Building hope against fear and devastation.* Athens, Greece: Solidarity for All.

Serdedakis, Nikos and Myrsini Koufidi. 2018. "Protest and electoral cycles." *Greek Political Science Review* 44(1), 7–30 (in Greek).

Simiti, Marilena. 2002. "New social movements in Greece: aspects of the feminist and ecological projects." Doctoral dissertation, London School of Economics and Political Science, London.

Stavrides, Stavros. 2016. *Common space: the city as commons.* London: Zed Books.

Taylor, Verta. 1999. "Gender and social movements: gender processes in women's self-help movements." *Gender and Society* 13(1), 8–33.

Taylor, Verta and Nancy Whittier. 1998. "Guest editors' introduction: special issue on gender and social movements, part 1." *Gender and Society* 12(6), 622–625.

Temple, Nick, Angelos Varvarousis, Chrysostomos Galanos, George Tsitsirigos and Georgia Bekridaki. 2017. *Greece: social and solidarity economy report.* London: British Council. https://www.britishcouncil.org/sites/default/files/greece_social_and_solidarity_economy_report_english_british_council_0.pdf.

Tronto, Joan C. 2013. *Caring democracy: markets, equality, and justice.* New York, NY: NYU Press.

Vaiou, Dina. 2016. "Tracing aspects of the Greek crisis in Athens: putting women in the picture." *European Urban and Regional Studies* 23(3), 220–230.

Vega Solis, Cristina, Raquel Martinez Bujan and Miriam Paredes Chauca, eds. 2019. *Cuidado, comunidad y comun: Extracciones, apropiaciones y sostenimiento de la vida [Care, community and common: extractions, appropriations and sustenance of life].* Madrid, Spain: Traficantes de Suenos.

4 Intersectional Perspective on Working Life

Poor, Black, Working-Class Women Remain on the Margins – The Case of Paid and Unpaid Domestic Labour

Nandi Vanqa-Mgijima

The history of African women in South Africa is a history of struggle against pass laws, forced removals, and separation from their husbands and families due to creation and administration of what was essentially a system of labour coercion, directed against Africans. Those conditions and consequences of coercion were central to the existence and change nature of South African capitalism (Lacey, 1981). With the development of capitalism, cheap black labour was realised by capital through state intervention by enacting coercive laws hence the forced proletarisation of African men (Callinicos, 1981). Under apartheid, the state separated production and social reproduction of labour by taking men away to work in the mines (Callinicos, 1981), leaving women behind to care for their households in the homelands (Cock 1980). This legacy has continued even after the democratic dispensation (Ally, 2008). Today, African women are still overwhelmingly responsible for the labour of social reproduction, and this work is shaped by the legacy of the development of capitalism, colonialism and apartheid. As a result of the draconian apartheid laws, most African women's lives were and are still invisible, undermined and undervalued. Globalization has systematically informalized work everywhere, and workers' protection in the formal economy is threatened by the impact of global deregulation. The findings of previous case studies suggest that workers have become increasingly differentiated into three categories-workers in the formal economy; workers in casual and externalized work arrangements; and workers in the informal economy where they are making a living instead of earning a living (Webster and von Holdt, 2005).

On the other hand there is a state through its neo-liberal policies, that has relinquished its responsibility of providing services, and is focusing instead on allowing the private sector to take over their provision (Newman, Pape and Jansen 2011). The African National Congress (ANC) led government came into power in 1994 already as a compromised former liberation movement, with its popular leader, Mandela in 1993 entering into a Faustian pact with global capital

(Kasrils 2013). It was during this time of complete global neoliberal capital dominance, when South Africans witnessed crafting and adoption of a neo-liberal economic policy called Growth Employment, and Redistribution (GEAR), dumping its initial developmental economic programme, the Reconstruction and Development Programme. In his book and a more recent article, academic social justice activists Patrick Bond (2000; 2016) argues that the neoliberal compromises demonstrably failed the South African society, economy and natural environment, no matter what one thinks of the ethics and politics of the Faustian Pacts.

Of-course as much as the dominance was not restricted to socio-economic policies only but at a political and psychological level – an emphasis on individualism was key. The theory of neoliberalism promoted individualism over societal collectivism and cohesions hence privatisation and other programmes, as Thatcher once said, 'there are no such a thing as society, there are only individuals.' Our daily lives were adversely affected not only in places of work but in our homes, societies, in our political spaces and at an individual level – with divergent views about what we were made to believe neo-liberalism brings – as a period of 'opportunism; self-reliance; volunteerism and vukuzenzele literally meaning 'Wake up and Act'.[1] Using its liberation credentials and political legitimacy, pushed through and implemented a full packaged of homegrown neoliberalism and liberalisation of the economy. But what became vivid were the dire consequences of the new philosophy, levels of poverty deepening, inequality widened, we witnessed closures of key industrial sectors such as textile and clothing (Kenny 2009); mass retrenchments, rise of precarious forms of jobs; decline in social and health sectors – rise in diseases such tuberculosis, HIV deaths, at the same time an empowerment of a handful of blacks was vivid, enabled by Black Economic Empowerment programmes.

In the world of work, many women are employed as casual and labour broker workers, and they are the first to be dismissed when economic crisis hits the markets hard. This has led to unprecedented growth of the informal economy, with women concentrated in the provision of services, as homebased carers, sex workers, waste pickers and vendors (Webster 2005; Bruneau, 2018). In addition to having to work to earn a pittance for survival, these women also shoulder the burden of housework, child rearing and parenting, and caring for the community at large. Both during apartheid and in the current phase of neoliberalism, laws have seldom been enacted for the benefit of working-class and poor women, yet have always benefited a handful of politicians and capitalists to maximize profits. Single-female-headed households are becoming the norm in Africa, but women's lower status means that they find it much harder to resettle because they have often been marginalised in growth strategies (Tsikata 2009).

The feminization of migration has become a global trend. Half of all migrants now arriving in South Africa are women, often accompanied by children, and they are among the most vulnerable and most marginalized (c.f Mbyoso 2018). In host countries like South Africa, these women work double shifts in order to keep just above the breadline. For example, in Cape Town, many female black domestic workers from Lesotho face insecure jobs in a wage-regulated sector, social exclusion and more overt forms of targeted nationalism, and gendered violence at the hands of their employers and employment agencies. Power imbalances at work still prevent the majority of domestic workers from claiming their legal rights, and the situation is dire for migrant workers (Vanqa-Mgijima 2011).

Another illuminating factor is that a number of trends have developed simultaneously in South Africa. In the case of home-based carers, continued reliance on poor Black women for social reproduction work extends beyond the household and into the community. Community-based care is not only seen as a 'cost-effective' way of supplementing poorly resourced public healthcare in marginalized communities, but also reinforces poverty and the gender-based division of labour in the home and in the community. In the sphere of social reproduction, growing unemployment is placing an added burden on women. As the state cuts its spending on healthcare, education, water and other municipal services, poor, working-class women bear the brunt of social reproduction. For example, research on home-based carers (Naylor and Vanqa-Mgijima, 2016) reveals that the state continues to rely on Black women for the underpaid, undervalued and dangerous work of social reproduction, while mobilizing apparently progressive language and policies, with schemes such as the Community Works Program (CWP) and the Extended Public Works Programme (EPWP) supposedly designed to alleviate unemployment.[2] However, research shows that these programmes have actually served to further entrench the gendered division of labour, trap workers in cycles of precarious employment and unemployment, and exploit forms of mutual aid and solidarity (Bhattacharya 2017).

Capitalism relegates women to unpaid reproductive labour, and indeed overburdens the vast majority of women. It relies on these unpaid tasks for the reproduction of labour power (see e.g Davis, 1981; Antonopoulos 2009; Murillo and D'Atri 2018). However, since no surplus value is extracted from this activity because it does not generate exchange value (i.e. it cannot be exchanged on the market), according to the logic of capital, it is thus unproductive labour (Marx 1887). This chapter reflects on the tension between paid and unpaid labour carried out largely by women in postapartheid South Africa and the continued multiple threats of discrimination.

Case Studies of Women Organizing

In the following, I draw on several research efforts carried out during the past ten years that explored the tension between paid and unpaid labour through political education workshops, interviews and focus group discussions with women activists involved in paid and unpaid domestic labour, homebased caring work and waste picking.

The Case of Paid Domestic Labour

Between 2009 and 2011, I conducted research in collaboration with the University of the Western Cape to explore connections in the organization and empowerment of domestic workers. This research revealed the dire working conditions of domestic workers working for Black 'madams', who were deplorable, inhumane and undermined women's privacy. Contraventions of almost every piece of legislation were discovered: the workers had no social security benefits, nor any other safety net to fall back on when their services were terminated. Their earnings were hardly enough to sustain them, and very little was left to take back home. I spoke to several domestic workers who worked for both White and Black 'madams' in Cape Town (see also Vanqa-Mgijima 2011).

Having worked for almost 40 years for one employer, Ma Mpinga (not her real clan name) was in her late fifties, a single mother of four children. She had no formal education, which made her totally reliant on her employer. She earned a meagre salary of R800 a month. She was not registered with the Department of Labour for unemployment insurance benefits. She worked from Monday to Monday, and her day started as early as 0700 and ended when the family had had dinner, around 1900. She was sometimes also called to work beyond these working hours. Throughout her working life, she had never had an opportunity to spend Christmas with her own family. She had never been entitled to take annual leave, paid sick leave or public holidays. Her daily chores included preparing all meals for the family, cleaning the house, making up beds for the employer and her children and guests, and looking after her employer's children and those of extended family members.

Ma Mpinga had been out of work for almost two months due to ill health as a result of losing two children: her daughter had died because of hospital negligence, and her only employed son had succumbed to HIV/AIDS. She never fully recovered from these losses and later died in hospital from hypotension, leaving behind two unemployed children and four grandchildren. Her employer did not pay her fully for the months that she was not at work, and she was unable to claim from the Department of Labour's unemployment insurance fund because her employer had never registered her. All Ma Mpinga expected from this longstanding employment relationship was to earn a decent salary and some benefits, but all her employer did was to pay her funeral costs and erect a tombstone. What an insult to the poor rural woman who had sacrificed her entire life, and that of her family, to looking after the employer's needs. Nthuso and other girls from Lesotho were trafficked for domestic labour exploitation by a black woman from Khayelitsha township. Nthuso said she had heard about a South African woman who was recruiting young women for employment in South Africa. She and other girls went to meet the 'lady' and were offered employment, but there was no mention of the type of work. Around 12 girls were driven to Khayelitsha in a taxi with the lady, Rhemaketsi.

Nthuso said, 'I do not think Rhemaketsi will ever afford you an interview. She is aware that what she is involved in is illegal. She has erected a shack that sleeps ten to 20 women. There are no beds, they sleep on the floors, and the living conditions for these girls are bad.' The living set-up of these young girls sounded like the migrant labour compounds erected during the apartheid era. Nthuso was very reluctant to provide me with Rhemaketsi's address and contact numbers. The address she gave was incomplete, but at least directed me to the section of Khayelitsha. She kept on saying, 'I do not think she will answer the call, I do not think that the number is still in use.'

Nthuso Funa had worked as a machinist in a Taiwanese-owned textile factory. She had been only 18 years old when she started working there. She was not a permanent worker, so she did not receive the benefits received by permanent workers 'which were also not good benefits. We earned very low salaries – it was equivalent to R300 per month.' She was born in Lesotho in 1988, and left school at the equivalent of grade 10 in the South African education system. She was the fourth child in a family of six children – four girls and two boys. Her parents and one sister, who had previously been a textile factory worker, were working in Rustenberg, South Africa, and another sister was working in Somerset West, in Cape Town. Back at home in Lesotho, they had left one elder sister with two younger brothers, and their children. Nthuso had been dismissed from the factory for operational reasons: 'this was very painful – I was thinking about how will I feed my child and be of help to my family?' In 2010 she had come to Cape Town as a survival strategy, on a journey organized by a notorious working-class woman also from Lesotho but based in Cape Town's working-class township, Khayelitsha, who was merely trafficking women into domestic labour. She initially worked for a family of five at Ilitha Park, Khayelitsha. Out of her first salary of R850, she had to pay R450 to the notorious trafficker for her employment, R30 for electricity and R50 toward groceries: 'I spend the R320 for my personal necessities and send R200 home towards maintaining my child. The "lady" does not allow us to come with our children to Cape Town.'

The life experiences of poor working-class women are often used to explore continuities and discontinuities between apartheid and the neoliberal, post-apartheid order in South Africa. The oppression of these women was and still is inextricably linked with multiple threats of discrimination, such as race, class, sexual orientation, ethnicity, nationality, education, health, economic status and other social characteristics. For example, Black lesbian, gay, bisexual, transgender, intersex and queer communities face higher levels of gruesome violence and discrimination than their White counterparts.

Today, labour movements in South Africa and elsewhere talk about the need to organize domestic and other vulnerable workers in the informal sectors. Since the 1990s, the largest labour federation in South Africa, Congress of South African Trade Unions (COSATU) has passed resolutions on the need to find new ways of organizing casual, domestic and farm workers, and to place more women workers in leadership positions, but with limited results. The picture that emerges is of a labour movement that has hardly begun to develop new forms of organization in response to the unfavourable labour market and economic conditions, and its failure to do so has weakened its position (Vanqa-Mgijima, Wiid and du Toit 2013). Greater priority appears to be given to servicing existing members by representing them in collective bargaining and, increasingly, in dispute resolution. According to Theron, trade unions are increasingly representing insiders employed by the 'core business', whose interests are perceived distinct, if not antagonistic, to those who are not, put differently segmentation in the workplace translates into a hierarchy, or 'pecking order', with workers in standard employment at the top (Theron 2009). For example, in the past decades there has been only two trade unions organizing domestic workers in South Africa, namely the South African Domestic Services & Allied Workers Union (SADSAWU) and the South African Domestic & General Workers Union (SADAGWU). According to general secretary, Myrtle Witbooi, SADSAWU has fewer than 70,000 members nationwide, with a minority paying union dues, while Nora Juries of SADAGWU claims that the union has a 10,000-strong membership in the Western Cape, with only two to three per cent being paid-up members. SADAGWU is an affiliate of the Confederation of South African Workers' Unions.

Although some domestic workers now belong to trade unions, membership of these unions remains low, and recruitment is often blocked by, among other things, lack of human and financial resources, which hampers daily union activities, including organizing. The unions rely on membership fees, which are too low to finance outreach programmes to service members and pay for salaries, child care facilities, office rentals, telephones and other necessities. Too few officials are employed to meet the intensity of union workloads and the dispersed nature of members' workplaces. Affiliation fees pose the biggest challenge to relationships between these trade unions and the federations. In some instances, trade unions operate in isolation from the public, other trade unions and NGOs, and civil society has done little to assist these vulnerable sectors.

The organizing strategies of both SADSAWU and SADGAWU are limited to recruitment and servicing, a difficulty that confronts trade unions everywhere and is in desperate need of an overhaul. In order to attract new members, trade unions need to adopt mechanisms to address the social, economic and political challenges faced by domestic and informal workers. Hence, their organizing strategies should involve building a leadership accountable to union members, empowering members through activism by sharing information, educating, and building global networks. For these reasons, we continued to explore organization and mobilization in this sector. Izwi Domestic Workers' Alliance was launched in 2018 as a network of domestic workers in Johannesburg. It was started by a group of domestic workers who wanted to change how they were treated by employers, and by society in general. On its website, Izwi states that in order to break down the isolation and vulnerability faced by domestic workers, it is building support networks of individual workers, neighborhood groups and partner organizations. A steering committee, elected from amongst the members, oversees Izwi's growth and direction. It provides information and advice on employment issues, and assistance with individual cases, training programmes and social activities, and collects and shares the stories and experiences of domestic workers. Since its launch, Izwi has built a network of around 1,000 female domestic workers to whom it provides labour rights education and support. It has supported over 400 individual cases of mistreated workers, has developed many active What's App groups to field questions and mobilize around issues, and has launched 12 neighborhood groups that provide peer support, training and social activities. It hosts monthly meetings to respond to individual concerns, and to discuss growth and advocacy issues. It has triggered extensive media coverage on domestic workers' challenges, allowing them to share their stories. It co-founded and coordinates the 'One Wage' campaign, a civil-society campaign against the exclusion of domestic, farm and EPWP workers from the national minimum wage, and has provided food assistance and rent support to members affected by the Covid-19 economic crisis.

It is hoped that Izwi will continue to grow and gain strength from the diversity of its partner organizations, such as the Casual Workers' Advice Office, the Goethe Institute South Africa, the Hlanganisa Institute for Development in Southern Africa, Lawyers for Human Rights, Luma Law, the Sexual Harassment Education Project, the Simunye Women Workers Forum, the Socio Economic Rights Initiative (SERI-SA) Solidarity Centre, SADSAWU and United Domestic Workers of South Africa (UDWOSA). Without workers' organizations representing the interests of the working class at large, rights will always be tampered with by policies seeking to undermine workers. Organizations of the working class are meant to guard against working-class exploitation and bureaucratic capitalists' tendencies.

The Case of Home-Based Care Workers

In 2016, Adrie Naylor and I, an intern at the International Labour Research and Information Group (ILRIG), started to carry out research in two main areas. The first was on home-based carers' types and conditions of work and areas of organizing. I have been working with home-based carers for some time, and this research was also the topic for three 'Building Women's Activism' political education workshops, which I facilitated. Adrie and I conducted four group discussions/interviews of between one and two hours' duration with groups of between four and home-based carers in two townships in Cape Town: three in Philippi and one in Gugulethu (see also Naylor and Vanqa-Mgijima, 2016).

In large and small discussions with home-based carers, we examined several related questions. We documented the work that they were doing in the two townships, and the risks associated with this work. Importantly, this emphasized the intersection between the occupational health and safety hazards experienced by these women workers, and the general health and safety issues they experienced as poor women in their communities. This opened up important space for organizing and discussion linking feminist, socialist, anti-racist, labour and community struggles, which are often not given adequate space owing to a perception that issues like rape and other forms of violence against women are not, properly speaking, labour nor genuinely anti-capitalist struggles. In my opinion this view is mistaken, and analysis of how this violence intersects with work and is exacerbated by the neoliberal healthcare system and the outsourcing of care work to poor and racialized women highlights these connections.

Another very illuminating theme of this research was how, in post-1994 South Africa, a number of trends developed simultaneously. The first is continued reliance on Black women for the underpaid, under-valued and frankly dangerous work of social reproduction, which in the case of poor and working class women in particular home-based care workers, this extends beyond the household and into the community either through state institutions (see Naylor and Vanqa-Mgijima). We also see the state mobilizing progressive-sounding language and policies, including schemes presented as being designed to alleviate unemployment, such as the CWP and the EPWP, and initiatives to enhance democratic participation in healthcare through the creation of community health committees. However, our research shows that these programmes have actually served to further entrench the gendered division of labour, trap workers in cycles of precarious employment and unemployment, and exploit forms of mutual aid and solidarity within communities. For example, many of the women to whom we spoke talked about doing this dangerous and thankless work 'for ubuntu' (discussed later), absolving the state of its responsibility for providing adequate healthcare and decent work. Community-based care is seen as a 'cost-effective' way of supplementing poorly resourced public healthcare in marginalized communities, but in doing so it reinforces poverty and the gender-based division of labour in the home and in the community, while enabling progressive sounding arguments about enhancing the 'continuum of care', or in other words extending care beyond the hospital or clinic to the home, and providing employment and training for unemployed and under-employed workers. Finally, we documented, discussed and began to analyse existing and potential forms of organization for women workers in home-based care.

In terms of their employment relationships, home-based carers in South Africa fall into various groups, and we interviewed women who either currently or had previously worked in each of these. Some home-based carers are either employed or are volunteers paid a stipend by faith-based or secular non-governmental organizations (NGOs) or by clinics. Some work as home-based carers while receiving a stipend from a public works programme (CWP or EPWP) run by the Public Works Department. Others work as volunteers providing safety and security in poor and working class townships of Cape Town, doing essentially the same work for no pay whatsoever. This is this an important area of research and activism, because it examines the links and overlaps between various struggles. The first are feminist struggles around gendered work in the home, such as women's expectations and the unequal distribution of work between men and women. The second are explicitly 'labour'-based struggles, around occupational health and safety, pay, and control of the labour process. Third, 'community' struggles are around both meaningful democratic control over public services, and the just, free and democratic provision of high-quality public healthcare. This also includes social grants, which are not necessarily seen as connected with discussions of social reproduction but are actually essential to it.

Virtually all of the women with whom we worked were receiving social grants. In some cases, social grants and debt were how they were supporting themselves and their families. They also frequently used those same grants to subsidize the public healthcare system, for example by using their own funds to buy food for those for whom they were caring, as well as to provide needed materials, for example by cutting up shirts to make bandages and makeshift masks, or using bags as gloves. As one worker told us:

As you go out to sick people they take treatment from the hospital and as they are discharged they take the treatment home … Only when you are terminally ill, that's when doctors will give you permission to get the social grant. It is given when you are on your deathbed, two months to die. Really people receive it one month, and the next month they die. When we as home-based carers do visits and we get [to the patient's place], they don't have food, absolutely nothing; and we are not in a position to give the medication on an empty stomach. And we take from our own pockets, and yet no one pays us for what we are doing. We prepare porridge so that we can start to administer medication.

Viewing social grants through this lens opens up fruitful questions that can be linked with other histories of organizing. These women were doing essential social reproductive work in the home and in the community and were, in a sense, being paid for it through social grants. This has interesting parallels with the 'Wages for Housework' campaign in Italy in the 1970s, and may also provide the basis for organizing and claim making around social grants, not as a bare minimum to prevent people, ineffectively, from starving, but as a way to acknowledge the need both for income in a context of high unemployment, and for compensation for the real labour that people, and especially women, undertake to reproduce and care for other people.

The employment relationships that I have described are transitory and porous. Most of the homebased carers whom we interviewed described experiences of falling into more than one of these categories in the course of their careers, and even simultaneously, placing them in a highly precarious position. Some long-term home-based carers had begun working for NGOs, but had become employed by CWP when funding was redirected away from home-based care. One had been employed by Healthcare Trust for about ten years during the 1990s, but when its funding had been cut it had shut down and she had begun to work for CWP. Another had been working for CWP for a stipend, but had been cut off by CWP while being paid for a couple of weeks' work at a hospital in Somerset West, after which CWP had refused to re-employ her. Another carer had applied to work for CWP and had been told that they were no longer funding home-based care because they were refocusing on waste picking. Seeing the need in her community and conscious of her skill set, she continued to do the daily work of home-based care, including reporting to CWP, in the hope that a paid position might result. This appeared to be a vain hope, but other home-based carers reported that they had already been working as home-based carers when they had begun to receive a stipend from CWP. Another worker was generally volunteering for no pay, but sometimes worked for two weeks here or there at a pensioners' home. Home-based carers employed by

CWP were working and reporting to CWP on average about 21 days each month; however, they were being paid a total of R600 per month for eight days' work, and sometimes that pay was delayed. They were not told in advance which days they would be paid for, and had to report every day for fear of missing out.

This way of coordinating care in the community is ludicrous. First, these precarious and uncertain employment relationships raise major issues for home-based carers. They also demonstrate the impact of the fragmentation and hyper-outsourcing of state services, making it extremely difficult to assert basic rights, such as the right to be paid, to enjoy protection under labour law, and to gain access to protective equipment. The workers whom we met were frequently denied these rights. Nor were they allowed to exert democratic control over the healthcare system and demand not only representation but meaningful participation, both as workers with a stake in the healthcare system and as residents of the country. It is especially difficult for workers employed through NGOs, as those organizations are directed by their funders. Funding for HIV/AIDS NGOs has decreased as a result of the global financial crisis, the move from aid to trade and the general downgrading of AIDS as a sexy fundraising issue in the global North (Vasilaki 2014). However, even in public-sector organizations, asserting control has been problematic. For example, we spoke to a group of home-based carers in Gugulethu who had formed a community health committee. They told us:

> We are coming from the community. The community elected us. We represent the community, report to the community. The community comes to us when they have problems, when they are shouted at or don't get the right care. Everyone will know there is a health committee. They will phone and say 'I have a problem. I was sitting here the whole morning and I didn't see the doctor.' Then I will have to leave everything and go. And even if the nurses didn't treat the people, they are rude. I was phoned by the sub-councilor and she said, 'there's no oxygen in trauma. You're the health committee, what can you do?' I had to phone the facility manager and say, 'Hello, wake up! Go to the day hospital because people are dying there.'

The committee members described monthly meetings with the clinic's facility manager. We asked them whether the facility manager generally addressed the issues they raised, and they responded that the issues were fixed. However, they carried on to describe the following event:

> You know, the other day we were called. This was in the maternity section there. The other woman was about to give birth. And she

was crawling on the floor, crawling. While she was crawling on the floor, they ignored her. And she messed the floor. She was in labour on the floor. And the nurse was just hitting her on her bum: 'Look, come and clean your mess.' The other woman phoned us. We ran to the hospital and we were so mad when we got into that ward and said 'what are you doing?' And the woman was crying, having to mop and clean up. We took photos and took over what she was doing. Then we said, 'Let the woman lie on the bed and leave the mop and leave everything there. Who's in charge?' The woman that was supposed to be in charge was not there. We laid a charge. We had that hearing; that nurse lost her job. It was not our intention, but the way she was rude.

A similar level of community involvement was not recounted in Philippi. These workers were not being paid to do this, and this work of direction was in addition to their work as home-based carers, for which they also received little or no pay. Yet even in instances where they were able to exert some kind of immediate direction, such as getting oxygen for the trauma room, this simply let the clinic's facilitator and/or the sub-councillor, both of whom were paid, off the hook. These workers were not privy to or able to dictate where and how funding was directed, how much funding there was, how the work was done, or what work there was, let alone discuss or direct healthcare in the province or nation as a whole.

In our interviews and in the 'Building Women's Activism' political education workshops, we asked home-based carers why they continued to do the work without being paid, or while being paid a pittance as a stipend. Many answered 'for ubuntu'. 'Ubuntu' is a Nguni word meaning 'compassion'. Genuine ubuntu, or responsibility for one's community, conveys a sense of giving back, but it can also be co-opted into a neoliberal form, in that these women would do it with no support. Through reciprocity and ties of care and responsibility, the community might be totally unresourced and abandoned by the state, but people will simply support each other. The health committee is another example that might be very positive if it were to have genuine power, resources and democratic control, perhaps as an elected body governing healthcare in the community. However, in practice, it is a way to pass other people's responsibilities on to these unpaid workers. I put this view to the workers in Gugulethu, and they responded that they were fed up that when things were good they did not hear from these officials, but were called only when there was a crisis.

Working-class women's rights have been severely compromised by neo-liberal capitalist policies and programmes, and progressive-sounding pro-grammes like the CWP are part of the broader problematic neoliberal agenda. In Philippi township, care workers were organizing to challenge this. Nozithembiso Diko, affectionately called sis Nozie[3] by her fellow care workers, was organizing with other women involved in care work. They felt that they were being exploited and unvalued, yet were 10 contributing enormously to the socioeconomic wellbeing of the nation's poor masses. As part of their organizing and mobilizing strategies, a group of about 50 women care workers started to attend feminist political education programmes run by ILRIG, a programme I oversee. This served as a vehicle for building and strengthening their organizing. In July 2015, they organized a march to the CWP offices in Philippi. This was another way in which women were challenging the exploitation and corruption endemic to the CWP. More than 9,000 community health workers in the Gauteng province of South Africa had been supplying community health services to poor, black communities for more than ten years. During this time, they were treated as volunteers and their work was not acknowledged. They were poorly paid, with no benefits in acknowledgement of the valuable nature of the work that they performed for communities and for the government. The 'Make Gauteng Community Health Workers Permanent' campaign was mobilized on a large scale with the help of an NGO, Khanya College. On 18 March 2018, the Labour Court in Braamfontein, Johannesburg ended the practice of treating these community health workers as volunteers, and confirmed their status as employees. This was an important step, recognizing the valuable contribution made by community health workers to the health system and the country.

The Case of Women Waste Pickers

Although my case study of waste-pickers is not as extensive as in the cases of home-based care workers and domestic workers, I also want to highlight this group as an important group for current organizing of women workers in South Africa because waste pickers represent women as being the backbones of their households and communities. When there is no food to feed the family, they go out in search of a meal; when there is no money to buy electricity and water, they go out to gather wood and fetch water from the rivers. Austerity measures imposed by the International Monetary Fund and the World Bank, and South Africa's home-grown neoliberal policies such as the Growth, Economic and Reconstruction (GEAR) programme have compounded the crisis of social reproduction, linked with jobless growth, and inequality in education, health and other basic services. This reflects a patriarchal culture in which care is still seen as women's work.

For the past 19 years, sis Mpumi Nompumelelo Njana, a woman waste picker, has been attempting to organize other waste pickers to fight for recognition of their work. Since 1986 she has been a resident of the Site B informal settlement in Khayelitsha, a working-class township outside Cape Town, South Africa, where she says almost everyone survives on waste picking. Sis Mpumi, as she is affectionately called, claims that women waste pickers are generally engaged in very risky and hazardous work. They often have no protective clothing and are exposed to hazardous material when collecting and sorting the waste. They are also at high risk of becoming victims of crime and sexual violence owing to their long, irregular working hours.

In 2010, sis Mpumi started talking to a group of women engaged in waste picking in her area about organizing themselves around the challenges they faced as waste pickers, and particularly as women. They formed a small group called 'Siyacoca', which means 'we are cleaning' in isiXhosa, and the group gradually grew. As part of organizing, they participated in the political education sessions I was conducting, aimed at strengthening women's leadership, analysing the constraints and limitations imposed on them by the state and business, and exploring different ways of organizing. Through Siyacoca, an autonomous organization, sis Mpumi and her comrades established local structures throughout Khayelitsha and other townships. These became platforms where people talked about the work they were doing and encouraged others to join the struggle. The strategies adopted as tools for organizing by these local Siyacoca structures included education, and writing letters to the authorities outlining their challenges and making demands. As they had no specific space in which to assemble the waste they collected, through Siyacoca they started to negotiate with the municipal authorities for space to be allocated for their collected waste.

Waste pickers are often looked down on by neighbours and the community. Sis Mpumi explains that 'we are ignored and looked down on because of the work we do; people often perceive us as dirty, vagrants and useless people who want to eat from the waste bins'. Waste pickers are also exploited and discriminated against by the state and the private sector, including middlemen, who are the small companies and well-off individuals who buy materials from waste pickers on the streets and sell them directly to big business. Waste pickers are paid very little by the middlemen, who resell the materials for much higher prices. Owing to discrimination, women in particular do not always have access to the highest value recyclables, which also impacts negatively on their income levels. Another problem is that waste pickers from the townships are often barred from other areas where there are more valuable forms of waste. Three of Cape Town's six landfill sites are closed to township-based waste pickers, and the pickers are often barred from entering predominantly white occupied leafy suburbs where the most valuable waste can be found.

Conclusions

The workers described here have traditionally not been well organized. The challenges of organizing are compounded by geographical isolation, migration status and the overall burden of care work, which falls squarely on the shoulders of marginalized black women from rural, urban and crossborder areas of South Africa. For domestic workers, the workplace is a private sphere, with high levels of insecurity, intimidation and collusion between employers and unions. There is an absence of strong unions organizing women in both the formal and informal economies. Domestic workers often mistrust unions, which are often perceived as being interested in taking membership fees but not in providing services to their members. However, levels of organization and resistance are growing amongst domestic workers and home-based care workers. In Cape Town in the Western Cape and Johannesburg in Gauteng province, levels of unionization are increasing through unions like SADSAWU, which was founded in 2000 and continues to provide services to domestic workers at local and national levels.

Home-based and community healthcare workers are also organized into various unions and organizations like the National Union of Public Service and Allied Workers Union (NUPSAW), and in forums and support initiatives provided to unions such as the National Union of Care Workers of South Africa by NGOs, including Workers World Media Productions. Khanya College is another NGO, based in Gauteng province, that provides support to Gauteng Community Health Care Workers Forum (the Forum). In 2012, healthcare workers under the banner of the Forum staged a successful strike that led to a doubling of their stipends, from R1,000 to R2,000, although this is still far below the living wage. The strike also led to community health workers being transferred from NGOs to clinics under the Gauteng Department of Health in 2013, with their stipends being paid directly by the provincial government. Most of the demands won by these workers are struggles faced by community healthcare across South Africa. Through support organizations like Women in Informal Employment: Globalizing and Organizing (WEIGO), women waste pickers are motivated to organize and fight for recognition as workers in local states and municipalities. These women have attempted to form cooperatives, organizations and movements of waste pickers. The political education that they have received from NGOs such as ILRIG and WEIGO have made women waste pickers realize that they are a force to be reckoned with. The political education workshops were a result of research I conducted in 2010, which looked at how waste pickers were organizing in the streets of Cape Town. Through their exposure to political education workshops, they formulated key questions that are imperative for any movement: around what are they organizing, whom are they struggling against, and how do they organize and in what forms of organization? Through these interventions by NGOs to provide political education, the women gradually became sufficiently confident to take up their struggles and organize themselves to voice their demands to the local authorities. As a result, a women-led waste pickers' movement was formed in 2013, in a township in Cape Town, working closely with ILRIG, WEIGO and the South African Waste Pickers Association (SAWPA).

The life experiences of women care workers, students and other working-class unemployed women are often used to explore continuities and discontinuities between apartheid and the neoliberal, post apartheid order in South Africa. The research work I have conducted with domestic workers, waste pickers and home-based care workers reveals the push and pull factors of migration from rural to urban areas. Women cite poor living conditions and lack of opportunities for paid employment in rural areas as push factors. The rural masses, and women in particular, move away from rural areas because of poor healthcare and scarce economic opportunities, as well as environmental changes such as droughts, overall lack of rural development by the state, and other pressures specifically affecting women, such as traditional patriarchal rulers. The main pull factors perceived by women in the research are employment opportunities in the cities. They are attracted to the urban lifestyle and the bright city life. Although they find it difficult to secure permanent and decent employment, the women still feel that urban life provides them with opportunities, and they become active in the informal economy, for instance by collecting and selling waste so as to have something to feed their families.

Internationally, the 'Wages for Housework' campaign, run by Italian socialist feminists in the 1970s, brought together organizing and political analysis in arguing that women's unpaid work within the home was not outside capitalism, but actually contributed directly, and indeed subsidized, the state and capital by providing the unpaid work of reproducing the working class (Federici 1975). Thus, cooking, cleaning, sex, childcare and healthcare within the home were not outside capitalism but actually inherent to it. Politically, this was important because it allowed socialist feminists to argue for expanding the idea of labour beyond the bounds of the factory, warehouse or port and into the community and the home (Federici 2017). This has proved to be a very fruitful area for thinking about feminist activists when working with women and unemployed people around 'non-labour' issues like housing and service delivery.

Traditional labour unions have a very limited understanding of what work is, what organizing might happen beyond the traditional workplace, how workers like these might be organized and what gains might be made. Their issue with regard to organizing relates not only to the question of the employment relationship, but also to the work itself. Where is the boundary between the work done by women in their own homes and the same work done in the community? How does this square up with expanded families where people care for cousins, and uncles and aunts, or where children head up households in the crises of HIV/AIDS and tuberculosis and the primary care providers are less clear? If one were to gauge the political and organisational extent of the failure of unions address segmentation, the appropriate place to begin would be at the bottom of hierarchy; in the case of the steel mill, with the 'cleaning' workers; in the case of the shopping mall, with the car guards who pay for the privilege of working. To evaluate the legislative roots of this failure, on we would have to conclude that the law has more often than not been used to seal organisational space than regulatory 'quick-fix', if today's established union movement is to carry on the tradition in which the emergent unions were founded, they will need to open up new spaces, in the work place as it has been reconstituted (Theron 2009).

Reproductive labour does not need to generate surplus value to be socially recognized and valued. On the other hand, some feminist theorists argue that if reproductive labour 'produces' labour power as a commodity, it should be considered productive. Yet as these theorists claim, patriarchal (ideological, cultural) oppression prevents reproductive labour within private homes, performed by women without compensation, from being seen as 'productive' (Valiani 2012). As French Marxist, Daniel Bensaïd (cited and translated by Murillo and D'Atri 2018) points out:

> The norms between labor that is actually subject to capital within the market and a private activity are nevertheless difficult to compare (Taylorization of kitchen and hotel work). The instruments of measurement depend on an unsatisfactory arbitrary choice, i.e. it involves calculating what a person could earn in the labor market during the time periods devoted to domestic activities (cost in potential earnings), as well as calculating how much should be paid in the market to obtain an equal service (cost of purchase in the market).

In line with her specific interpretation of 'masculine bias' in defining productive labour in capitalism, Federici wonders 'what the history of capital development would be like if seen not from the viewpoint of the formation of the waged proletariat but from the viewpoint of the kitchens and bedrooms in which labour power is daily and generationally produced'. In this question, she critiques what she sees as Marx's (and later, Marxism's) vision of, or rather blindness to, women's place in the reproduction of labour power and in social reproduction within the capitalist system.

Despite not delving into how labour power is produced as a commodity, Marx (1887) considered that the sexual division of labour – a characteristic of patriarchal societies – existed prior to capitalism and did not emerge for the first time during primitive accumulation. The patriarchy was already there. Capitalism adapted these relationships to its own logic and subordinated them to its needs. The challenge facing both paid and unpaid women workers is to build movements across geographical and sectoral divides. While there are pockets of resistance and organizations, there is no united voice drawing together women in these and other sectors to challenge the root causes of discrimination and patterns of accumulation.

Notes

1 President Thabo Mbeki speech, 6 January 2002, http://www.suntimes.co.za/ 2002/01/06/anc/anc14/asp, consulted December 2003. In a speech by President Thabo Mbeki, 6 January 2006 on the 90th anniversary of the founding of the African National Congress in Durban, then President Thabo Mbeki made the following call: 'During this year we must focus on the mobilisation of our people actually to engage in the process of continuing to be their own liberators, of occupying frontline in the popular struggle for the reconstruction and development of our country.' In his speech Mbeki declared 2002 they year of the volunteer. The according Mbeki was a call for South Africans to engage in volunteer work in the spirit of 'letsama or ilima.' http://www.suntimes.co.za/2002/01/06/anc/anc14/asp. The Black Economic Empowerment (BEE), now Broad-Based Black Economic Empowerment still provides legislative framework for the transformation of South Africa's economy. The B-BBEE Act No.53 of 2003, aims to advance economic transformation and enhance the economic participation of black people in the South African economy.
2 The Extended Public Works Programme – The Expanded Public Works Programme (EPWP) has its origins in Growth and Development Summit (GDS) of 2003. At the Summit, four themes were adopted, one of which was 'More jobs, better jobs, decent work for all'. The GDS agreed that public works programmes 'can provide poverty and income relief through temporary work for the unemployed to carry out socially useful activities'. This Programme is a key government initiative, which contributes to Government Policy Priorities in terms of decent work & sustainable livelihoods, education, health; rural development; food security & land reform and the fight against crime & corruption. EPWP subscribes to outcome 4 which states "Decent employment through inclusive economic growth." The EPWP has been established and mandated by Cabinet to create work opportunities according to the set targets and across all its four sectors, namely, infrastructure, non-state, environment and culture, and social sectors. One of the prescripts of the EPWP is to use labour-intensive methods which allow the drawing of a significant number of participants into the Programme to do the work. Source: http://www.epwp.gov.za/.
3 Permission was granted to use her real name. Pseudonyms are used to protect other informant's identities.

References

Ally, Shireen, 2008. "Domestic work unionisation in post-apartheid South Africa: demobilization and depoliticization by the democratic state." *Politikon* 35(1), https://doi.org/10.1080/02589340802113014.

Antonopoulos, Rania. 2009. "The unpaid care work – paid work connection." Working Paper No. 86, Policy Integration and Statistics Department, International Labour Organization, Geneva.

Benson, Koni and Nandi Vanqa-Mgijima. 2010. "Organizing on the streets: a study of reclaimers in the streets of Cape Town." WIEGO Organizing Brief No. 4, Women in Informal Employment Globalizing and Organizing, Cambridge, MA.

Bhattacharya, Tithi. 2017. "Mapping social reproduction theory." In *Social reproduction theory*, ed.Tithi Bhattacharya, 1–20. London: Pluto Press.

Bruneau, Camille. 2018. "How do patriarchy and capitalism jointly reinforce the oppression of women?" CADTM [website], 13 September. Available at: https://www.cadtm.org/How-dopatriarchy-and-capitalism-jointly-reinforce-the-oppression-of-women.

Bond, Patrick. 2002. *Elite transition: from apartheid to neoliberalism in South Africa*. London: Pluto Press and South Africa: University of Natal Press.

Bond, Patrick. 2016. *"Why South Africa should undo Mandela's economic deals."* University of Witwatersrand, Johannesburg.

Callinicos, L. 1981. *Gold and workers, 1886–1924: a people's history of South Africa*, Vol. 1. Ravan Press: Johannesburg.

Cock, Jacklyn. 1980. *Maids and madams: domestic workers under apartheid.* Johannesburg, South Africa: Ravan Press.

Davis, Angela Y. 1981. *Women, race and class.* London: The Women's Press.

Federici, Silvia. 1975. *Wages against housework.* Bristol: Falling Wall Press.

Federici, Silvia. 2017. "Capital and gender." In *Reading "capital" today*, eds.Ingo Schmidt and Carlo Fanelli, 79–96. London: Pluto Press.

ILRIG. 2001. "PPPS: A questionable strategy for service delivery." Unpublished paper, International Labour Research and Information Group, Cape Town, South Africa.

Kasrils, R. 2013. "How the ANC's Faustian Pact sold out South Africa's poorest," The Guardian Post.

Kenny, B. 2009. "Mothers, Extraordinary Labor, and Amacasual: Law and Politics of Nonstandard Employment in the South African Retail Sector," Paper presented at Annual ILRIG Rosa Luxemburg Cape Partners Conference 2009. Available also from Law & Policy, Vol. 31, Issue 3 https://papers.ssrn.com/sol3/papers.cfm?abstract_id=1418731.

Lacey, Marian. 1981. *Working for Boroko: the origins of a coercive labour system in South Africa.* Johannesburg: Ravan Press.

Marx, Karl. 1887. *Capital: a critique of political economy.* Moscow, USSR: Progress Publishers.

Marx, Karl and Engels, Fredrich. 1973. Selected Works in Volume 1 Origins of the Family, Private Property and the State.

Mbyoso, Aimée Nöel. 2018. "Gender and migration in South Africa: talking to women migrants." Institute for Security Studies. Available at: http://issafrica.s3.amazonaws.com/site/uploads/sar16.pdf.

Murillo, Celeste and Andrea D'Atri. 2018. "Producing and reproducing: capitalism's dual oppression of women." Left Voice, 11 September. Available at: https://www.leftvoice.org/onreproductive-labor-wage-slavery-and-the-new-working-class.

Naylor, Adrie and Nandi Vanqa-Mgijima. 2016. "Homebased care workers research." Unpublished paper, ILRIG, Cape Town, South Africa.

Newman, Neil, John Pape and Helga Jansen, eds. 2011. *Is there an alternative? South African workers confronting globalisation*. Cape Town, South Africa: ILRIG.

Theron, Jan. 2009. "Space for organisation: trade unions in South Africa and the prospects for renewal," Paper presented at Annual ILRIG-Rosa Luxemburg Cape Partners Conference 2009.

Tsikata, Dzodzi. 2009. "Gender, land and labour relations and livelihoods in sub-Saharan Africa in the era of economic liberalisation: towards a research agenda." *Feminist Africa Journal* Issue 12, December 2009.

Valiani, Salimah. 2012. *Rethinking unequal exchange: the global integration of nursing labour markets*. Toronto, Canada: University of Toronto Press.

Vanqa-Mgijima, Nandi. 2011. "Race, class and gender relations then and now: the case of domestic labour." South Africa Today: how do we characterise the social formation? Paper presented at ILRIG Conference, Cape Town, South Africa, 29–30 April.

Vanqa-Mgijima, Nandi, Yvette Wiid and Darcy du Toit. 2013. "Organising for empowerment." In *Exploited, undervalued – and essential: domestic workers and the realisation of their rights*, ed.Darcy du Toit, 265–320. Pretoria, South Africa: Pretoria University Law Press.

Vasilaki, Christina. 2014. "Funding cuts create a ticking time bomb for HIV patients." Equal Times, 1 December. Available at: https://www.equaltimes.org/funding-cuts-create-a-tickingtime?lang=en#.V1V-zlfwySMhttp://www.equaltimes.org/funding-cuts-create-a-ticking-time.

Walker, Cherryl, 1990. "Gender and the development of the migrant labour system c.1850–1930." In *Women and gender in Southern Africa to 1945*, ed.Cherryl Walker, 168–196. Cape Town, South Africa: David Philip.

Webster, Edward. 2005. "New forms of work and the representational gap." *Beyond the apartheid workplace: studies in transition*, eds. Edward Webster and Karl von Holdt. Pietermaritzuburg: University of KwaZulu Natal Press.

Webster, Edward and Karl von Holdt, eds. 2005. *Beyond the apartheid workplace: studies in transition*. Pietermaritzburg: University of KwaZulu Natal Press.

5 The Logic of Intersectional Marginalization

Palestinian and Israeli Practitioners' Observations of Inequitable Labour Practices in Grassroots Peace Organizing

Ambreen Tour Ben-Shmuel and Manar Faraj

Introduction

While women are underrepresented in leadership in government and negotiations, studies have pointed to the prevalence of women in grassroots and civil society organizations and the importance of including them in all levels of peace organizing (Hunt and Posa 2001; UNSCR 1325; Krause, Krause and Bränfors 2018). Grassroots peace organizations often seek to equip and empower women to take leadership roles and be more active in civil society, and studies exploring gender mainstreaming and women in peace and conflict often do so from a *gender* angle (United Nations, Security Council, 2019; Webster, Chen and Beardsley 2019). However, having a high percentage of women in grassroots movements and programming does not accurately reflect equity and equality within peace organizations, and an intersectional analysis of labour practices along both national and gender lines can elucidate this (Ben-Shmuel 2019). In this study we seek to fill an important gap in the literature, asking: What does intersectionality as a theoretical framework and methodology offer researchers studying peace organizations? Looking at our context, how are intersectional gender-national groups, Israeli and especially Palestinian women, marginalized in the management, implementation, and labour practices of peace organizations in Palestine and Israel? Secondarily, how is this marginalization manifested in the movement of bodies from peripheralized to more central spaces for the needs of peace organizations?

We argue that it is essential to apply an intersectional perspective to the field of Palestinian and Israeli peace organizing as it broadens the study of power relations and inequality beyond the existing studies focusing exclusively on national groups, particularly as addressing women's roles in grassroots peacebuilding can be translated into participation in other initiatives, also affecting their political participation (Anderson 2016). While the existing literature points to the roles of women in peace negotiations, both their positive influence and invisibility (Sharoni 1996; Aharoni 2011; Paffenholz et al. 2016), it overlooks the way organizational ideology is practiced in the workplace and activities of grassroots peacebuilding organizations; for example, how people are promoted, the distribution of labour, how people move between peripheries and centres, and additional responsibilities and opportunities outside of work hours. While all our interviewees said the 25 organizations in which they worked exhibited sensitivity with regard to the asymmetric power imbalance between Palestinians and Israelis, our findings point to the disconnect between this sensitivity toward a *national* power imbalance and the power imbalance that is experienced at a gender-national intersectional level. In effect, we found a prevalent organizational logic that negatively discriminates against Palestinian and Israeli women in wages and professional mobility, disproportionately allows Palestinian women to be subject to harassment and humiliation when moving from peripheries to centres for the sake of the organization, and largely assumes non-compensation for Palestinian and Israeli women in necessary care work, including for the sake of effective organizational activities.

This study draws on our dual commitment to the field, as academics seeking to contribute to the literature by exploring intersectional outcomes in peace organizing, and as practitioners pointing to challenges that can be addressed to mitigate inequality. This research has implications for other peace and conflict contexts, illuminating the ways multidimensional perspectives can better help practitioners, researchers, and policy makers understand and address unique gender-national intersectional challenges and needs.

Intersectionality as Theory and Method

In this section, we review relevant theories, provide context for our field site, reflect on our positionality, and outline our data and research method. As a theory, intersectionality makes visible power relations that are otherwise neglected or explicitly ignored, calling attention to privilege and equity, and by extension, the lack thereof, as they manifest at the intersection of multiple identity categories, like gender, race, or class. Drawing on the intersection of gender and nationality in organizational policies, we will also address the spatial aspects of power relations by identifying the movement between geographical and organizational centres and peripheries.

Theoretical Background

While power relations and marginalization have been discussed at length within the context of peacebuilding in Palestine and Israel (Rouhana and

Korper 1997; Abu-Nimer 1999; Maoz 2000; Suleiman 2004), studies have largely focused on the *two national groups*, overlooking other social categories, like gender. However, peace and security research has indicated the importance of a gender perspective (Tickner 1992; Willett 2010). At the same time, there are limited studies of gender in grassroots peacebuilding (McKay and Mazurana, 2001; Mazurana et al. 2005), particularly in ongoing conflict contexts, and likewise, few articles highlighting the impact of gender on peacebuilding between Palestinians and Israelis (Pearson D'Estree and Babbitt, 1998; Golan and Kamal, 2005; Golan 2011). This limited research on *gender* has largely focused on trends and reflections as opposed to in-depth empirical work. As the majority of peace organizations in Palestine and Israel conduct mixed-gender activities, a gender and gender-national perspective can enhance our knowledge of power relations embedded within peace organizing.

A gender-organizational perspective is important as it can explain how gender and inequality persist and are reproduced in organizations. As Acker has argued, "Gender is a constitutive element in organizational logic, or the underlying assumptions and practices that construct most contemporary work organizations" (Acker 1990, 147), and organizations that operate in a shared space tend to have similar logics (DiMaggio and Powell 1983). An important aspect of this is the conceptualization of the "ideal" or "abstract worker" that organizations envision when hiring, namely, desirable characteristics for a job position that tend to be gendered, with inherent assumptions regarding availability and the presence or lack of competing interests (around childcare, for example) (Acker 1990).

More recent research on gendered organizations has pointed to the inseparability of one identity, like gender, from other identities and categorizations based on race, class, or religion (Acker 2006; Britton and Logan 2008; Tariq and Syed 2018). Acker (2012) has pointed to the ways that organizing processes and culture, like the value attributed to particular tasks, wage assignments, beliefs about gender differences, purported gender-neutral policies, and attitudes and behaviours, among others, contribute to inclusion and exclusion within an organization and the gendered organizational logic that perpetuates gender inequality. These concepts, she argues, can also be applied to other identities, in our case, the way assumptions about gender, nationality, citizenship, or religion are simultaneously embedded in organizations. This is important because the intersection of multiple identities, like gender *and* nationality, can result in gender-national organizational logic, including assumptions, procedures, and tasks, that can uniquely and adversely impact particular members of an organization.

Yet organizations are not divorced from geopolitical spaces, and as people move to and from organizations, they also move between centres and peripheries, which is particularly relevant in a conflict-ridden context. Peripheries are characterized by economic polarization, social inequality, and a lack of political power (Kühn 2015), and geographical research draws our attention to spatial relations that can produce and reproduce inequality (Blomley 2006; Valentine 2007; Kühn 2015). Valentine (2007) has noted the importance of considering intersectional subjects as bodies experience space differently, but research on inter-sectional studies has largely ignored the role of space. Yet it is in space, Valentine argues, where different aspects of subjects' intersectional identity become salient or disappear, are claimed or rejected, or are made relevant or irrelevant. Exploring intersectionality as lived experiences in space adds another dimension to intersectional studies, also allowing for more subject complexity and agency.

As a method, intersectionality offers us a number of approaches for analysis, aptly summarized by Choo and Ferree (2010), as group, pro-cess, and system centred. We draw on all three aspects, first by fore-grounding the most marginalized gender-national subgroups, Israeli and especially Palestinian women; second, by exploring how marginalizing practices are expressed across contexts; and third, by examining the prevalence of gendered organizational logic in peace organizations.

Contextualizing the Field

The Palestinian-Israeli conflict has been characterized as an intractable conflict, meaning that it is protracted, violent, identity-based, cultivates a zero-sum mentality, and is central in a society (Bar-Tal 2000). While numerous peace proposals have been initiated over the years, the Oslo peace process, which started in 1993, and the two-state solution it pro-posed, garnered significant attention and was initially hailed as a great success. Numerous grassroots and civil society organizations emerged and engaged in peacebuilding initiatives with governmental and institutional support, allowing Palestinian and Israeli civilians to meet one another, marking a particularly optimistic period. However, the situation has largely deteriorated since then, marked by intifadas, wars on Gaza, expanding Israeli settlements in the West Bank, and numerous Israeli unilateral policies. Many political pundits and peace practitioners often note that the two-state solution is no longer viable. Under the ongoing Israeli occupation, Palestinians are subject to Israeli political, economic, and social control, and face increasingly constrained rights.

In the current political environment, there is much less institutional support for or civilian belief in peace. Peace organizations that continue to engage in this work are perceived as "leftist," although many of the organizations do not explicitly embrace a political position. Palestinian political principles reject the meeting of Palestinians and Israelis except in cases where they seek to resist or expose the Israeli occupation and oppression of Palestinians.

While civilian engagement in peacebuilding initiatives is permitted, people who participate in peacebuilding programs, particularly Palestinians, are often subject to suspicion, criticism, and at times, harassment. In this context, in the absence of a governmental peace process, some peacebuilding organizations still seek to lay the foundation for a shared future, seeing the value in ongoing people to people engagement to allow Palestinians and Israelis to meet to reduce dehumanization, educate participants, and explore alternatives to the current political situation. However, this work is conducted in an atmosphere that lacks the institutional support it once had and is often responded to with derision, cynicism, or rejection.

Positionality

We recognize the sensitivities of this joint co-write, both the disproportionately high social cost for Faraj as a Palestinian refugee woman compared to Ben-Shmuel, and the politics of Ben-Shmuel as an Israeli-American writing about the occupation (Handel and Ginsburg 2018). Our writing is not divorced from our context, and as we have worked on this chapter, we have faced disruptive and traumatic events as our young children grow and see the ugly face of the occupation we oppose. The very writing of this project was affected by checkpoints, frequent Israeli electricity cuts in the West Bank, and increasing challenges to conduct peace research in a period of limited funding for peace and humanitarian work. All of these issues affected our ability to work together, particularly for Faraj, living in the West Bank, which is economically and socially peripheralized by the Israeli occupation, resulting in inequitable power imbalances and access to resources we take for granted in Israel. One of the strengths and limitations of this study is that we draw on our experiences as women working and researching the field, which causes us to be more attentive to what other women are experiencing.

Data and Method

In this study, we are informed by our 13 (Faraj) and 12 (Ben-Shmuel) years in the field and the combined 400+ binational meetings in which we have participated and worked as adults. From 2017-2019, we collected field notes during research observations and conducted 36 semi-structured interviews with select Palestinian and Israeli men and women, including participants, facilitators, and staff from various organizations. The staff interviewed, including both employees and freelancers, have an average 13 years of experience, and combined, have worked in 25 different organizations that engage in binational dialogue between Palestinians and Israelis.

It is important to note that in subsequent sections, we will discuss Palestinians based on nationality and citizenship. This distinction is important, as in our context, when both Israelis and Palestinians use the word "nationality," they see this as something distinct from citizenship. In our context, nationality refers to Israeli Jews or Palestinian Arabs, and both would agree that they do not share the same *national* identity, even when they both share Israeli citizenship. Thus Palestinians, regardless of their citizenship status or place of residency, including in the diaspora, are considered within the Palestinian national group. Similarly, Israeli Jews would generally see all Jews, including those in the diaspora, as sharing in their nationality.

The organizations studied varyingly coordinate binational encounters between Israeli Jews and Palestinian Muslims and Christians with Israeli citizenship, and/or between Israeli Jews and Palestinian Muslims and Christians from the occupied Palestinian territories. These encounters include children's camps, youth and adult trips, lectures, and extended dialogue meetings (ranging from a few times to regular meetings over the course of a few years). All names of interviewees and organizations have been changed to protect their privacy.

We chose to study peacebuilding organizations that coordinate mixed-gender dialogue groups in particular, not only because the vast majority of peace organizations coordinate mostly mixed-gender programs, but also because we believe in the importance of mixed-gender participation and representation in peace and conflict resolution. Less than one-third of the organizations that we studied regularly coordinate all-women's groups, although, *even* in these organizations, mixed-gender projects comprise the vast majority of their work. In order for grassroots peace work to scale, women must be able to equitably and effectively participate and work alongside men. Mixed-gender groups offer the unique opportunity to not only model equitable engagement between binational groups, but also between women and men, elevating the perspective of Palestinians, the national minority, and women, the gender minority, to ensure that a wide range of opinions, needs, and contributions are brought to the fore.[1]

The field of Israeli and Palestinian peacebuilding is a largely secular endeavour in which primarily secular Israelis engage in programs with secular to more religious Palestinian participants. The exception to this is interfaith initiatives, which recruit Jewish, Christian, and Muslim participants who range from culturally to more devoutly religious. However, there are fewer interfaith or religious peace organizations compared to their secular counterparts; likewise, most of the organizations we studied are secular.

Drawing on interviews, observations, and field notes, we applied thematic analysis to generate codes, identify patterns, and search for themes to interpret the data (Braun and Clarke 2006). Relying on Choo and Ferree (2010), we foregrounded the experiences of Palestinian women (group centred), explored intersectional power relations across contexts (process centred), and assessed the prevalence of these phenomena across numerous organizations, which are largely representative of binational peace initiatives, essentially the institution of peacebuilding (system centred). In order to engage in methodological reflexivity in our research, we shared our findings with experienced Palestinian and Israeli practitioners to solicit feedback and critique, and we are grateful for their comments, which we took into consideration in the writing process.[2]

Exclusionary Organizational Logics and Labour Practices

Our findings point to exclusionary gender and intersectional gender-national labour practices that affect Israeli and especially Palestinian women. These practices comprise part of the gender-national organizational logic (Acker 2012) that perpetuate inequality in Palestinian and Israeli peace organizing. Three primary themes emerged when considering the way organizations manage and implement their programs: gender discrimination and essentialism that exclude women from management positions; unrecognized spatial movement labour performed by Palestinian women as they travel from peripheries to centres; and gendered care and non-compensation related to childcare and emotional labour. These themes permeated various areas of the organizational structure and work environment, the way the organizations built their programming, and the requisite influences on participants, resulting in various stratifications of exclusion and inclusion, which promoted or constrained women in their work.

Gender Discrimination: The Gender-National Ideal Worker

The first finding points to the logic of the "abstract" or ideal worker (Acker 1990) in peace organizations, which manifests in male-dominated executive positions and female-dominated mid- to low-level positions. While this is not particularly surprising considering the prevalence of gendered work and management in most organizations and peace negotiations, the field of grassroots peacebuilding is considered a sphere for women's agency and empowerment, and in Palestine and Israel, is female dominant with regard to participants and workers. At the same time, the management hierarchy privileges men while marginalizing women, particularly those at the intersection of a double minority, Palestinian women.

A number of long-term practitioners noted the feminization of peace work, discussing how Israeli men and women and Palestinian men were more dominant 30 years ago, and men had the most senior positions.

Liat, an Israeli female facilitator and academic with 30 years of experience in the field said, "If there is money and a little bit of prestige [...] within a peace organization, there are only men. Women are conducting all the work, and men are directing that organization," a trend which she said continues to this day. While men, "got all the credit, the international credit, the awards, the economic incentives were given to them," women filled mid- to lower-level positions. However, over time, as the prestige of the field began to wane corresponding with failed peace processes, and financial cuts followed, she noted shifting trends, as Israeli men who initially led organizations moved on to more lucrative and prestigious positions in other fields, while Israeli women, if they stayed, even with their long time commitment and expertise, continued to work "more or less in the same organizations, in the same position, and [for] the same salary."

A few of those interviewed pointed to the shift over time, and how, particularly in the 2000s, Palestinian women began to work in the field alongside Palestinian men. Ahmed, a Palestinian facilitator and evaluator who has worked in the field for nearly two decades, noted, "In recent years, maybe the last five years, you see more women taking over program positions; managers, facilitators, but again not at the top level of the director." In spite of the shift with women taking over more mid-level positions in particular, both Palestinian and Israeli women echoed Liat's sentiments about women's labour, noting that women continue to do most of the work for which Palestinian and Israeli men get credit.

Discrimination in the Organization

While most of the staff interviewees noted how women in the field excelled in their work, Chaim, an Israeli male group leader and practitioner, reflected that gender also "influenced the way they [women] were evaluated or assessed for a certain position." There is a "view [in the organization] that if you're a woman you have pre-assigned roles in society – mothers – but whatever else you are or do – those are already there. Gender played a role in a way that you do or don't meet gendered expectations," he noted.

While many of those interviewed pointed to the very gendered nature of the staff structure, the Palestinian women in particular began to note distinct acts of marginalization and discrimination within the field. This contrasted with the way Israeli women discussed issues, as Israeli women might discuss *gendered* issues, but Palestinian women noted the way *they* as *Palestinian* women were singled out in unique ways.

Luna, a Palestinian female project manager, noted that in her experience working with some prominent organizations in the field, Palestinian women would often take support roles, and they were encouraged to volunteer their time with the potential of this becoming more permanent; however, in her experience, "so many [Palestinian] women worked for free, and were promised a paid job, but they never got any." However, even when Palestinian women were employed, they could face uniquely difficult conditions with limited recourse. A few women addressed this in their interviews, discussing how asking for a raise, a better title, or promotion tended to be refused, and this negatively affected Palestinian women in particular, because they were less confrontational and more willing to continue working in spite of their frustration over their circumstances. It was easier for men to leave the organization and find other employment compared to women in the organization; however, while Israeli women would stay due to ideological commitment to the peace organization, Palestinian women would stay both out of ideological commitment and the challenges of the labour market that limited their work possibilities elsewhere.

When reflecting on how women tended to remain in spite of difficult conditions with male superiors, Mary noted, "maybe their endurance was higher" and women were more likely to "get along" with management, which was one of the main reasons she thought women were more likely to be employed in the organization. She contrasted this with male staff who tended to have more conflict with male management. Khaled, a Palestinian manager from a different organization with 14 years of experience in the field, reflected on his years of work and explicitly indicated his preference for working with women, as "men have too much ego" and "it isn't as hard to work with women as it is with men."

These patterns indicate gender essentialism that reduces women to certain roles based on perceived biological or socialized capabilities, supportive and voluntary roles. Furthermore, the preference for working with women, particularly Palestinian women, points to an "ideal type" of worker in mid- to low-level positions. This preference for those lacking in ego, who are less confrontational, and who will work for less money without advancement opportunities, point to an ideal type of "abstract worker" (Kanter 1977; Acker 1990). These criteria are most often filled by women, and particularly Palestinian women, who have the least recourse for comparable employment opportunities, which is also a result of the economic peripheralization in the West Bank and the limited work opportunities they have. While some of this is comparable to other contexts regarding gender discrimination in the workforce (Williams and Multhaup 2018; Heilman and Chen 2005), Palestinian women, like other minority women in the literature on women of colour, face a "double jeopardy" due to their identity as gender and national minorities (Beal 1970; Maume 1999; Berdahl and Moore 2006).

Gender-National Disparities in Movement

Movement is an inherent part of labour and participation in organizations. This is made particularly salient in cross border peace organizing in conflict contexts, and issues that often arise here are uncommon in other contexts, in which there are large disparities in the travel time and experiences of workers and participants due to their intersectional identities. Throughout our research, four central axes or spectrums, which granted advantage or disadvantage, indicating differential power relations, emerged as most salient: citizenship, nationality, gender, and religiosity. In effect, we found that Palestinian women, and especially Palestinian women who express piety through their dress (*hijab* and/or *abaya*), undertake significant hidden labour in the time and effort they invest in moving to and from peripheries for the sake of the peace organization.

In order to work and meet, there is significant movement between political centres and peripheries. Drawing on Kühn's (2015) conceptualization of peripheries as marked by economic polarization, social inequality, and a lack of political power, *centres* are characterized as areas under complete Israeli control and hegemony. Peace organizing largely occurs in these centres, and on this scale, Palestine is the political periphery, comprised of administrative divisions established in the Oslo Accords, Areas A and B, the densely populated areas under Palestinian civil and some security control, and Area C, which comprises 60% of the West Bank and is under full Israeli civil and security control. Palestinian peace workers and participants move from more to less peripheral areas, toward centres (*from* Areas A or B *to* C or Israel), and Israelis move within Israel or to Israel-controlled areas of the West Bank (Area C). Most meetings occur in Area C, and on occasion, groups meet in Israel if the organization can obtain permits for workers or participants. If organizations have funding for international events, they sometimes send workers and participants abroad.

Workers' Movement for Organizational Activities

While Palestinian men and women from the West Bank were the most marginalized of all the workers, spending the most time and effort to arrive at work, they often saw this as justified, as jobs in Israel offer higher compensation. As Nour, a female facilitator employed by a Jerusalem-based organization noted, "My work started at nine, and I had to go to the checkpoint around five or six in the morning. Most times, I chose six, because so many workers go around four or five, [...] and they are mostly men. I wanted to avoid that judgment of a woman being at the checkpoint that early. Sometimes they [Israeli soldiers] close the checkpoint for hours and hours, and I will be late to work." Then, often on the commute, Nour would be one of the only women on the bus, "It was very uncomfortable, and some men had their eyes on me, some harassing, some sexually harassing me. This experience was also difficult." She continued, "My boss was always mad if I'm late. Many times, I heard him saying, 'Why don't we hire a person from Jerusalem? It will be much easier for us, and she will be on time,' [...] which made me hide my challenges, because I wanted this job."

Other interviewees spoke about working as freelancers, being based in the West Bank, or going into a West Bank office, which made their commute easier. Yet in order to conduct much of the work, which entailed coordination with Israeli colleagues, Palestinians would meet Israelis in Area C or cross checkpoints to go into Israel. Some organizations tried to address the additional effort of the commute by sending a taxi for the worker or a volunteer group leader, and a Palestinian taxi would pick them up from their home, bring them to the checkpoint where they would cross on foot to be met by a staff member or Israeli taxi on the other side to continue the commute. While this was often seen as a helpful way of ameliorating the situation as much as possible, Palestinian women from the West Bank noted that even this could not neutralize the challenge of the commute.

A few Palestinian female facilitators discussed the challenges Palestinian women encountered by being picked up early in the morning or dropped off late at night. Sometimes the organization would send a private car, and the women would express their discomfort, as people in the neighbourhood would begin asking why a particular man always picked her up, which could lead to neighbourhood gossip. They would often prefer a taxi to a private car, which on one hand, did not imply their overfamiliarity with a driver, but on the other hand, meant that she was constantly encountering strangers on her early morning or late evening commutes, which could result in a measure of uncomfortable questioning or harassment. Additionally, since afternoon and evening activities entailed returning home late, it was challenging because it is culturally unacceptable for women to be out alone or return late in the evening.

While Israeli Jews, both men and women, did not often need to pass through checkpoints where they were stopped in order to get to Area C, Palestinians with Israeli citizenship often had the most mobility, due to their citizenship and nationality, freely going in and out of Areas A, B, and C to meet with Palestinian colleagues or participants. However, while this particular identity granted them more mobility, this same identity, their citizenship and nationality, resulted in additional scrutiny when traveling abroad.

Traveling Abroad

Palestinians and Israelis in peace organizations sometimes travel abroad to attend conferences, fundraise, and accompany groups of Palestinian and Israeli participants in a peace encounter. While Palestinians and Jews with Israeli citizenship or permanent residency can travel through Israel's international airport, Palestinians from the West Bank must first cross into Jordan and travel to Amman, since there are no airports in Palestine, and it is rare for Israel to grant a permit for Palestinians to travel through Israeli airports.

Our Palestinian interviewees spoke at length about the challenges of traveling abroad. Travel through Israel's international airport strongly favours Israeli Jews compared to Palestinians with Israeli citizenship or residency. Higher security flagging, represented on a numerical system, ranges from more intrusive questions, opening and going through each item in one's luggage, to a lengthy interrogation and full strip search. As Mary, a Palestinian woman with Israeli citizenship, noted about her frequent trips abroad, "Any Israeli Jewish participant or leader is more credible with me. So in a group setting, I might be first to talk to the airport security, but they always asked for an Israeli Jewish person to verify [what I said] and be their credible source. The nationality was more important than the gender. One time, I was traveling with a Jewish co-leader, and he was just out of the army, and the security asked him to point at the people he knew before the trip, and those he did know got a lower clearance, and those he didn't know before trip were flagged as higher security risks."

While Palestinians from the West Bank could obtain a permit to travel through Israel on occasion, this was still a difficult journey. While it was less expensive and shorter to travel this way, saving two additional commuting days, Palestinians from the West Bank are often subjected to more, often humiliating, security checks. Nasreen, a Palestinian project manager, noted that even though she could sometimes obtain a permit, she and other Palestinian women preferred the longer trip through Jordan to avoid the harassment that she and other Palestinians experienced on multiple occasions. The organization, despite its extensive work with Palestinians and sensitivity to power dynamics, would respond in a patronizing way, "The Palestinian women were asked to feel lucky they even have a chance to travel and see the world," and when they asked to travel through Jordan, "they said that we have to pay for it ourselves because the budget only covers travel through Israel."

Often, Palestinians from the West Bank and those who are Israeli citizens cannot travel together, as their citizenship requires them to cross to Jordan via land bridges in different locations. Thus, even when Israeli Jews or Palestinians with Israeli citizenship might want to defer to their Palestinian colleagues from the West Bank and travel the longer route together in solidarity, it is impossible to do so.

Participants' Movement for Peace Organization Meetings

While Israelis can drive to and from Area C, easily passing Israeli military checkpoints, Palestinians must move from the more residential

Areas A and B to Area C, facing additional checkpoints in between their towns and cities, as well as flying checkpoints randomly implemented by Israeli forces (Bishara 2015). These checkpoints significantly lengthen their journeys. Palestinian men, much more than Palestinian women, are accustomed to long commutes and checkpoints, both within Palestine and, at times, into Israel with work permits. Thus, while commuting to Area C from the north or south West Bank can be tiring for all workers and participants, it is often more challenging for Palestinian women who are less accustomed to long trips in the West Bank, as they do not work far from home as often as Palestinian men.

Luna summarized sentiments raised by several Palestinian staff interviewed, referencing how the particular needs of religious Palestinian women were rarely taken into consideration. She discussed how, "in the summer time, when we travel to areas farther away, the Palestinian women would ask to stop somewhere to freshen up," which was needed because of the heat and was compounded due to the amount of clothing the women wore. She continued, noting that the Palestinian male manager accompanying the group would refuse these requests, saying "They are waiting for us, and we don't want to be late […], or why are you wearing your hijab in the first place?"

When Palestinian participants come into Israel for a peace organization's meetings, they need to obtain permits from the Israel Civil Administration. While it is often easier for Palestinian women to obtain a permit than men, they face additional challenges when crossing the checkpoint, both because they do not cross into Israel as frequently, and because they face greater scrutiny due to the amount and types of clothing they are wearing (Faraj 2019), including undergarments that have any metal wire or hooks. This is an issue for Muslim women who wear the *hijab* or *abaya*, as their hairpins and decorative accessories on clothing can affect their ability to cross the checkpoint and the amount of time their inspection will take. Israeli soldiers can ask women to remove articles of clothing, including head coverings, in front of men, and women often acquiesce in order to cross the checkpoint. However, this can also anger religious men or family members traveling with the women, thus the women risk denial of entry from Israeli soldiers or angering other Palestinians.

These accounts illustrate the gender-national and gender-national-religious complexity Palestinian women in particular can experience, resulting in unique and compounding intersectional pressure. As Valentine (2007) noted, intersectionality is a lived experience, and space is experienced differently by various bodies. Spatial inequality is manifested in bodies, not only along national lines, but across other stratifications as well. Similar to earlier geographical literature on women's movement and spatial restrictions (McDowell 1993), Palestinian women live in much more spatially restricted ways than Palestinian men or their

Israeli counterparts due to the Israeli occupation alongside patriarchal gender norms as expressed through religious or cultural expectations. While gender and nationality are often prominent axes of identity for Palestinian women, religiosity becomes another axis, particularly as it manifests in cultural and traditional dress as they cross boundaries, moving from being part of the hegemonic, traditional, Muslim culture in Palestine to more secular centres where peace organizations meet. As movement for the sake of peace organizing is *toward* areas of Israeli control, asymmetric power relations favouring Israeli Jews are manifested in the ease of Israeli movement compared to other groups, and significant hidden and unrecognized movement-labour occurs by Palestinians.

Gendered Care and Non-compensation

There is a wide literature focusing on gendered care and labour in the workplace, the roles that women fill (and are stereotypically expected to fill), and the ways this maintains their exclusion and male dominance (Budlender 2010; Chopra and Sweetman 2014). It is not surprising that this occurs within Palestine and Israel, including in grassroots peace organizing. However, the literature looking at grassroots peace movements, particularly in Palestine and Israel, largely ignores this, failing to explore inequitable patterns and practices with regard to women's work and responsibilities in the organization, also failing to address the intersectional challenges that arise.

Women's Challenges around Work and Childcare

In both Israeli and Palestinian societies, as in much of the rest of the world, the burden of childcare falls disproportionately on women. As researchers have noted in various corporate and other workplace contexts (Taneja et al. 2012; Amaram 2019), women seeking to balance professional and personal responsibilities around childcare face unique barriers in professional advancement. This extends to work in the nonprofit sector, as Chopra and Sweetman (2014) have noted, "Care work also constrains women's ability to participate on equal terms with men in development interventions supported by international and national nongovernment organizations." Similar to other contexts, in grassroots peace movements, constraints on women due to care work is relegated to the private sphere and beyond the concern of the organizations seeking to recruit women. However, this is an organizational issue as work-family practices can be intentionally adapted to address or overlook women's needs and obligations (Allen and Martin 2017). Peace organizations regularly recruit participants or select staff or organizational members as group leaders or facilitators in projects extending for a full day, a weekend, or a few days inside or outside of the country. This is particularly ironic in that peace organizations often believe in and engage in work surrounding women's equality and empowerment, however without always accommodating their needs surrounding childcare.

Our research points to the ways both Palestinian and Israeli women with young children (and grandmothers who take care of grandchildren) often faced the most challenges when committing to participate, perform staff-related tasks, or fill semi-volunteer positions as group leaders or facilitators. While most organizations we researched did not actively accommodate this demographic, notably, a few of the organizations attempted to by intermittently providing babysitters for staff when they had work-family conflicts, by allowing female participants to bring a babysitter and children to meetings, and the most generous, by providing programs with babysitters so mothers with young children could take a (often unpaid) leadership role in meetings or obtain training.

Reflecting on inner work dynamics in one organization, Chaim noted that having children influenced the roles and opportunities allocated to staff, which specifically influenced women. He said, "You might not have the same opportunities available to you because there would be assumptions," for example, assuming that a woman should (or would rather) "stay home and take care of their kids." In some cases, he noted women were told, "'You need to think about your family,' or 'Are you sure you can do this project because you are going to start having babies soon?'" A few Palestinian women echoed this due to their extensive experience in a few different organizations, and Nora, a Palestinian project coordinator, noted the ways pregnancy inhibited her ability to work, not due to health reasons or a lack of desire to participate, but because her workplace explicitly limited the types of positions and opportunities she could have had.

When discussing the way organizations recruit group leaders and facilitators from among organizational members, Ortal, an Israeli female project manager with long-term experience in the field, noted that there was not a gendered pattern to who they chose, although she qualified, "some of them are [facilitating] more than others. It depends on how available they are." This issue – availability – turned out to be key, as several other figures in the organization noted the gendered nature of availability, and the fact that nearly half of the facilitators, who happened to be women, tended to have specific constraints around their time due to childcare.

Studies in other contexts have noted that geographical distance between mothers and mothers-in-laws is correlated to a woman's attachment to the labour force, as she can rely on family for childcare (Compton and Pollak 2014), and we have observed similar dynamics in our contexts. If Palestinian women with young children would attend a peace organization's meeting, in the event the organization did not provide childcare, they would often leave their children with family members, as Palestinian families, particularly in the occupied Palestinian territories, live in closer proximity to family than Israelis. Israeli women, in the event they could not make arrangements for their children, would often hire a babysitter, and if these mothers would come out of their ideological commitment to the organization and its vision, they knew that they would ultimately receive less money as part of their earnings would go to childcare.

Liat noted the challenges around times of meetings, where after a full day of work, staff go out to eat and continue to discuss important issues regarding who should be invited to sit on the organization's board, brainstorm about important topics and come to consensus on it prior to raising it during office hours, or decide which staff member should be sent abroad to lead a binational peacebuilding meeting. Women, "if they choose motherhood, [are] excluded from that," she said. Hind expressed something similar, "What bothered me is that after every meeting, when there is an evaluation, men meet at night or go to a restaurant, [...] and of course I can't go. I'm single and from a very conservative family and village, but they [male co-workers] never really pay attention." While most of these anecdotes address challenges around childcare, particularly in this last reference, it is, more generally, challenges due to family obligations, and a lack of consideration for how issues affect Palestinian women.

Emotional and Uncompensated Staff Labour

The final prevalent category of gendered labour entails the emotional and uncompensated invisible labour of women and men in organizations who are involved in recruiting participants for events. One of the most time consuming and critical aspects of building a program is participant recruitment, and organizations seek to recruit an equal number of Palestinians and Israelis. National representation is always the highest priority in recruitment, and then, secondarily, gender. Some of the more veteran practitioners interviewed noted that, in the 1990s, there was "no effort to have a gender balance" (Liat), while most of those who have worked in the field for the past five to ten years indicated that a gender balance in participation is important, following national representation, indicating a shift in organizational priorities.

Sometimes organizations must ensure a gender balance due to a quota imposed by the donor organization funding the meetings, and other times, the organization seeks to enforce this balance on its own. Oftentimes, Israeli staff or facilitators in an organization recruit Israeli participants while Palestinian staff or facilitators recruit Palestinian participants. However, we have noted that Palestinian women, much more than Palestinian men or Israeli men and women, invest the most time and money in recruitment, particularly in recruiting Palestinian women. The challenges around Palestinian women's recruitment stem from the particular national and gender-national challenges Palestinian women face in attending, as they must often obtain the approval of their spouse or father prior to participation.

Israeli recruitment most often entails publicizing the event on social media, sending emails to former participants to suggest new people that might wish to attend, and waiting for participants to respond. Palestinian recruitment, in contrast to Israeli recruitment, is much more relationship based. For Palestinian women, recruitment of Palestinians often includes lengthy phone conversations, learning about the woman and her life, meeting with her during and outside of work hours, and taking a vested interest in her situation. While those interviewed also noted that they enjoyed building these relationships, they also noted, "The phone calls sometimes took too long, asking about the kids, and the family, and the personal life. Sometimes I even had to go for lunch with this person if it was a female. I also had to be interested in what the women do. For example, there was this woman who I was recruiting [who] had a hair salon. I went to her hair salon to do my hair more than once so she [will] participate in the group. There is this woman that cooked at home and sold homemade food, so more than once, I had to buy from her, so we can have this relation[ship] that will convince her to come to the group" (Nasreen). She continued, providing more examples from her experience across multiple organizations.

When asked if her Palestinian male colleague had similar experiences, she said, "No, he didn't, and that's the difference. I *had* to do it. [...] He would get invited to social events *after* he had a relationship with them." She continued, "We would envy him, [saying] 'Oh you have the skill for it.' Maybe it is a skill. Or maybe it's the culture. Women are expected to build relationships." This was a topic of conversation among Palestinian female workers in organizations, who would discuss the significant amount of uncompensated time, money, and energy invested in recruitment. Nasreen recalled an exchange where another senior employee, a Palestinian woman, argued with her director, saying, "'I spend so much time and energy and emotions [...] and you don't even know this, and you don't even recognize it.'" Nasreen continued, reflecting on her own experience, "They [the men] say it should be easy, 'It's part of your job.' So, this was really frustrating, the recruitment part."

Luna echoed these sentiments. "For a man in our organization, it was very simple and very easy. He is known as a hero," by which she meant he was either in an Israeli jail or was a former combatant (or both), and as a result, "his reputation is very respected. So [if] he goes to men and tells them 'We want the women in your family to participate in some of the activities that we are doing,' the men do not even ask him what are the activities. They tell him, 'If they are with you, then they are safe.'"

These examples indicate the emotional labour (Hochschild 1983) Palestinian women in particular invest in recruitment, seeking to build relationships and address culturally mediated norms in which they cannot rely on their status or reputation like men would, but must build a relationship with women in order to recruit them. Beyond the emotional unseen labour, there was also invisible labour (Cherry 2016), which looks at unrecognized or devalued labour performed within contexts of employment that are crucial to the success of the position. Finally, there was also uncompensated labour, expenses the women had to pay in order to successfully recruit other women, but as these tasks were often perceived as personal, they were not compensated.

These findings point to the unique care practices that influence Israeli and Palestinian women, particularly the financial challenges Israeli women face, as they are less likely to have family close by that can assist with childcare. Palestinian women also noted these challenges, and overall, organizations failed to address this. Additionally, Palestinian women in particular face further emotional, invisible, and uncompensated labour in recruitment practices, and while recruitment was a part of their job, they were not compensated for the additional time and expenses they had to invest in order to perform their positions well. Both Palestinian and Israeli women struggled with these challenges, which had a direct effect on their opportunities within the organization and on their ability to earn the same amount of money as their male counterparts.

Conclusion

Applying an intersectional and spatial inequality perspective to peace organizing provides a number of unique insights, raising issues that are generally overlooked, while highlighting marginalization, discrimination, and disproportionately performed hidden labour by Palestinian women in particular. These processes coalesce into an overarching organizational logic of "underlying assumptions and practices" (Acker 1990) that perpetuate gender and gender-national inequality in peace organizing. This includes exclusionary practices in gendered leadership and gender discrimination that confines women to mid- to low-level positions, the discomfort gender-national and gender-national-religious minorities experience in their movement for work and participation, and the gender and gender-national components of care and emotional labour. While external hegemonic policies, like secular, patriarchal norms and the occupation influence society and organizations, by failing to counter the negative and inequitable effects in their influence on Palestinian women, organizations, ironically, reproduce them while struggling for social justice and better relations between Palestinians and Israelis.

Bringing together a gender-intersectional and organizational analysis to highlight dynamics *within* the organization and *in movement* between peripheries and centres for the needs of the organization sheds light on a number of phenomena we would otherwise fail to see. Isolating one stratification, whether nationality, gender, or religion, would overlook the compounding effects of these identities when combined. Together, we can see implicit and explicit power relations and inequality patterns as they manifest in organizational practices and logic in peace organizations.

Despite the challenges we have identified in our research, as academics who have come to our studies due to our work as practitioners and our awareness of how gradual, positive changes can and have been made, we are optimistic that organizations can apply an intersectional analysis to their work and programming to create more effective and inclusive programs for Palestinians and Israelis. There is already an awareness that national groups have different needs, which has led to increased uninational meetings within binational encounters; additionally, the field has long-recognized the different needs of women by creating all-women's programs. We argue that it is important to account for these sensitivities in binational *mixed-gender* programs as well, particularly as this is the dominant form of programming, looking at the myriad ways that these needs and challenges are expressed, not only in the interactions between participants, but at all levels of peace organizing.

This research has implications for all those involved in peace organizing: staff, participants, and donors who can encourage organizations to address intersectional challenges and needs. Beyond the boundaries of Palestine and Israel, this research can point to ways other organizations operating in binational or other complex intersectional environments, especially conflict zones, can critically examine their organizational choices despite political and societal constraints. In these contexts, people already struggle with numerous challenges due to fear, discrimination, and oppression, and peace organizations play an important role in trying to address these issues. Peace organizing is a field that is committed to social justice and creating a better future. In order to get there, it is important to understand, name, and address injustice, particularly as it is expressed in organizational logic and practice to mitigate further intersectional marginalization.

Notes

1 We discuss this in terms of sociological minorities, which takes into account issues such as inequality and ascribed status, with particular attention to distribution of resources and power relations (Wagley and Harris 1958; Healey, Stepnick and O'Brien 2018); thus, for example, while women are not

necessarily a *numerical* minority relative to men in a society, due to patriarchal structures privileging men over women, women are a *sociological* minority.
2 We are especially grateful to Huda, Gal, Walid, Shireen, Michal, and Shadia for their feedback.

References

Abu-Nimer, Mohammed. 1999. *Dialogue, conflict resolution, and change: Arab-Jewish encounters in Israel*. New York: Suny Press.

Acker, Joan. 1990. "Hierarchies, jobs, bodies: a theory of gendered organizations." *Gender and Society* 4(2): 139–158.

Acker, Joan. 2006. "Inequality regimes: gender, class, and race in organizations." *Gender and Society* 20(4): 441–464.

Acker, Joan. 2012. "Gendered organizations and intersectionality: problems and possibilities." *Equality, Diversity and Inclusion* 31(3): 214–224.

Aharoni, Sarai. 2011. "Gender and 'peace work': an unofficial history of Israeli-Palestinian peace negotiations." *Politics and Gender* 7(3): 391–416.

Allen, Tammy D. and Angela Martin. 2017. "The work-family interface: a retrospective look at 20 years of research in JOHP." *Journal of Occupational Health Psychology* 22(3): 259–272.

Amaram, Donatus I. 2019. "Attracting and retaining women talent in the global labor market: a review." *Journal of Human Resources* 7(1): 1–10.

Anderson, Miriam J. 2016. *Windows of opportunity: how women seize peace negotiations for political change*. New York: Oxford University Press.

Bar-Tal, Daniel. 2000. "From intractable conflict through conflict resolution to reconciliation: psychological analysis." *Political Psychology* 21(2): 351–365.

Beal, Frances M. 1970. *Double jeopardy: to be black and female*. Detroit, MI: Radical Education Project.

Ben-Shmuel, Ambreen. 2019. "Centering intersectionality when organizing peace: how gender and nationality shape participation in peacebuilding in Israel and Palestine." (Unpublished master's thesis). The Hebrew University.

Berdahl, Jennifer L. and Celia Moore. 2006. "Workplace harassment: double jeopardy for minority women." *Journal of Applied Psychology* 91(2): 426–436.

Bishara, Amahl. 2015. "Driving while Palestinian in Israel and the West Bank: the politics of disorientation and the routes of a subaltern knowledge." *American Ethnologist* 42(1): 33–54.

Blomley, Nicholas. 2006. "Uncritical critical geography?" *Progress in Human Geography* 30(1): 87–94.

Braun, Virginia and Victoria Clarke. 2006. "Using thematic analysis in psychology." *Qualitative Research in Psychology* 3(2): 77–101.

Britton, Dana M. and Laura Logan. 2008. "Gendered organizations: progress and prospects." *Sociology Compass* 2(1): 107–121.

Budlender, Debbie. 2010. "What do time use studies tell us about unpaid care work? evidence from seven countries." In *Time use studies and unpaid care work*, ed.Debbie Budlender, 23–67. New York: Routledge.

Cherry, Miriam A. 2016. "People analytics and invisible labor." *St. Louis University Law Journal* 61(1): 1–16.

Choo, Hae Yeon and Myra Marx Ferree. 2010. "Practicing intersectionality in sociological research: a critical analysis of inclusions, interactions, and institutions in the study of inequalities." *Sociological Theory 28*(2): 129–149.

Chopra, Deepta and Caroline Sweetman. 2014. "Introduction to gender, development and care." *Gender and Development 22*(3): 409–421.

Compton, Janice and Robert Pollak. 2014. "Family proximity, childcare, and women's labor force attachment." *Journal of Urban Economics 79*: 72–90.

DiMaggio, Paul J. and Walter W. Powell. 1983. "The iron cage revisited: institutional isomorphism and collective rationality in organizational fields." *American Sociological Review 48*: 147–160.

Faraj, Manar. 2019. "The Israeli checkpoint fashion runway." Unpublished manuscript.

Golan, Galia. 2011. "Asymmetry in cross-conflict collaboration: is there a gender factor?" *Peace and Conflict Studies 18*(2): 164–191.

Golan, Galia and Zahira Kamal. 2005. "Women's people-to-people activities: do we do it better?" *Palestine-Israel Journal of Politics, Economics, and Culture 12/13* (4/1): 58–64.

Handel, Ariel and Ruthie Ginsburg. 2018. "Israelis studying the occupation: an introduction." *Critical Inquiry 44*(2): 331–342.

Healey, Joseph F., Andi Stepnick and Eileen O'Brien. 2018. *Race, ethnicity, gender, and class: the sociology of group conflict and change*. 8th ed. Thousand Oaks, CA: Sage Publications.

Heilman, Madeline E. and Julie J. Chen. 2005. "Same behavior, different consequences: reactions to men's and women's altruistic citizenship behavior." *Journal of Applied Psychology 90*(3): 431–441.

Hochschild, Arlie Russell. 1983. *The managed heart: commercialization of human feeling*. Berkeley, CA: University of California.

Hunt, Swanee and Cristina Posa. 2001. "Women waging peace: inclusive security." *Foreign Policy 124* (May/June): 38–47.

Kanter, Rosabeth Moss. 1977. *Men and women of the corporation*. New York: Basic Books.

Krause, Jana, Werner Krause and Piia Bränfors. 2018. "Women's participation in peace negotiations and the durability of peace." *International Interactions 44*(6): 985–1016.

Kühn, Manfred. 2015. "Peripheralization: theoretical concepts explaining socio spatial inequalities." *European Planning Studies 23*(2): 367–378.

Maoz, Ifat. 2000. "Power relations in intergroup encounters: a case study of Jewish–Arab encounters in Israel." *International Journal of Intercultural Relations 24*(2): 259–277.

Maume, David J., Jr. 1999. "Glass ceilings and glass escalators: occupational segregation and race and sex differences in managerial promotions." *Work and Occupations 26*(4): 483–509.

Mazurana, Dyan, Angela Raven-Roberts and Jane Parpart, eds. 2005. *Gender, conflict, and peacekeeping*. New York: Rowman and Littlefield.

McDowell, Linda. 1993. "Space, place and gender relations: part I." *Progress in Human Geography 17*(2): 157–179.

McKay, Susan and Dyan Mazurana. 2001. "Gendering peacebuilding." In *Peace, conflict, and violence: peace psychology for the 21st century*, eds.Daniel J.

Christie, Richard V. Wagner and Deborah DuNann Winter, 341–349. Englewood Cliffs, NJ: Prentice Hall.

Paffenholz, Thania, Nick Ross, Steven Dixon, Anna-Lena Schluchter and Jacqui True. 2016. *"Making women count – not just counting women: assessing women's inclusion and influence on peace negotiations."* Geneva: Inclusive Peace and Transition Initiative (The Graduate Institute of International and Development Studies) and UN Women.

Pearson d'Estree, Tamra and Eileen F. Babbitt. 1998. "Women and the art of peacemaking: data from Israeli-Palestinian interactive problem-solving workshops." *Political Psychology* 19(1): 185–209.

Rouhana, Nadim N. and Susan H. Korper. 1997. "Power asymmetry and goals of unofficial third party intervention in protracted intergroup conflict." *Peace and Conflict* 3(1): 1–17.

Sharoni, Simona. 1996. "Gender and the Israeli-Palestinian accord: feminist approaches to international politics." In *Gendering the Middle East: emerging perspectives*, ed. Deniz Kandiyoti, 107–126. New York: Syracuse University Press.

Suleiman, Ramzi. 2004. "Planned encounters between Jewish and Palestinian Israelis: a social-psychological perspective." *Journal of Social Issues* 60(2): 323–337.

Taneja, Sonia, Mildred Golden Pryor and Jennifer Oyler. 2012. "Empowerment and gender equality: the retention and promotion of women in the workforce." *Journal of Business Diversity* 12(3): 43–53.

Tariq, Memoona and Jawad Syed. 2018. "An intersectional perspective on Muslim women's issues and experiences in employment." *Gender, Work and Organization* 25(5): 495–513.

Tickner, J. Ann. (1992). *Gender in international relations: feminist perspectives on achieving global security*. New York: Columbia University Press.

United Nations, Security Council, Women and Peace and Security: Report of the Secretary-General, S/2019/800 (9 October 2019), available from https://undocs.org/pdf?symbol=en/S/2019/800.

United Nations Security Council resolution 1325, Resolution 1325 S/RES/1325 (31 October 2000), available from https://undocs.org/S/RES/1325(2000).

Valentine, Gill. 2007. "Theorizing and researching intersectionality: a challenge for feminist geography." *The Professional Geographer* 59(1): 10–21.

Wagley, Charles and Marvin Harris. 1958. *Minorities in the new world: six case studies* New York: Columbia University Press.

Webster, Kaitlyn, Chon Chen and Kyle Beardsley. 2019. "Conflict, peace, and the evolution of women's empowerment." *International Organization* 73(2): 255–289.

Willett, Susan. 2010. "Introduction: Security Council Resolution 1325: assessing the impact on women, peace and security." *International Peacekeeping* 17(2): 142–158.

Williams, Joan C. and Marina Multhaup. 2018. "For women and minorities to get ahead, managers must assign work fairly." *Harvard Business Review*. https://hbr.org/2018/03/for-women-and-minorities-to-get-ahead-managers-must-assign-work-fairly.

6 From the Body to the World, from the World to the Body
Ethnography, Migration, and Care[1]

Camila Esguerra Muelle

The Route

In this chapter, I reflect on the ways of performing multi-sited ethnography in the field of migrations from an investigation that began nearly ten years ago in Spain and Colombia on '(trans)national care plots' (Esguerra Muelle, Ojeda and Fleischer 2021). Further, I present an embodied reflection, both epistemological and methodological, on what it means to build an investigative agenda and, simultaneously, on the place of the body in ethnography. I examine how, ultimately, we are body and how local and global policies are embodied. This follows the premise of Minh-ha (1989, 36): 'We do not have bodies, we are bodies and we are ourselves while we exist in the world'.

In the first section of this chapter, I conduct a reflective exercise on my place in the field, the process of setting up a research agenda, and my idea of a 'border epistemology'. In the second section, I address the question of how to conduct research from a series of perspectives such as the following: 1. the intersectional (Crenshaw 1991; Viveros Vigoya 2016); 2. the situated (Haraway 1988); 3. the heterarchical[2] (Kontopoulos 1993); 4. the multi-scalar[3] (Haidar and Berros 2015); 5. the inter- and transdisciplinary, in order to achieve collaborative action research; and 6. the multi-sited that goes beyond the comparison between particular dynamics of certain places, that is, beyond an ethnological perspective and allows an enquiry on how to use the ethnographic method to understand migration dynamics and trajectories that go from the micro to the macro and from the local, through the transnational, to the global. In the third section, I examine the place of the body and the politics of space in the ethnographic experience. In the last section, I propose a balance of what it means to know and build knowledge from rational as well as sensory and emotional registers, aiming at a decentred practice as part of the cognizant experience, which implies a commitment to understanding that the substance, performativity, materiality, and embodiment constitute the flesh and bone of knowledge.

My Situation in the Field: Research Agenda and Border or Migrant Epistemology

I choose a first-person narrative through which I aim to present the conditions of the production of 'situated knowledge' (Haraway 1988). I engage in a form of writing that aims at radical objectivity (Harding 2018) and politics of location (Rich 1984). I am inclined towards responsible knowledge, which understands that the cognizant subject is not located outside the field of knowledge or in a position of 'modest witness', and plays the trick of a laboratory staging. Further, I lean towards a partial knowledge that is not closed but is rather exposed to negotiation (Haraway 1988), as well as towards a contingent knowledge and contingency. Moreover, I am drawn towards creating a traffic of theories (Lima Costa 2002). Bearing all this in mind and using the Borderland/*La Frontera de Anzaldúa* (1987) metaphor, I try to develop my idea of what a border epistemology can be (Esguerra Muelle 2015) and how I situate myself in the sutures of the epistemologies, theories, and politics figured in the long western tradition as seamless places.

My proximity to the fields, first of migration and subsequently of care, has meant a political evolution and an embodied experience. Next, I relate the way in which I came to build, little by little, a research agenda on migrations, sexualities, and care. It is not a whimsical autobiographical exposition but rather a pedagogical exercise shared with you to understand how, in my case, one enters a field of research and how this field is embodied. When I began studying migration in 2007, I engaged in it based on my migratory experience as a student. This led me to deepen my awareness of how the colonial system worked. Over a short period, I felt a 'colonial wound' opening (Mignolo 2005). At that point, I began my master's degree in gender in Spain and continued my studies in Holland thereafter. I was aware that I was immensely privileged but also dislocated on the border of contradictory linguistic competences that my family heritage, on the one hand, and my place in ableism as hard of hearing, on the other, had imposed on me. My position as a privileged white-mestizo from Bogotá in the Colombian context was questioned, and my position as a person with a nonnormative sexuality and gender situation, despite what I had initially assumed, continued to be threatened and seen as a threat. Conversely, I had a sufficiently cognitive and political mental structure that had been built from my experience: first, in 1995 with lesbian feminist organisations and subsequently through the movement of people with dissident sexualities and gender experiences, which at that time, was not even called a movement; and later, in 2001, with the start and transformation of the Planet Peace Project, also known as the LGBT sector, and subsequently, the LGBT movement.

Within my migratory experience, my cultural and symbolic capital were not minor. They provided me with a place in the field. I managed to build myself from sufficiently westernised, but also ladino capitals, from the aforementioned experience and my academic and political reflections around sexualities and non-normative identities and gender expressions[4]. At that time, within the framework of my master's degree, I had proposed a study on the idea of family, which was the subject of much debate in Colombia, and the transnationality of families constituted by same-sex couples. For this reason, my place in the field forms the crossroads of my activism and academic work around sexualities and migration.

However, it was not long before I realised that my position as an agent in the field (Bourdieu 1997) and the field itself had changed and that the rules were different. I was a migrant, and my white skin colour – not my whiteness (Echeverría 2010) – turned dark in that environment where I was nothing other than a *sudaca*, (pejorative term for South Americans mainly by Spaniards) where the ghost or Franco's social phantasmagoria still saw me as 'inverted', such as those that, in Spain, were the subject of social danger laws (Osborne Verdugo 2009). In this new old-world that was difficult for me to listen to while simultaneously rendering me inaudible, both in Spanish and English, my *sudaca* accent and bad English were not phonetic or grammatical problems but geopolitical ones.

At the time, I understood my privilege when I saw myself for the first time in my academic trajectory, with all material conditions of existence covered by a scholarship. I had no care or provision responsibilities, as I had left them behind, and I know that I fled. I understood that this was not the situation of the migrants who lived in or came to reside in western Europe that began its descent into xenophobic and racist panic given the misnamed 'economic crisis' of 2007, which more than economic, was a financial and stock market crisis. It was not long before I began to see the subtle, and sometimes not-so-subtle, manifestations of that structured racism and xenophobia, which turned on my existence-*sudaca* body from time to time, although without the inconsideration that afflicted others more 'markedly *sudaca*' than me, or certain Africans, Eastern Europeans, or Asians.

A wound, and with it, 'anger and tenderness' (Rich 2002, 113) had opened up. I began an active and clumsy opposition to these symbolic and material forms of colonialism and began to understand that migration was a re-actualisation of colonial relations (Esguerra Muelle 2009). I proposed my project on 'lesbian existence' (Rich 1996) and migration, with the aim of weaving with this warp what had been built and destroyed in my research agenda, from 1995 to 2007, to understand this new crack, this wound – this new frontier that I inhabited and that inhabited me. Therefore, I continuously engaged in ethnography and living, and I remembered that they were the same thing.

Along this path, I came face-to-face with the notion of the 'global care chain'[5] (Hochschild 2000). It emerged first as an empirical reality rather than as a theoretical category, as I had the news of it from Gloria Wekker – my master's dissertation co-director – when I already had the preliminary text of my manuscript ready. I found the theory after two years of field work. I found in the field that those 'migrant women and non-women who inhabited lesbian existence', as I called them back then, were chained to that spectacular apparatus that up to that moment I had not been able to see in my family: the global care chain.

I also found that Wittig's (2006) maxim 'Lesbians are not women' insofar as they do not dedicate their sexual and any kind of energies to men, fell apart before the evidence: there were those women and not-women paying tribute with their energies and their work to a 'sex-gender system' (Rubin 1975) that is somewhat more complex than a simple patriarchal system. It is a system that, through the 'technologies of gender' (De Lauretis 1987) of race, class, and ableism, configures women as caregivers, particularly women from the South, marked in ethnic-racial terms, and all feminised beings. Being a woman does not simply mean a place in gender but a place in production-reproduction-system.

Upon my return to Colombia, I was faced with the diagnosis of my mother Lucía's disease that began to incubate a couple of years before I left for Europe, but which now received me as a welcome pass to my Bogotá reality of dense clouds; those deep skies that I had lost sight of in the blue seasonal firmaments of the Cantabrian, Manzanares, and Mediterranean basins and the short days of autumn, and even shorter days of the Dutch winter of frozen channels: Amyotrophic Lateral Sclerosis. Gradually, I understood the excessive burden that Lucía had carried for years. In my house, there was a great load of caregiving and provision because my great-aunt and grandmother suffered from incurable Alzheimer's. My uncle had a cognitive disability. Although he was quite self-sufficient, he had been poorly educated in a dependency that he himself detested. There were also those of us who, without such marked dependencies, demanded caregiving and care-provision. I unscientifically diagnosed that all of her unrecognised care work had finally killed her.

Where is Lucía's killer? Can this be a research question? I understood that research questions are often emotions, concerns, discomforts, twists, and turns.

That question was quarantined after her death, when, for four years, I tried to perform part of the work that she did as a caregiver and care-provider while writing my doctoral thesis on exile and non-normative sexualities. It was an approximation to kinder things – I thought – such as the representations of women with exiled non-normative sexualities, through poetry, music, performance, and photography, in short, through multimodal discourses.

I chose to focus on the work and life of women who eroticised me, that is, those who made me feel alive. That somehow helped me fight death. A strategy of disobedience and resistance against the necropolitics (Mbembe 2011) and the thanatopolitics (Foucault 1991), understood from a trafficked (Da Lima Costa 2002) and intersectional perspective

(Carbado et al. 2013), helped me understand death as a good mother. That doctoral thesis led me to see a subject that I had wanted to avoid, head-on, namely the transnational war waged in Colombia. That war exiled two of my brothers and wounded my younger brother, who tortured my father and besieged my adoptive mother, Sabina, a woman who had fled her town owing to the continuum of violence, and who was trying to leave behind her Muisca-peasant existence, in exchange for a false promise of urbanity that served as a link in the local and global care chains installed within my creole family from Bogotá.

At this moment, I am striving to understand how global care chains work and how to build the notion of (trans)national care plots[6] (Esguerra Muelle 2020). It is along a political, emotional, and academic path, embodied for over 20 years, that sexualities, gender, migrations, care, and armed conflict are tied to my current research agenda.

By 2015, the question on the caregiving women in my family, especially centred on Lucía and Sabina, and migration and war had become an increasingly pressing concern that questioned my political value as a researcher. An epistemological strategy was to find the relationships among care, migration, armed conflict, and health. In 2016, I began my postdoctorate and with it, the possibility of materialising the continuity of this investigative path[7] with my project on migration and global care chains.

With this narrative, I do not intend to do an autobiographical overexposure but rather aim to show how research agendas arise from complex existential processes or, at least, that is how it has been in my case. Research agendas – which are also political – are neither the product of rational choices nor of suitable scientific plans for knowledge industries. They are not the result of neutral circumstances but of deep discomforts or joys and pleasures, all embodied. This has been my experience. They are not methodical or scrupulous choices but are rather a part of the fabric of life itself. Thus, there is no perfect linearity between theory and empirical work but rather a loop that is most of the time a little consistent with the positivist narrative, which is ultimately epistemic violence and colonialism of knowledge, not to speak of 'coloniality of knowledge' (Lander 2000); simultaneously, the theory is not the seamless corpus of ideas that we have been made to believe it to be. Theoretical dialogues and epistemological awareness, in my experience, have to resonate with that embodied trajectory that gradually becomes a research agenda.

Relying on the developments in feminist epistemologies, particularly of situated knowledge (Haraway 1988), standpoint epistemology (Harding 2008, Hill Collins 2000), and location politics (Rich 1984) – which are very much an academic systematisation of the thinking of Afro, Black, *Chicana*, Latin American and Latin women, and feminised individuals – of the Aimará Chi'xi' thinking (Rivera Cusicanqui 2010) of the theoretical-poetic coined as Borderland/*La Frontera* (Anzaldúa 1987) and of trafficking (Da lima Costa 2002), debasing, and 'misinterpreting' the social science theories that I inherited, is what I call a *border or migrant episte-mology*, where, in addition, emotions and sensations, being a body, living and dying a little every day, are present and not denied.

It is an epistemology in which strategies are privileged over ordered and controlled methods and by which lapses, errors, interstices, and silences are considered more than the certainties. Here, questions are fundamental rather than answers; testimonies, narratives, rumours, and secrets have a more prominent place than the motionless, closed, and regulated photographs of society, as proposed by the parents of anthropology.

Multi-Sited Ethnography: A Methodological Strategy for Collaborative Action

In this section, I present a brief account of how and why I, or we, gradually built, the means of being able to conduct multi-sited ethnography on global care chains and (trans) national care plots that articulate Colombia, Spain, and the USA. Though my research began in 2009, I commenced more systematic fieldwork in 2016. I wonder how to make a multi-sited ethnography with an intersectional (Manalansan 2006), inter- and transdisciplinary, and situated (Haraway 1988), heterarchical (Kontopoulos 1993), multi-scalar (Haidar and Berros, 2015), and collaborative perspective.

Once the operation of global care chains between Colombia and Spain and between Colombia and the USA were recognised, I initially proposed to conduct the study in three Colombian cities: Medellín, Cali, and Bogotá. These are the three main cities of arrival for internal migrant women after they are displaced or banished.[8] Most migrants leave from these three cities as well, either as people seeking refuge in or as those who have been exiled to Europe and the US. Subsequently, I added Ibagué and Cartagena,[9] two cities in Spain (Barcelona and Madrid, the main cities where migrants are in charge of care work), and one in the USA (either Los Angeles or New York, but I have not managed to conduct fieldwork there yet).

After drawing a map of the field and establishing the research questions, I realised, thanks to my conversations with Sergio Montero[10], that what I was proposing was a multi-sited ethnography (Marcus 1995). Gradually, I understood that this ethnography had already begun a few years ago (Esguerra Muelle 2009). I understood that multi-sited ethnography goes beyond a comparison between particular dynamics of certain places, that is, beyond an abstract, non-embodied ethnological view, and allows the use of the ethnographic method to understand migration dynamics and trajectories that go from the micro to the macro and from the local, through the transnational, to the global.

With this multi-sited ethnography, I seek to understand three phenomena of different scales: a) the social determinations of health and disease of these women; b) how global and local care chains operate

(Hochschild 2000)[10], that is, the trans nationalisation of care; and c) its impact on national migration, occupational health, and care policies.

This multi-sited ethnography, which has become a life project, has sought to pursue an approach built on the dynamics of care trans nationalisation, its effects on the health[11] and living conditions of migrant care workers, as well as on the public policies of care, migration, and health. A multi-sited ethnography is based on a method that 'constructs the mobility trajectories and histories of its subjects located in different places, to establish aspects of the system through the suggested associations and connections between the different places' (Marcus 1995, 96). Furthermore, multi-sited ethnography necessarily implies a triangulation method, in this case, between the oral and cartographic accounts of the subjects of the investigation, a review of the various empirical and theoretical academic sources and of public policy documents, as well as with national and international statistical data processed by means of econometric and statistical models[12], in addition to an inter- and transdisciplinary approach. The latter implies breaking multiple borders and even the overflowing of academy borders.

The heterarchical perspective (Kontopoulos 1993) was inescapable and challenged us to assume that different levels of power operated simultaneously. Thus, the study involved an approach to the interrelation between the anatomopolitical (body), Micropolitical (collectivities), biopolitical and geopolitical (care trans nationalisation), and multi-scalar levels, which implies a locus of analysis, such as the body, the local, and the global. The interdisciplinary perspective involved addressing the phenomenon through methods used in different disciplines: anthropology, critical epidemiology[13], public health, and statistics. Transdisciplinarity, as I have already pointed out, involved an approach where the limits between some disciplines and others are diluted, which means putting into crisis epistemological, theoretical and methodological disciplinary approaches. In this way, transdisciplinarity is a fertile field for the 'traffic of theories' (Da Lima Costa 2002) and what I call 'border epistemology'. This border epistemology undoubtedly fed by fields such as feminist, cultural, and artistic studies. The latter have opened up the possibility for me to think about the field of critical studies of migration as an emergency field[14]. Conducted from an intersectional perspective, this study implies an understanding of how oppression systems that are simultaneously systems of representation – gender, age, class, race, ableism, ethnicity, and sexuality – are co-produced within the framework of global care chains (Hochschild 2000) and (trans)national care plots (Esguerra Muelle 2020).

As I have already indicated, it has not been a linear decision to perform an ethnography on migration and care but rather an outcome crossed by a series of questions linked to my trajectory. It is one thing to build a research agenda from a reflexive exercise – a process that I presented in the previous section – and another to convince the institutional environment that this agenda is relevant. Being able to communicate the political and structural issues that are tangled in the stories, sensations, and emotions that give flesh to the research agenda is both a political challenge and one that centres on being able to find the relationship between the personal and the general, which is an opportunity to configure and share a relevant research agenda. This decision was accompanied by the search for conditions of knowledge production and the necessary strategies to investigate these dimensions.

I identify two major apparatuses in the construction of my methodological strategy: the symbolic academic research apparatus (methodology, theoretical, and epistemological corpus), which I referred to in the last section, and the apparatus for the production of knowledge. The latter is determined by the material and symbolic conditions of knowledge production. It is largely a bureaucratic apparatus that Flórz 6 Olarte (2020, 15-58) addressed in a very pertinent way in her chapter titled 'For a policy of the murky. Feminist Research Practices' and identified as the practice of 'questioning and circumventing authoritarian administrative procedures'. These two apparatuses are personified in the networks of social and political relations woven by the research subjects, that is, by the 'agents' (Bourdieu 1997) and research actors.

It was necessary to manage extremely diverse resources, both material and financial,[15] and especially networks that, ultimately, were care networks comprising many people who were to be the subjects of the study. The first category included Colombian migrants, displaced people, exiles, care workers such as domestic workers, 'Community mothers' or care workers precarised by the ICBF and hotel room attendants (cisgender, heterosexual, lesbian, mestizo, Afro, black, 'indigenous' women of different ages, and transsexual men and women), and residents of Bogotá, Cartagena, Medellín, Cali, Madrid, and Barcelona. The second category comprised people from the research team, young professionals and students from Bogotá, Cartagena, Medellín, Cali, and Madrid – whom I selected because in one way or another, they had reflected, acted politically, and experienced migration and care – academics from different universities, and friends living in different cities. The research was a scale model of migratory and care networks of which I was a part, and to a large extent, a subject of care.

I speak of transnational work because this ethnography involved me following the (trans)national care plots, which meant going back and forth through the transnational relationships that transsexual women and men wove between their cities of origin in Colombia and their lives in Spain.

One of the first steps, in addition to establishing the research map, was to write an ethical, political, methodological, epistemological, and security protocol (Esguerra Muelle, Sanabria, Guerrero, María de Los Ángeles, Majul, and Enache 2016). Each of these elements were elaborated from a critical feminist perspective. For this study, this step was intended to serve as a guide that could be collectively adjusted by the team.

The fact that this would be a collaborative investigation was stated on the map and in the protocol. In previous experiences, it was easier for me to find my political place as part of the collective subject to which I belonged and from which I acted in political terms. For this investigation, my political place had changed, as although I had seen closely how the local care plots were embodied in the trajectory of my mother Lucía and my mother Sabina, this investigation was no longer about my experience as in other investigative experiences (Esguerra Muelle 2002; Esguerra Muelle 2009). For this reason, in addition to conducting basic research, I proposed a series of strategies that could somehow benefit the people and groups with whom we worked.

Our research aimed at forms of co-working, as Diana Ojeda (2020, 167–184) pointed out in her chapter titled 'Counter-cartographies: Conduct critical and collaborative socio-spatial research' and sought to integrate not community researchers, as Flórez & Olarte (2020, 15–58), but young researchers involved in the field. A collective and negotiated work is also proposed, which exceeds the margins of the research itself to become direct political action that involves building knowledge together and being a workforce for the organisations and people with whom we build that knowledge. That becomes collective capital to the extent that it is put into play in different fields. We can then talk about **collaborative action research**. At this point, I would like to emphasise that it was owing to my conversations with Diana Ojeda[16] that I managed to maintain a critical distance with the Participatory Action Research, not to dismiss it but rather to understand the power relations that are thoughtlessly naturalised in it.

Thus, engaging in this multi-sited ethnography has implied the deployment of contingent strategies of collaboration, many times transnational and other times corporal, that are not one-way. It is not that the researchers donate one-sided work. We were also lavished with care and knowledge from the women and people who participated in the study. Research is always a plot of social and political relations.

Some of the actions we carried out in Cartagena, Bogotá, Cali, Medellín, Madrid, and Barcelona comprised co-working management[17] in order to achieve spaces of political incidence,[18] pedagogical spaces,[19] strengthening of the organisation,[20] diffusion,[21] artistic[22] and financing.[23] Further, we carried out direct assistance actions;[24] design and implementation of participatory workshops, many of which were on body and self-care,[25] support for the generation of communicative pieces,[26] and participant observation.[27] We strive to broaden the scope of the research further.[28]

With this account I want to demonstrate that for those of us who have been part of this agenda, conducting research does not simply involve participatory observation. Rather, it involves a commitment to political action woven from initiatives and strategic drifts that fill the daily work and that extend through time and space, that are truncated and fail many times, and for which the knowledge production industry rarely dedicates funds.

The conditions of this collaborative action work have been complex. Owing to the lack of resources, many of the aforementioned initiatives have been fading. However, we continue to insist, with the awareness that our resources are limited and that a multi-sited investigation always forces us to disengage, disjoin, twist, fracture, and break, that it implies a spatial paradox contained by spatial policies, including border policies.

Somatic and Space: Mapping, Listening, Perceiving, and Feeling

A few days after I arrived in Spain, in 2007, the year when I began exploring this path, I ended up in a bar where a transgender show was taking place. The woman presenter shouted with her Spanish flair, 'Welcome all to the parlour'. She immediately began to make jokes on the expressions typical of Latin American and Caribbean countries. I remember the 'qué oso' (what a shame) that alluded to Colombia. That bar made me feel at home. I did not feel strange. I recorded that image because it would be the border that I would inhabit for several years and by which I gradually gained awareness: the queer and parlour border, the place from where one could communicate with one's home in the distant country (Field diary 2007)

In this section, I reflect on the body place of the research subjects, of the body as existence, of the body located in the migration trajectories, and in particular, on how and why bodies should be mapped. I talk about the qualitative methods and techniques used in the research on (trans)national care plots, that is, individual and collective corporal cartographies and semi-structured interviews.

Spatial Paradoxes

One of the most striking factors of this research is understanding how people entangled in (trans)national care plots experience a 'spatial paradox' (Esguerra Muelle, Ojeda and Fleischer 2021), a dislocation of the body-being, consistent in that on the one hand, they travel long and, often, multiple distances from their place of origin to other cities or countries or within the same cities – the case of Medellín for example, where intra-urban displacement and invisible borders mark the dynamics of permanent confinement and expulsion – and simultaneously end up confined in domestic spaces. This paradox also has to do with how these domestic spaces are dispossessed, for example in the case of early childhood care workers by the Colombian Institute of Familial Welfare (ICBF), or through home expropriation as many of them only have the workplace, which is a bedroom but not a house or a home. This is evident in the case of internal workers engaged in transnational domestic service. They often do not have a place to spend their rest days, so they choose to stay at their workplace where they remain isolated and exploited. Further, because they may face the threat of deportation, they may prefer to remain confined while trying to regularise their situation in the country where they are seen as upstarts, in this case, Spain. Alternatively, they may choose strategies such as not using certain routes in the city, or even never walking the streets to avoid police raids and feel a sense of estrangement from the new world.

Thus, while these women and people travel long distances while migrating, or when they are trafficked, displaced, or exiled, their mobility in these destinations is often reduced because of the lack of space, accessibility problems, precarious transportation, internment, and surveillance (home and Detention Centers for Foreigners CIE scale). Simultaneously, there is also a spatial and political home-work continuum.

Performing the role of a researcher in a multi-sited ethnography implies another spatial paradox that comprises two things. On the one hand, it involves matching the different locations of the research team as well as constant displacements. Thus, spaces are experienced in different ways. I was the mobile element in the team, as I was present in approximately 90 of the 130 interviews that had been conducted in 7 cities. On the other hand, it comprises the impossibility of being in certain spaces when required, for which it is necessary to resort to dislocation, twisting, and trans nationalisation strategies that migrants use in their journeys. These strategies include the use of social media that is sometimes disrupted by differences in time zones. Simultaneously, it implies confronting spatial policies and experiencing forms of production in urban spaces (Esguerra Muelle, Camila, Ojeda and Fleischer 2021), as well as the discontinuities and exclusions established across the borders and networks of cities involved in (trans)national care plots.

Hear and Listen

I know I do not hear well. However, I know how to listen, and that makes me feel valuable. One of the best-known strategies in western and westernised fields of knowledge, such as psychoanalysis or ethnography, is to listen. When I began the Migration and Global Care Chains project (2016), I was afraid that this research, the first attempt at which was not circumscribed within the confines of my social universe, would end up being a good example of extractive research. I expressed this concern to Eliza Enache, a colleague and field assistant in Madrid, who told me the following: 'By listening to the stories of these women, you will have already done a lot'. I thought that this was a way to comfort me. However, I gradually understood the value that listening had for these transsexual men and women who were isolated in their migratory and work trajectories and their existence as feminised beings. After each interview, we asked them what they liked or disliked about the experience. An overwhelming majority of respondents told me that they had never been able to tell their story, and being heard in these interviews provided them immediate relief. Some ended up feeling removed and tired. Beyond this relief, I doubt that the investigation had any larger impact on their lives. I still talk to some of them and even support them, while often keeping a distance, in their losses and achievements. However, this still seems meagre compared to what they donated: their time, history, and knowledge. On the other hand, as Flórez and Olarte (2020) noted, we cannot vainly assign ourselves the place of saviours.

What I experienced in corporal-existential terms with this listening is perhaps similar to psychoanalytic transference (Kristeva 2006). It refers to a kind of empathy that is made substantial through emotions and perceptions. It made me experience forms of sympathy and compassion but not in the religious sense. It involves embodying the pain, emotions, or passions of my interlocutors for a moment. It was not only anguish or harm but also joy and courage. When we discussed the research protocol with the team (Esguerra Muelle, Sanabria, Guerrero, María de Los Ángeles, Majul, and Enache 2016), I remember suggesting that we should never cry or try to comfort people but allow silence. Rather, I recommended that we had to be careful not to interrupt or show empathy in our counter-questions (we were guided by a semi-structured interview instrument); that we had to seek to elicit responses to the discomfort by drawing from the tools of the people with whom we were conversing (we set the interview as a conversation); and that we should show attention, not lose eye contact, and let them know, with our body language, that we were there and that their story was valuable. I knew beforehand that these stories were going to be replete with sad and sometimes even terrifying passages. They were not alien to me. I had somehow experienced them with my mother Sabina's story, and from many stories that I have known as a Colombian. I knew what could emerge. It became increasingly evident that war and the continuum of violence would be a common substrate for all. The interview instrument was designed to investigate this continuum of violence that I knew in advance would be misogynistic, racist, transphobic, lesbophobic, classist, ageist, and xenophobic. We did not want to induce responses using our academic categories, but we had to take the conversation forward to see how this 'matrix of oppressions' operated (Hill Collins, 2000). I was constantly surprised at the capacity of representation, resistance, transformation, disobedience, and invention of my interlocutors against the scenes of oppression and domination they faced. I understood then that I did not have to save them. However, they were counting on me, on us, on being a network, to ensure that their voices were heard.

As I had already pointed out, we conducted approximately 130 interviews in seven cities, each of which lasted between three and five hours. I personally conducted approximately 90 of those interviews, sometimes alone or with another team member. By the end of the fieldwork, I felt that all these interviews had become a part of my substance, that something in me had definitely changed, and that these stories had incarnated me.

Death, Impoverishment, Disease, and Imprisonment

It is difficult to deal with the impossibility of alleviating certain pains, tragedies, and discomforts. Shortly after finishing the interviews in Cali, I received news that Carlos, Guacho's brother, a boy who lived with Ruth, a 'substitute mother', and Miss Elvia Ochoa, who gave me a book by Jehovah's Witnesses, had died. Further, I learnt that other ICBF workers had died waiting for the Colombian government to recognise their right to receive a pension. Some were sick when we interviewed them. One request that I have not been able to fulfil came from Aunt Africa, Yaneth Blanquicet, to make a documentary on the community mothers – or better still, ICBF precarious workers – in Cartagena, who are dying without a pension or retirement.

I lived closely and at a distance from the imprisonment and illness of María del Mar, a Venezuelan migrant. She was unjustly imprisoned as a result of an obviously manipulated process and now suffers from cancer. We were able to weave networks at a distance to manage resources. She received solidarity meals and got legal representation and psychological counselling, particularly from the members of SEDOAC. Marta Álvarez, from Cali, the Vice President of SEDOAC at that time, put me in touch with María del Mar, in 2017. She was worried about her and was overwhelmed by the multiple forms of violence to which her Spanish employers – former and current – had subjected and continued subjecting her. I witnessed the prison in which she worked, an apartment by the Guzmán El Bueno metro station. It exuded oppression, from the Spanish flag hanging on its balcony to the surveillance cameras with which María could see if her employers were approaching. When she was imprisoned, I visited her at the MECO women's prison in Madrid. All of us who visited her had the feeling that she was less confined in MECO than she was in the houses where she worked. Now that she has cancer, I have tried to talk to her, but I have also broken down and given up. How can we support this from a distance?

I could tell other similar stories, against which we have been able to do something or nothing. However, what I am interested in highlighting here is that collaborative action research implies knowing that, as researchers, we are only a small part of a network that is sometimes maintained and sometimes not. The possibility of weaving these networks tightly does not correspond only to the will of the people who integrate them but rather to the structural and material conditions of existence. It is not by chance that the places where such networks can bear fruit without many difficulties were cities such as Madrid, Barcelona, and Bogotá. This implies understanding the multi-scale dimension of space that we face in a multi-sited ethnography. It seeks continuities and links and often meets geopolitical fractures that are not under our government.

Body Maps

One of the tools that yielded the most moving and revealing results during fieldwork were the individual and group corporal cartographies (Gastaldo et al. 2012) that we built with women and feminised individuals. These cartographies were an opportunity to identify the pains and the ability to invent and respond to the precarious, isolated, and impoverished conditions generated by the (trans)nationalised care regime in the bodies-that-are-these-people. It was particularly revealing how women repeatedly identified emotional and psychological rather than physical pain, woven with their migration, exile, displacement, and deportation trajectories as with their history of job insecurity. They also showed the marks that misogyny, transphobia, lesbophobia, racism, xenophobia, and ableism have left in their existence, in their bodies.

We made these cartographies using coloured pencils and the collage technique, by pasting magazine clippings and coloured paper. Afro, black, and Afro-indigenous women put forth the representations of their ethno-racial marks with a political conscience – some were shy, others determined – such as their hair, dress, ancestral knowledge, and the colour of their skin. On this collective map where they recognised themselves and their diasporic consciousness, they proceeded to tell us their history and emphasised their emotions, feelings, and trajectories, as migrants and care workers.

I remember how a woman who had been displaced from the Colombian Caribbean coast, and who at the time of the interview lived in Cali, titled her corporal cartography *La siempreviva* (The always alive). It was a strategy to preserve her anonymity and highlight her ability to survive and resist the insidious persecution of paramilitaries that led her to experience displacement and different acts of victimisation in the context of armed conflict. *La siempreviva*: like the flower that grew in the territory she was dispossessed of. Her territory was not taken from her: she was ripped from there, banished[29], and as one who was always alive, she learnt to live without being sown in the ground.

At the time of the construction of her corporal cartography, she was in a kind of informal contract with a substitute mother in Cali, who paid her in currency and in kind for her support in the care of children with disabilities who had been abandoned and internally displaced. When María de los Ángeles and I finished this interview, sometimes collective and individual, we were relieved with food. *La siempreviva* even gave me a massage that lasted approximately 20 minutes, and with it, all her blessings. In Madrid, another woman also offered me a massage in gratitude for my having listened to her story.

Liveliness is resistance, like that of a wonderful and energetic indigenous Coconuco, from Cauca province 'community mother', Lucelly Bambagüé, living in Cali, who came to our appointment, overflowing with vigour, driving a car, and apologising for arriving a little late to her house in El Vallado, a slum where we had agreed to meet. An exquisite political conscience, delicious *empanadas vallunas*, (regional dish of Valle del Cauca, it is corn patty, stuffed with potatoes and meat) and songs of resistance from her people made this interview festive. Her daughters and her romantic partner, a white man of European origin, also participated in the interviews.

In general, we find the manifestation of a regime of corporality comprising working-keeping-swallowing-silencing a deep process of subalternisation in the testimonies and corporal cartographies. This process is observed in inflamed and stagnant bodies. Knowledge and care practices that maintain life in general make it contagious.

Sense and Feel Bodies

I had another invaluable knowledge experience through the body workshops that we conducted in Madrid and Cartagena. Negotiated spaces formed a part of our collaborative research actions. The sometimes hardened and stagnant bodies of these working women who cared but were not cared for impressed me. The refusal of some Afro women to dance for a prolonged mourning, a social rule in the face of death that many women keep with zeal, was also embodied. Though they could not dance, they did not lose their humour. At least this was what we experienced in a workshop in Cartagena. It was full of affection and laughter, though grief also had a place. Aside from Cartagena, the topic of love and death did not appear persistent.

Another form of contact with their bodies was crying. It was present in most interviews. As I have already pointed out, we agreed with the team not to cry during the interviews. It seemed that it was a means of invading and stripping them of their pain. I learnt to dry cry, without my eyes getting wet. It is a transfer experience that has undoubtedly been registered in my body. Despite not crying, I could feel a looped movement going from them to me and vice-versa, a form of empathy that did not need to be pronounced. Sometimes, that cry seemed collective and without tears. That was what I felt in the Nelson Mandela slum, under a fig tree, where I attended a group mourning for the displacement and death of a 'community mother' exploited by the Colombian government. In another workshop, we tried to avert that sadness with a few children's games that we invited them to participate in. It was a moment of laughter. The strategy of dislocating oneself in age and making a fool of oneself is well known to those of us who engage in educational work.

Finally, I want to highlight another somatic mode of migration and care. One of the things I learned from this research is that the continuum of migration, displacement, exile, and trafficking that these women and feminised individuals have lived is an experience that turned into substance and was both embodied and incorporated:

> Sometimes intellectual experience exceeds understanding. Cognitive processes and corporal or emotional experience produce contradictory responses that disorient the mind. Uncontrolled gut reactions occur due to the explanatory schema [or lack thereof] in the film. Broadly speaking, these reactions are normally taken as abnormalities.
>
> (Nichols 1994, 76).

On the other hand, migration becomes body, gesture, and food, and implies a transformation of the corporal *hexis*, at the point when this continuum turns them into migratory fodder.

Migratory fodder is the least visible face of the Border Industrial Complex. With the idea of migratory fodder I make an analogy in the neo-colonial context, with the so-called 'cannon fodder' of wars and 'prison fodder' of prisons[30]: From migration, as from a prison, you never get out, not entirely, migration is a journey that begins and does not end. The Border Industrial Complex is hungry for beings, for bodies. Fodder for the 16th century bulldogs and now fodder for the sex feast, fodder for the *maquilas*, fodder for the sex tourism, fodder for servitude, organs for sale, fodder for sex trade and pornography, fodder for kitchens, fodder for servile couples, 'mule' fodder for drug trafficking and fodder for care work that gives shape to the (trans)national care plots (Esguerra Muelle 2020).

In the stories of these women and people, we find the operation of a micro policy of armed conflict: the logic of war/capitalism underlying the destruction of life and territory. The armed and social conflict and the continuum of violence form the scene of the social determinations of the health of these people. The armed conflict and the operation of community homes and neighbour networks characterise the (trans)national care plots in the Colombian case: the 'Colombian link of local and global care chains' or what configures the particularity of Colombian (trans) national care plots. There is a continuum of migration-trafficking-displacement-exile-care work (work in the domestic area) which, in turn, supposes a continuum of violence. Dedication to a (trans)national plot of care work encompasses exploitation for the purpose of servitude, domestic employment, early childhood care, people with disabilities, sick or elderly, hotel and hospitality industry, health, trades that are inherited or transferred from some women to others within their family, and neighbourhood circles.

Writing about Embodied Knowledge: Sensations, Emotions, and Ideas

In this last section, I will try to reflect on the corporal and embodied experience of knowledge, the policies of care, and their writing. I try to balance what it means to know and build knowledge from both rational as well as sensory and emotional registers, aiming at a dislocated practice to understand that the substance, performativity, materiality, and embodiment is the flesh and bone of knowledge.

I would like to point out – by closing what I consider to have been part of the epistemological and methodological reflection that is a drift in my research experience – that, beyond the organisation and rational government of investigative techniques, there is a non-logocentric way of knowledge, namely, ¿Embodied? knowledge. It becomes and also comes from experience. By this, I mean that, as I have previously indicated, research agendas are always political and come from an existential trajectory, from the reflected and reflective experience; not of course, from pure experience, as there is no such thing. Simultaneously, I believe that knowledge transforms, in terms of substance, the existence, that is, the body. At least, this is the case in the process of knowledge construction based on ethnography and existential experience. For this reason, doing ethnography is like living.

Being there (Geertz 1989) cannot simply be a maxim for the validation of authority and authorship; instead, being there, in the field, implies an embodied experience and, in my perspective, getting there must be an evolution of the existence itself; the way in which we construct our political and research agendas must reflect an ethical aim. Simultaneously, the way in which one is and exists 'there' implies a commitment, in this case, to care. Care cuts across the collaborative action research that I have discussed in this chapter. Dual-track care is understood as a political and knowledge relationship between the knowledge subjects.

In this configuration, border epistemology forms a part of this 'renunciation of' or a 'traffic of theories' and epistemologies that invite us to maintain a lying distance between what we are and what we do. It is an interpellation with the place we occupy in relationships, always political and of power and the construction of knowledge. Border epistemology can be seen, simultaneously, as *migrant epistemology*. Recognising care as a fundamental political act for the maintenance of life is 'learnt through bodies' (Bourdieu 1999). Somehow, my voracity while interviewing so many people is a sign of an anthropophagic knowledge. I feel that my eagerness for several interviews responds to my quest for, beyond filling out extensive field diaries or recording countless testimonies of women and feminised individuals, developing a performative act that, through the repetition and saturation of migration and care-work stories, will allow me to understand what these lives are like and embody their stories by an act of transference, transmutation, and transformism.

I hope to conclude this section of my research agenda, turning, with both the words of the care-work migrants and my own – which are formed from theirs – these experiences into a testimony on what it means to be part of (trans)national care plots and become migratory fodder. Hopefully, this collective narrative can explain how (trans)national care plots, entangled in the transnational conflict that we live in in Colombia, have been a form of dispossession of the existence, the knowledge, and the work of women and feminised individuals, geared towards political and economic apparatus such as the hegemonic and colonial sex-gender system (dimorphic, binary, cisgender, hetero-centred, and androcentric) and to a racist apparatus of (trans)nationalisation of care, which expropriates bodies, existences, energies, and knowledge from women and feminised individuals, regardless of the whiteness and through migration, displacement, exile, trafficking, banishment, and deportation. We speak of the global dispossession of care – as work and knowledge, of care as the primary common for the maintenance of life; and of life as maximum common. This is a narrative on how migratory trajectories go from the body to the world and to the body, again.

Notes

1 This chapter was translated from Spanish to English and reprinted in this book with the curtesy of Carlos Arturo López, editor of the book *Investigar a la intemperie. Reflexiones sobre métodos en las ciencias sociales desde el oficio,* Editorial Pontificia Universidad Javeriana(2020).

2 In this chapter, I understand it as the analytical consideration of the different levels of power (micro and anatomopolitical, and meso and macropolitical) without establishing a relationship of hierarchy among them but rather establishing one of inter-correspondence, that is, none of the levels is more relevant than the other in the analysis.

3 I use the word 'multi-scalar' to denote the analytical approach that allows an understanding of how the corporal, the local, and the global are interconnected.

4 Before and after my stay in Europe, I also participated in the construction of LGBTI public policies, trying to distance myself from the 'marriage' agenda adopted by some organisations of the so-called LGBT sectors. I also became aware that the State apparatuses (government, parastatal business or military organisations, supranational entities, institutionalised civil society, etc.) are always ready to betray and undermine aspirations and creations of social movements that are functional within that machinery and even form a part of that machinery itself when we trade with it. I continue to believe that the State – which is not a monolithic space but rather a network of complex

relationships of different political positions of groups and individuals – is a battlefield that we must not abandon.

5 Following Hochschild (2000), I understand that global care chains constitute the complex network of local and global flows of care work, which generates both care leaks and deficits. The care deficit of industrialised countries or the global north – given by issues such as demographic aging and the insertion of women in the labour market – is covered by the precarious work of women from countries in the global south. However, it is important to consider that these flows also occur between southern countries and to a lesser extent, between northern countries, as well as between rural and urban areas in the same country. Simultaneously, the migration, displacement, and exile of rural women mostly from the global south, supposes leaks in care, in terms of not only the workforce but also the knowledge of care, which is known as the drain of care (Bettio, Simonazzi and Villa 2006).

6 The threads that constitute these plots are as follows: first, the institutional structures and social networks present in care work linked to migration and supporting the trans nationalised care system and global and local care chains; second, the minimal flesh and bone stories of migratory trajectories and the networks and provision of care woven by women and feminised individuals both to migrate and to care; and finally, (neo) colonial power devices present in the migration.

7 I owe my gratitude to Professors Luz Gabriela Arango, Marta Zambrano, Mara Viveros, Isabel Carrera, and Gloria Wekker, for this.

8 Women from Cali, in particular from the *El Chontaduro* foundation, use this name to refer to the dispossession processes in the context of the armed conflict in Colombia.

9 I decided to include Cartagena in the study because Alí Majul, who later became my research assistant, invited me to work with his group *Contextos* with women from the peripheral region of Cartagena. I recommended working particularly with the 'community mothers' – or better still, precarious workers of the ICBF. I paid for this trip with my resources. I also took advantage of a trip to Barranquilla on an invitation from the Caribbean Women's Network, to transfer to Cartagena and to continue the field opening with a body workshop for these ICBF workers. I treated the invitation to Ibagué and other cities as a means to begin my fieldwork.

10 Cider Researcher at the University of Los Andes.

11 In engaging with occupational health, we relied on particular categories in classical epidemiology such as ergonomic, chemical, physical, and psychosocial risks. We also inquired about the health notions of transsexual women and men. Thus, we concentrated on analysing social determinants of health following suggestions in the field of critical epidemiology (Peñaranda 2013).

12 I will not cover these methods in this chapter.

13 We assume a critical epidemiological approach (Breilh 2013) that goes beyond the causality and multi-causality of the disease to analyse the economic, social, and cultural systems as determinations, in the Marxist sense, of health or disease.

14 The reflection of the lecturers on the master's degree in artistic studies at the District University of Colombia, over 10 years ago, allowed me to propose the master's degree in Critical Studies on Migration at the *Pensar* Institute, whose creation process I lead, as a program that contributes to the construction of an emerging critical field.

15 Funding granted by the Vice-Rectory for Research of the University of Los Andes, through the 2017–2018 internal interdisciplinary call: for fieldwork

in Colombia and Spain. The support of the CiSAL of the Pompeu Fabra University: to strengthen the research in the health field. I had the collaboration of Sara Zamora and María López to strengthen my knowledge of health anthropology and epidemiology. María López, researcher at the Centre for Health Research, CISAL of the Pompeu Fabra University, made arrangements for me to do an internship there, in two different periods, where I managed to partly cover the transnational fieldwork.

16 Researcher at the *CIDER*, Los Andes University.

17 In Cartagena, Alí Majul, a research assistant, together with his group CONTEXTOS, held talks with SENA, with the Technological University of Cartagena, and the UNAD to try to agree upon educational spaces for migrant care workers. He also held talks with the MUTUAL SER-SISBEN to promote the application of the SISBEN survey to migrants, and displaced and exiled care workers. Further, talks were also held with the Unit for Victims, where he attempted to build agendas with migrant, displaced, and exiled female care workers.

18 Through the Intersectoral Board on Care Economy, we carried out permanent advocacy work on public policies that link migration, care, and occupational health, particularly in the fast track process of peace agreements (point 1 rurality and care), noting that displaced and exiled women cannot be excluded from measures favouring rural women who are victims of armed conflict. This led me to a discussion on how these migrant women did not stop being peasants by virtue of exile. I have also participated in the discussion on the formation of the National System of Care (SINACU) and with the Ministry of Health, in a meeting with Alejando Gaviria, who was the Minister of Health at the time, Angela María Robledo, representative of the chamber, and Yolanda Cardozo, a nurse member of the intersectoral Board of Care Economy, and with the Truth Commission at the technical table on gender and LGBT issues. We accompanied the substitute mother Ruth Sánchez to discuss the specific situation of this type of service with a lawyer of the UTL and member of parliament Alexander López.

19 At the time of writing this chapter, we completed, jointly among Dejusticia, UTRASD, and the *Pensar* Institute, the *Escuela Camina (Walk School)* for the leaders of domestic work, who mostly belonged to the Bogotá-UTRASD branch.

20 In particular, with UTRASD and Sintrahín, I developed a pedagogical proposal to strengthen the organisation and advocacy that is being supported by the alliance for decent domestic work in Bogotá, constituted by three university lecturers, two students, and an independent researcher since 2018. Currently, only another member and I are active. We participated in the creation of the Bogotá UTRASD branch.

21 In Medellín and Bogotá, I participated in various events on domestic work and workplace violence, organized by National Union School and UTRASD (Union of Afrocolombian Women Domestic Workers), in which I showed part of the research results. We conducted an investigation on workplace harassment for the Unitary Central of Workers (CUT) together with Alexandra Chocontá, in which part of the testimonies of migrant care workers with whom a made the multisited ethnography were included and discussed. This research was presented in the 108th session of the International Labor Conference in the framework of the discussion on violence in workplace, in Geneve, 2019. Together with Laura Castrillón, field assistant in Bogotá of my project, we participated in the communication initiative *Mutante*, of which some communication students from the

Javeriana University take part, dealing with domestic work and migration. More recently, we participated in an international symposium on migration and mental health at the Javeriana University in which we showed some results of the multisited ethnography on the impact of migration and care work in mental health. I also participated in the documentary by the Catalan group *La Direkta* titled *Entre Terres*: the storyline relates to the argument in our investigation on migration and global care chains. On my last trip to Barcelona, in June 2019, I attended the launch of this documentary, which was simultaneously launched in Colombia, in the best way of transnational plots.

22 In association with lecturer Eliana María Sánchez Aldana from the design department of the University of Los Andes, a project called *Embroidery for the memory of care and care of the memory* was established. In Cali, María de los Ángeles Balaguera, field assistant and daughter of a migrant woman in Chile, was honoured by the ICESI for her thesis on migration. The thesis focused an exhibition of the corporal cartographies built with the women who participated in the investigation, that was held on 8 March 2018.

23 We formulated the research intervention project in conjunction with the *Néctar* Foundation, with the purpose of presenting it to funders such as UN Women, OIM Colombia, and the Open Society Foundation. Funding was not awarded.

24 María de los Ángeles Balaguera provided individual support to women domestic workers in critical conditions of survival. I contributed remotely and on-site to the management of personal, legal, and psychological support for a Venezuelan migrant domestic service employee in Madrid, a victim of sexual violence, and workplace and sexual harassment, who was unjustly imprisoned and accused of theft, which is a releasable crime in Spain.

25 In Bogotá, I designed and conducted several workshops with the National Association of Workers of the Care Economy (ANTEC), the National Afro-Colombian Union of Domestic Service Workers (UTRASD), and Sintrahín. With the Active Domestic Service association, SEDOAC, we conducted a workshop on body and corporal cartography, together with Nekane Rius, physiotherapist and founder of the *Maison Medicale* in Belgium. I also held a couple of workshops on care economy with TRUNCUVIC (United Care Workers).

26 I developed a script for a video on care economy for care workers. A team from the Confederation of Workers of Colombia was in charge of the production.

27 In Barcelona, I supported the systematisation of the occupational health survey developed by Las Libélulas and carried out participant observation for several days in the Barcelona migrant confine (In Catalan, Tancada Migrante), with the aim of understanding how the context for the search of Catalan independence had affected migrants. I briefly accompanied a migrant woman from Cali to obtain legal support to regularise her immigration status. I also attended demonstrations by 'those who clean the hotels' in Barcelona and the SITRACIHOBI protest days in Bogotá, since 2016.

28 We contacted HOCAR, the union of hotel workers in Colombia to expand the investigation to hotel room attendants in Cartagena and Bogotá, there was significant reluctance on part of the leaders of these organisations. Alongside Laura Castrillón, we wanted to give continuity to some initiatives that had been proposed within the project. This was integrated into the *Pensar* Institute's agenda.

29 This category emerged in Cali, because women victims of displacement,

especially women associated with the *El Chontaduro* foundation, speak of exile and not of displacement (Collected by María de Los Ángeles Balaguera, in an approach with this organisation that did not allow us to work with them, as they rightly pointed out that they already had their researchers).

30 Bello Ramírez, (2013, p. 74) quoted the following testimony from an inmate at the District Prison in Bogotá, about what prison fodder means: 'In jails you are going to find people who became prison fodder. That is when you go in and out of jail several times and then you realise that your youth is gone, your life is gone, being eaten by these walls (...) (Wilson, aged 21 years)'.

References

Anzaldúa, Gloria. 1987. *Borderlands - La frontera: the new mestiza*. San Francisco: Aunt Lute Books.

Bello Ramírez, J. 2013. "Cuerpos encerrados, vidas criminalizadas. Interseccionalidad, control carcelario y gobierno de las diferencias." Master's Thesis. Escuela de Esudios de Género. Universidad Nacional de Colombia. http://bdigital.unal.edu.co/45378/1/80857966.2013.pdf.

Bettio, Francesca, Annamaria Simonazzi and Paola Villa. 2006. "Change in care regimes and female migration: the 'care drain' in the Mediterranean." *Journal of European Social Policy 16*(3), 271–285.

Bourdieu, Pierre. 1997. *Razones prácticas. Sobre la teoría de la acción*. Barcelona: Anagrama.

Bourdieu, Pierre. 1999. "Conocimiento por cuerpos." In *Meditaciones pascalianas*, eds. Pierre Bourdieu and Thomas Kauf, 169–2014. Barcelona: Anagrama.

Breilh, Jaime. 2013. "La determinación social de la salud como herramienta de transformación hacia una nueva salud pública." *Revista Facultad Nacional de Salud Pública 31*(1), 13–27.

Carbado, Devon W., Kimberlé Williams Crenshaw, Vickie Mays and B. Tomlinson. 2013. "Intersectionality." *Du Bois Review: Social Science Research on Race 10*(2), 303–312.

Crenshaw, Kimberlé. 1991. "Mapping the margins: intersectionality, identity politics, and violence against women of color." *Stanford Law Review 43*(6), 1241–1299.

De Lauretis, Teresa. 1987. *Technologies of gender*. Bloomington: Indiana University Press.

Echeverría, Bolivar. 2010. *Modernidad y blanquitud*. Mexico: Editorial ERA.

Esguerra Muelle, Camila, Diana Ojeda and Friederike Fleischer. 2021 "Forced displacement, international migration and (trans)national care networks: the urban other in Colombia and Spain." In *A feminist urban theory for our times: reconsidering social reproduction, the urban and its constitutive outside*, eds. Linda Peake, Elsa Koleth and Patrick Darren. New York: Wiley Blackwell.

Esguerra Muelle, Camila. 2002. "Del pecatum muntum al orgullo de ser lesbiana: Grupo Triángulo Negro de Bogotá (1996–1999)." Tesis para optar por el grado de antropóloga. Universidad Nacional de Colombia.

Esguerra Muelle, Camilla. 2009. "Dislocation and Borderland: Latin Americans migrants in Spain inhabiting the territory of the lesbian experience." Master's Thesis, MA Gender and Ethnicity, Utrecht University, Oviedo University.

Esguerra Muelle, Camilla. 2015. "Mujeres imaginadas: mujeres migrantes, mujeres exiliadas y sexualidades no normativas." Tesis de Doctorado en Humanidades. Universidad Carlos III de Madrid.

Esguerra Muelle, Camila, Ivette Sepúlveda Sanabria, Laura Castrillón Guerrero, María de Los Ángeles Balaguera, Alí Majul and Eliza Enache. 2016. *Protocolo metodológico, ético, de seguridad y operativo de investigación Proyecto Migración y cadenas Globales de Cuidado.* Cider: Universidad de Los Andes (unpublished manuscript).

Esguerra Muelle, Camila, Ivette Sepúlveda Sanabria and Frederike Fleischer. 2018. "Se nos va el cuidado, se nos va la vida: Migración, destierro, desplazamiento y cuidado en Colombia (No. 3)." *Documentos de Politica.* https://cider.uniandes.edu.co/es/publicaciones/node%3Atitle%5D-81#gsc.tab=0.

Esguerra Muelle, Camila. 2020. "Complejo industrial fronterizo, sexualidad y género." *Tabula Rasa 33*, 107–136.

Flórez, Juliana and Carolina Olarte. 2020 *"Por una política de lo turbio: Practicas de investigación feministas"* In Lopez Carlos (ed) *Investigar a la intemperie: Reflexiones sobre métodos en las ciencias sociales desde el oficio.* Bogotá: Editorial Pontificia Universidad Javeriana, pp 15–58.

Foucault, Michel. 1991. *Historia de la sexualidad. I La voluntad de saber.* Mexico: Siglo, Editores Mexico.

Gastaldo, Denise, Lilian Magalhães, Christine Carrasco and Charity Davy. 2012. *Body-map storytelling as research: methodological considerations for telling the stories of undocumented workers through body mapping.* Toronto: Creative Commons.

Geertz, Clifford and Alberto Cardin. 1989. *El antropólogo como autor.* Barcelona: Anagrama.

Haidar, Victoria and Maria Valeria Berros. 2015. "Hacia un abordaje multidimensional y multiescalar de la cuestión ecológica: la perspectiva del buen vivir." *Revista Crítica de Ciências Sociais 108*, 111–134. Accessed October10, 2019, https://doi.org/10.4000/rccs.6133 https://journals.openedition.org/rccs/6133.

Haraway, Donna. 1988. "Situated knowledges: the science question in feminism and the privilege of partial perspective." *Feminist Studies 14*(3), 575–599.

Harding, Sandra. 2008. *Sciences from below: Feminisms, postcolonialities and modernities.* London: Duke University Press, p. 296.

Harding, Sandra. 2018. "State of the field: Latin American decolonial philosophies of science." *Studies in History and Philosophy of Science 78*, 46–63, accessed September7, 2019, https://journals.openedition.org/rccs/6133 https://doi.org/10.1016/j.shpsa.2018.10.001.

Hill Collins, Patricia. 2000. *Black feminist thought: knowledge, consciousness, and the politics of empowerment.* New York: Routledge.

Hochschild, Arlie Russell. 2000. "Global care chains and emotional surplus value." In *On the edge: living with global capitalism*, eds.Anthony Giddens and Will Hutton, 130–146. New York: Vintage.

Kontopoulos, Kyriakos M. 1993. *The logics of social structure.* London: Routledge.

Kristeva, Julia. 2006. *Historias de amor.* Siglo XXI.

Lander, Edgardo. 2000. *La colonialidad del saber: eurocentrismo y ciencias sociales.* Buenos Aires: CLACSO.

Lima Costa, Claudia de. 2002. "Repensando el género: tráfico de teorías en las Américas". In Claudia de Lima Costa, ed. *Perfiles del feminismo iberoamericano*, 189–214. Buenos Aires: Catálogos.

Manalansan IV, Martin F. 2006. "Queer intersections: sexuality and gender in migration studies." *International Migration Review 40*(11), 224–249.

Marcus, George. 1995. "Ethnography in/of the world system: the emergence of multi-sited ethnography." *Annual Review of Anthropology 24*(1), 95–117, accessed September 7, 2019, https://doi.org/10.1177/1463499605059232.

Mbembe, Achille. 2011. *Necropolítica*. Tenerife: Melusina.

Mignolo, Walter. 2005. "La idea de América Latina." *Crítica y emancipación 2*, 251–276.

Minh-ha, Trinh. 1989. *Woman, native, other, writing poscoloniality and feminism*. Bloomington e Indianapolis: Indiana University Press.

Nichols, Bill. 1994. *Blurred boundaries: questions of meaning in contemporary culture*. Bloomington: Indiana University Press.

Ojeda, Diana 2020. *"Contracartografía: Métodos en investigación socioespacial crítica" In Lopez Carlos (ed) Investigar a la intemperie: Reflexiones sobre métodos en las ciencias sociales desde el oficio*. Bogotá: Editorial Pontificia Universidad Javeriana, pp 167–184.

Osborne Verdugo, Raquel. 2009. "La sexualidad como frontera entre presas políticas y presas comunes bajo los nazis y el franquismo." *Política y Sociedad 46*(1–2), 57–77.

Peñaranda, Fernando. 2013. "Salud pública y justicia social en el marco del debate determinantes – determinación social de la salud." *Revista Facultad Nacional de Salud Pública, 31*(1), 91–102.

Rich, Adrienne. 1984. 'Notes towards a politics of location'. In *Blood, Bread and Poetry: Selected Prose 1979-1985*. London: Virago Press, 210–232.

Rich, Adrienne. 1996. "Heterosexualidad obligatoria y existencia lesbiana." *Duoda: Revista d'estudis Feministes, no. 11*, 13–37.

Rich, Adrienne. 2002. *Poemas (1963–2000)*. Editorial Renacimiento.

Rich, Adrienne. 2003. "Notes towards a politics of location." In *Feminist postcolonial theory a reader. A Reader*, eds. Lewis Reina and Mills Sara, 29–42. Edinburgh: Edinburgh University Press. Accessed June 15, 2020. doi:10.3366/j.ctvxcr9q0.6.

Rivera Cusicanqui, Silvia. 2010. *Ch'ixinakax utxiwa: una reflexión sobre descolonizadores*. Buenos Aires: Tinta Limón.

Rubin, Gayle. 1975. "The traffic in women: notes on the 'political economy' of sex." In *Toward an anthropology of women*, ed. Rayna Relter, 157–210. New York: Monthly Review Press.

Viveros Vigoya, Mara. 2016. "La interseccionalidad: una aproximación situada a la dominación." *Debate Feminista 52*, 1–17.

Wittig, Monique. 2006. *El pensamiento heterosexual y otros ensayos*. Translation Sáez, Javier and Vidarte, Paco. Editorial Egales: Barcelona.

7 The Imbrication of Gender and Nationality Where the Pay Gap Is Concerned

The Case in Malta

JosAnn Cutajar

Introduction

This chapter uses postcolonial and intersectional theory to explore how the legacies of the past perpetuate institutionalized racism and sexism and result in neocolonial forms of racism in the particular context of Malta. By looking at Malta's positionality within the European Union (EU), it explores the interconnection between North and South in Europe to delineate how they are mutually constitutive. The first part of the chapter explains that although Malta is in the Global North, its size and geopolitical location locate it at the periphery. Southern European countries are considered to form part of the Global North, yet in reality they are 'subordinated in economic, political and cultural terms' (De Sousa Santos 2016: 17).

Malta's economy is booming, forcing employers to import foreign workers and facilitate the employment and retention of Maltese women. The second part of this chapter analyzes the intersecting relationship between gender and nationality, in view of the EU's differentiation between North and South, West and East, and also between EU and non-EU. This relationship is explored by examining how workers differentiated on the basis of gender intersecting with their regional origin are located within the Maltese labour market, and how this impacts on their average wages. This chapter illustrates how small South European countries like Malta are subordinated in the EU. This subordinate position in conjunction with heteropatriarchal, postcolonial and neocolonizing practices is imbibed by employers and policymakers to legitimize and justify the maldistribution of income within Malta. The EU differentiates between two categories of migrant workers – those who originate from within the EU, and those who do not. This differentiation is taken into consideration and problematized. This chapter helps demonstrate the intercategorical complexity of the terms 'Global North' in conjunction with 'male' and 'female' by taking gender intersecting with regional origin as an analytical starting point to document inequality between and within various social groups with regard to employment and wages.

Feminist Postcolonial and Intersectional Theories

Postcolonial feminist theory consists of a framework of intersecting theories and discourses used to explore 'conflicting, competing, co-opting, intersecting spaces of identity nexus formations, whether geo-political, socio-economic, cultural or ideological' in nature (Parekh 2007: 142). Feminist postcolonial theory departs from the idea that a binary and essentialist approach to identity is conceptually flawed and inconsistent, and has undesirable moral and political consequences (Sisson Runyan 2019). This theory is used here to study the historical, socioeconomic, and cultural legacies of European colonialism in a previously colonized and neocolonial nation. It is used in conjunction with intersectional theory to study the hegemony within the EU, namely the power wielded by northwestern countries over southern and eastern member states.

Postcolonial theory is used to study the context diachronically, that is by tracing the economic and social development of the South vis-à-vis the North within Europe, focusing mainly on Malta. An intersectional analytical approach is also adopted to enable synchronic analysis of the Maltese labour market to determine how gender together with national and regional origin are used as a basis for discrimination. Together, these theoretical approaches help make transparent the matrices of oppressive, hierarchical and discriminatory ideologies, practices and politics (Parekh 2007).

Postcolonial feminist theory is a useful tool for drawing attention to the economic, political and sociocultural forces of recolonization that tend to work in conjunction with nationalist discourses (Sisson Runyan 2019: 43). It enables researchers to demonstrate how gender, class, nationalist and imperialist hierarchies 'are interwoven to undermine the lives of people [who are] physically, politically, economically and culturally' peripheralized (Sisson Runyan 2019: 44). Intersectionality helps analyze and politicize meanings attributed to particular bodies located in a particular time and space. Gendered, racialized and migrant bodies tend to be coded differently when it comes to employment (Parekh 2007).

Postcolonial theory requires attention to be given to a state's positionality within the international system, since this positionality tends to impact on the state's behaviour (Sisson Runyan 2019: 39). Malta's positionality in the EU affects how Maltese policymakers and employers perceive themselves, and this in turn impacts on which workers they actively seek to employ, and how much they decide to pay them. Grewal and Kaplan (2006) maintain that we must study specific locations, rather than speaking about ahistorical and essentialized category identities such as the Global South and the Global North, male and female, national and migrant workers. According to Sisson Runyan (2019: 37–39), essentialized notions of group identities tend to erase differentiations within them, and 'subject and object gain their meaning and agency according to their locations in a system of meaning (discourse, norms and rules)'.

Intersectional theory enables researchers to adopt 'both/and' thinking to theorize from a position of simultaneity (Nash 2008). The focus here is on the interplay between gender, regional derivation and nationality, as simultaneous sites of oppression. The objective is to analyze multiple systems of oppression, namely postcolonialism, neocolonialism, heteropatriarchy and nationality, within and beyond Malta. Analyzing the imbrication of these systems of oppression provides scope to demonstrate how they operate within a 'matrix' of domination.

Intersectional theory helps uncover how identities are interconnected. Hill Collins (1991) suggests that identities are constituted of multiple vectors of power, meaning that they are simultaneously partially privileged and partially oppressed. It is important to keep this in mind when studying localized imbrications. Sisson Runyan (2019: 7) underlines that multiple gender variations in pay emerge when gender is studied in intersection with nationality. Intersecting gender with regional origin reveals gendered variation within regional origin, as well as regional and gender ordering among the categories studied.

Methodology

Textual analysis of 'grey' literature and secondary data was undertaken for this study. Paez (2017: 233) defines grey literature as consisting of 'academic papers, including theses and dissertations, research and committee reports, government reports, conference papers, and ongoing research, among others'. Reports by EU agencies and the Maltese government, as well as by civil-society and non-governmental agencies, were analyzed to interrogate and question the power dynamics playing out in Maltese labour. Reliance was placed on these sources because relevant data are 'not found within commercially published literature' (Paez 2017: 233). Statistics provided by national and EU entities are used to illustrate and explore the inter-categorical complexity of wages in Malta, where gender and regional origin are involved.

Context: Malta

Malta consists of an archipelago of islands, the Maltese Islands, located in the middle of the Mediterranean Sea between Sicily and Libya. Until 1964 it was part of the British Empire, and had previously been ruled by the French, The Order of St. John, and other powers that historically held sway over the Mediterranean. The British imposed fortress economic policies in Malta, which remained in operation until the late 1950s (Cutajar 2009).

Malta's first phase of industrialization occurred between the mid-1950s and 1980, and a second phase commenced in the 1990s (NCPE 2006). In the latter, a number of economic and fiscal policies were implemented to facilitate the country's entry into the EU in 2004 and its joining of the Eurozone in 2008.

The first decade of the second millennium led to a decline in the direct production sector, which was counterbalanced by the flourishing of market services. According to Harper (2019):

> By the time the country's membership in the EU was formally approved in 2004, Malta had already crafted a place for itself within Europe's economy, and the nation's attractive tax schemes – effective rates as low as 5 percent for foreign-owned companies, vs. an average of 22 percent for other European countries – helped attract investment funds, banks, and financial services firms from all over the world.

In the 2010s Malta was highly ranked in the EU with respect to high- and medium-low-tech goods. The services sector grew further when a number of key players in the i-gaming industry (online gaming and gambling) set up shop in the country, capitalizing on its European first-mover advantage, (European Commission 2018). Apart from the i-gaming industry, which in 2016 accounted for 12% of value added, the buoyant services sector also included tourism and transport (European Commission 2018). Harper (2019: 4) adds that in 2014:

> Malta began a three-year run as Europe's fastest-growing economy. Binance Holdings, the world's largest cryptocurrency exchange, announced it was moving its headquarters from Hong Kong to Malta and within weeks, Morgan Stanley analysts were reporting that a majority of the world's cryptotrading volume was moving through companies based in Malta.

And according to Borg (2019a: 2):

> Malta is the only European country to feature in a top 20 worldwide list of wealth growth driven by the migration of wealthy people over the past ten years. According to the list, published by research group New World Wealth, while Malta experienced migration driven wealth growth of 95% between 2007 and 2017, European countries with high tax regimes experienced negative growth.

The EU started to take issue with Malta's emerging status as an international financial and remote i-gaming centre. The European Commission's (2018) country report stated that Malta's corporate tax rules were being used by companies engaging in aggressive tax planning to avoid paying taxes in recipient countries. It cited the absence of withholding taxes on dividends, interest and royalty payments as the reason for these companies moving to Malta. Western-based agencies such as the European Commission and European Parliament, among others, have a propensity to determine, dictate and define what should be done in countries perceived as 'deficient' (McEwan 2019: 16). The European Parliament's Special Committee on Financial Crimes, Tax Evasion and Tax Avoidance accused Malta of facilitating aggressive tax planning (European Commission 2019). Bullier (2019) suggests that tax harmonization is often promoted by high-tax member states to fight tax competition, thereby protecting their own economic interests to the detriment of other EU countries.

Malta's citizenship and residency schemes also came under attack. These allow non-domiciled individuals to avoid paying tax on foreign-derived income (Borg 2019a). An OECD report published in 2018 blacklisted Malta and Cyprus for this reason, and the European Commission stated that such schemes pose security, money-laundering and corruption risks (Caruana 2019). All these negative reports had an impact on Malta's Transparency International Corruption Perceptions Index ranking, which dropped from 37 in 2010 to 51 in 2018 (Borg 2019b). A quick look at the map of rankings shows how South and East European countries fare, with Italy, Slovakia, Croatia, Romania, Hungary, Greece and Bulgaria ranked lower than Malta. The Global North usually creates and manages such indices, making use of them as 'dispossessing actions' (Meekosha 2011: 669) to discredit countries that it feels threatens its economic supremacy, including newly-evolving economies. Criteria on how to create, maintain and run an economy are defined by countries that have already attained supremacy in the global economy, which use these criteria to mitigate competition. This means that the leaders of countries in the Global South operate within an international framework not of their own making (Islam and Hossain 2016: 37).

The objective of this chapter is threefold. It will start by illustrating how in the case of Malta, small South European countries are subordinated in the European Union. The colonization of the South by the North, and the West over the East is inherent in the EU itself. It leads to hierarchies within the Union, resulting in the subaltern colonialism of the South (De Sousa Santos 2016: 17) and the East. Southern Europe is treated as a periphery, a subordinate rather than an equal, and Malta is a case in point. As De Sousa Santos (2016) underlines, the colonialization of the South by the North is based on a ranking order that justifies the domination and oppression of countries perceived as inferior. This perceived inferiority helps legitimize their domination. Small Southern states retain some power when it comes to managing their economy. However, its decisions are constantly monitored and undermined by international and supranational watchdogs. As noted above, Malta's small size, its location in the South of Europe, and its colonial status until 1964 are constantly used to question its economic progress. As a small country that was prevented from developing industrially under British rule, it had to find a means of building an economy that would help ameliorate its citizens' standards of living.

In the process of defining themselves as 'modern nations' and finding their niche in the global economy, 'newly' independent nation states straddle the old and the new (Parekh 2007: 154). The old means dependency, having historically been constantly dependent on their colonial masters for ideas and investment. The new means forging closer alliances with the EU while not ignoring investment from other parts of the world. Whatever actions new economies take, these are often subject to surveillance, classification and hierarchization (Barker 2010: 22). Countries that have more access to and control over symbolic and material resources retain power over the stabilization and institutionalization of particular norms, rules and practices (Sisson Runyan 2019: 37).

The European Union not only differentiates between the North and the South, but also between workers - those deriving from within the European Union, and those without. This differentiation will be taken into consideration and problematized. This chapter will help demonstrate the inter-categorical complexity of the term Global North in conjuction with male and female by taking gender intersecting with regional derivation as analytical starting points to document inequality between and within the various social groups with regards to employment and wages. By studying inequality along multiple and conflicting dimensions, the objective is to expose the relationship between inequality and the categories themselves (McCall 2005).

Borg 2019Meekosha 2011Islam 2016
De Sousa Santos 2016De Sousa Santos 2016
Parekh 2007Barker 2010Sisson Runyan 2019

The subordinate position as well as or heteropatriarchal, postcolonial and neo-colonizing practices are imbibed by employers and policy makers in Malta who use these to legitimize and justify the maldistribution of income in Malta. The men governing Malta (Malta has one of the lowest numbers of women in government in the EU, see Cutajar 2014) oppress others within the nation. Female and male workers, and Maltese, EU and third-country nationals tend to be valorized differently and employed in specific economic sectors and occupations in the Maltese labour market. People's regional origin and gender impact on the types of employment they find and the remuneration they receive. Gender is shaped by nationality, and nationality is gendered, as explained below. The focus is on regional origin rather than race because the valency given to different groups of migrant workers depends not only on their levels of education, experience and/or race, but also on their country of origin.

Overall, politicians and policymakers tend to be perceived as masculine because the majority are male. However, Connell (1995) differentiates between hegemonic and subordinated masculinities. Only a minority of men have 'hegemonic masculinity', and these embody 'the currently most honored way of being a man', requiring 'all other men to position themselves in relation to it' and 'ideologically legitimat[ing] the global subordination of women to men' (Connell and Messerschmidt 2005: 832). Economically-, ethnically-, racially- and geopolitically-privileged men control power and decision making. Men subordinated by class, race, sexuality, non-normative gender and/or (neo)colonization must conform with the economic status and conditions created by economic elites. Sisson Runyan (2019: 113) concludes that subordinate masculinities may react to this subordination by controlling the bodies of non-elite men and women to reclaim some sense of masculine authority.

Maltese policymakers are perceived as subordinated masculinities because of their peripheral positioning in the EU. They use gender, race, class, as well as national and sexual privilege to subordinate other groups in order to assert, maintain and retain power. Masculinisms justify gender hierarchies. At the same time, those who are not perceived as forming part of the hegemonic masculinity are placed in feminized positions or positions categorized as feminine. This means that men who are non-rich, non-white, non-Christian, non-middle-class, non-heterosexual, non-European and/or non-able-bodied are feminized.

Policymakers who form part of subordinated and hegemonic masculinisms tend to criticize the way they are subordinated by global and regional agencies, while neglecting to see how they themselves are implicated in subordinating others through the policies and decisions they make which promote hierarchies of gender, race, class, nation or sexuality. Gender as a power relation combines with other structural power relations, such as colonialism, imperialism, racism and economic and environmental exploitation, to help normalize social, political and economic divisions, inequalities and injustices (Sisson Runyan 2019: 10). This will be discussed when analysing the location of men and women, native and 'foreign' migrant labour in the Maltese labour market. The next section focuses on the location of native and 'foreign' workers in the Maltese labour market to determine how regional origin intersecting with gender affects who does what and how much they are paid. This chapter distinguishes between EU and non-EU workers to establish whether they occupy the same labour market economic sectors and/or occupations, and how this location affects their access to the basic average wage.

Location of 'Foreign' Labour in the Maltese Labour Market

The Maltese economy has grown in the last decade, pushing more women into joining a buoyant labour market. During the 2010s, Malta experienced the highest increase in female employment of all EU states (European Commission 2019: 29). However, although the percentage of women in the labour market increased, this did not address all the country's labour and skills shortages, so foreign labour had to be brought in. This influx of foreign workers was crucial in mitigating labour market shortages. Foreign labour increased sharply, from 1.7% in 2012 to 22.5% in 2018 (Central Bank of Malta 2019: 35).

According to Jobsplus (2018), 68% of foreign workers originated from the EU, and the rest (31%) were third-country (non-EU) nationals. Figure 7.1 gives a breakdown of migrant workers' continent of origin. While 78% were European, 14% came from Asia, 6% from Africa and 2% from the Americas and Australia. Importantly, not all European workers are EU nationals. In 2017, foreign workers constituted '14% of the working age population and 31% of total employment' (Borg 2019c: 5).

The majority of EU nationals working in Malta came from Italy (16.8%) and Britain (12.6%) (European Commission 2018).Bulgarian, German, Swedish, French, Romanian, Hungarian, Spanish and Polish workers were also among the top ten EU nationalities working in Malta. A smaller proportion of foreign workers came from non-EU countries, originating mainly from Serbia and Montenegro, the Philippines, India and Libya (Jobsplus 2018).

Sectors that depend heavily on foreign workers include healthcare, finance and ICT (European Commission 2019). The European Commission

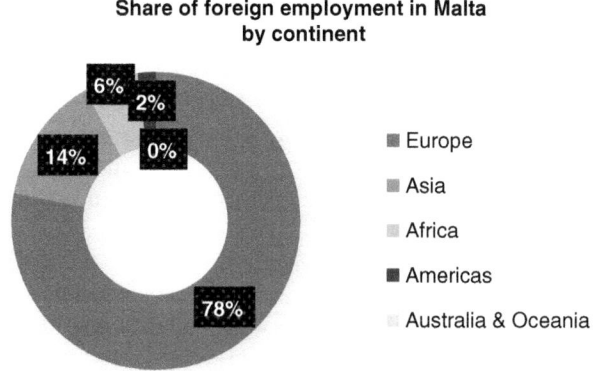

Figure 7.1 Share of foreign employment in Malta by continent.
Source: Jobsplus 2018.

(2018) states that this dependence on imported high-skilled workers is due to Malta's lower proportion of tertiary graduates when compared with the rest of the EU. The tertiary education rate for 30–34 year olds stood at 33.5% in 2018, compared with an EU average of 39.9%. It is important to note that in 2017 Maltese women were more likely to have received tertiary education (35%) than native men, and that 39.7% of foreign workers were also educated to tertiary level (European Commission 2019: 31).

The European Institute for Gender Equality (EIGE 2017) compared the work participation rates of native male and female workers with those of foreign workers, using data from the 2014 Labour Force Survey. It reveals that the full-time equivalent employment rates for male and female foreign workers in Malta (63.4% and 41% respectively) were higher than for native men and women (59.5% and 33% respectively) (EIGE 2017). The propensity of foreign workers to work longer hours may result from the fact that '27% of all foreign workers that were engaged in the period 2002–2017 were below 25 years of age, while 43% of them fall within the 25–34 cohort' (Borg 2019c: 4). At this age, EU workers are less likely to have dependents, while non-EU workers are more likely to leave their dependents at home to enable them to save enough money before bringing them over. 'Official policy states that to apply for a residence permit for a family member, third country nationals are required to earn €19,000 annually (the average salary in Malta) as well as €3,800 for each dependent' (Abela 2019), meaning that only non-EU workers with substantial salaries can afford to reunite their families.

Labour force statistics also demonstrate work segregation on the basis of regional origin (Figure 7.2). In 2018, EU nationals worked mainly in retail, transport and tourism, professional and administrative support activities, and the arts, entertainment and recreation sectors (Central Bank of Malta 2019: 38). Maltese workers were concentrated mainly in retail, transport and tourism, together with public administration, education and the health economy. Maltese often opt for jobs in the civil service, even though pay prospects are not particularly lucrative, because they are more likely to retain their jobs during economic crises (Cutajar 2009). Non-EU and third-country nationals are strongly represented in professional and administrative support, as well as the retail, transport and tourism sectors.

The Central Bank of Malta (2019: 39) suggests that the extent of reliance on migrant workers varies by sector. In 2018, 58.6% of the workforce in the arts, entertainment and recreation sector were foreign, as were 34.4% of those in professional and administrative support services. While the arts, entertainment and recreation sector was reliant on (non-Maltese) EU nationals, the construction and administrative support service sectors tended to rely on non-EU workers.

Figure 7.3 demonstrates a link between the distribution of the workforce by occupational position and regional origin. Third-country

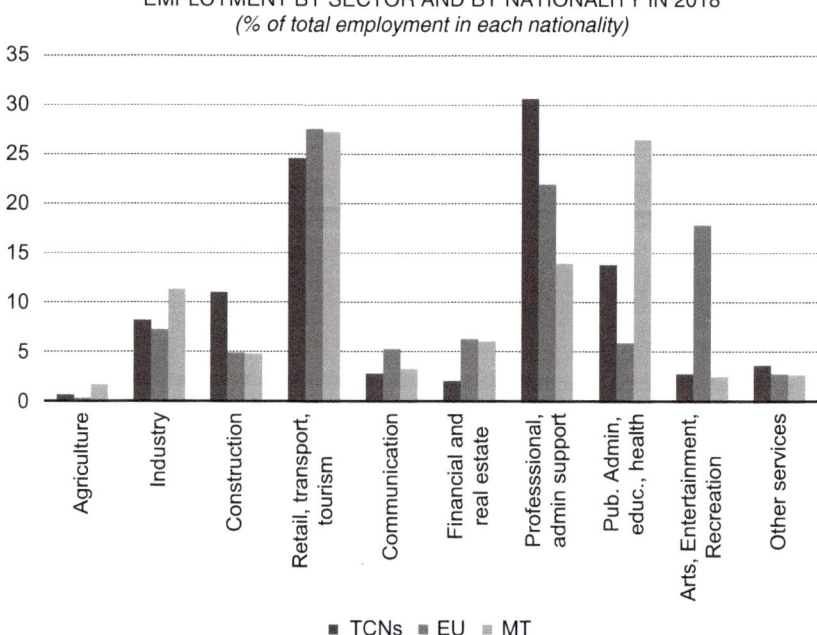

EMPLOYMENT BY SECTOR AND BY NATIONALITY IN 2018
(% of total employment in each nationality)

Figure 7.2 Employment by sector and regional derivation in 2018 (% of total employment in each nationality).

nationals (non-EU workers) were over-represented in elementary occupations, as well as the services and sales sectors, whereas Maltese and EU nationals had a 'higher probability of being employed in more advanced positions' (Central Bank of Malta 2019: 38). With regard to employment in managerial and professional positions, the figures were 13.2% and 16.9% respectively for EU nationals, and 8.2% and 18.5% for Maltese nationals. Thus, EU nationals were more likely than Maltese nationals to have managerial jobs. The data also indicate that EU and Maltese nationals were more likely than non-EU workers to be employed in more advanced occupations. Borg (2019c: 16) notes that a large proportion of EU workers 'tend to be high-skilled, with managers, professionals, and technicians forming almost 40% of the total number of workers that come from EU countries'. Non-EU workers were more likely to be low-skilled. They find it harder to find employment in financially lucrative sectors because they either do not have the necessary educational qualifications and/or work experience or, if they do, these are not recognized by the Maltese authorities.

Sectors requiring high skills, namely the financial and insurance, arts

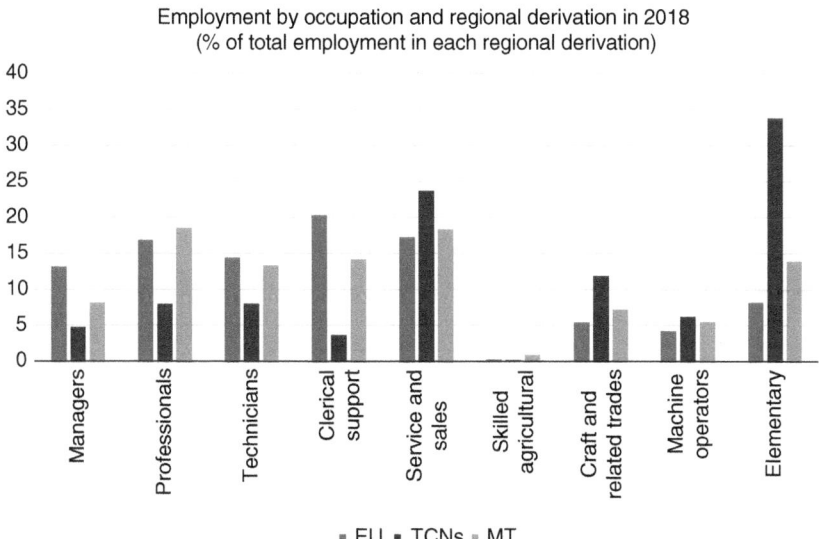

Figure 7.3 Employment by occupation and regional derivation in 2018 (% of total employment in each regional derivation).
Source: Central Bank of Malta 2019: 37.

and entertainment (represented by Other) and information and communications sectors, had the highest average basic annual salaries (Table 7.1). Average sectoral wages are used here as an indication of the wages that workers might obtain in Malta, but as Borg (2019c: 19) notes, this can only be used as a proxy since 'foreign workers might get a different wage than the native population and hence, the average sectoral wage could be biased'. This is the only viable solution in the absence of micro-level evidence. EU and Maltese nationals were more likely to be working in financially more lucrative sectors such as finance and insurance, and Other services, the best paid sectors highlighted in Table 7.1.

The data show a hierarchization of the Maltese labour market on the basis of regional origin. EU nationals were more likely to find employment in financially more lucrative niches of the labour market, while third-country nationals were concentrated in less lucrative ones, and Maltese workers were located somewhere between these two categories.

This section has mapped out where national, EU and non-EU workers were located within the labour market. The next section examines the imbrication of regional origin with gender with regard to pay.

Table 7.1 Average annual basic salary of employees by gender and economic activity of main occupation, October–December 2017

Economic activity	Males average (€)	Females average (€)	Total average (€)
Agriculture, forestry and fishing	::	::	::
Manufacturing, mining and quarrying and other industry	18,181	13,430	16,761
Construction	17,147	::	16,955
Wholesale and retail trade, transportation and storage, accommodation and food service activities	17,058	12,765	15,386
Information and communication	21,967	16,869	20,047
Financial and insurance activities	29,335	24,300	26,741
Real-estate activities	::	::	::
Professional, scientific, technical,	18,105	15,882	16,987

Table 7.1 (*continued*)

Economic activity	Males average (€)	Females average (€)	Total average (€)
administration and support service activities	20,383	17,404	18,757
Public administration, defence, education, human health and social work activities			
Other services	25,592	15,805	21,827
Total	**19,289**	**16,041**	**17,911**

Source: Adapted from NSO 2018, Table 10

Gendered Division of Labour in Malta

Malta's accession to the EU and its recent economic boom have expanded employment opportunities for women in Malta. Many still opt out of labour market participation because they internalize the stereotypical idea that they must be the primary carers for children. They opt out of the labour market because of 'the low availability of flexible hours and teleworking and equally important – job satisfaction' (Mangion n.d.). Gendered beliefs and cultural practices also affect whether they work part-time or full-time, and in which economic sectors and occupations. Data show that these cultural beliefs are more prevalent among Maltese (NCPE 2012) and migrant women from sub-Saharan and North African countries (Migrant Women Association Malta 2017), although gender data de-segregated for EU and non-EU workers are unavailable to confirm this.

Male and female workers were concentrated in different sectors of the labour market (NSO 2018). Over a third of female workers were in public administration, defence, education, human health and social work activities, while men worked in wholesale and retail trades, transportation and storage, accommodation and food service activities. With regard to their main occupation, while women were more likely to work in services and sales, as professionals and clerical and sales workers, men were more likely to find jobs as technicians and semi-professionals, professionals and craft and related workers.

The average salary for the different economic and occupational sectors differed by gender (see Table 7.1), with women tending to be paid substantially less than men working in the same economic sector. The economic sector offering the highest pay was the financial and insurance sector, where men received an average of 29,335 euros, whereas women's basic average annual salary was 24,300 euros. The second-highest average wage was for other services (21,827 euros). These two sectors both had a high percentage of EU workers. The gender pay gap was over 20% in the three economic sectors in which female workers were concentrated (Figure 7.4). Women with tertiary-level education were more likely to be affected by this pay gap (18.7%), while women with a basic level of education were less likely to do so, suffering only a 10.3% pay gap (Magro Cuschieri 2018).

Interestingly, Figure 7.4 shows that the gender pay gap was negative for clerical support workers and service and sales workers, which are sectors in which non-EU nationals were concentrated (see Figure 7.4). The statistics do not provide information on the gender of foreign workers in these types of occupation. Jobsplus (2018) suggests that they tended to be male, so in this case, the presence of non-EU men working in these sectors led to a reversal of the gender pay gap in a feminized sector of the labour market. More data are needed to verify what is happening here. Statistics need to be gender de-segregated not only by occupation and economic sector, but also by nationality.

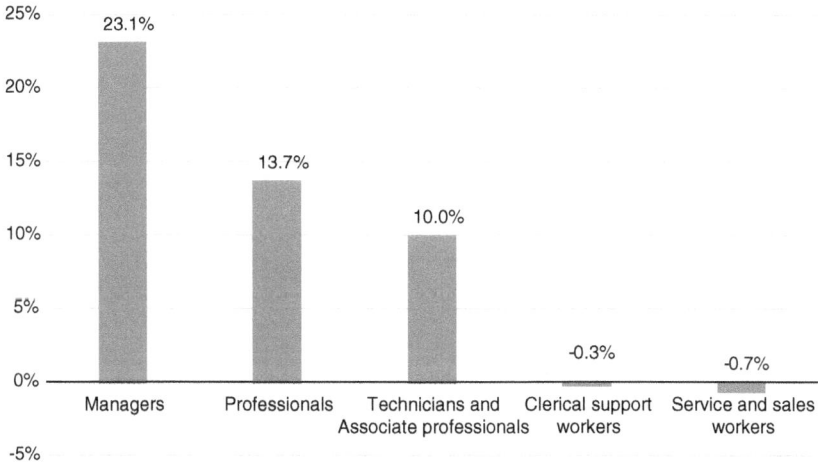

Figure 7.4 Gender pay gap among the more common occupational groups for all
economic activities, 2014.
Source: Magro Cuschieri (2018).

As these statistics establish the feminization of employment has not
altered the gender division of labour, nor the valorization of masculinized work over women's work (Sisson Runyan 2019: 45). The data also
indicate that Malta still has a gender-polarized valorization of skills and
work, although non-EU men who work in these sectors fare worse than
native women. This gendered valorization of skills, work and bodies is
linked with racialization and neocolonialism, as discussed in the next
section.

Regional Origin and Gender Wage Differentials

As previously discussed, native, EU and third-country nationals were
concentrated in different economic sectors and occupations. The EIGE's
(2017) data also reveal a tiered salary scale based on regional origin and
gender (see Table 7.2). Maltese women were paid less than Maltese men,
consolidating the previous findings; and EU-born men were paid more
than EU-born women and native workers. Non-EU born men were paid
the least, which is probably because this segment of the working population consists largely of young African men who lacked 'acceptable'
academic qualifications and/or prior work experience. EU and non-EU
women received higher incomes than native women. This is an important
issue requiring more detailed exploration. While native men's work is
valorized less than EU but more than non-EU men, Maltese women are

Table 7.2 Mean monthly and equalized net income (PPS) in euros, 2015

	Native born	Foreign born	
			Non-EU born
Women	1,737	1,966	17,633
Men	2,336	2,550	16,709
	Native born	**EU born**	
Women	17,577	19,919	
Men	18,395	21,597	

Mean equivalized net income in euros – data derived from EU SILC

Source: Adapted from EIGE 2017; mean monthly earnings based on Labour Force Survey.

located at the bottom of the pay hierarchy, even though they have a higher standard of education than Maltese men.

Statistics for 2017 reveal consistent results. Data provided by the Maltese National Statistics Office (NSO) for 2018 (personal communication with Charlene Abela, January 2019) show that the average annual basic salary was 18,019 euros for native workers, around 20,695 euros for EU workers and only 17,099 euros for third-country nationals. Unfortunately, gender de-segregated data for this year are difficult to obtain. EU workers earned more than Maltese workers, and Maltese more than non-EU. The data clearly show that EU nationals were more likely to be recruited to high-income jobs, Maltese nationals were concentrated in middle-income jobs, and non-EU nationals were more likely to be working in financially less lucrative ones.

Neither the NSO nor service providers and employers de-segregate their data by gender, nationality and race (The People for Change Foundation 2017: 9). These data are needed to study the intersection of gender with nationality and race, in order to determine how these factors affect access to employment and income in Malta, and to help render visible the exploitation of gendered and racialized bodies.

According to the European Commission (2018), foreign workers are dampening the upward pressure on wages, although not all sectors are equally affected. Sectors affected by this dampening are usually those employing foreign workers from countries with poorer working conditions and income than Malta. This seems to be happening in feminized sectors of the labour market, such as clerical support, services and sales. Sisson Runyan (2019) maintains that working conditions tend to deteriorate in feminized sectors of the labour market, and the effect is evident in sectors with a high concentration of third-country nationals.

Conclusion

This chapter has looked at the intersectionality of regional origin and gender with regard to employment and wages in Malta. This analytical exercise started by delineating Malta's 'liminality' (Bhabha 1994) within the EU/Global North. As a southern European country within the Global North, it is 'subordinated in economic, political and cultural terms' (De Sousa Santos 2016: 17) to more powerful EU countries that define and determine what should be done at the local level.

Entities within the Global North retain moral legitimacy to dictate to countries they perceive as being morally, culturally and socio-politically lacking and lagging (McEwan 2019: 38). South European countries tend to internalize this definition of themselves. In attempting to emulate Western countries that set themselves up as the epitome of democratic and capitalist development, South European countries end up embracing and appropriating the same colonizing and exploitative techniques that

helped the Global North gain and retain power. The Othering and ordering of less deserving 'bodies' on a gender and nationality basis have
consequences for those involved, leading to wage differentials between
EU, native and third-country nationals, and between men and women
within these categories.

This study reveals that Maltese nationals receive lower average basic
salaries than European nationals, but they enjoy better incomes in relation to third-country nationals. When regional origin is imbricated
with gender, European men emerge as dominant masculinities in relation
to salaries, while Maltese men have an edge over male third-country
nationals. Maltese women are the most marginalized group in terms of
aggregated basic average salary. They receive a lower basic average
salary even though they have higher levels of education than their male
co-nationals.

From the data presented, it is evident that sectors with a high concentration of women (whatever their origin) and male third-country
nationals are badly paid in relation to other sectors. The data also demonstrate that those with the necessary educational qualifications and
experience to meet the demands of post-industrial and informational
capitalism tend to receive more lucrative salaries than those working in
feminized sectors, and in semi- or unskilled occupations in the case of
third-country nationals. Technical, informational and knowledge-based
skills are valorized, masculinized and reserved for certain nationalities
and genders but not others.

The data show marked regional origin striations within the Maltese
labour force. They also reveal a gendered division of labour marked by a
distinction between a core of skilled, mainly EU and Maltese male
workers, and a marginalized Maltese female and non-EU male workforce. Women and men, colonized and colonizers occupy different positions in the Maltese labour market.

McClintock (1995) regards men in liminal positions as dangerous.
People in such positions attempt to maintain their power by segregating
and subordinating others whom they perceive as inferior, in this case
Maltese women and non-EU men. Fear of being found wanting at an EU
level leads to a knee-jerk reaction that symbolically reduces gendered and
other bodies to an inferior status. Non-EU people and Maltese women
are defined as the other, as inferior on a nationality and gender basis,
perceived as temporary and hence subsidiary workers.

This chapter has explored the implications of the simultaneous privilege (being part of the Global North) and oppression (of gendered or
racialized bodies) of workers in Malta. Hill Collins (1991) maintains
that identities are constituted by the intersections of multiple vectors of
power, in this case geographical location, gender and nationality. A shift
toward the global should not sanction the subordination and/or

exploitation of others. However, globalization does indeed appear to be predicated on sanctioning such subordination.

References

Abela, Kristina. 2019. "My child would be worse off in Serbia." *Times of Malta*, 21 December. Available at: https://timesofmalta.com/articles/view/my-child-would-be-much-worse-off-back-in-serbia.758554.

Barker, Clare. 2010. "Interdisciplinary dialogues: disability and postcolonial studies." *Review of Disability Studies: An International Journal* 6(3), 15–24.

Bhabha, Homi. 1994. *The location of culture*. London: Routledge.

Borg, Jacob. 2019a. "Malta flagged as popular tax destination for the rich and famous: Greens call on EU to harmonise tax rules." *Times of Malta*, 2 April. Available at: https://www.timesofmalta.com/articles/view/20190402/local/malta-flagged-as-popular-tax-destination-for-the-rich-and-famous.706271.

Borg, Jacob. 2019b. "Malta tumbles to record low on corruption index: PN reaction – Government condemned according to its own yardstick." *Times of Malta*, 29 January. Available at: https://www.timesofmalta.com/articles/view/20190129/local/malta-tumbles-to-record-low-on-corruption-index.700539.

Borg, Ian. 2019c. *The length of stay of foreign workers in Malta: Policy note*. Malta: Central Bank of Malta.

Bullier, Guillaume. 2019. "Rather than tax harmonisation, the case for budgetary federalism." *Thinking Federalist*, 7 March. Available at: https://www.thenewfederalist.eu/rather-than-tax-harmonisation-the-case-for-budgetary-federalism.

Caruana, Claire. 2019. "Malta displays traits of tax haven, says EP committee: Report to be discussed later this month." *Times of Malta*, 8 March. Available at: https://timesofmalta.com/articles/view/malta-displays-traits-of-tax-haven-says-ep-committee.703882.

Central Bank of Malta. 2019. *Quarterly review 2019: Quarter 4*. Malta: Central Bank of Malta.

Connell, Raewyn W. 1995. *Masculinities*. Cambridge: Polity Press.

Connell, Raewyn W., and James W. Messerschmidt. 2005. "Hegemonic masculinity: rethinking the concept." *Gender and Society* 19(6), 829–859.

Cutajar, JosAnn. 2009. "Social inequality." In *Social transitions in Maltese society*, eds.JosAnn Cutajar and George Cassar, 225–258. Malta: Agenda.

Cutajar, JosAnn. 2014. *Women and political participation in Malta*. Paper commissioned by OSCE Office for Democratic Institutions and Human Rights. Available at: https://www.osce.org/odihr/126803.

De Sousa Santos, Boaventura. 2016. "Epistemologies of the South and the future." *From the European South: A Transdisciplinary Journal of Postcolonial Humanities 1*, 17–29.

EIGE. 2017. *Intersecting inequalities in Malta: Money indications in Malta*. Vilnius, Lithuania: European Institute for Gender Equality. Available at: https://eige.europa.eu/gender-equality-index/2015/domain/money/MT.

European Commission. 2018. *Country report Malta 2018*. Commission staff working document SWD(2018) 216 final, European Commission, Brussels,

Belgium. Available at: https://ec.europa.eu/info/sites/info/files/2018-european-semester-country-report-malta-en.pdf.

European Commission. 2019. *Report from the Commission to the European Parliament, the Council, the European Economic and Social Committee and the Committee of the Regions*. Document COM(2019) 12 final, European Commission, Brussels, Belgium. Available at: https://ec.europa.eu/info/sites/info/files/com_2019_12_final_report.pdf.

Grewal, Inderpal and Caren Kaplan. 2006. *An introduction to women's studies: gender in a transnational world*. New York, NY: McGraw-Hill Education.

Harper, Jo. 2019. "Malta in the eye of a financial tempest." *Deutsche Welle Business*, 25 March. Available at: https://www.dw.com/cda/en/malta-in-the-eye-of-a-financial-tempest/a-47979126.

Hill Collins, Patricia. 1991. *Black feminist thought: knowledge, consciousness and the politics of empowerment*. New York, NY: Routledge.

Islam, Saidul and Ismail Hossain. 2016. *Social justice in the globalization of production: labor, gender, and the environment nexus*. Basingstoke: Palgrave Macmillan.

Jobsplus. 2018. "Foreign nationals employment trends." *Jobsplus* [website]. Available at: https://jobsplus.gov.mt/resources/publication-statistics-mt-mt-en-gb/labour-market-information/foreigners-data#title1.1.

Magro Cuschieri, Joslyn. 2018. *The gender pay gap in Malta: a partial analysis of occupational and industry characteristics*. MEP seminar on the gender pay gap in Malta, University of Malta, 8 June.

Mangion, George M. n.d. "Female participation." *PKF Malta* [website]. Available at: https://pkfmalta.com/female-participation/.

McCall, Leslie. 2005. "The complexity of intersectionality." *Signs* 30(3), 1771–1800.

McClintock, Anne. 1995. *Imperial leather: race, gender and sexuality in colonial contest*. Abingdon: Routledge.

McEwan, Cheryl. 2019. *Postcolonialism, decoloniality and development*. London: Routledge.

Meekosha, Helen. 2011. "Decolonising disability: thinking and acting globally." *Disability and Society* 26(6), 667–682.

Migrant Women Association Malta. 2017. *Stepping up: an investigation of female asylum seekers and employment in Malta*. Santa Venera, Malta: Migrant Women Association Malta.

Nash, Jennifer C. 2008. "Re-thinking intersectionality." *Feminist Review* 89(1), 1–15.

NCPE. 2006. *Gender pay review*. Blata l-Bajda, Malta: National Commission for the Promotion of Equality.

NCPE. 2012. *Unlocking the female potential*. Blata l-Bajda, Malta: National Commission for the Promotion of Equality.

NSO. 2018. "Labour force survey: Q4/2017." News Release 048/2018, National Statistics Office, Valletta, Malta.

Paez, Arsenio. 2017. "Gray literature: An important source in systematic reviews." *Journal of Evidence-Based Medicine* 10(3), 233–240.

Parekh, Pushpa Naidu. 2007. "Gender, disability, and the postcolonial nexus." *Wagadu: A Journal of Transnational Women's and Gender Studies* 4, 142–161.

Sisson Runyan, Anne. 2019. *Global gender politics*. New York, NY: Taylor and Francis.

The People for Change Foundation. 2017. *Ethnic minorities: the case of Malta*. San Ġwann, Malta: The People for Change Foundation. Available at: http://www.pfcmalta.org/uploads/1/2/1/7/12174934/ethnic_minorities_beyond_migration_-_final.pdf.

Transparency International. 2018. *Corruption perceptions index 2018*. Berlin, Germany: Transparency International. Available at: https://www.transparency.org/cpi2018.

8 Intersectional Perspectives on Northern Swedish Rural Men's Working Life Narratives

Lisa Ridzén

Introduction

This chapter explores, through an intersectional lens, the working life narratives of two men living in peripheral parts of northern rural Sweden. The northern part of Sweden, *Norrland*, includes five regional counties that together take up about two thirds of Sweden's land area but contain only 12 per cent of the population (SCB 2017). The interviewees live in the southern inland of Norrland, in the county of *Jämtland* in mid-west Sweden and in the southern part of indigenous Saami land, Saepmie. Conflict continues over the Saami people's right to land and the rights of colonial powers such as the state, private land-owners and mining companies (Sjöstedt Landén and Fotaki 2018). The western parts of Jämtland are mountainous, and with an area of 34,000 square kilometres it is the second biggest county in Sweden, with 117,000 inhabitants. Although it has one of the largest rural populations, most inhabitants live in or near the only city, Östersund (63,000 inhabitants).

Following a significant population increase arising from forestry, since the mid 1900s the population of Norrland has steadily decreased, and for decades the area has suffered from out-migration, closure of welfare services, and young people moving away to larger cities. One recurrent 'issue' in Norrland has centred around the 'survival' of the region (Nilsson and Lundgren 2015: 85). As a result of wider social phenomena such as urbanization and neoliberal discourses, including implementations of New Public Management (NPM) focusing on purchaser–provider models and cost efficiency, local municipalities are struggling to sustain services and welfare, especially in rural areas (Giritli Nygren and Nyhlén 2015), and schools and healthcare facilities are closing down. For instance, maternity care is increasingly centralized in larger towns (Larsson 2018). However, in these sparsely populated areas with big distances between small towns, there are also growth zones such as the regional centres of Umeå and Östersund. Geographical inequality in Norrland is therefore problematic. Globalization has led to increased competition and centralization, and large-scale businesses are part of broader international processes (SOU 2017: 73). These are typical characteristics of what is described as peripheral in relation to urbanity. Peripheral places in Norrland are extremely important for the growth of global markets, and mining and forestry create considerable economic growth for both the Swedish state and private companies (Sjöstedt Landén 2020).

Wage work has been described as central to the constitution of gender and as a crucial aspect of patriarchal societies (Campbell 2006). Inability to live up to certain working life expectations may therefore affect people's gender constructions (Andersson 2003; Collinson and Hearn 2005), as well as their general wellbeing. As in many Western countries, declining employment in industries such as forestry and manufacturing in rural areas has led to structural changes in the labour market. These have resulted in a decline in the sorts of jobs traditionally done by men and an increase in those done by women (Little 2017). Norwegian researchers argue that these economic changes have affected gender norms associated with rural areas, in that women tend to be seen as more modern, capable, influential and independent, whereas rural men are pictured as backward, lonely, vulnerable and marginalized (Brandth and Haugen 2005:14, 16). Similarly, being affected by local gender norms, some peripheralized rural parts of Sweden traditionally dominated by agriculture are described as having 'untraditional gender contracts', as more women than men are small company owners, mainly in tourism (Forsberg, Lundmark and Stenbacka 2012: 19). Traditionally, rural cultures have centred around 'physically defined masculinities' and the 'heroisation of the work-hardened bodies of men' (Brandth and Haugen 2005: 16). In this chapter, I explore working life narratives that challenge normative and stereotypical descriptions of when 'men are most male' (Bull 2009: 448). The interviews for this study focus on the men's experiences of mental health issues while struggling to live up to masculinity norms and stressful working conditions. It has been highlighted that men in rural areas face health disadvantages, and mental health is of particular concern in Sweden and other Western countries (O'Callaghan and Warburton 2017). Men account for about 71 per cent of all suicides in Sweden, and they are much more common among men living in rural than urban areas (Folkhälsomyndigheten 2018).

It has been argued that continued discrepancy between rural and urban areas, including unequal access to welfare such as healthcare and education, may have extensive consequences for people's trust in society and democracy (SOU 2017). In the context of urbanization, working life conditions and changing masculinity norms, I explore through working life narratives how these men experience and identify with processes of peripheralization. What do these local stories say about work, masculinity, whiteness and rural living conditions?

The Ideal Worker in Relation to Masculinity, Place, Class and Whiteness

Work norms have been described as some of the strongest and most present ideologies in today's society (Paulsen 2010: 50), and wage work has been highlighted as crucial in reproducing men's symbolic and economic power in society. Losing a job, or not having the 'right one', may therefore play a large role in a subject's gender construction (Andersson 2003; Collinson and Hearn 2005: 294). I find the term *work society* (Paulsen 2010) helpful for analyzing and better understanding the role of *work*. This term addresses work norms that consider the will to work to be an almost essential aspect of being human (Andersson 2003: 38). I also find Acker's (1990: 152) concept of the *abstract worker* fruitful. This characterizes a full-time, highly qualified man (Olofsdotter and Sjöstedt Landén, 2014: 10), a type of bodiless worker who does not have to think about reproductive work. In relation to gender, I understand the abstract worker as being closely linked to a form of hegemonic masculinity, a type of *masculine work ideal* characterized by independence and autonomy, whose domination is justified through the marginalization of women and minorities (Connell 1995). The literature on men in relation to rurality tends to focus on hegemonic and traditional aspects of men's doing of gender, such as normative constellations of relationships and sexuality, and hegemonic and gender-conservative ideas and perceptions of men living in rural areas (Brandth 2016; Campbell, Bell and Finney 2006; Little 2002; Nilsson 2001; Nordin 2007; Pini 2008; Stenbacka 2011). As a result, we know little about how men living in these areas deal with vulnerable aspects of life, prompting calls for treatments of rural gender identities that fully engage with ideas of fluidity and movement without reproducing stereotypes (Little 2002: 667). Rather than understanding gender constructions of men living in rural areas as 'rural masculinities', inspired by Campbell and Bell (2000: 539), I focus on how subjects' gender constructions – masculinities – interact with aspects such as (rural and urban) place, work, class and whiteness on a 'symbolic level'.

Vallström and Vallström (2014: 8) suggest that rural areas in Sweden are often understood and described as the opposite of urban growth regions, and I understand the (abstract) ideal worker as strongly associated with *urbanity*. This also applies to ideas constructed around work, as specific areas and regions are associated with career building and more or less successful types of jobs. The peripheralization of work contributes to making urbanity central to success for the ideal worker. The literature on men's work in rural places focuses on hard physical work and hegemonic forms of masculinity in agriculture (Little 2002: 667), or investigates traditionally masculine unpaid work activities associated with rurality, such as fishing and hunting (Bye 2003). In focusing on processes of peripheralization in working life narratives, this chapter contributes to this field by challenging stereotypical descriptions of when 'men are most male' (Bull 2009: 448) and highlighting that peripheralization does not automatically (only) mean subordination.

In the literature on men, gender and rurality, white men are often in focus but are not necessarily the departure point for the analysis (Agyman and Spooner 1997). I understand Jämtland and rural northern Sweden as institutionalized by Swedish whiteness – a place where white bodies feel at home and alike (Ahmed 2011). In this respect, the ideal worker is also Swedish and white. *Race* and *ethnicity*, as well as *class*, seem to intermesh and play a crucial role in peripheralizing place. An American study of popular cultural media shows that privilege and power among whites seem to be stratified according to rural versus urban identities. In the labelling of white people into categories such as 'white trash', 'redneck' and 'hillbilly', the study highlights that a normative status of whiteness is affirmed (Hartigan 2003: 110–111). Hegemonic whiteness – the centre – assumes a non-racist position by ascribing racism to peripheralized groups of white people. This kind of political disgust and stigma is nothing new: forms of abjection change in relation to the constantly changing social and economic imperatives of neoliberalism and capitalism (Tyler 2013), and take different forms in different contexts. By portraying places such as rural Norrland and its inhabitants as unmodern, gender-conservative, problematic and dependent on welfare (Eriksson 2008; Stenbacka 2011; Vallström and Vallström 2014), and American 'rednecks' as unsophisticated and obsolescent (Jarosz and Lawson 2002), urban places are positioned as modern, progressive and liberal. In this process of othering, the poor white worker subject becomes peripheralized in relation to the middle-class white urban work subject of the centre.

Exploring Intersections of Place, Masculinity, Whiteness and Work Through Life Stories

In exploring how the interviewees in this study articulated their identities in relation to work, gender and place, I adopted a constructionist life course approach (Gubrium and Holstein 1998; Holstein and Gubrium 2007). This helped me to read how life courses were narrated and how the interviewees drew on different discourses in order to give meaning to experiences over time. The interview material drawn on here consists of six in-depth interviews (three with each interviewee), which were the first data collected for my ongoing PhD project focusing on rural men's gender constructions. The interviews were conducted in Jämtland between November 2018 and January 2019, and lasted between 1.5 and 2.5 hours. The participants were selected using various sampling methods, including traditional pinboards in libraries and healthcare centres in local villages, virtual pinboards on Facebook, and local media such as television, radio and newspapers. In addition, by handing out information flyers to people around me, I used my background experience of having grown up in the countryside myself as a way to start several snowball samples (Kvale and Brinkmann 2014). Ethical clearance to conduct the research was provided by Umeå University, requiring informed consent, confidentiality and anonymity. The participants are therefore anonymized.

The interviews took place in public places such as the university library and in the participants' work places. I understand interviews as a discursive practice and a situated language activity (Johansson 2005: 250). This means that I see emotions, ideas and values that circulate during the interviews as products of an active interplay between myself and the participant. I do not regard interviews or research as an objective process in which the narratives are solely those of the participants (Goodall 2003: 58–59). On the contrary, they are the result of jointly formulated interactions between myself as a researcher and the participants in the interview situation. For instance, I participated in and contributed to 'where the story was going' (Gubrium and Holstein 2008: 257) by asking follow-up questions, such as 'how did that make you feel?', and 'why do you think rural men are worse off when it comes to mental health?' In the initial interviews, my opening question – 'Please tell me about who you are and what you like to do' – focused on how the participants narrated themselves, important aspects of their lives and constructions of gender. By asking what work meant to them, as well as about the places in which they were and had been living, I sought to capture their everyday lives and processes of identity.

Participants and Analytical Framework

The life stories analyzed in this chapter were narrated by two people identifying as heterosexual men: Kjell aged 67, and Jan aged 42. Kjell grew up in a village about 40 minutes' drive from the city of Östersund. He left home at 14 and moved to Östersund, which is still common for youths starting their three years of gymnasium (secondary school) studies, since most schooling takes place in towns. After gymnasium, to find work he went to Stockholm, where he has lived for more than two decades. He has two adult children with a woman from whom he was divorced a couple of decades ago, and one young child with another women from whom he separated some years ago. The child stays with him every other week. For several years he has lived in a neighbouring village to where he grew up.

Jan grew up in Östersund and in a smaller town 20 minutes by car outside the city. He spent a lot of time with his grandparents, who lived in the countryside in the eastern part of Jämtland. He has never lived outside the county. He has been married twice, and has two children with his first wife and one with his current wife. They live in a village about 45 minutes outside Östersund.

Jan and Kjell are both from white Swedish working-class back-grounds. Kjell's father was a truck driver and his mother worked in the local grocery store. Jan's father was an assistant nurse, and after gaining a university degree in teaching, his mother worked as a teacher her whole life. Neither Jan nor Kjell studied at university. Despite having no tertiary education, Jan made a career in a local media business, with well-paid jobs throughout his working life. Kjell has mainly been self-employed, for instance driving a taxi, truck or bus, managing a petrol station and working as a door man. The areas in which they live are traditionally farming areas, as well as important places for the forestry and mining industries.

Methods of Narrative Analysis

I used narrative ethnography to interpret my data (Gubrium and Holstein 2009). A first reading of the transcribed interviews gave me a broad framework around how the interviewees narrated their selves and their life courses. During this step, I came to see that both Kjell and Jan had experienced *life crises* in relation to work and masculinity norms. When talking about work, Kjell told me that his business partner (also his girlfriend at the time) falling sick had led to a three-month period of 18-hour working days, after which he 'crashed'. The company went bankrupt and Kjell was hospitalized for several weeks. He described his life at this time as a 'catastrophe' where 'nothing in life worked'. About a year after the crash he made his first suicide attempt, and he made further attempts over the next four years. To escape a destructive relationship, during this period he lived and worked in Norway. Owing to the ser-iousness of his diagnosed burnout depression, Kjell has been living on governmental sick pay, and has helped friends with work-related tasks for more than ten years.

Jan too experienced a kind of existential crisis, partly due to a com-bination of what he called 'a dysfunctional masculine work culture' in a 'highly competitive environment' and the 'unquestionable expectation that you would want to work at least eight hours a day at the cost of life outside work', such as family and friends. He strongly disliked his workplace, a local media station, where the only right thing to do was, in his words, to 'perform'. On top of this, he was also struggling with the experience of socially destructive aspects of his childhood: alcoholism in the family resulting in emotionally distant relationships with his parents and, later in life, a difficult divorce from the mother of his two oldest children. As a result, he had ended up having to deal with a severe 'identity crisis', as he called it, where he had come to question all aspects of life, resulting in 'anxiety and chest pain'. After a couple of years in a newly-built house in a rural area close to Östersund, Jan and his wife had decided to move even further away from the town to 'the real country-side', as he described it. They had left 'all kind of modernity' and moved into a nineteenth-century, wood-heated croft in the middle of the forest.

In the second step of the analytical process, in focusing on the inter-viewees' narrative practices, I tried to understand how and when the participants drew on different discourses to narrate their ideas and ex-periences of going through life crises. The two men's processes of iden-tification and how they structured their life stories were practical and took place in lived circumstances, or narrative environments, the varied content of which affirmed or challenged new and old stories or dis-courses in social worlds. According to Gubrium and Holstein (2008: 254), 'Self stories come from somewhere, relate to larger stories, are shaped by other stories, and are affirmed and challenged through time by yet different and transformed narratives.' In this part of the process, since I was explicitly focusing on aspects of work, gender, place and whiteness, I approached the narratives analytically by conducting a *part content reading* (Gubrium and Holstein 2008: 246). Rather than fo-cusing on the form of the narratives, the meanings associated with the content were my primary interest. Inspired by Gubrium and Holstein (2008: 255), I used concepts such as *narrative linkage* (using the key cultural constructs of white urban middle-class career masculinity, work society, the gender-equal man and anti-Stockholm), *narrative footing* (how interviewees referred to the stories 'that can be told' about certain cultural constructs), *narrative maps* (ways of narrating life after dis-ruptive life changes) and *preferred narratives* (commonly used dis-courses, such as anti-Stockholm). As shown in O'Callaghan and Warburton's (2017) narrative ethnographic study of how aging Australian farming men construct their situations and self-identity in specific narrative environments, masculinity is a process of negotiation. By drawing on concepts such as class, heteronormativity and whiteness, I explored the process of negotiating masculinity, work and place in ev-eryday talk as a way to manage the narrative self in relation to processes of peripheralization.

Stories are never isolated, but exist within a broader social context, which I see as laden with globalized discourses. The interviewees' nar-ratives revealed layered interplays of the local, national and transna-tional (Gubrium and Holstein 2008: 253). Narratives are therefore relational rather than personal, in that they mirror aspects and accounts with which people engage in their everyday lives (Gubrium and Holstein 2008: 243). Furthermore, as Riessman Kohler (1990) highlights, rela-tional selves are not only shaped by but also shape their social worlds; they are *active relational selves*. In reading the narratives, I therefore tried to see not only *what* the participants' social experiences were like, but also *how* they amalgamated these social experiences (Gubrium and Holstein 2008: 245), for instance how they negotiated their positions in the processes of peripheralization.

In exploring peripheralization – a process I see as a set of changing, potentially contradictory and multi-layered discourses (Kellington 2002: 157) – I combined an intersectional perspective with a narrative approach. To better understand discrimination and address expressions of power structures, in the late 1980s black post-colonial feminists such as Kimberlé Crenshaw (1989) developed intersectional theory to highlight, for example, the interplay of race and gender (McCall 2005; Yuval-Davis 2006). Thus, to explore how gender, class, whiteness and place interact with and complicate each other, I adopted an intersectional approach to better understand processes of peripheralization in the working life narratives of two men living in northern rural Sweden.

Work, Place and Gender Through a Life Crisis

Listening to Kjell (67) and Jan (42), it was apparent that their experiences of going through life crises, which Kjell referred to as a 'crash' and Jan as an 'identity crisis', continued to pose challenges as they went about their lives. However, the consequences of these crises differed. Owing to the seriousness of his burnout depression, Kjell had been unable to return to work for over a decade and was about to retire. Jan still suffered from anxiety and chest pain, but was functioning well in the sense that he worked about 65 per cent of full-time. Despite differing experiences, both Kjell and Jan composed their stories using narrative linkages to the key cultural constructs of *white urban middle-class career masculinity, work society, the gender-equal man* and *anti-Stockholm*. I see these cultural constructs as discourses on the abstract worker (Acker 1990). Referring to these discourses enabled them to establish a firm narrative footing in these themes and to provide the listener with 'the kind of stories that could be told' (Gubrium and Holstein 1998: 169). These linkages, developed and positioned throughout their life stories, gave their stories coherence (O'Callaghan and Warburton 2017: 449).

Both interviewees said that before their breakdowns, despite strongly disliking it, wage work had been an important part of their identities. For instance, Kjell described work as a 'necessary evil'. Throughout his working life, he had often held several jobs simultaneously. He had often worked longer days or done overtime, not necessarily to further his career, but rather because 'that is what you do'. Similarly, although Jan 'had to share [his] everyday life with colleagues [he] was not comfortable with' and sometimes 'hid crying by the computer because people were so mean', it was still important to him to climb the career ladder, to gain status and make money. They had both followed the norm of working hard and for long hours, despite not liking it. Jan expressed this duality of safety and discomfort when following work norms:

> For me, as for many others, it was the norm, of course, and security; it was the way it was supposed to be, that culture, society is based on it. ... A man takes responsibility, a man provides for the family, takes care of himself. How important status symbols are to fit in ... attributes like jobs and cars and all these stereotypes are actually true, you know? I've also carried with me ... all these expectations of how it is to be a man. I'm an incredibly performance-focused person, which has sprung from a survival instinct. Perform, perform, perform.

By reflecting on the discourse of *white urban middle-class career masculinity* and norms of *work society* (Paulsen 2010), parts of their work stories, such as working more than full-time and being in work cultures that had made them ill, can be understood as constructed within their narratives. Qualities of the ideal worker – autonomy, hard work, not asking for help and not showing vulnerability – are embedded in the culture and in the construction of a masculine work identity, and can be seen as being central to norms of what a masculine work subject should be and do to become successful. As Jan put it, 'I did not have any time to reflect; it was not in my world that I could do things differently.' They never really questioned either moving to urban areas to find work or the amount of time they worked. In their ways of relating to wage work and narrating rurality as a place 'where you can't live' to either be successful or to be able to find a job, I trace discourses of performance and norms of 'work society', where the countryside is seen as inefficient and lagging behind at the periphery, while the modern city represents the centre. The culture around work society, with the unquestioned role of wage work in their lives and, especially for Jan, white urban middle-class career masculinity, provided not only a firm footing for their stories, but also guidelines on how to behave, think and act as a man in relation to work. Whereas building a career was highly important to Jan, Kjell described the expectation of autonomy and independence – not showing vulnerability and not asking for help – as more important to him, as indicated when he talked about how he had handled his work-related breakdown: 'I did not talk very much. I closed up emotionally, sat at home. Today I wonder what I was actually doing [during these years] ... I guess it was a way of keeping everything at a distance.' In the interviews, Kjell said that he had attempted suicide several times, which speaks to previous research suggesting that health issues are given lower priority and suicide is more common among men in rural areas than among men in general (Folkhälsomyndigheten 2018; O'Callaghan and Warburton 2017).

In the same way that Kjell and Jan positioned paid work as an essential part of their identities, studies show that wage work and being a breadwinner constitute an important part of many men's identities (Brandth and Haugen 2005: 14). Going through a work-related life crisis like Kjell and Jan, being unable to either work at all or as much as previously, may therefore affect future identifications with work. For instance, a study of Australian farmers shows that despite losing their physical strength as they aged, they tried to regain 'narrative control' over what an aging body is and hoped to retain their farming identities (O'Callaghan and Warburton 2017: 451). This did not seem to apply to Jan and Kjell. After experiencing their respective crises, it had become increasingly difficult for them to live up to the notion of the ideal worker. However, they did not seem to call their masculine/gender identities entirely into question. Rather, they seemed to articulate new *narrative maps* of how to go about their lives, where wage work had become something different from before. In the process of downshifting in terms of wage work and consumption and moving back to the countryside, Jan described how he had come to change many views on how a man can be and act:

> Men are really shit at talking. ... I've had to learn that, which has built all my new relationships. Good, healthy relationships are with women. ... I'm seen and included. ... And now I think it's uncomfortable to talk about myself, ... because I feel like I'm taking up too much space ... [And] the benefit of asking for help has become much more obvious ... and has helped me, hopefully, to change into a – I shouldn't say that I'm neutral and gender-equal, it has to be ... up to others to judge that – but I feel like we've made a project of what we've said that we're trying to be [more gender-equal] just by working [less].

Jan frequently highlighted how he had changed, as a man, after his 'identity crisis'. Through his wife and her contacts, he had come to think differently about friendships, focusing on making new kinds of relationships and ending some old friendships with men. He also said that he had changed as a parent, as he had gone from 'almost giving up on his parenthood' [being a good parent] to becoming a 'house wife' who 'spends a lot of time at home' and does most of the reproductive work. In his story, different relationships with work were coarticulated with various forms of masculinity and a kind of disidentification from 'other men'. In Jan's positioning as different from other men, whom he described as 'really bad at talking about feelings' and 'asking questions', I trace the presence of the *gender-equal man*, closely related to national discourses on the new gender-equal man (Järvklo 2008) and the good gender-equal man (Dahl, 2005). These discourses characterize a heterosexual man who is encouraged and expected to incorporate traditionally feminine duties of domestic work and parenting. I also see the discourse on the gender-equal man as a masculine subject who takes emotional responsibility, challenging the idea that men must be emotionally closed. This type of discourse, of a communicative, present, gender-equal father who does his share of the domestic work, is associated with status in the kinds of environment in which Jan moved – 'academic', 'politically conscious' and 'opinion-builders', as he put it. Although Kjell did not articulate the same kind of academic approach to gender equality and men as Jan, he also appeared critical of men's behaviour. He talked about masculinity norms as something that he had to 'deal with' in his everyday life in the village. When talking about the stereotype of the 'northern rural man' as tough and emotionally closed, I asked: 'Do you know of any such men?' Kjell answered:

> Yes, unfortunately. … Every day when I go into ICA [the local grocery store] in [village name], I see some of them, and then I'm reminded about them and I laugh. On the inside, imagine that it can be so … the blinkered horse … But … I've even got friends there, in that group. … Sometimes I can't resist telling them what I think. I say 'that's not fucking you', 'you're talking shit' … So it's – I'm pretty direct!

Listening to Jan and Kjell's narrations of new narrative maps following their crises makes me think of Andersson's (2003: 102) description of how being unemployed may create a discrepancy between norms and experiences, which gives room for reflexivity. This 'resistance of reflexivity', as Andersson describes it, can be found in Jan storying a revaluing of relationships and work norms, and Kjell talking critically about other men. They had also become more critical of urbanity, and had developed a kind of *Stockholm hatred* around which they structured their narratives of work, place and gender. Even though Kjell had lived in the capital for over two decades, he described Stockholm as 'horrible' and as:

> a jungle, because it's so overgrown … When I'm out walking in the city [Stockholm] and I don't have time to look at people because they've already passed me. Everything goes so, like this the whole time [waving quickly with hands]. People don't have time … for other people; they've hardly got time for the people they have to have time for. The pace is terrible. No one can leave without being affected. … No, I just think the city is disgusting, today.

This kind of local, *anti-Stockholm* discourse was frequently used by the interviewees and can be seen as a *preferred narrative* (Gubrium and Holstein 2008: 225). Being critical of Stockholm is very common in

Jämtland, and it is therefore easy to structure experiences and other narratives of one's life around it. However, it can also be seen as a critical response to negative ideas associated with Norrland and stereotypical ideas of northern rural men, often described in negative terms and depicted and understood from (urban) normative viewpoints (Eriksson 2010; Stenbacka 2011; Vallström and Vallström 2014). Therefore, the process of going through a crisis and being unable to live up to certain expectations of the abstract worker had not only made the interviewees peripheralized, but had also given them an observer position from where they seemed to have developed critical perspectives on work, place and masculinity norms.

Class, Heteronormativity and Swedish Whiteness in Negotiations of Peripheralization

Listening to Kjell and Jan talking about the places where they lived made me reflect on their ways of negotiating peripheralization, a process in which *class*, *heteronormativity* and *whiteness* seem to play a crucial role. At the time of the interviews, being younger and with a media business background, Jan was seen as more valuable in the labour market. His marriage to a woman with a stable monthly income afforded him many social privileges, and he had a wide safety and support network. Jan and his wife had moved to the village where they lived partly because his wife had relatives there, but also because they knew other people who lived there – cultural, political people who were critical of normative ways of working and living. This had probably contributed to enabling Jan to see the move to the countryside as a way 'to downsize economically and decrease his consumption habits ... because [he] wants to be completely free'. Jan narrated rurality as a place where he could fulfil himself – 'feel the seasons and recover in nature' – and described his home as a 'strongly spiritual place'. For Kjell, on the other hand, who had fallen sick when fairly close to retirement age and had no partner to share the costs of living, living in the countryside of Jämtland may have been a kind of 'last choice' because he could not afford anything else. Although Kjell said it was easier to live in his old home village after he had 'stood up to his old bullies' who still lived there, he described the village as 'terrible'. Fragments and comments like these are a reminder of the narratives of class and heteronormativity in Jan's and Kjell's life stories, and highlight their different positions in the process of peripheralization. This resonates with research by Jarosz and Lawson (2002: 15), who identify a gap between the views of people who live and work in the countryside and those of middle-class people who see it as a place for leisure, recreation, aesthetics and spiritual renewal. Jan talked very positively about other people in the village, some of whom did not necessarily have a historical connection with the place. Jan and his wife had become part of a creative class, and living in a picturesque croft in a farmyard afforded them status. Having grown up in the area and being older than Jan, Kjell seemed to relate differently to the place and the people living in the area. He knew many of them and their ancestors. Jan talked about how he had been 'healed' by 'living in a village where everyone is dependent on one another … for everyday life to function', and felt like he belonged, whereas Kjell was more critical of other people in the village, especially men. Talking about what it was like being a man living there compared with living in a city, Kjell said:

> Yeah, there's a big difference [between the village and the city]. In the city they [men] don't have to hide from someone they know, because there are just so many people around, so they can show a little empathy and some emotions and so on. But if you have grown up in the countryside with 200–300 people and all the men have been hunters for generations, and they know best and they've ordered their wives around and all of that, well, some people are strong enough to resist all that, but there's also those who don't resist it, and I see so many [of those men] in [village name].

Kjell's ways of relating to other men can be understood similarly to Sohl's (2014: 173) descriptions of working-class women's ways of distancing themselves from other working-class people who are 'trashy' or just 'regular working class' (Swedish 'arbetarklassvensson'). When talking about 'what men in the village are like', rather than describing a kind of belonging to a certain group (or class), Kjell *distanced* himself from the other 'hicks' (Swedish 'karlar') in the village, whom he described as traditional 'northern rural men', who 'can't talk about feelings'. In contrast, by drawing on the gender-equal man and positioning his life crisis as a kind of personal development, Jan described a kind of *belonging* to a modern, middle-class Swedish masculinity, a type of masculine subject associated with status in the creative class surrounding him. Thus, Jan identified with a modern, middle-class masculinity associated with higher status, while Kjell dis-identified from a working-class, rural masculinity associated with lower status. The latter can be seen as an expression of dissimulation: Kjell hid his class position by 'giving the appearance of being something else' (Sohl 2014: 173).

Interestingly, in this process of negotiating peripheralization, Jan seemed to take on a form of underdog position, which gave him certain privileges; whereas Kjell, who might actually be described as less socially and economically well-off than Jan, did not. By using a politically conscious type of language, with words such as 'patriarchal and capitalist structures', and by referring to 'power relationships between urban and rural', Jan positioned himself as subordinated, a position he enjoyed:

I kind of like being in a subordinated position. Because if you're subordinated then you get the right to criticize the powerful [Swedish 'sparka uppåt'], as everyone does. It doesn't matter where in the hierarchy you are, everyone is subordinated in relation to something, ... even if you're a billionaire.

Being an *active storyteller*, Jan assembled his life story and skilfully constructed narratives of being unable to live up to a certain masculinity and work norms as a political struggle. When talking about national identity, he described himself as 'Swedish of rural origin', despite having lived in town most of his life. Without denying that Jan had suffered and continued to suffer mentally in relation to masculinity norms and work norms, he was well-functioning and had a wide network of social connections:

> We save rivers, and we are really engaged. ... We're involved in a pretty big community engaged in urban versus rural issues. ... It's a pretty big academic community, ... we're strong opinion-builders who have linked arms, so we're creating a new – God this sounds elitist – ... community, with a pretty clear set of goals around how the countryside should be and be perceived.

In relation to this show of some bravado, Jan name-dropped nationally and locally famous cultural people, such as musicians and politicians, whom he knew or had met. This heroization of himself was also present when I asked him how he thought of being Swedish on colonized Saami land: 'I am probably the journalist who has written most about the Saami issue in Jämtland', he said. However, as he continued to talk, he questioned indigenous and Swedish peoples' differing rights to fishing and hunting in certain areas of Jämtland:

> The Saami people I grew up with, I can guarantee they're not reindeer herders. They own reindeer, but they live in houses in town. ... We've been to parenting group together. He [Saami man] works as a teacher; I'm a journalist. ... He has inherited a right: he can fish whenever and wherever he wants in these areas ... and [has] many big individual privileges, which I can only dream about. He can brag about it and say 'I can fish wherever I want.'

Without reflecting on his own position and behaviour, or individual rights, Jan criticized Saami people's rights based on how they lived. This not only illustrates his privileged position as Swedish, but also echoes the discourse of 'lapp ska vara lapp'(Lapps should be Lapps)[1] – ideas of what Saami people, culture and lifestyle are and should be (Lantto 2012). Coined in the early 1900s, the slogan was used as an argument for sustaining the 'natural' Saami cultures, and is still present in their exotification (Lundmark 2008). Jan said that he had 'read Saami literature', knew about 'the social heritage', sympathized with Saami people and 'would not for a second change life with a Saami person'. Yet he described Jämtland as 'just as much mine as the Saami people ... see it as theirs'. At times he found it unfair that he did not have access to fish in certain areas of Saepmie, and worried about what would happen if the Saami people gained the right to control more land in the mountains. Jan was also very critical of Saami male culture, which he described as 'patronizing of women [and] far from what he identifies with [as a man]'. In distancing himself from what he saw as the non-gender-equal Saami male culture, Jan reproduced a normative status of Swedish whiteness as gender-equal and better (Hartigan 2003: 110–111). These narratives of negotiating peripheralization – Jan's and Kjell's different ways of handling life crises – should therefore not be seen as simply doing a more or less privileged *Swedish whiteness* marked by class and heteronormativity (Hartigan 2003; Kellington 2002). They also say something about the possibilities for those who do not fit into the Swedishness and whiteness that Jan and Kjell have. Their move/return to rural areas can therefore be understood as a practice done just because they *can* (Kellington 2002), because this place is 'ready for their bodies' (Ahmed 2011: 135).

Conclusion

This chapter has shown that in the process of positioning themselves in relation to the ideal worker – the centre – the interviewees negotiated peripheralization differently. Through an intersectional lens, I have shown men's various options when experiencing the aftermaths of mental health issues. Using narrative linkages to discourses relating to the abstract worker, I have shown the reflexive interplay of lived experiences and material and social realities as these men created new narrative maps following their crises. This process included resistance of reflexivity (Andersson 2003: 102) to certain work and masculinity norms, and to positioning the urban gaze of rural people as less modern. How these men handled and coped with mental health issues was affected by heteronormativity and class. The chapter has also shown what the privileges of being Swedish and white may mean in relation to place and gender, and what kinds of bodies and subjects are unquestioned in certain areas. This means that peripheralization does not automatically mean subordination, but may also be a way, as for Jan, to gain status in certain narrative environments.

From a wider societal perspective, Kjell's and Jan's life stories of going through crises, being vulnerable and struggling to live up to certain masculinity and work norms, challenge traditional, stereotypical and normative descriptions of rural men (Little 2002: 667), and can be seen as challenging normative stories of 'when men are most male' (Bull 2009: 448). Despite mirroring themselves and trying to live up to aspects of work society and white urban middle-class career masculinity embodied in the ideal worker, which in many ways resonates with traditional masculinity, the men in this study did not simply cling to traditional masculinities. Rather, they seemed to draw on a wider repertoire of masculine storylines. For these men, it was evident that gender equality and being able to talk about vulnerable aspects of life were important and positive. The findings therefore also partly challenge ideas of Swedish gender equality associated with urbanity.

Exploring the narrative work and practices of these two men, and what they said about aspects of gender, work, place, class and whiteness, provides a better understanding of individuals' differing options for handling and creating healthy lives. Their stories are hardly singular. Their significance, although partially local, echoes the broader stories and circumstances in which their experiences and narratives are embedded.

Note

1 'Lapp' is a Swedish term for a Saami person, now considered derogatory and racist.

References

Acker, Joan. 1990. "Hierarchies, jobs, bodies: a theory of gendered organizations." *Gender and Society* 4(2), 139–158.

Agyman, Julian and Rachel Spooner. 1997. "Ethnicity and the rural environment." In *Contested countryside cultures: otherness, marginalisation and rurality*, eds. Paul Cloke and Jo Little, 197–217. London: Routledge.

Ahmed, Sara. 2011. *Vithetens hegemoni [The hegemony of whiteness].* Hägersten, Sweden: Tankekraft.

Andersson, Maria. 2003. *Arbetslöshet och arbetsfrihet: moral, makt och motstånd [Unemployment and being free from work: morality, power and resistance.* Uppsala, Sweden: Uppsala University Press.

Brandth, Berit. 2016. "Rural masculinities and fathering practices." *Gender, Place and Culture* 23(3), 435–450.

Brandth, Berit and Marit S. Haugen. 2005. "Doing rural masculinity: from logging to outfield tourism." *Journal of Gender Studies* 14(1), 13–22.

Bull, Jacob. 2009. "Watery masculinities: fly-fishing and the angling male in the South West of England." *Gender, Place and Culture* 16(4), 445–465.

Bye, Linda Marie. 2003. "Masculinity and rurality at play in stories about hunting." *Norsk Geografisk Tidsskrift – Norwegian Journal of Geography* 57(3), 145–153.

Campbell, Hugh. 2006. "Real men, real locals, and real workers: realizing masculinity in small-town New Zealand." In *Country boys: masculinity and rural life*, eds. Hugh Campbell, Michael Mayerfeld Bell and Margaret Finney, 87–104. University Park, PA: Penn State University Press.

Campbell, Hugh and Michael Mayerfeld Bell. 2000. "The question of rural masculinities." *Rural Sociology* 65(4), 532–546.

Campbell, Hugh, Michael Mayerfeld Bell and Margaret Finney. 2006. *Country boys: masculinity and rural life*. University Park, PA: Penn State University Press.

Collinson, L. David and Jeff Hearn. 2005. "Men and masculinities in work, organizations, and management." In *Handbook of studies on men and masculinities*, eds. Michael S. Kimmel, Jeff Hearn and Robert W. Connell, 289–310. Thousand Oaks, CA: Sage.

Connell, Raewyn. 1995. *Masculinities*. Berkeley, CA: University of California Press.

Crenshaw, Kimberlé. 1989. "Demarginalizing the intersection of race and sex: a black feminist critique of antidiscrimination doctrine, feminist theory and antiracist politics." *University of Chicago Legal Forum* 1(8), 139–167.

Dahl, Ulrika. 2005. "Scener ur ett äktenskap: Jämställdhet och heteronormativitet" [Scenes from a marriage: Equality and heteronormativity]. In *Queersverige [Queer Sweden]*, ed. Don Kulich, 48–71. Porvoo, Finland: WS Bookwell.

Eriksson, Madeleine. 2008. "(Re)producing a 'peripheral' region: Northern Sweden in the news." *Geografiska Annaler: Series B, Human Geography* 90(4), 369–388.

Eriksson, Madeleine. 2010. "(Re)producing a periphery: popular representations of the Swedish North." PhD thesis, Umeå University, Umeå, Sweden.

Folkhälsomyndigheten. 2018. "Statistik om suicid." Available at: https://www.folkhalsomyndigheten.se/suicidprevention/statistik-om-suicid/ (accessed 24 March 2020).

Forsberg, Gunnel, Mats Lundmark and Susanne Stenbacka. 2012. *Demografiska myter: Föreställningar om landsbygden – mer myter än faktiska fakta [Demographic myths: Conceptions of the countryside – more myths than actual facts]*. Estland, Sweden: Printon.

Giritli Nygren, Katarina and Sara Nyhlén. 2015. "Tärandets kartografi: styrningsrelationer med betydelse för arbetsmiljö i glesbygdens äldreomsorg" [The cartography of the tavern: governance relationships of importance to the working environment in rural elderly care]. In *Sprickor, öppningar och krackeleringar [Cracks, openings and crackles]*, eds. Angelika Sjöstedt Landén, Malin Bolin and Gunilla Olofsdotter, 49–68. Sundsvall, Sweden: FGV.

Goodall, H. Lloyd, Jr. 2003. "What is interpretive ethnography?" In *Expressions of ethnography: novel approaches to qualitative methods*, ed. Robin Patric Clair, 55–64. Albany, NY: SUNY.

Gubrium, Jaber F. and James A. Holstein. 1998. "Narrative practice and the coherence of personal stories." *The Sociological Quarterly* 39(1), 163–187.

Gubrium, Jaber F. and James A. Holstein. 2008. "Narrative ethnography." In *Handbook of emergent methods*, eds. Sharlene Nagy Hesse-Biber and Patricia Leavy, 241–264. New York, NY: The Guilford Press.

Gubrium, Jaber F. and James A. Holstein. 2009. *Analysing narrative reality*. London: Sage.

Hartigan, John. 2003. "Who are these white people? 'rednecks', hillbillies', and 'white trash' as marked racial subjects." In *White out: the continuing significance of racism*, eds. Ashley W. Doane and Eduardo Bonilla-Silva, 95–112. New York, NY: Routledge.

Holstein, James A. and Jaber F. Gubrium. 2007. "Constructionist perspectives on the life course." *Sociology Compass* 1(1), 335–352.

Jarosz, Lucy and Victoria Lawson. 2002. "'Sophisticated people versus rednecks': economic restructuring and class difference in America's West." *Antipode* 34(1), 8–27.

Johansson, Anna. 2005. *Narrativ teori och metod: med livsberättelsen i fokus [Narrative theory and method: with life stories in focus]*. Lund, Sweden: Studentlitteratur.

Järvklo, Niclas. 2008. "En man utan penis: heteronormativitet och svensk maskulinitetspolitik" [A man without a penis: heteronormativity and Swedish masculinity politics]. *Lambda Nordica* 13(4), 16–35.

Kellington, Stephanie. 2002. "Looking at the invisible: A Q-methodological investigation of young white women's constructions of whiteness." In *Working through whiteness: international perspectives*, ed. Cynthia Leviny-Rasky, 153–178. New York, NY: State University of New York Press.

Kvale, Brinkmann and Svend Brinkmann. 2014. *Den kvalitativa forskningsintervjun [The qualitative research interview]*, 3rd ed. Lund, Sweden: Studentlitteratur.

Lantto, Patrik. 2012. *Lappväsendet: tillämpningen av svensk samepolitik 1885–1971 [Patchwork: the application of Swedish Sami policy 1885–1971]*. Umeå, Sweden: Centrum för Samisk Forskning, Umeå Universitet.

Larsson, Emelie. 2018. "(De)politicising pregnancy-related risk: gender and power in media reporting of a maternity ward closure." *Health, Risk and Society* 20(5–6), 227–240.

Little, Jo. 2002. "Rural geography: rural gender identity and the performance of masculinity and femininity in the countryside." *Progress in Human Geography* 26(5), 665–670.

Little, Jo. 2017. *Gender and rural geography*. New York, NY: Taylor and Francis.

Lundmark, Lennart. 2008. *Stulet land: Svensk makt på samisk mark [Stolen land: Swedish power over Sami land]*. Stockholm, Sweden: Ordfront.

McCall, Leslie. 2005. "The complexity of intersectionality." *Signs* 30(3), 1771–1800.

Nilsson, Bo. 2001. "Män och (otidsenlig?) maskulinitet på norrländsk landsbygd" [Men and (old-fashioned?) masculinity in the rural countryside]. In *Sprickor i fasaden: Manligheter i förändring [Cracks in the facade: masculinities in change]*, ed. Claes Ekenstam, 106–123. Hedemora, Sweden: Gidlunds.

Nilsson, Bo and Anna Sofia Lundgren. 2015. "Logics of rurality: political rhetoric about the Swedish North." *Journal of Rural Studies* 37, 85–95.

Nordin, Lissa. 2007. "Man ska ju vara två: Män och kärlekslängtan i norrländsk glesbygd" [There should be two: Men and longing for love in the rural north]. PhD dissertation, Stockholm University, Stockholm, Sweden.

O'Callaghan, Zoe and Jeni Warburton. 2017. "No one to fill my shoes: narrative practices of three ageing Australian male farmers." *Ageing and Society* 37(3), 441–461.

Olofsdotter, Gunilla and Angelika Sjöstedt Landén. 2014. "Gender as headline and subtext: problematizing the gender perspective in an occupational health project." *Vulnerable Groups and Inclusion* 5(1), art. 23261.

Paulsen, Roland. 2010. *Arbetssamhället: hur arbetet överlevde teknologin [Work society: how work survived technology]*. Malmö, Sweden: Gleerups.

Pini, Barbara. 2008. *Masculinities and management in agricultural organizations worldwide*. London: Routledge.

Riessman Kohler, Catherine. 1990. *Divorce talk*. New Brunswick, NJ: Rutgers University Press.

SCB. 2017. "Folkmängd i landskapen den 31 december 2017" [Population in the landscape, 31 December 2017]. *Statistics Sweden* [website]. Available at: https://www.scb.se/hitta-statistik/statistik-efter-amne/befolkning/befolkningens-sammansattning/befolkningsstatistik/pong/tabell-och-diagram/helarsstatistik--forsamling-landskap-och-stad/folkmangd-i-landskapen-den-31-december-2017/ (accessed 24 March 2020).

Sjöstedt Landen, Angelika. 2020. "Taking to the woods: towards decentralized research in protest movements." Unpublished manuscript, Mid Sweden University, Sundsvall, Sweden.

Sjöstedt Landén, Angelika and Marianna Fotaki. 2018. "Gender and struggles for equality in mining resistance movements: performing critique against neoliberal capitalism in Sweden and Greece." *Social Inclusion* 6(4), 25–35.

Sohl, Lena. 2014. "Att veta sin klass: Kvinnors uppåtgående klassresor i Sverige" [Knowing their class: women's upward class mobility in Sweden]. PhD thesis, Uppsala University, Uppsala, Sweden.

SOU. 2017. *För Sveriges landsbygder: en sammanhållen politik för arbete, hållbar tillväxt och välfärd [For rural Sweden: a coherent policy for work, sustainable growth and welfare]*. Stockholm: Elanders Sverige AB.

Stenbacka, Susanne. 2011. "Othering the rural: about the construction of rural masculinities and the unspoken urban hegemonic ideal in Swedish media." *Journal of Rural Studies* 27(3), 235–244.

Tyler, Imogen. 2013. *Revolting subjects: social abjection and resistance in neoliberal Britain*. London: Zed Books.

Vallström, Maria and Mikael Vallström. 2014. "Hållbar utveckling på kartan och i verkligheten" [Sustainable development on the map and in reality]. In *När verkligheten inte stämmer med kartan: lokala förutsättningar för hållbar utveckling [When reality does not match the map: local conditions for sustainable development]*, ed. Mikael Vallström, 7–24. Lund, Sweden: Nordic Academic Press.

Yuval-Davis, Nira. 2006. "Belonging and the politics of belonging." *Patterns of Prejudice* 40(3), 197–214.

9 Risky Subjectivities

Peripheralization and Appropriation of Small-Ward Midwives' Work Practices in the Closure of a Rural Area's Maternity Ward

Emelie Larsson

Introduction

> I had the feeling it was already decided. It felt like they [the politicians] were sitting there, arms crossed, like 'we do this because it looks good'. That was my experience. No matter how much we presented, showed them statistics and numbers ... We provided medical care that I felt I could stand for, with good results. But in the debate, the actual reason [for closing] was lost (Malin, midwife).

On 31 October 2016, midwives from the maternity ward at a hospital in Sollefteå, Sweden met in one of their houses to collectively await a political decision on whether or not BB Sollefteå, the hospital's maternity ward, would close. It was not the first time that closing the ward had been discussed: over the years, this had been presented as a measure to decrease costs in the region. Yet this time everything seemed to indicate that the closure would actually be carried out. Thus, when the decision came, no one – at least not the staff working at BB Sollefteå – was surprised.

Sollefteå, a town with a population of 8,000, is located in the inland of the Swedish region of Västernorrland. The closure of BB Sollefteå followed that of the hospital's emergency ward, and was scheduled for 1 February 2017; much earlier than the staff and people living in the area had expected. Several protest actions were initiated. For example, in cooperation with The Worker's Educational Association (Sweden's biggest educational association), midwives from BB Sollefteå started a course on how to give birth in a car, and the day before the closure, locals occupied the hospital entrance. As I write this chapter, the occupation is still active, four years since the closure. Fear that the decision will lead to women giving birth in cars or en route to hospital is rooted in the longer distance that women must now travel to the closest ward. Women in Sollefteå must travel 100 kilometres by car or bus to reach a neighbouring town with a maternity ward, a journey that takes between an hour and 40 minutes and two hours, depending on the weather conditions. For women living outside Sollefteå, in the opposite direction from neighbouring towns with maternity units, the distance can be up to 220 kilometres.

Swedish healthcare is organized into regional assemblies, and political decisions regarding healthcare are made independently in the regions. Nevertheless, the regions follow national guidelines when it comes to organization, and since the 1980 and 1990s, when New Public Management (NPM) was introduced into Swedish healthcare, mathematical models and measurements have increasingly been used to improve efficiency (Hood 1991). Following the logic of NPM, everything that an organization produces, as well as human values such as care, is approached in terms of efficiency in an economic market (Sjöstedt Landén 2016). There is thus little room for less measurable values, such as emotional work or the social effect of maintaining healthcare services in rural municipalities. The fact that it had become harder to justify smaller health units on economic grounds was the reason for closing BB Sollefteå and several other wards and health units formerly located in Sweden's sparsely populated northern inland. Today, there are two maternity wards in Västernorrland, both located on the Baltic coast. As Västernorrland stretches from the west coast to halfway into Sweden, the inland (where BB Sollefteå was located) is now poorly provided for.

In this chapter, I explore midwives' subjectivities in a process in which work practices associated with smaller maternity wards were initially described as *risky* in political discussions prior to the closure, but were subsequently adopted in a risk-prevention programme after the ward closed. The analysis builds on interviews with midwives who were working at Sollefteå hospital when the closure decision was made. Following the notion of previous research that neoliberal organizational patterns adapt efficiently to new conditions and contexts (e.g. Bondi 2005; Sjöstedt Landén 2016), this study uses the closure of BB Sollefteå to show how power structures such as gender, class, race and place operated in the simultaneous peripherialization and appropriation of small-ward midwives' work practices. The overall aim is thus to investigate how midwives' subjectivities were formed in the context of healthcare restructuring, alongside the overlapping processes of centralizing healthcare units and constructing work practices in large, specialized hospitals at the centre of discourse on Swedish maternity care.

The Closure of BB Sollefteå

The closure of BB Sollefteå not only sparked local protests, but also soon became a national symbol of both a perceived gap between Sweden's rural and urban areas and a perceived crisis in Swedish maternity care, manifested in few beds in big city hospitals and the closure of wards in smaller towns (Larsson 2016). As the protesters refused to accept the economic rationale for the ward's closure, politicians in the regional assembly started to stress that the ward could not guarantee patient safety. One reason that was brought to the fore was Sollefteå hospital's difficulty in recruiting physicians, and another was the relatively low number of births in the ward, averaging one per day. The latter was deemed both costly and risky, because midwives at the hospital did not have the same practice in delivering babies as midwives on bigger, more specialized wards.

At the time BB Sollefteå closed, 11 midwives were working on the ward, and two midwives were working on the gynaecological ward. Shortly after the closure, a researcher-led project, 'Barnmorska hela vägen' ('Midwife all the way'), which was partly financed by the region, was introduced at the hospital. The project included five midwives responsible for women who were about to give birth for the first time, or were afraid of giving birth or travelling to give birth. When it was time for a woman to travel to one of the closest hospitals with a maternity ward, the midwife would follow her car (driving behind it), and once at the maternity ward would deliver the baby. Midwives involved in the project also took turns to be on call by telephone, enabling parents to call for consultations, for example concerning when to travel to the hospital. The project followed the caseload model, which stipulates that a single midwife should be responsible throughout a woman's pregnancy and labour, from early consultation to delivery (Hildingsson 2018). Thus, seven midwives remained at the hospital after the closure: two in gynaecology and five on the caseload project.

Together with the union, the hospital management decided that the five positions on the project and one in the gynaecology department (one midwife from the gynaecology department had recently left her position) would be offered to the midwives who had been working at the hospital for longest. The remaining midwives would be offered other positions at the hospital (but not as midwives). However, the positions on the project proved to be harder to fill because, according to a hospital manager, many of the midwives 'viewed it as a betrayal against the fight for BB [Sollefteå] if they had joined the project'. Many midwives were still actively protesting against the closure and were unwilling to collaborate with the region. However, the positions were eventually filled with midwives from BB Sollefteå.

Interviews with Midwives

This chapter builds on four interviews with three midwives whom I interviewed in January and February 2019. These were part of my dissertation project, which used the case of BB Sollefteå to explore how risk is constructed alongside power structures such as gender and centre–periphery. I interviewed two of the midwives on a single occasion, and did a follow-up interview with one of them by telephone in May the same year. In addition, I interviewed one of the managers at Sollefteå hospital to gain details about the closure, such as how many midwives worked on the ward prior to and after the closure. I started to contact midwives for interviews at the beginning of 2017, but in dialogue with researchers working on the recently initiated caseload project, I agreed not to interview midwives involved in the project, as they were already carrying a heavy workload. I thus ended up interviewing midwives who were working at Sollefteå hospital when the decision to close the ward was made but had subsequently quit their employment at the hospital. The midwives differed in the time they had spent in the profession and at Sollefteå hospital, as well as their work roles as midwives at the hospital. To ensure anonymity, I provide no further details of the individual midwives, as relatively few (11) were working on the ward when the political decision to close it was announced.

My three initial interviews were quite open, yet I suspected that the discussion would somehow be about resistance, so I asked some questions about that. However, the experiences that the midwives shared with me were more complex than I had expected: they *did* talk about resistance, but also about not having the energy to resist, and about wishing life could just go back to normal. I processed the transcribed interview material through a thematic narrative lens (Riessman 1993), exploring the political narration of midwives' subjectivities (as perceived by themselves) in contrast to midwives' own narration of their subjectivities, which can be read as a counter-narrative. Within both narratives, I explored the theme of risk, and how this linked with power structures.

Importantly, the chapter reflects the experiences of only some of the midwives. The fact that the midwives I interviewed had all left BB Sollefteå is likely to have affected the themes that appeared in the interviews. Interviewing midwives still employed at BB Sollefteå, especially those working on the caseload project, might have evinced different answers to my questions, and different themes might have been highlighted.

Changing Terms for Midwifery in Sweden

Midwifery in Sweden is closely connected with the development of the welfare state, and the organization of today's maternity care must be understood both in light of the 1930s welfare project, and the neoliberal restructuring of the healthcare system in the 1980s and 1990s. In 1938, the state started to provide financial support for maternity units as part of the welfare programme, yet birth institutions were already very common in Swedish cities by this time. In Western countries where the institutionalization of childbirth did not take place in a welfare context, for example the USA, middle- and upper-class women were the first to start to give birth in institutions. In Sweden, on the other hand, the early institutions were meant for poor and unmarried women, and were often connected with orphanages. As mortality rates were reported to be lower among women giving birth in institutions, women of higher classes soon started to request institutional births. In the mid 1920s, 80% of births in Sweden's larger cities took place in an institution (Wisselgren 2005). The initial setting for midwifery in Sweden, where midwives cared for poor and morally rejected women, contributed to the construction of midwifery as a profession building on a middle-class, white femininity.

It took a little longer for institutionalization of childbirth to spread as an option in northern Sweden; yet in the 1930s, with the establishment of state support, many units were set up in smaller northern towns (Wisselgren 2005). Nevertheless, not all women gave birth in an institution, or even with assistance of a midwife, as midwives would often be unable to reach those in remote areas in time, and helpers (elders with traditional knowledge) were forbidden (Lindroth 1907). Reindeer-owning Sami[1] women often continued to move with their families with the changing seasons, and thus gave birth without institutional assistance (Sköld et al. 2011). Institutionalized maternity care was therefore not primarily a classed matter, but a matter determined by place (densely populated areas) and race.

The institutionalization of childbirth meant that midwives who had previously worked independently were now positioned below physicians in the institutions. To some extent, midwives retained their positions as being ultimately responsible for childbirths, in contrast, for example, with England, the US and Canada, where physicians often took over responsibility for childbirths (Milton 2001); yet they regularly needed to consult physicians before making decisions (Öberg 1996). The institutionalization and medicalization of childbirth were driven largely by political decisions, such as forbidding helpers and giving financial support to institutions. However, as we have seen, institutionalization was also requested by women (Vallgårda 1995). Nevertheless, it is important to remember that such requests came from middle- and upper-class married women in the bigger cities. The poor and unmarried women who initially gave birth in institutions did so because they had little choice, and for rural and Sami women living in remote, sometimes roadless areas, travelling to an institution was simply not an option.

In feminist studies of the institutionalization of childbirth, the transition from midwife-led births to births in medical environments is often described as a patriarchal 'take-over' and an appropriation of traditional female knowledge inherited over generations (e.g. Cahill 2001). In the Swedish context, such claims may be misleading, as the women who became midwives at the end of the nineteenth century had not inherited knowledge from their elders and would have been unlikely to have become helpers if they had not studied to become midwives. Thus, class-based appropriation (overlaid by geography) was already at work in the origin of midwifery as a profession in Sweden. A postcolonial feminist analysis of its institutionalization and professionalization may thus be more useful. For example, Hill Collins (2005) notes that the knowledge on which institutionalized maternity care was built was not only inherited over generations of women, but also often developed within indigenous communities, who are poorly represented among midwives and physicians. She also suggests that how institutionalized childbirth is organized sets a Westernized, white agenda for how childbirth should be (Hill Collins 2005). In the Swedish context, this is expressed both through an unquestioned linking of safety and technology (Kopare 1999), and through normative practices such as encouraging fathers (while discouraging others) to attend births (Sandell 2018).

Since the reorganization of Sweden's healthcare system in the 1980s and 1990s when the welfare model was replaced by one inspired by NPM, resulting in mixed welfare and neoliberal ideals, it has become harder to justify smaller wards economically (Wingborg 2017). Midwife-led homebirths are now only options in the capital, Stockholm, and in Umeå, the biggest town in northern Sweden, and they are still very uncommon even in these two cities. Thus, the large, urban, highly medicalized and specialized institutions have come to set the agenda for Swedish maternity care. The historical and contemporary organization of maternity care in Sweden must therefore be understood not only as Westernized and white (following Hill Collins' theorization of institutionalized maternity care), but also as gendered, classed, determined by geographical place, and embedded in a specific ideological context.

Small-Ward Midwives' Work Practices as Risk and Risk Prevention

In Sweden, like other Nordic countries, the 1990s restructuring of maternity care resulted, as previously noted, in a mixture of neoliberal and welfare ideals that set the rules for how care work is performed: on the one hand, patients' options are still quite strictly controlled, and on the other, choice and individual responsibility are emphasized (Leppo 2012). Characteristic of neoliberal models are their flexibility and ability to coexist with other, sometimes apparently contradictory, ideological values, whether totalitarian or social democratic (Bondi 2005). The Swedish case is thus no exception.

The introduction of NPM guidelines into Swedish healthcare, which has led to a focus on specialization and efficiency, places smaller wards at the periphery of the healthcare discourse. It makes practices associated with work on these wards appear to be a risk to patients, because specialization is assumed to go hand-in-hand with advanced skills. Thus, feminist risk scholars observe that how we construct risks is linked to ideology and norms in society (e.g. Douglas 2002; Boholm 2003), which is highly relevant to understanding the effect of healthcare restructuring. Furthermore, as has been noted by risk scholars using an intersectional approach, risk is *done* in parallel with categories such as gender and race (Giritli Nygren et al. 2017). Drawing on the work of intersectional feminist theorists (e.g. Crenshaw 1989; McCall 2005), the *doing risk* theory acknowledges how power structures interact with each other, and with risk as a concept. In analyzing the construction of the BB Sollefteå midwives' work practices as unsafe, I am interested in how understanding certain worker subjectivities as *risky* contributed to such a construction, and to what extent gender, class, race and place were at work in this process.

In her research on nurses' identities, Selberg (2012: 67) notes that nurses occupy a 'semi-independent middle position', meaning that they are positioned above assistant nurses (a profession labelled as working class, which is not associated with whiteness to the same extent as nursing or midwifery) but below physicians (a high-skilled, masculinized profession). In addition, midwives working on smaller wards maintain a specific position in relation to other midwives in the region. Giritli Nygren and Nyhlén (2017: 340) show how their interviewees – public-sector managers working in elderly care in rural areas in Sweden – navigated a discourse where the rural was understood as the periphery, viewing themselves as 'a drain on the public purse'. Applying this understanding of urban centre and rural periphery as a division based on both place and power, in terms of distance/closeness to social norms and institutions (Langholm 1971), the midwives at BB Sollefteå were positioned as peripheral in relation to the midwives working on the region's large, specialized ward.

The 1990s restructuring also brought about a *professionalization* of healthcare, meaning that nurturing was deprioritized in favour of medical practices. Physicians, nurses, midwives and assistant nurses all perform body work, in the sense that they work *on bodies*, yet their practices vary, ranging from very instrumental and practical interactions with bodies, to sitting down and talking with patients (Selberg 2012). Again, midwives are located on a middle level, and their work is not always easily defined. Some aspects are instrumental, some are nurturing, and the two are often combined. In Sweden, nurses perform advanced tasks that were previously assigned to physicians, yet are also expected to cover for assistant nurses as cuts are made in the healthcare sector. Although labelled as a skilled profession, the care work embedded in nursing is consistently viewed as a 'feminine quality', and thus as unskilled (Granberg 2014: 140). For midwives, who are often more highly trained than nurses but work exclusively on or with women's bodies, this clash is even more salient.

However, workers' identities, in terms of categories such as gender, class, race and place, are not only determined by the idelological organization of work. Employees do not form their identities only in line with managerial naming, but also in meetings with clients and patients (Williams 2006, cited in Selberg 2012). In the case of midwives at BB Sollefteå, their identities (gendered, classed, racialized and geographically bound) are likely to have been shaped in relation to management, patients, each other, and the protests that took place in and around the hospital.

Feminist research on worker subjectivities suggests that because workers move between spheres even when at work, and respond to managers as well as to others, their identities are complex to the extent that they may conform with some managerial naming, while resisting others. Identities are thus fluid and can be perceived as contradictory (Salzinger 2003). Following a neoliberal organizational logic, female workers are often understood as mainstays, and are generally not perceived as *risky* in terms of troublemakers and carriers of resistance (Walkerdine 2010). To some extent, resistance among female workers may thus be seen as resistance against neoliberal constructions of (feminine) worker identities. Yet, as worker subjectivities are complex, resisting some power orders does not automatically mean resisting others. Granberg's (2016) research on nurses' strikes in northern Sweden reveals how the ethics of care embedded in nursing was used against nurses in managers' rhetoric, yet was simultaneously appropriated by nurses, who constructed the protest as a form of care. They thus resisted certain notions of femininity, while drawing on others. In theorizing risk, Giritli Nygren et al. (2017) claim that just as risk can be done, it can also be undone; and just as the undoing of risk may intersect with the undoing of power categories, it may also intersect with a doing of categories. Thus, following Salzinger's (2003) notion that worker subjectivities are complex and sometimes contradictory, resisting *risky worker subjectivities* may intersect with an undoing of some power structures and a doing (intentionally or unintentionally) of others.

Small-Ward Midwives as Risky Subjectivities

Returning to the day of the decision to close BB Sollefteå, although it was highly expected by the midwives, one of those I interviewed said it felt good to be gathered together when the decision was finally announced. The midwives I interviewed all talked about a good working environment, and described how they were close to each other. However, one midwife also said that the process prior to the closure had led to 'paranoia' amongst them. Differing priorities and efforts to resist had created tensions between them, as had the poor self-esteem resulting from the politicians' labelling of BB Sollefteå as *risky*. All three midwives to whom I talked described having experienced an attack on their professional identities as a means to legitimize the closure. Malin, a midwife who had recently chosen to quit her job at Sollefteå hospital, explained the procedure as follows:

> It was a big savings plan, that was what it was. But then the other came, and it was hard to handle. I remember this [politician's name] said something like 'Look at Sollefteå, they have so little to do, they don't do anything' – something like that. Like there we were, at our work shifts, waiting around. ... I think that in the debate, they lost what it was really about. Is it economy? Is it patient safety? They mixed those two *all the time* ... [I think it was] to get the citizens on the train. You understand better if they say 'This is not safe – it's not enough staff.' You understand that as a citizen. As a tax payer, you want the maximum; but as a patient, you want it to be safe. So I think the concepts became too many.

This quote reflects a narration of safety which is rooted in the Nordic welfare context, where a large workforce and a high-tech environment are seen as indicators of safety. Hill Collins (2005) suggests that ideas of what maternity care should be commonly build on white, Westernized ideals, and the narration of BB Sollefteå as unsafe mirrors the same ideals in illustrating what maternity care in Sweden *should not be*. Thus, following Giritli Nygren et al.'s (2017) theorization of how risk is *done,* the doing of small maternity wards as risky leads to a doing of the large, specialized ward at the centre of Swedish healthcare discourse, while small, local wards and the alternative health ideals they substantiate, such as equal distribution/closeness of care and integrated care practices, are made peripheral.

The group of patients that Malin and her politicians depicted appeared to take such a discourse for granted, as they equated few staff with lack of safety. It therefore seems reasonable to assume that they had grown up in Sweden, or a country with a similar health discourse. The health narrative in which large, specialized wards are the norm is less likely to be perceived as a given by some groups of newly arrived immigrants,[2] who may be used to other forms of maternity care, and may lack the wherewithal (e.g. a car) to travel safely to a distant ward. The narration of patient safety thus reflects an imaginary (white) group of reflexive female patients, who may question political decisions but are also able to reconsider if their initial position proves to be counterproductive.

When talking about their work, all the midwives mentioned delivering babies as one of several work tasks. Besides deliveries, they mentioned abortions, caring for pregnant women hospitalized for observation and gynaecology patients, and nurturing/talking to patients. Nevertheless, deliveries were repeatedly used as a measure of efficiency in political discussions. The number of deliveries a day (one) was repeated, and the rest of the day was assumed to be filled with 'waiting', as Malin expressed it. Deliveries, being the most critical and skilled part of midwifery, and also one of the most easily measurable, seemed to outcompete other forms of care in political discussions, following a neoliberal logic that Selberg (2012) notes is characterized by neglect of feminized work such as caring for patients. However, the single focus on births also reflects a patriarchal societal ideal where deliveries are seen as midwives' *real* work task or calling, while other skilled work, such as abortions, is seen as (bad) work that is included in the deal. This may be linked with the ethics of care so deeply associated with midwifery and other forms of nursing (Granberg 2016). From a patriarchal point of view, deliveries are associated with care more than, for example, abortions. The fact that small-ward midwifery inevitably includes a greater diversity of integrated, less measurable tasks ('everyone does a little of everything', as one midwife put it) makes it *risky*, in the sense that it does not fit into the neoliberal (masculine, urban) model of care.

Although the midwives did not see deliveries as their single work task, they still mourned the fact that this task was being taken away from them. In a follow-up interview, Malin said that assisting in deliveries is not just fun and emotionally rewarding, but is also the 'most technically and intellectually advanced' part of midwifery and is highest ranked by midwives. She also highlighted that deliveries are a sphere in which the midwives themselves have most power:

> The delivery is the midwives' playing field, fully. We take care of the deliveries by ourselves – as long as they are normal, we take care of them. The physicians come, and we consult each other and work together, but ... it is us who decides and tells when ... like 'Now I need help.'... Then a physician arrives, and you get that help, and you do it together. You feel very *important* in healthcare there. You have a central ... place.

In her initial interview Malin said that she had sometimes considered quitting her job as a midwife, as she was so tired of 'savings, savings, budget, budget', and of 'being a cost who does not contribute enough'. Her feelings connect with the findings of Giritli Nygren's and Nyhlén's (2017) study of Swedish public managers working in rural units, who had to navigate a discourse in which their work was seen as a cost and a burden for urban areas. Malin's experience of navigating such a discourse was evident in her experience of being in the delivery room as a 'safe zone', free from the neoliberal demands for cost-cutting and efficiency that made her feel unimportant. It was a space where she felt important and had 'a central place'.

Following Selberg's (2012) notion that nurses occupy a semi-independent middle position, above assistant nurses and below medical doctors, deliveries can be seen as the practice that distinguishes midwives from other professional groups in the hospital. In light of feminist research that theorizes deliveries as a space performed by midwives yet controlled by doctors (e.g. Öberg 1996), it is interesting that Malin highlighted that midwives and physicians work collaboratively, side by side during deliveries. Deliveries were thus narrated as a space where midwives are professionally equal to physicians. In her follow-up interview, Malin explained that the midwives' desire to continue assisting in deliveries had made them want to join the caseload project at Sollefteå hospital. Although they had to spend time driving rather than being on the ward, and even though it might be tough to lead a delivery in a new place and with new people, it might still be worth it for some midwives, as they would get to continue with deliveries. In order to uphold a rewarding worker identity in terms of both emotional and technical stimulation and status, midwives are willing to accept uncomfortable working conditions and compromise their own ideals, given that the manager I interviewed said that it had been difficult to fill the positions on the project. The fact that deliveries are a relief from neoliberal demands for cost-efficiency also, ironically, makes midwives more prone to conform with new, neoliberal ways of organizing their work.

Midwives themselves valuing deliveries so highly thus formed the basis for both resistance to the closure, because being able to continue with deliveries was so important, and conformity with a neoliberal perspective in which the number of deliveries has come to define midwifery. This proves that maintaining a certain worker identity may mean simultaneous resistance and conformity with managerial naming, as Salzinger (2003) notes. Maria, who besides working at Sollefteå hospital had experience of working as a midwife on a bigger ward, said that she had sometimes experienced that the attitude toward small-ward midwives who carry out few deliveries a day was internalized by those working at the region's bigger hospital in Sundsvall:

> I have always felt a bit that they ... that they think they are a bit better. Maybe more people have told you that? It's not all of them, I shall say ... not all of them. Many of them I have had good contact with, so it's not *all* midwives at Sundsvall, but ... Some of them. They think Sollefteå should close because it's so small, that's what I've heard when I've been there [at BB Sundsvall].

Valuing high numbers of deliveries and high-tech, bigger wards constructs small-ward and big-ward midwives' worker identities differently. The fact that midwives on bigger wards take care of more deliveries and work in a more technological environment labels them as more skilled than small-ward midwives. After the interview, Maria emailed me to say that when she had worked on a bigger ward herself, she had thought the same way about small-ward midwives: this mentality was internalized by those working on the bigger ward. The doing of specialized care as the centre of the Swedish health discourse, and more holistic 'do-a-little-of-everything' practices as *risky* thus follows urban and masculinized ideals that contribute to constructing small-ward midwifery as a peripheral other in healthcare. Maria's quote illustrates that the professionalization of healthcare (rooted in 1990s neoliberal restructuring) contributed to a deprofessionalization of small-ward midwifery that began long before the closure of BB Sollefteå, yet could be used as a tool in political discussions before and after the closure.

Renegotiating Professional Identities

When I interviewed the midwives, they all agreed that the working environment at BB Sollefteå had been good, and they sometimes offered a counter-narrative to the political narration of small wards as *risky*. Seen from the perspective of risk being something that can be done as well as undone (Giritli Nygren et al. 2017), the midwives were trying to *undo* risk by highlighting how BB Sollefteå was a *safe* and patient-friendly environment. Maria often compared her experience of the environment on the big ward with that at BB Sollefteå. Like the other midwives, she often returned to the issue of time:

> Working with the women was the same, but then we had more deliveries, so you were very pressured. So yes, the work rate is higher, or was higher then, at the bigger clinic. Then you didn't have time to be with the women all the time, as you might have wished – you had to run between them. It was very efficient. In Sollefteå you had that time. But that is a luxury today. You should not be allowed to have that, it seems.

Maria highlighted that although there were fewer midwives working at BB Sollefteå, they had more time to care for the women. She also distinguished between deliveries, as the more technical and skilled part of midwifery, and 'being with the women', suggesting that on the bigger ward, the latter form of care had been phased out. How she managed to *undo* small-ward midwifery as a risk and instead *do* risk in the environment of the bigger ward can be seen as resistance to the neoliberal and urban narration of midwifery. Her *undoing* of BB Sollefteå as risky thus intersected with the undoing of this narrative. Malin also stressed that having few deliveries a day does not necessarily mean that the work is less skilled, as small wards require midwives to do a little of everything. Being able to perform many different tasks may make one more flexible and confident, skills that are useful when managing deliveries. Petra, who had also quit her employment at Sollefteå hospital following the closure, offered an alternative image of BB Sollefteå, describing it as safe and explaining the working environment on the ward as follows:

> It's a shame they closed, because I think Sollefteå hospital was an incredibly good hospital … If the patient was there, they always got help because you saw a gain in that. I think we worked in a good, effective way and … and we all knew each other, everyone who worked there was important for the *care* – I think it was really good what we had.

Like Maria, Petra emphasized that there was always time to care for patients. She thus also drew on a narrative of 'being with the women' as a social rather than economic *gain*. Both Malin's and Petra's narrations of the smaller ward as safer and more patient-friendly than the large, specialized ward can be read as attempts to shift the current health discourse, highlighting the centrality of integrated practices on the small ward.

Petra also highlighted the value of feeling important, as did Malin when explaining why deliveries are so central for midwives. The fact that being important kept being repeated indicates that the neoliberal restructuring of midwifery, which Malin referred to as being seen as a cost, collided with the very core of midwifery's professional identity – being needed and doing something important.

Sometimes the midwives also mentioned acts of resistance that they or their colleagues had undertaken before the decision had been made, when political discussions had still been under way. Malin explained that she had eventually got so tired of hearing talk about BB Sollefteå's low number of births that she had decided to check the statistics herself. Before a meeting with politicians, she had prepared statistics from BB Sollefteå and from the other two hospitals in the region:

> As it was about how many deliveries each midwife had – it was a lot about that in the media – I sat down and counted [the deliveries] in the region. How many does every midwife in the county have? … [BB Sundsvall] has so many staff, I knew how many midwives were employed there, I knew how many babies were born at each clinic, and then it was quick to do a computation: this is how many it is. And then you also know that there are locums and temporary

> doctors, who also deliver babies. And from that [the calculation], it was exactly the same [number per midwife]!

Malin's initiative to present the statistics is a concrete example of attempting to *undo risk* as a tool for resistance. The accusation that there were too few midwives at BB Sollefteå lost legitimacy, as it turned out that the number of women giving birth per midwife was the same in the county's three hospitals. However, Malin's resistance required her to follow a neoliberal logic that used the number of childbirths to define midwifery. Again, resistance was mixed with conformity, which Salzinger (2003) notes is common in the formation of worker identities. Although Malin was *undoing* BB Sollefteå as risky, she was not undoing the terms of midwifery, which encompasses other ideals like those presented above.

Overall, resistance was not unproblematic and easily performed; it was embedded in both the power orders within which midwifery is located, and the ideological playing field on which all health workers move. On the one hand, the fact that the midwives were so active, both in public protests against the closure and in continued resistance to the decision at their workplace, meant that they rejected neoliberal (feminine, conforming) subjectivities (Walkerdine 2010). Yet on the other hand, the form of their resistance was loaded with other power narratives, and might, as in the example above, strengthen the neoliberal logic behind closing the ward, even if the true reason was not the low number of births.

New Work Tasks, New Worker–Patient Relations

At the same time as work practices in the small maternity ward were being targeted as a risk in political discussions prior to the closure of the ward, decision makers in the regional assembly were acknowledging that the longer distance to obtain maternity care was worrying expectant parents, and thus the caseload project was initiated immediately before the closure. Working as a midwife at BB Sollefteå had previously been described as *risky*, but now the argument was increasingly directed toward risk prevention. The midwives I interviewed all mentioned the project and had differing opinions on it; they were also firm in pointing out that opinions differed amongst them. Maria said that travelling with the women to the hospital is not a particularly new practice, as it was common in northern Sweden in the early days of midwifery; and Malin stressed that the midwives on the project have to deliver babies in a 'new' work environment, which she said was 'tough'. Petra said there were benefits to how work was organized on the project, with the same midwife being assigned to the women throughout pregnancy, birth and aftercare; yet she also felt that the long journeys to the hospital made this work harder. She reflected as follows:

> I think it [the way of working] is good both for the expectant parents and the midwives ... It's a better work environment. It's not as stressful, but like I said ... it doesn't work as well when we have long distances, because the workload becames so heavy. Partly because the midwives also have to travel far, and because you need to count ... there's a limit to how much you're allowed to work, it's 12 hours I think. And it's quite some time that is dedicated to sitting in the car, and going back and forth. So you lose a lot of time in the car that you could have spent in the delivery room.

The organization of work on the project seemed partly to follow a logic similar to the integrated, less specialized work practices that had previously been described as risky. The project offered a clearly defined alternative to specialized work, and had the 'do-a-little-of-everything' approach that Malin captured as characteristic of work at BB Sollefteå prior to the closure. For midwives enrolled on the project, the new way of working meant that they could continue to deliver babies, but they also had to perform unskilled tasks, such as driving three or four hours to deliver a baby at another hospital. Working on the project also meant that the midwives met a more homogeneous group of patients than previously. As the project was directed toward first-time mothers and women suffering from birth anxiety, they now handled some of the more complex patient cases. However, the fact that the project was also largely directed toward couples planning to drive to the hospital had the effect of excluding some expectant mothers from the project's patient group. In line with theorization of how risks may be neutralized or *undone* (Giritli Nygren et al. 2017), the patient group on which the project focused seemed to consist of parents who were well established in the area, as they owned a car and were familiar with the potential obstacles presented by driving to the hospital. The region's funding for the project thus offered an *undoing* of risk that intersected with prioritizing patients according to a heteronormative and white logic.

When interviewing the midwives, it became clear that the patients they perceived as most *at risk* were newly arrived, non-Swedish-speaking women. Both Malin and Petra mentioned the difficulties that the longer travelling time meant for these women, and the new demands for information placed on the midwife. Petra explained the effects on the women and herself as follows:

> We have many foreign-born here. And it becomes ... to sit and explain every meeting that 'You need to go to Sundsvall or Örnsköldsvik' and they don't know where that is. Many meetings

I need to talk about this: where they should go, how they should go there, what they need to do. Many think they can call an ambulance, but we don't have that many ambulances here for them to be able to go with an ambulance. It takes a lot of energy for them as well. Because they often don't have a car or ... those kind of things. Some don't speak Swedish, they don't... they need to call the delivery ward and announce [that you are coming in] – yes, it becomes really hard, just a thing like that, when it's a much, much longer travel.

Petra emphasized that a project focusing on information in different languages had been initiated, facilitating both her own work and the situation for newly arrived pregnant women. However, the difficulties associated with not owning a car remained, necessitating individual solutions that did not take access to a car and driver for granted. As the public care that BB Sollefteå offered was removed from the area, and risks with the new situation were neutralized through project money, the distribution of economic resources made certain priorities visible. Women who were well-established in the area became the normative image of those living in Sollefteå, while newly arrived women were a second priority. In the aftermath of the closure, the construction of risks – and the bodies targeted as *at risk* – reflect how care in a rural northern context affected by the politics of centralization builds on power inequalities such as gender, race, and social and economic resources. It also shows how small maternity ward practices that were made peripheral and risky in political debate prior to the closure might be appropriated and used as a risk-prevention strategy when needed.

Conclusion

The three midwives' experiences of and resistance to a process attacking their professional identities as small-ward midwives reveal power structures that are integrated into the Swedish healthcare system, which all agents, including politicians and midwives, must navigate. The process through which small maternity wards were constructed as *risky* took place within a discourse that favours large, specialized wards, while constructing the practices and ideals of smaller wards as peripheral. In the political construction of small-ward midwifery as risky, this discourse was reproduced alongside neoliberal ideals and power structures such as gender, class, race and place. Consequently, small-ward midwives' subjectivities, which differed from the neoliberal subjectivity, were constructed as ideologically risky. These risk constructions were resisted by the midwives, who provided examples of how work practices at the smaller ward were safe and good for both staff and women.

The midwives' recollections of political discussions and initiatives before and after the closure of BB Sollefteå, and their own reactions to it, also illustrate how some bodies have been peripheralized in the process. Beside the fact that maternity care has suffered badly from cuts in the healthcare sector, women living in the northern inland are peripheralized as patients when the logic of the large, urban ward becomes the norm for maternity care. At the utmost periphery are the newly arrived women, whose difficulties in travelling long distances for maternity care were highlighted by two of the midwives, yet seemed to be ignored in political discussions of patient safety. The specific difficulties that closing smaller inland wards might cause for reindeer-owning Sami women, who sometimes need to work far from the bigger towns for part of the year, was not discussed by the midwives I interviewed.

In conclusion, the process through which small maternity wards and small-ward midwives' working practices were constructed as *risky* intersected with two peripheralization processes: one where small-ward maternity care practices were made peripheral, and the other where certain patients were peripheralized. In both these processes, ideology and power structures such as gender, class, race and place were at work, and although the midwives I interviewed resisted the political risk narrative, they nevertheless took part in reproducing neoliberal ideals and power structures.

Although the holistic way of working with women, with no midwives on the ward specializing solely in deliveries, had been targeted as unsafe in political discussions prior to the closure, after the closure it was used in a project specifically aimed at first-time mothers and women suffering from birth anxiety (or 'travel anxiety', as one midwife called it). This reflects how small-ward work practices relying on values other than efficiency and cost-cutting were peripheralized in favour of practices on urban, specialized wards, yet could be appropriated to legitimize healthcare centralization, ultimately resulting in the closure of smaller wards where integrated work practices were first developed.

Notes

1 The Sami people are the indigenous people of Saepmie, a territory stretching across northern parts of Norway, Sweden, Finland and northeast Russia. Sollefteå is located in southern Saepmie.
2 The period of 2017–2020, a total number of 995 refugees were granted housing in the Västernorrland region (Länsstyrelsen Västernorrland 2020).

References

Boholm, Åsa. 2003. "The cultural nature of risk: can there be an anthropology of uncertainty?" *Ethnos* 68(2), 159–178.
Bondi, Liz. 2005. "Working the spaces of neoliberal subjectivity: psychotherapeutic technologies, professionalisation and counselling." *Antipode: A Radical Journal of Geography* 37(3), 497–514.

Cahill, Helen. 2001. "Male appropriation and medicalization of childbirth: an historical analysis." *Journal of Advanced Nursing 33*(3), 334–342.

Collins, Patricia Hill. 2005. "Black women and motherhood." In *Motherhood and space: configurations of the maternal through politics, home, and the body*, eds. Sarah Hardy and Caroline Wiedmer, 149–160. New York, NY: Palgrave Macmillan.

Crenshaw, Kimberlé. 1989. "Demarginalizing the intersection of race and sex: a black feminist critique of antidiscrimination doctrine, feminist theory and antiracist politics." *University of Chicago Legal Forum 1989*(1), art. 8, 139–167.

Douglas, Mary. 2002. *Risk and blame: essays in cultural theory*. London: Routledge.

Giritli Nygren, Katarina and Sara Nyhlén. 2017. "Mapping the ruling relations of work in rural eldercare intersections of gender, digitalization and the centre–periphery divide." *Journal of Rural Studies 54*, 337–343.

Giritli Nygren, Katarina, Susanna Öhman and Anna Olofsson. 2017. "Doing and undoing risk: The mutual constitution of risk and heteronormativity in contemporary society." *Journal of Risk Research 20*(3), 418–432.

Granberg, Magnus. 2014. "Manufacturing dissent: Labor conflict, care work, and the politicization of caring." *Nordic Journal of Working Life Studies 4*(1), 139–152.

Granberg, Magnus. 2016. *Care in revolt: labor conflict, gender, neoliberalism*. Doctoral thesis, Sundsvall, Sweden: Mid Sweden University.

Hildingsson, Ingegerd. 2018. *Barnmorska hela vägen: halvtidsrapport [Midwife all the way: half-time report]*. Sundsvall, Sweden: Region Västernorrland, Mid Sweden University and Uppsala University.

Hood, Christopher. 1991. "A public management for all seasons?" *Public Administration 69*(1), 3–19.

Kopare, Tellervo. 1999. "*Att rida stormen ut: Förlossningsberättelser i Finnmark och Sápmi*" *[Riding the storm: Birth stories in Finnmark and Sápmi]*. Doctoral thesis, Göteborg, Sweden: Göteborg University.

Langholm, Sivert. 1971. "On the concepts of center and periphery." *Journal of Peace Research 8*(3–4), 273–278.

Larsson, Margareta. 2016. "Autonomy, agency and choice: kvinnors självständighet, handlingsutrymme och valmöjligheter [Women's independence, freedom of action and choice]." *Jordemodern 9*, 34–35.

Leppo, Anna. 2012. *Precarious pregnancies: alcohol, drugs and the regulation of risks*. Doctoral thesis, Helsinki, Finland: University of Helskinki.

Lindroth, Karl. 1907. *Medicinalstyrelsens förslag till ett nytt reglemente för barnmorskor [The Swedish Medicines Agency's proposal for a new regulation for midwives]*. Stockholm, Sweden: K L. Beckmans Boktryckeri.

Länsstyrelsen Västernorrland. 2020. *Mottagande och etablering av nyanlända*. Link: https://www.lansstyrelsen.se/vasternorrland/samhalle/social-hallbarhet/integration/mottagande-och-etablering-av-nyanlanda.html [Downloaded 200406].

McCall, Leslie. 2005 "The complexity of intersectionality." *Signs 30*(3), 1771–1800.

Milton, Lena. 2001. "*Folkhemmets barnmorskor: den svenska barnmorskekårens professionalisering under mellan- och efterkrigstid*" *[The People's Home midwives:*

professionalization of the Swedish midwife corps during the mid- and post-war years]. Doctoral thesis, Uppsala, Sweden: Uppsala University.

Öberg, Lisa. 1996. *"Barnmorskan och läkaren: kompetens och konflikt i svensk förlossningsvård 1870–1920" [The midwife and the doctor: competence and conflict in Swedish childbirth care 1870–1920]*. Doctoral thesis, Stockholm, Sweden: Stockholm University.

Riessman, Catherine K. 1993. *Narrative analysis*. Newbury Park, CA: Sage.

Salzinger, Leslie. 2003. *Genders in production: making workers in Mexico's global factories*. Berkeley, CA: University of California Press.

Sandell, Kerstin. 2018. "Att veta som den jag är: Reflektioner över ett misslyckat fältarbete [Knowing who I am: Reflections on a failed field job]." In *Kritiska gemenskaper: att skriva feministisk och postkolonial vetenskap [Critical communities: writing feminist and postcolonial science]*, eds. Kerstin Sandell, Maja Sager and Nora Räthzel, 247–256. Johanneshov, Sweden: MTM.

Selberg, Rebecca. 2012. *Femininity at work: gender, labour, and changing relations of power in a Swedish hospital*. Lund, Sweden: Arkiv Academic Press.

Sjöstedt Landén, Angelika. 2016. "Nyliberal styrning och ideologi i offentlig verksamhet: Teman för feministisk arbetslivsforskning [Neoliberal governance and ideology in public activity: Themes for feminist working life research]." In *Ambivalenser och maktordningar: feministiska läsningar av nyliberalism [Ambivalences and systems of power: feminist readings on neoliberalism]*, eds. Siv Fahlgren, Diana Mulinari and Angelika Sjöstedt Landén, 30–56. Stockholm, Sweden: Makadam.

Sköld, Peter, Per Axelsson, Lena Karlsson and Len Smith. 2011. "Infant mortality of Sami and settlers in Northern Sweden: the era of colonization 1750–1900." *Global Health Action* 4(1), art. 8441, 1–6.

Vallgårda, Signhild. 1995. "Fødælsehjælp og modernisering i Danmark och Sverige, 1900–1950 [Birth aid and modernization in Denmark and Sweden, 1900–1950]." *Den Jyske Historiker 1995*, 75.

Walkerdine, Valerie. 2010. "Re-classifying upward mobility: femininity and the neoliberal subject." *Gender and Education* 15(3), 237–248.

Williams, Christine. 2006. *Inside toyland: working, shopping and social inequality*. Berkeley: University of California Press.

Wingborg, Mats. 2017. *Marknadiseringen av den svenska sjukvården – så gick det till*. Stockholm: Arena idé

Wisselgren, Maria. 2005. *"Att föda barn – från privat till offentlig angelägenhet: Förlossningsvårdens institutionalisering i Sundsvall 1900–1930" [Giving birth to children – from private to public affairs: the institutionalization of childbirth care in Sundsvall 1900–1930]*. Doctoral thesis, Umeå, Sweden: Umeå University.

10 On the Margins of Mine Work: Organizational Peripheries in a Globalized World of Work

Kristina Johansson and Lisa Ringblom[1]

Feminist organization scholars have a long history of investigating power inequalities in organizations from the perspective of divisions of work. In a study of the male-dominated food production industry, Baude (1992) found that the limited number of women employees were allocated to specific parts of the workplace, where they performed repetitive tasks with no prospect of vertical or horizontal advancement. There, in 'their place', women were allowed to work without challenging men's position as the 'real' workers at home and at work, and the employer could benefit from their cheaper labour. Similarly, in a study of a supermarket, Johansson and Lundgren (2015) found that the pre-store, where only women worked, was precluded from the job-rotation system that dominated the rest of the organization. The exclusion of the pre-store meant that the women spent their whole workday in an enclosed and controlled space, both organizationally and physically separated from the store's other activities.

These and similar studies (e.g. Abrahamsson 2009; Kanter 1993) offer important insights into the spatial practices of peripherialization in specific organizations and their relation to gendered hierarchies and relationships. However, in exploring intra-organizational practices without considering how these relationships are linked to other places and other organizations, these analyses do not consider power relations and inequalities that transcend the specific location or situation. This tendency becomes further problematic as contemporary organizations are increasingly entangled in global neoliberal networks. To avoid narrow analyses of power inequalities relating to organizations, Acker (2012: 221–222) urges researchers to reflect on:

> What counts as 'an organization'? Within what boundaries do we focus investigation? Are the locations of outsourced functions part of the original organization or a different organization? ... What jobs constitute the workforce of a particular employer? Does it include contingent, contract, temporary, and part time workers? Does it include all levels of employees, from the top to the bottom?

In addition, emphasis on the gendered division of work risks losing sight of how gender is intertwined with other social power relations in organizations, such as class and race/ethnicity (Holvino 2010; McCall 2005). Acker (2006, 2012) introduces the concept of *inequality regimes* to comprehend the complex dynamics of inequalities in organizations. These are defined as 'loosely interrelated practices, processes, actions, and meanings that result in and maintain class, gender, and racial inequalities within particular organizations' (Acker 2006: 443). The specific processes and practices that constitute the inequality regimes of specific organizations tend to vary in accordance with 'the severity of inequalities, their visibility and legitimacy, and the possibilities for change toward less inequality' (p. 459). The result of these intertwined processes and practices is persistent, but fluid and changing, closely connected with the surrounding society and its culture, politics, norms, etc. In addition, Acker (2006) suggests that ongoing progression toward a globalized world of work, production and technologies is likely to lead to greater variation in inequality regimes in and between organizations, making them more subtle, and therefore more difficult to challenge.

Linking Acker's thoughts together, the primarily intra-organizational focus of inequality regimes, combined with her reminder of the fluidity of organizational boundaries, helps us understand the leakage or entanglement between organizations and their surroundings. Acker's hands-on approach to analyzing racialized and gendered class practices in the specific context of organizations offers the potential to construct vital intersectional knowledge on organizational practices and processes that maintain (and potentially challenge) inequalities at work. Studying the specific and local, in this case the Swedish mining industry, and the ongoing organization of work reveals the production of complex, interconnected practices and processes that result in inequalities in work organizations. This is thus an analytical strategy to identify inequality-produced practices in a concrete and delimited context. However, importantly and somewhat contradictorily, the delimited context also provides an opportunity to determine how it is entangled in its surroundings, and how organizations can be understood as producers of inequality not just within their own organizational boundaries, but also beyond these imagined margins.

This chapter explores different meanings of organizational peripheries in the globalized world of work from an intersectional perspective. Empirically, we focus on examples of the Swedish mining industry in the literature. The first example explores inequalities at the centre of mining work and major mining companies, and the second investigates inequalities at the margins of mining work and scrutinizes the mine as a 'multi-employer work site' (Nygren 2018). Following an introduction to the spatiality of the mining industry from an intersectional perspective, we chart the social relations involved in each example, and end by reflecting on how a focus on organizational peripheries helps to nuance our understanding of power inequalities within *and* across organizations.

Introducing Intersecting Practices of Gender, Class and Place in the Swedish Mining Industry

Sweden's mines produce about 90% of all iron ore produced in Europe, and several of the country's most well-known technology companies, including ABB, Sandvik and Atlas Copco, have their origins in the mining industry (Ringblom and Abrahamsson 2017). The Swedish mining industry competes in the global market, and its management is part of an international business elite, with seemingly seamless flows of communications and capital. At the same time, the localities of natural resources make mining a place-bound and material activity. The majority of the 14 mines currently operational in Sweden are located in the two northernmost counties, Norrbotten and Västerbotten, which are both vast and sparsely populated, especially in the hinterland. They are thus situated in a form of national periphery, contrasting with the (urban) centres in the south and along the country's coastline. Together, Norrbotten and Västerbotten, cover almost a third of Sweden's 450,000 square kilometres of land, but are home to no more than five per cent of its 10 million habitants. In these regions, the mines are in many ways the centre of economic activity and infrastructure with their flows of workers, capital and natural resources (cf. Pini and Leach 2011), offering employment and relatively high salaries. The regional importance of mining is given greater prominence because the region is otherwise marked by struggles relating to high unemployment, net out-migration of young people, skewed age structures and weak local economies (Beland Lindahl 2008).

Mining also plays a central role in the conflicts that characterize the region, especially in relation to environmental and land-use issues. One cause of conflict is the fact that most mines are located in Sapmí, the land of the indigenous Sami people and their reindeer pastures (Beland Lindahl et al. 2016; Sjöstedt Landén and Fotaki 2018). The conflicts surrounding mining is longstanding, relating to historical as well as contemporary issues. According to Beland Lindahl (2008), conflicts over natural resource extraction tend to be rooted in contestations of values, characterized by actors with widely diverging perceptions of nature and the role and function of its resources, including fundamental concerns such as 'what is a necessity?' and 'what is worth protecting and on what grounds?' Should the job opportunities created by the mining industry be protected because they enable people to live and work in otherwise de-populated areas? Or should nature preservation and protection of the rights of the indigenous Sami people and their reindeer pastures be prioritized? These lines of conflict are sometimes sharp, but take shape in the everyday lives of people living in the region in often complex and contradictory ways (Jensen and Sandström 2019). Hence, conflicts surrounding the mining industry, its organizations and their geographical locations highlight that a location is never just a geographical area, but is also a place of temporal social relations in the past, present and future.

The mining industry's dominant role in certain localities is particularly evident in the town of Kiruna, located in the northernmost part of the country close to both the Norwegian and Finnish borders. According to Hägg (1993), in 1900 state-owned Luossavaara-Kiirunavaara AB (LKAB), one of Sweden's major mining companies under the management of Hjalmar Lundbohm, led the building and founding, as well as the social and cultural development, of Kiruna. The great mine complex of LKAB still dominates Kiruna culturally and economically, as well as its visual skyline. As new ore deposits have been discovered in the surrounding mountains of Luossavaara and Kiirunavaara, the distance between town and mine has gradually diminished, to the point where the town is now being relocated further up the valley. A similar collision between the locality of ore deposits and the built environment is also occurring in the nearby community of Malmberget. In other national and urban-oriented discourses, rural regions such as Norrbotten and Västerbotten, which are frequently associated with problems such as depopulation and unemployment, tend to constitute the outside against which meanings of modernity, development and equality are established (Nilsson and Lundgren 2015; Rönnblom and Sandberg 2015). Discourses of the problematic rural also tend to have a gendered dimension, as rural men are often represented as backward, outdated and the opposite of modern urban masculinities (Campbell and Bell 2000; Pini and Leach 2011; Stenbacka 2011).

The mining industry is dominated by men as experts, entrepreneurs, investors and workers, and is intertwined with various intersecting symbols of masculinity, class and place, along the lines of organizational and geographical divides. The taken-for-granted role of men, together with major capital investments, the conquest of lands, the establishment of large production sites and the use of big machines and considerable human capital, make industrial mining itself an articulation of the discourse of hyper-masculinity (Lahiri-Dutt 2011). However, miners on the shop floor consisting only of rural, working-class men is a relatively modern construction. Prior to industrialization, mine work took place only during a short and intense period of the year. In order to secure enough labour, families of men, women and children were hired to conduct the very strenuous and dangerous work (Karlsson 1997). The prohibition on women working underground began with industrialization, when mining became more capitalized, centralized and mechanized (Abrahamsson 2007; Blomberg 1995; Hägg 1993; Karlsson 1997). This law, constituting a joint agreement between the state, the union and the employer, was seen as a way to protect women (and children) from the hazards underground, and to steer them in the direction of tasks better suited to their reproductive and moral responsibilities. This prohibition began to be repealed during the 1960s, when women workers were allowed back underground, not as miners but as nurses and cooks, serving in the dining and healthcare facilities set up underground to improve the comforts and services of the male miners. In 1978 the law was totally repealed, motivated by women's otherwise poor opportunities for paid labour in the mining communities. Women began, to a limited extent, to take part in more mechanized mine work that was perceived as not requiring physical strength (Karlsson 1997). The (con)temporary exclusion of women from underground work is not specific to Sweden, but is also a reality in other countries, including Great Britain, China and Peru (Gier and Mercier 2006; Mercier 2011; Mercier and Gier 2007). Thus, the masculinization of mining is evidently far from a natural circumstance, but is the result of an ideological and very active exclusion of women from mining.

As mines became an exclusively male domain, the masculinization of mining work, skills, ideals and symbols intensified (Abrahamsson 2007; Abrahamsson and Johansson 2006; Eveline and Booth 2002; Mayes and Pini 2010; Wicks 2002). In a study of representations of miners in union publications between 1919 and 1949, Blomberg (1995) analyzed the construction of male miners' identity as built on being simultaneously miners, union members, patriots of the local community and men. At this time, the everyday lives of miners were characterized by great insecurity and the status of 'permanent temporaries'. Their pursuit of a masculine identity was a means for them to regain a sense of the power, respect and control (over their existence and over working-class women) of which their class position deprived them, which Blomberg calls the 'power of the powerless'.

Macho Men and Wanted Women at the Centre of Mine Work

Mining work is traditionally represented as dark, dirty and dangerous, and the first Swedish miners worked the rock using hand-held tools. Rural working-class men constructed their identities as miners and men in relation to the practical knowledge, physical strength, risk-taking and endurance required by the dangerous and strenuous working conditions in the mines (Abrahamsson 2007; Abrahamsson and Johansson 2006; Abrahamsson et al. 2010, 2015; Abrahamsson and Somerville 2007; Andersson 2012; Lahiri-Dutt 2012). The twentieth century saw increasing mechanization and the presence of machinery. Today's mines are high-technological activities, characterized by automatization and digitalization, which have considerably changed the miners' working conditions (Abrahamsson 2007; Abrahamsson and Johansson 2006; Abrahamsson et al. 2010, 2015). New production technology has brought new demands and competences that have changed workers' role in the production system, making it more about surveillance than manual labour. Over time, mining machinery 'has tended to become bigger and more technologically sophisticated', and 'work processes have become automated, remotely controlled and dependent on the technologies and techniques of closed circuit television, computers and advanced electronic measurement and calculation' (Abrahamsson and Johansson 2006: 699). This process of digitalization is marked by a spatial redistribution and gradual distancing of the miner from the rock, symbolized not least by the establishment of remote operational control centres above ground. This spatial reconfiguration also brings changes to skills and knowledge, from bodily and tacit to abstract and theoretical (Lööw and Nygren 2019). In these centres, the miners sit behind computers in office-like rooms, overlooking and operating the activities of machines underground.

The reduction of strenuous, physically demanding work tasks has had complex and contradictory effects on the gendering of mining work and related identities. Technology tends to be robustly associated with men and masculinity (e.g. Cockburn 1983; Wajcman 1991), and the technology of mine work has also been found to play a part in the industry's masculine connotations (Mayes and Pini 2010), as in the exclusion of women in a North American setting (Tallichet 1995, 2000). However, in Abrahamsson and Johansson's (2006) study, the miners working underground tended instead to perceive the introduction of new technology and new skills requirements as a threat and in conflict with the manual labour that constituted the core of their identities as both men and miners. Their resistance to new technology was demonstrated in their description of the mine work that had been transformed to the remote operational control centres above ground as 'velour work', contrasted with the 'real' mining work still executed underground (by men). Andersson (2012) found that although strenuous and hazardous work tasks had been reduced, men who embodied a type of macho-masculinity built on risk taking and physical strength continued to be celebrated as 'real mine workers', while men (and women) who expressed other identities were subordinated and positioned as weak, girly, or simply incompetent and disloyal to the workers' collective.

In a recent study drawing on interviews with men and women miners, Ringblom (2019) found that the increase in women miners was made sense of predominantly in relation to the improved working environment and the new technology. The reduction of physically strenuous work tasks had altered the demands on miners and challenged dominant ideas of who can do mining work. At the same time, aligned with previous studies, idealized images of masculinity continued to be constructed in relation not to the modern technology, but to traditional tools, work methods and manual labour. Furthermore, while the gendered divide described by Abrahamsson and Johansson (2006) worked to construct real mining work as undertaken by men underground, in contrast to the work mediated by modern technology above ground, Ringblom (2019) also found indications of divisions of work along gender lines underground. According to this meaning making, mining work still had a more manual character associated with men, while mining work carried out with technical aids and large machinery was associated with both men and women. Work tasks that required less muscle strength were perceived as non-bodily, and therefore 'simple', 'easy' and something 'almost anybody could do'. This suggests that, despite the transformation of mining work, men's bodies as big and strong still form part of the dominant narrative of mining work and its essence among miners themselves.

Women Miners Wanted

Although Abrahamsson and Johansson (2006), Andersson (2012) and Ringblom (2019) saw signs of greater variation in expressions of masculine identity, a traditional, 'hyper-' or 'macho-masculinity' still plays a predominant role in the shop floor culture of big mining companies. The symbolic gendering of mine work has created space for the construction of women (and feminized men) as a sexualized Other in relation to mine work, as is evident in descriptions of women miners (Andersson 2012; Ringblom 2019; Ringblom and Abrahamsson 2017; Eveline and Booth 2002; Mayes and Pini 2014; Norberg and Fältholm 2018; Saunders and Easteal 2013; Tallichet 1995, 2000).

At the same time, women currently hold prominent positions elsewhere in today's mining industry, and will perhaps do so even more in future. According to Andersson et al. (2013: 12):

> Mining companies have to be and want to be modern and attractive employers for both men and women. During the last years, LKAB and Boliden have implemented several ambitious gender initiatives, both within the companies and in collaboration with the local community. They have many years of experience in gender equality measures (e.g. wage mapping systems, women's networks, gender awareness training, recruitment efforts for female executives and technology experts, and support for a high school program for mining with 50% girls) and are strategically communicating that women are an important part of the new modern mining industry.

Often framed as a 'business case', Johansson and Ringblom (2017) describes how taking an active stand in favour of gender equality has become part of mining companies' branding strategies and their overarching desire to be perceived as 'modern' and 'attractive' (cf. Mayes and Pini 2014). A more or less explicit part of this argument is that women are assumed to bring to these organizations something 'other' than the men who are already there (Andersson 2012; Eveline and Booth 2002; Fältholm and Norberg 2017; Mayes and Pini 2014; Norberg and Fältholm 2018; Tallichet 1995, 2000). In the mining companies' portrayal of themselves as modern and attractive, a certain type of woman and the specific qualities that she is assumed to bring are celebrated as solutions to the problem created by the working-class masculine ideals that dominate the shop floor.

Alongside a focus on women within and outside the mining companies, these organizations' 'doing' of gender equality is to a growing extent a matter of men and masculinity. Feminists, as well as critical masculinity scholars, have long argued for the necessity to 'name men as men' and scrutinize the masculine values embedded in most organizations (cf. Collinson and Hearn 1994). However, Ringblom and Johansson (2020) suggest that when men are the focal point of gender equality in the context of mining (and forestry), it is mainly rural blue-collar workers who are described as 'the problem'. Hence, rather than problematizing how intersecting masculinities are intertwined in dominating organizational practices and processes, gender equality measures draw on an individualistic focus targeting specific groups of men. Especially evident is the assumption that men on the shop floor lack the requisite knowledge and attitudes relating to gender equality, preventing them from 'getting everybody on board' and 'making sure we are all on the same page'.

Contractors at the Margins of Mine Work

So far, analyses of Swedish mining companies have focused on the work processes of mining work (and miners). The sophisticated industrial processes of modern mines have transformed them into huge complexes, with myriad more or less auxiliary tasks carried out within and in relation to the mine. An abundance of activities take place beneath the surface in Sweden's vast underground mines, which have expanded downward and sideways as new deposits of ore are mined at depths of over a kilometre. LKAB's mine in Malmberget, for example, has 600 kilometres of roads, workshops, control rooms, canteens, break rooms and other staff facilities. At the start and end of each shift, buses transfer workers from the gate at ground level to where their work takes place underground. These bus rides take approximately half an hour each way, and workers stay underground for their entire shifts, including breaks.

Shifting the analytical focus to these activities at the margins of mine work enables different meanings of peripherialization to unfold. Today, tasks seen as auxiliary tend to be conducted not by the mining company itself, but by the many suppliers, contractors and entrepreneurs also operating in the mining sector. Thus, the modern mine constitutes 'a multi-employer work site' (Nygren 2018) made up of not one but many interacting and interconnected organizations. Nygren's (2018: 12) definition of contractors is used here, as 'any third party organization that performs work tasks and services for another organization on a contractual basis and that formally operates under its own management control'.

While all statistics point to the fact that the use of contractors has increased considerably in the mining industry since the 1980s, determining precise numbers is difficult in the absence of verified records (Lööw and Nygren 2019; Nygren 2018). Based on companies' own estimations, SveMin (2016), the industry's association of mines, mineral and metal producers, states that in 2010, 14% of total working hours in the mining industry were performed by contractors. However, it is unclear whether these figures include contractors from all sectors or only from the mining industry. According to Nygren (2018), unofficial figures from SveMin's representatives suggest that 40% of production-related work in the mining industry is performed by contractors. The mining company in Nygren's study estimated that approximately 4,300 contractors and other suppliers had delivered services or goods to its mining complexes within the previous year. According to Andersson et al. (2013), in LKAB's daily business, half of the workers involved in the activities were hired not directly but by another company.

In the context of the mining industry, contract work is said to involve mainly construction contractors, equipment manufacturers and transport companies (STRIM 2016). The expansion and modernization of the Swedish mining companies and their facilities have meant that large construction projects take place in and in close relation to the mine, and in these projects the work is carried out mainly by contractors (Nygren 2018). Another predominant category of contract work is repair and maintenance work, necessitated by the mechanized production processes and large machinery. Transport companies include truck drivers, and to some extent train drivers, who handle the logistics of getting equipment and minerals in, to and from the mines. In addition, contractors are involved in rock cleaning, drilling and blasting, as well as providing expertise in rock mechanics (Andersson et al. 2013: 12), suggesting that they include not only blue-collar workers and craftsmen, but also academically trained professionals.

The sectors most commonly referred to in relation to mining contractors are almost entirely male-dominated. Yet although big mining companies have increased the percentage of women amongst their personnel, statistics on the gender composition of their contractors is not provided. One might also argue that the companies used as contractors may be less able to work on issues of gender equality and diversity than the big mining companies. Although researchers and policymakers advocate a need to include the gender patterns and activities of contractors in the industry's gender equality programme (Andersson et al. 2013; STRIM 2016), no such initiative seems to have been implemented.

Although most contractors are from male-dominated industries, some are not. Of course, all the facilities of underground mines need cleaning, but cleaners working in mines do not appear to have been scientifically studied. A short glimpse into their reality is provided by Träff (2019) in a report on cleaners working in the Kiruna mine, hired by a contractor to clean underground staff facilities and offices. This focuses on how keeping the mining space neat, free from dust and dirt is an important part of the safety protocol. Apart from wearing helmets and using protective equipment in certain parts of the complex, the cleaners working underground use the same cleaning methods as they would aboveground. The environment is described as 'clean and bright', like any other office. Yet according to the interviewed cleaners, it is difficult to keep the facilities clean because workers coming into the canteen often bring in heavy, black dirt from their work clothes. One interviewee said that 'You can't stand everywhere like a police officer, demanding that they must clean their shoes', so instead they keep cleaning thoroughly throughout the day. While the dominant representation of mine workers in Sweden tends to be white, all cleaners portrayed in the article are racialized. Although no conclusions can be drawn from only one news article, this suggests that gendered and racialized class relations in this type of contract work may produce other types of inequalities from those of the mine workers at the centre.

Nygren (2018) states that the contracting companies range in size from small firms with only a few individuals to multinational corporations with thousands of employees. His focus is on local companies involved in safety management, which have evolved as a result of their proximity to the mining industry. Although these companies may depend heavily on the mining company as their single large client, in order to compete with other employers in the same region they must presumably offer their employees attractive contractual conditions. However, Nygren (2018) also highlights another category of contracting companies that provide 'fly-in/fly-out' contractors who travel to the mining sites only to work. It is unknown how many immigrant workers are employed by contractors and sub-contractors, although since immigrant workers form a significant part of both the construction and transport sectors at large, one might expect this also to be the case for activities relating to the mining industry. This hypothesis is supported by informal reports from a major mining area of a constant stream of 'bus-in/bus-out' workers from Eastern Europe.

Concluding Discussion

In analyzing inequalities at the centre and margins of Swedish mining companies, this chapter explores various meanings of organizational peripheries from an intersectional perspective. The results suggest that in the literature on inequalities in the context of miners and mine work, working-class male and female miners are the focal point for processes of differentiation. With this focus, analyses of inequalities have described, for example, how hierarchization of the different types of work tasks involved in the mining process is played out in accordance with their association with traditional or modern mine work. In the struggle to define 'real mine work' on the shop floor, the women and men workers who perform the 'modern' and more technologized mine work are subordinated. This focus also reveals how mining companies' increased efforts to improve gender equality tend to construct women miners as sought-after labour and as solutions to the problems created by the 'backward' macho men who dominate the shop floor.

Employment as a miner in a major mining company brings greater social and financial security than most other working-class jobs in the region. Analyzing the margins of mine work and non-representation in mining organizations also enables us to shift the focus to less researched experiences and positions among the growing number of contractors working in and in relation to the mines. These contractors come not only from traditionally male occupations such as construction, transport and maintenance, but also from female-dominated occupations such as cleaners.

Consideration of the margins of mine-work enables additional questions to be asked about mining organizations' 'doing' of gender equality (Ringblom and Johansson 2020). How can the fact that a significant part of the workforce of contemporary mining workplaces are contractors be understood in relation to the gender-equality initiatives taking place in the industry? For example, a frequently cited indicator of gender (in) equality used in the industry is the numbers of men and women, showing an increase in women over the last decade (cf. Ringblom and Abrahamsson 2017). However, the numbers used to describe gender patterns in the industry only consider employees within the core organizations, whereas, as suggested, 40% of production-related work in the mining industry is performed by contractors, most of whom are men. What do gender statistics really say about representation in these organizations' day-to-day activities? This also opens up new questions about the centre and periphery of gender equality at work. While pursuing gender equality has become a way for mining companies (and similar male-dominated organizations) to construct themselves as 'modern' organizations (Johansson and Ringblom 2017), the use and activities of contractors tend not be included in these narratives. Using contractors may thus lead to 'outsourcing' inequality away from company agendas. As well as revealing a necessity to acknowledge the role of contractors, this shows how power relations are interrelated and simultaneously constituted in the organizational practices and processes of gender-equality measurements. Measures designed to change gender patterns are situated in specific organizational contexts, but are likely to be relevant to the production and counteraction of inequalities in a broader sense. It is therefore important that gender-equality measures in organizations maintain awareness of the interconnectedness of other social power relations.

The division of work, income and status is crucially important for the creation and reproduction of power hierarchies structured through the intersections of gender, class and race/ethnicity. As these patterns are shaped partly by organizational practices, the gendered processes and practices of organizations continue to be an important field of research, in Nordic countries as elsewhere (e.g. Abrahamsson 2009; Gunnarsson et al. 2003; Kvande 1999; Korvajärvi 1998). Within this literature, organizations are not simply stages on which inequality plays out, or on which gender and/or the formation of gendered identities are practised. Rather, such studies thoroughly interrogate how gender structures, norms and identities are constituted in relation to, and as part of, specific organizational practices and processes, involving work requirements, job evaluations, wage setting, supervision, recruitment, and the more informal 'doing the job' (Acker 1990, 2006).

Where power, money and men cluster, feminist scholars must be present, asking critical questions and making the 'inside' of these organizations visible to the outside world. Hence, from this perspective, the fact that mining is a contested and conflicted industry strengthens the need for feminist working-life scholars to scrutinize its organizations. The literature on patterns of inequality in contemporary mining organizations is substantial (e.g. Abrahamsson and Johansson 2006; Abrahamsson and Somerville 2007; Mayes and Pini 2014; Tallichet 2016), not least in the Swedish context, where major mining companies such as LKAB and Boliden have a long history of providing researchers with the access needed for detailed analysis of work processes, workplace cultures and miners' identities, including how they contribute to or challenge predominant power relations (Abrahamsson and Johansson 2006; Andersson 2012; Ringblom 2019). As well as reviewing how this literature enables us to explore processes of peripherialization in mining companies, this chapter has also tried to go beyond approaches adopted in the existing literature. The latter has a blind spot relating partly to the fact that the industry and companies tend to focus on 'core' activities, and partly to issues of access, and the tendency for (any) employer to steer organizational scholars away from the more hidden corners of the labour market. Both of these factors provide a reminder that researchers interested in understanding patterns of inequality must not only analyze the complexity going on before their eyes, but must also constantly search for and scrutinize practices and processes that are *not* obvious.

This chapter has shown that going to the 'margins' of mine work reveals a number of critical questions with the potential to nuance existing knowledge on intersections of gender, class and place in the mining industry, as well as the organizational peripheries intertwined in the inequality regimes of large industrial mining organizations. Inspired by Acker's (2006, 2012) theory, the inequalities produced by organizational practices and processes have been approached as 'leaking in-betweens', entangled in their surroundings and produced within and beyond the imagined margins of organizational boundaries. In doing so, the mining industry becomes not a number of demarcated companies, but a material and discursive interconnected organizing of work and people who relate to each other in complex spatial webs of power and (inter-)dependency. Organizing of the work and people entangled in the mining industry goes far beyond the contractors working within the mines analyzed in this chapter. Depending on scale, it may also include, for example, tourism vendors and reindeer herders who live off the land in the mining regions, and the welfare and service sectors of mining communities. Importantly, focusing on reciprocity does not eliminate the power and conflicting interests beneath a shimmer of mutual dependency. On the contrary, teasing out the complex ways in which the organizing of work and people are entangled together in relations of power and spatial dimensions of interdependency is a way to nuance understanding of the processes and practices that produce inequalities at both the centre and margins of the mining industry.

Note

1 The authors contributed equally to this work and are listed in alphabetical order.

References

Abrahamsson, Lena. 2007. "Gruvarbetets historia ur ett genusperspektiv: hur gruvarbetet blev och förblev manligt" [The mining history from a gender perspective: how mining became and remained male]. In *Oplogat: Spår av kvinnors liv och arbete i Norrbotten [Unplowed: Traces of women's lives and work in Norrbotten]*, ed. Helen Doktare, 130–158. Luleå, Sweden: Oplogat Produktion.

Abrahamsson, Lena. 2009. *Att återställa ordningen: könsmönster och förändring i arbetsorganisationer [Restoring order: gender patterns and work organization changes]*. Umeå, Sweden: Borea.

Abrahamsson, Lena and Jan Johansson. 2006. "From grounded skills to sky qualifications: a study of workers creating and recreating qualifications, identity and gender at an underground iron ore mine in Sweden." *Journal of Industrial Relations* 48(5), 657–676.

Abrahamsson, Lena, Jan Johansson and Eira Andersson. 2010. "Från bergets djup till sjunde himlen" [From the depths of the mountain to seventh heaven]. *Arbetsmarknad and Arbetsliv* 16(4), 11–29.

Abrahamsson, Lena, Jan Johansson and Eira Andersson. 2015. "Identitet och genus under förändring i en gruvlig miljö" [Identity and gender changing in a horrible environment]. In *Sprickor, öppningar & krackeleringar: nya perspektiv på arbetsmiljö [Cracks, openings & crazing: new perspectives on work enviroment]*, eds. Angelika Sjöstedt Landén, Gunilla Olofsdotter and Malin Bolin. Sundsvall, Sweden: Forum for Gender Studies, Mid Sweden University.

Abrahamsson, Lena and Margaret Somerville. 2007. "Changing storylines and masculine bodies in Australian coal mining organisations." *Norma* 2(1), 52–69.

Acker, Joan. 1990. "Hierarchies, jobs, bodies: a theory of gendered organisations." *Gender and Society* 4(2), 39–158.

Acker, Joan. 2006. "Inequality regimes: gender, class, and race in organizations." *Gender and Society* 20(4), 441–464.

Acker, Joan. 2012. "Gendered organizations and intersectionality: problems and possibilities." *Equality, Diversity and Inclusion: An International Journal* 31(3), 214–224.

Andersson, Eira. 2012. *Malmens manliga mysterium: en interaktiv studie om kön och tradition i modernt gruvarbete [The male mystery of mining: an interactive study of gender and tradition in contemporary mining]*. Luleå, Sweden: Luleå Tekniska Universitet.

Andersson, Eira, Lena Abrahamsson, Ylva Fältholm and Malin Lindberg, 2013. *Breaking ore and gender patterns: a strategic and sustainable R&I-agenda for the Swedish mining industry*. Luleå, Sweden: Luleå Tekniska Universitet.

Baude, Annika. 1992. *Kvinnans plats på jobbet. [The woman's place at work]*. Stockholm, Sweden: SNS.

Beland Lindahl, Karin. 2008. *Frame analysis, place perceptions and the politics of natural resource management: exploring a forest policy controversy in Sweden*. Uppsala, Sweden: Sveriges Lantbruksuniversitet.

Beland Lindahl, Karin, Anna Zachrisson, Roine Viklund, Simon Matti, Daniel Fjellborg, Andreas Johansson and Lars Elenius. 2016. *Konflikter om gruvetablering: lokalsamhällets aktörer och vägar till hållbarhet [Mining conflicts: local community actors and paths to sustainability]*. Luleå, Sweden: Länsstyrelsen i Norrbotten.

Blomberg, Eva. 1995. *Män i mörker: arbetsgivare, reformister och syndikalister –politik och identitet i svensk gruvindustri 1910–1940 [Men in the dark: employers, reformists and syndicalists – politics and identity in the Swedish mining industry 1910–1940]*. Stockholm, Sweden: Stockholms Universitet.

Campbell, Hugh and Michael Mayerfeld Bell. 2000. "The question of rural masculinities." *Rural Sociology* 65(4), 532–546.

Cockburn, Cynthia. 1983. *Brothers: male dominance and technological change.* London: Pluto.

Collinson, David and Jeff Hearn. 1994. "Naming men as men: implications for work, organization and management." *Gender, Work and Organization* 1(1), 2–22.

Eveline, Joan and Michael Booth. 2002. "Gender and sexuality in discourses of managerial control: the case of women miners." *Gender, Work and Organization* 9(5), 556–578.

Fältholm, Ylva and Cathrine Norberg. 2017. "Gender diversity and innovation in mining: a corpus-based discourse analysis." *International Journal of Gender and Entrepreneurship* 9(4), 359–376.

Gier, Jaclyn J. and Laurie Mercier, eds. 2006. *Mining women: gender in the development of a global industry, 1670–2005.* New York, NY: Palgrave Macmillan.

Gunnarsson, Eva, Susanne Andersson and Annika Vänje, eds. 2003. *Where have all the structures gone? doing gender in organisations, examples from Finland, Norway and Sweden.* Stockholm University.

Holvino, Evangelina. 2010. "Intersections: the simultaneity of race, gender and class in organization studies." *Gender, Work and Organization* 17(3), 248–277.

Hägg, Kerstin. 1993. *Kvinnor och män i Kiruna: om kön och vardag i förändring i ett modernt gruvsamhälle 1900–1990 [Women and men in Kiruna: gender and everyday life in a modern mining society 1900–1990].* Umeå, Sweden: Umeå Universitet.

Jensen, Tommy and Johan Sandström. 2019. "Organizing rocks: actor–network theory and space." *Organization* 27(5), 701–716, doi:10.1177/1350508419842715.

Johansson, Jan, Bo Johansson, Joel Lööw, Magnus Nygren and Lena Abrahamsson. 2018. "Attracting young people to the mining industry: six recommendations." *International Journal of Mining and Mineral Engineering* 9(2), 94–108.

Johansson, Kristina and Anna Sofia Lundgren. 2015. "Gendering boundary work: exploring excluded spaces in supermarket job rotation." *Gender, Place and Culture* 22(2), 188–204.

Johansson, Maria and Lisa Ringblom. 2017. "The business case of gender equality in Swedish forestry and mining: restricting or enabling organizational change." *Gender, Work and Organization* 24(6), 628–642.

Kanter, Rosabeth Moss. 1977 1993. *Men and women of the corporation*, 2nd ed. New York, NY: Basic Books.

Karlsson, Lynn. 1997. "I gruva och på kontor: genusstämpling av arbete" [In the mine and in the office: the gendering of work]. In *Mot halva makten: elva historiska essäer om kvinnors strategier och mäns motstånd – rapport till utredningen om fördelningen av ekonomisk makt och ekonomiska resurser mellan kvinnor och män [Towards half of the power: eleven historical essays on women's strategies and men's resistance – report to the inquiry into the distribution of economic power and financial resources between women and men]*, ed. Ingrid Hagman, 89–104. Stockholm, Sweden: Fritze.

Kvande, Elin. 1999. "In the belly of the beast: constructing femininities in engineering organizations." *The European Journal of Women's Studies* 6(3), 305–328.

Korvajärvi, Päivi. 1998. "Reproducing gendered hierarchies in everyday work: contradictions in an employment office." *Gender, Work and Organization* 5(1), 19–30.

Lahiri-Dutt, Kuntala. 2011. "The megaproject of mining: a feminist critique." In *Engineering earth: the impacts of mega engineering projects*, ed. Stanley D. Brunn, 329–351. Dordrecht, Netherlands: Springer.

Lahiri-Dutt, Kuntala. 2012. "Digging women: towards a new agenda for feminist critiques of mining." *Gender, Place and Culture* 19(2), 193–212.

Lööw, Joel, Magnus Nygren and Jan Johansson. 2017. *Säkerhet i svensk gruvindustri: 30 år av sänkta olycksfallsfrekvenser – och den fortsatta vägen framåt [Safety in the Swedish mining industry: 30 years of reduced accident rates – and the continued way forward]*. Luleå, Sweden: Luleå Tekniska Universitet.

Lööw, Joel and Magnus Nygren. 2019. "Initiatives for increased safety in the Swedish mining industry: studying 30 years of improved accident rates." *Safety Science* 117, 437–446.

Massey, Doreen. 1994. *Space, place and gender*. Oxford: Polity Press.

Mayes, Robyn and Barbara Pini. 2010. "The 'feminine revolution in mining': a critique." *Australian Geographer* 41(2), 233–245.

Mayes, Robyn and Barbara Pini. 2014. "The Australian mining industry and the ideal mining woman: mobilizing a public business case for gender equality." *Journal of Industrial Relations* 56(4), 527–546.

McCall, Leslie. 2005. "The complexity of intersectionality." *Signs* 30(3), 1771–1800.

Mercier, Laurie. 2011. "Bordering on equality: women miners in North America." In *Gendering the field: towards sustainable livelihoods for mining communities*, ed. Kuntala Lahiri-Dutt, 33–48. Canberra, Australia: Australian National University.

Mercier, Laurie and Joan Gier. 2007. "Reconsidering women and gender in mining." *History Compass* 5(3), 995–1001.

Nilsson, Bo and Anna Sofia Lundgren. 2015. "Logics of rurality: political rhetoric about the Swedish North." *Journal of Rural Studies* 37, 85–95.

Norberg, Cathrine and Ylva Fältholm. 2018. "'Learn to blend in!' a corpus-based analysis of the representation of women in mining." *Equality, Diversity and Inclusion: An International Journal* 37(7), 698–712.

Nygren, Magnus. 2018. *Safety management on multi-employer worksites: responsibilities and power relations in the mining industry*. Luleå, Sweden: Luleå Tekniska Universitet.

Pini, Barbara and Belinda Leach. 2011. *Reshaping gender and class in rural spaces*. Burlington, VT: Ashgate.

Ringblom, Lisa. 2019. *Utmanad ordning? en studie av kön och jämställdhetsarbete i den svenska gruvindustrins arbetsorganisationer [Challenging the gendered order? a study of gender and gender equality work in the Swedish mining industry]*. Luleå, Sweden: Luleå Tekniska Universitet.

Ringblom, Lisa and Lena Abrahamsson. 2017. "Omförhandling i gruvan? om kön, arbete och förändring i den mansdominerade gruvnäringen" [Renegotiations in the mine? gender, work and change in the male-dominated mining industry]. *Tidskrift för Genusvetenskap 38*(1–2), 33–54.

Ringblom, Lisa and Maria Johansson. 2020. *"Who needs to be 'more equal' and why? doing gender equality in male-dominated industries."* Equality, Diversity and Inclusion: An International Journal 39(4), 337–353, doi:10.1108/EDI-01-2019-0042.

Rönnblom, Malin and Linda Sandberg. 2015. "Den nödvändiga jämställdheten" [The necessity of gender equality]. *Tidskrift för Genusvetenskap 36*(3), 57–82.

Saunders, Skye and Patricia Easteal. 2013. "The nature, pervasiveness and manifestations of sexual harassment in rural Australia: does 'masculinity' of workplace make a difference?" *Women's Studies International Forum 40*, 121–131.

Sjöstedt Landén, Angelika and Marianna Fotaki. 2018. "Gender and struggles for equality in mining resistance movements: performing critique against neoliberal capitalism in Sweden and Greece." *Social Inclusion 6*(4), 25–35.

Stenbacka, Susanne. 2011. "Othering the rural: about the construction of rural masculinities and the unspoken urban hegemonic ideal in Swedish media." *Journal of Rural Studies 27*(3), 235–244.

STRIM. 2016. *Strategic research and innovation agenda for the Swedish mining and metal producing industry*. Luleå, Sweden: Strategic Innovation Programme for the Swedish Mining and Metal Producing Industry.

SveMin. 2016. *Occupational injuries and sick leave in the Swedish mining and mineral industry 2015*. Stockholm, Sweden: GRAMKO.

Tallichet, Suzanne E. 1995. "Gendered relations in the mines and the division of labor underground." *Gender and Society 9*(6), 697–711.

Tallichet, Suzanne E. 2000. "Barriers to women's advancement in underground coal mining." *Rural Sociology 65*(2), 234–252.

Tallichet, Suzanne E. 2016. "Digging deeper: rural Appalachian women miners' reconstruction of gender in a class based community". In *Reshaping gender and class in rural spaces, eds.* B. Pini and B. Leach. Ashgate Publishing Group.

Träff, Matilda. 2019. "Så bidrar städarna till Kirunagruvans säkerhet" [This is how the cleaners contribute to the safety of the Kiruna mine]. *Fastighetsfolket*, 7 May. Available at: https://fastighetsfolket.se/2019/05/07/sa-bidrar-stadarna-till-att-kirunagruvans-sakerhet/.

Wajcman, Judy. 1991. *Feminism confronts technology*. Cambridge: Polity Press.

Wicks, David. 2002. "Institutional bases of identity construction and re-production: the case of underground coal mining." *Gender, Work and Organization 9*(3), 308–335.

11 Inequality Regimes in Equality Work

New Public Management and Peripheralization Processes in Swedish Schools

Ulrika Schmauch, Björn Ahlström, and Britt-Inger Keisu

In her classic text, *Feminist theory: From margin to center*, bell hooks (2000) describes how, while the feminist movement has rallied for gender equality, it has tended to centre on the experiences of white middle-class women at the expense of working-class women and women of colour; and how, despite its overall aim of empowering women, it has tended to disregard the multiple ways in which some women are privileged over others. A similar critique is voiced by other critical race scholars, as well as postcolonial scholars, who argue that ideals of individual freedom and the sanctity of human life have long co-existed with the brutal exploitation and oppression of people of colour. This shows that claiming commitment to equality and justice does not necessarily mean that equal rights prevail. It also implies that different dimensions of power, such as gender, race and class, must be studied in relation to each other, since in many ways they are mutually constitutive (Crenshaw 1988; De los Reyes and Mulinari 2005). Mudimbé (1988), Said (1978) and others argue that production of knowledge about Others is linked with the discursive and material domination of people and space, whereby some perspectives on the world are given precedence over others. What is considered a problem worthy of political intervention thus relates to the power to define and describe reality. In Sweden, issues of inequality in education, which are the topic of this chapter, tend to be studied in relation to an assumed lack of integration of migrant youth, and to racialized neighbourhoods in larger cities, while organizational factors within the education system are seldom examined from an intersectional perspective.

Ahmed (2012) shows that while many institutions claim to be committed to diversity, it is often given peripheral importance in their everyday operations. Such work is conducted in separate committees, often by people who are seen as signifying diversity in their very being, thus allowing privileged employees to avoid dealing with diversity altogether. Taking Butler's concept of performativity as a point of departure, Ahmed argues that a lot of diversity work is non-performative, ensuring that the institution as a whole continues to be non-diverse and non-equal. In this chapter we are interested in these processes of peripheralization (Kühn 2015; Kühn and Bernt 2013), where the (re-)production of inequality within organizations is linked with the (re-)production of silence about inequality, power and privilege. We discuss equality work on three different but interrelated levels: first, understanding of what equality work is and what it should aim at (discourse); second, the consequences of how the work is conducted and the implications for the reproduction of inequality within the school organization (inequality regimes, material space); and finally, how these understandings and practices relate to wider societal discourses of inequality. We therefore focus on peripheralization processes located in what Lefebvre (1991) terms *lived space*, at the intersections between material practices on the one hand, and discourses and imaginations on the other (Giritli-Nygren and Schmauch 2012; Schmauch and Giritli-Nygren 2014). Tyler and Cohen (2010) argue that power relations in organizations, such as gender, are materialized in work practices and constantly enacted. Looking more closely at how diversity work is performed in institutions, Ahmed (2012, 2019) shows that it often creates an illusion of the institution being committed and 'behind' diversity. In reality, however, diversity work is pushed to the margins, and thus functions as a way of 'not bringing something to effect' (Ahmed 2012: 117) or a 'way to separate diversity work from institutional work' (Ahmed 2012: 87). In looking at equality and diversity work in Swedish schools, and how the work is perceived and practised, we aim to gain deeper knowledge of the processes that locate ideals and organizational goals of equality in a peripheral position in schools' everyday lives.

Inequality Regimes in Neoliberal School Organizations

Organizational intersectional research has tended to focus on individual subjectivities and identities at the expense of organizational structures. There is a need to redirect attention toward socioeconomic conditions, economic and political processes and their materiality (Kantola and Lobardo 2017). Rodriguez et al. (2016: 205) call for research that 'moves beyond subjectivities to capture micro-level encounters, structures, systemic processes and institutional arrangements', in order to denaturalize ideals of efficiency and economy that tend to be at the centre of organizational research. In this chapter, we focus on the institutional level and how 'race, gender and class relations and stratification are built into organizational structures, processes and ways of working, which seem normal at the same time that they produce particular relations of inequality and privilege' (Holvino 2010: 262). Starting with Acker's (2006) concept of inequality regimes, in relation to equality and diversity work in Swedish schools we are interested in 'disparities between participants in power and control over goals, resources, and outcomes; workplace decisions such as how to organize work; ... pay and other monetary rewards; respect; and pleasures in work and work relations' (Acker 2006: 443).

Linked with wider neoliberal economic policies, new public management (NPM) has become a strong discourse in formulating how organizations, not least public institutions such as schools, should be managed (Ahlbäck Öberg, Shirin and Sten Widmalm 2016). Dahl (2009) argues that two, somewhat contradictory, logics are central – one focusing on detailed, often bureaucratic ways of organizing work, and the other on self-governance and individual responsibility for continually enhancing performance. While a core function of the educational system is to discipline students into certain ways of thinking and acting (*styles of the flesh*; Foucault 1977), the conduct of the school itself and the work carried out within it are also governed. Management of public organizations, such as schools, has largely been integrated into a logic of governance, through specific governmentalities (Foucault 1982) that focus on creating certain mentalities rather than using coercion. Rule is practised in a decentralized manner. In Sweden, the introduction of audit and evaluation systems, systems of management by objectives and results, and the idea of professional leadership and leadership of local processes (Thedvall 2015) have led organizations to organize their work in more auditable ways (Power 1999). Audits tend to govern what kind of work is conducted and how, giving rise to what Strathern (1997) calls an 'audit culture'. Issues that are not explicitly part of the audit tend to be peripheralized, both in relation to understanding their importance and centrality to the organization's aim and focus, and consequently to the material resources allocated to them.

In the Swedish curriculum, the mission of Swedish schools has two main strands: academic objectives and social/civic objectives (Skolverket 2011). Social objectives concern human interactions and how to treat others, and oblige schools to work against bullying, racism, gender inequality, and other forms of abuse and discrimination (SFS 2010). Swedish schools also have a compensatory assignment – a responsibility at the school level to compensate for students' differing preconditions, for example due to their class background. In other words, it is the schools' responsibility to ensure the provision of equal opportunities to enable students to learn what is taught. School principals have a responsibility to design and implement policies to promote gender equality and diversity that align with the Discrimination Act and the School Law (SFS 2008, 2010). These policies are formulated within a broader equality and anti-discrimination framework that covers gender, ethnicity, religious and other beliefs, disability, sexual orientation, gender identity and age (Skjeie and Langvasbråten 2009). Schools are obliged to conduct equality work to remediate discrimination and harassment that has already taken place, to prevent discrimination and harassment from happening, and to promote equality (SFS 2008).

The contradiction between schools' obligation to work for equality on the one hand, and their reproduction of inequalities on the other is, of course, neither a new nor a particularly Swedish phenomenon. The fields of social justice and multicultural education, developed mainly in the United States, have studied what schools need to do to ensure that minoritized and underprivileged groups' rights and needs in education are catered for. These aspects involve the curriculum itself, school staff and their beliefs and actions, and organizational factors such as testing procedures, counselling programmes, teaching strategies and home–school–community relationships (Banks 2013). In this field, intersectional perspectives are gaining momentum (Banks 2013). Kumashiro (2000) distinguishes between four approaches to inequality and power in relation to educational content: *education for the other*, e.g. helping students who are or may be at risk of being victims of oppression; *education about the other*, e.g. focusing on reaching those who may be oppressors by teaching about stereotypes, etc.; *education that is critical of privileging and othering*, where taken-for-granted norms and privileges are explored; and *education that changes students and society*, remodelling students' perceptions. It can be argued that these approaches are in line with Swedish schools' obligations in relation to equality work, mentioned above. In Sweden, however, issues of diversity and multiculturalism in relation to schools are studied mainly in ethnically segregated areas in major cities (see e.g. Bunar 2011; León Rosales 2010; Öhrn 2011) and often focus on social relations between young people, youths' identity work, neighbourhood stigmatization, etc., rather than on school organization or the organization of education *per se*. Issues of equality are thus peripheralized, not only from schools' everyday work, but also in relation to the kinds of school contexts in which issues of diversity are considered and tackled.

Analyzing Equality and Diversity Work

As required by the Discrimination Act and the School Law (SFS 2008, 2010), all the schools in this study engaged in some sort of equality and/ or diversity work, although how the work was organized and the centrality it took in their everyday work differed. Four schools were selected based on analysis of their plans for gender equality and diversity work (Keisu 2018) and whether they mentioned equality and/or diversity issues as part of their marketing, for instance on their websites. The issues were thus part of the schools' identity. The schools were located in different parts of the country and in towns and cities of different sizes in order to gain material from a broad range of organizational settings. The research was framed within a qualitative case study approach, where we were interested in understanding actors in different positions, and the contradictions between different actors' experiences and perspectives on equality work. A total of 41 individual and focus group interviews were conducted. Although students were also interviewed, in this chapter we focus on our interviews with school staff, including teachers, school principals, student health teams and other key actors. The data analysis was inspired by Bacchi's (2012) 'What's the problem represented to be?' approach, and focused on 'the unexamined assumptions and deep-seated conceptual logics within implicit problem representations' (Bacchi 2012: 22) and the lived effects of these problem representations (Bacchi 2010). Through this approach, on the one hand, we aimed to gain a deeper understanding of what the schools viewed as problems (how is the 'problem' that equality/diversity work is aiming to solve represented; on what assumptions is this based; what is left unproblematic; can the 'problem' be thought about differently?). On the other hand, we were interested in how this impacted on the enactment of equality work and its effects in changing and/or reproducing inequality in the schools and beyond.

Two of the schools were compulsory schools, and the other two upper secondary schools (see Table 11.1). The first school, '*North*' was located in a town dominated by industry. As in most northern towns, the student body was ethnically diverse with regard to the indigenous population, national minorities, the Swedish majority population and students of migrant background. The school had recently been rebuilt in a way that aimed to eliminate bullying by ensuring that the students were always visible to staff. The second school, '*South*' was located in the far south of the country, an area where racist and xenophobic political parties have long had wide support. In this school we conducted interviews with staff teaching on the introduction programme for recently arrived migrants, many of whom had arrived as unaccompanied minors. Most students were male. The school's diversity and equality work focused mainly on issues of gender equality, sexuality and religious freedom. The third school, '*East*' was located in a medium-sized town dominated by the cultural class and with a strong identity of tolerance and political awareness. This school had recently been criticized by the national school inspectorate for how it dealt with incidents of sexual harassment, and several staff had difficulty understanding why. Finally, the fourth school, '*Centre*' was located close to a larger city and was one of two upper secondary schools in the municipality. It had a relatively large proportion of students from working-class and migrant backgrounds, and a relatively low standing in comparison with the other school in the municipality. Prior to our interviews, its equality work had consisted of two strands, one based on norm-critical teaching led by a devoted teacher, and the other on administrative procedures for incidents of discrimination and harassment.

Table 11.1 School informants and gender division

	North Compulsory	South Upper secondary	Centre Compulsory	East Upper secondary	Total
	6 focus groups	3 focus groups	3 focus groups	5 focus groups	17 focus groups
	3 individuals	3 individuals	4 individuals	2 individuals	12 individuals
	9	6	7	7	**Total: 29 interviews**
	32 female	13 female	16 female	18 female	79 women (80%)
	2 male	No male	2 male	16 male	20 men (20%)
	34	**13**	**18**	**34**	**Total: 99 individuals**

The interviews focused on how the work was conducted in practice, by whom and for what reasons. The interviews were recorded and transcribed verbatim. In order to safeguard participants' anonymity, information on which participant related to which school is not disclosed in the analysis.

Centring Equality and Diversity Work

When asking staff to describe their schools' equality and diversity work, the focus was on the organization's response to incidents of harassment and bullying, often outside the classroom. An important part of the work was to deal with incident reports of harassment, discrimination and bullying filed by school staff and reported to the school principal, and on documentation required for the process following an incident. The focus here was on helping the victims, discussing what actions needed to be taken with regard to the students involved, and how staff could be vigilant over the relationship between victim and abuser, as well as over the culture within the group in particular and the school in general. In one of the schools, a person was hired to help structure the equality/diversity work:

> What was prioritized, and which I think we were also successful with, was to discover, investigate and remediate insulting behaviour, once it had happened. I think we were good at that. … What we were also successful with last year, was that we, really insistently, informed all staff about the importance of actually reporting insulting behaviour, writing those incident reports, handing them in and reconnecting and following up, and that it really… that they actually followed up on students (Equality coordinator).

It was unclear from our interviews how distinctions were made between behaviours that should be reported and interactions that were perceived to be acceptable. In one interview, members of the equality team in the same school discussed the prevalence of racism and homophobia, and concluded that although there had been racist and homophobic name calling in the corridors, they could not recollect any incidents of homophobia or racist discrimination. Similarly to Ahmed's (2019) argument, this suggests that what is considered worth reporting is indicative of the culture regarding harassment in the organization. Interestingly, this incident also highlights that although a lot of equality work was taking place, it was dealing with incidents after they had occurred, rather than focusing on preventing discrimination in the first place.

Another set of activities involved evaluating the status of equality and diversity for students. As previously mentioned, according to Swedish school regulations, school principals are responsible for establishing, implementing, following up and evaluating not only academic but also social objectives (Skolverket 2011). A common way to evaluate this was to distribute surveys to students. These were distributed by several actors: the municipality (the entity responsible for schools in Sweden), national school agencies such as the Swedish School Inspectorate, the Swedish Agency for Youth and Civil Society, teachers and local health teams. Most effort was put into evaluating students' knowledge; equality and diversity work was also evaluated but was not prioritized in the same way (Keisu and Ahlström 2020). Furthermore, according to both staff and students, the students were tired of completing too many surveys. The students explained that the surveys were often distributed at the end of a class or semester, and feedback on the results was scarce or non-existent (see also Keisu and Ahlström 2020). Hence, the students did not take them seriously, which decreased the validity of the data. Surveys tend to focus on issues that are already accepted as being important, and tend not to address dimensions of power that are perceived as problematic to ask about, or those seen as unproblematic. As is the norm in Swedish surveys, issues of race/ethnicity are not asked about, but rather are redefined in terms of migration background. This tends to conceal the experiences of indigenous and national minorities, for example, and tends to conflate racist discrimination with a lack of integration into Swedish society. The surveys also risk being understood as 'box ticking' for the school's annual audit, and might therefore be understood as an example of the neoliberal discourse of performance culture (Ahmed 2012) that tends to conceal important aspects of diversity and equality in the school.

One way of dealing with problems identified from the surveys was to organize special theme days or weeks, where special guests were invited to give lectures, special films were screened, etc. In the schools we visited, issues that had received special focus included sexual consent and homophobia. While staff viewed this as a way to give special focus to important issues, the students were less enthusiastic. Although this strategy puts equality issues at the centre of the school agenda for a short time, it also peripheralizes them from everyday practice (see also Banks 1989; Ladson-Billings 1994). Interestingly, the focus on gender and sexuality tended to be strong, regardless of the schools' location and/or social context. Linking this to Kumashiro's (2000) dimensions of anti-oppressive education, we can see that the focus was on education for and about the Other. Although there were some examples of education on privileging, education aimed at helping students change society was never discussed. The theme days focused on teaching for and about the Other, in this case women and LGBTQI+-issues.

Several schools also had special committees to organize staff work on equality, but the students were not represented. Although the teams had various names, such as 'equal opportunity committee', 'group for safety' and 'gender team', they all met a few times per semester, discussed equality-related topics, planned activities (e.g. theme days) and later reported to their colleagues. At one school, several groups were working on related issues. Although those engaged in the teams put effort and time into equality work, the groups tended to be relatively isolated from the school's everyday work:

> Because the problem is that we as teachers get divided into these groups, I mean it becomes an information problem. We feel that, that we are not given the information. I, mean, what happened in the gender team? What... what... what is going on there? I don't doubt for a second that my colleagues wonder what the heck is going on in the equality team. I have no idea what happens in the library team. And everybody goes to the all these meetings (Member of Equality team).

Like the theme days mentioned above, the equality committees were understood as a way to take diversity issues seriously and give them special attention. However, as this quote shows, they tended to become a way to dislocate equality issues from the agenda (Ahmed 2012).

A fifth activity mentioned in the schools was working with the plan for equality work itself. Working with the plan often became an isolated activity separate from the school's everyday work. One school had been criticized by the Swedish School Inspectorate for not working with the plan on a regular basis:

> IP: The School Inspectorate said that it wasn't... I mean... during a long time that the equality and diversity plan had not been... used. That we hadn't worked on it. That it is neglected... I think we work on it from time to time!
>
> IP: Every year we work on it (Teachers).

This example also highlights what Ahmed (2012) describes as the plan as a manifest, and that 'you end up doing the document rather than doing the doing' (Ahmed 2006: 117) of equality work (see also Keisu and Carbin 2014; Lundin and Torpsten 2018). After the plan was written, in several schools we visited it was not used until it was time to work on its evaluation the following year. Clearly, equality and diversity work was not necessarily based on the school's own understanding of the problem, but was often performed in case the school was subject to external evaluation. While government requirements to work on diversity and equality issues forced the schools to conduct the work, the plans formed part of the documentation of inequality, and were also in themselves perceived as a way to combat it (see also Ahmed 2012).

Many activities focused on the actions of individual students, or on students' attitudes and knowledge. The problems identified often related to areas over which teachers and other staff had little control (and therefore limited responsibility), such as hallways, changing rooms and lavatory. Thus, structural problems of inequality tended to be individualized as a matter of student behaviour (Foucault 1982) and placed in spaces peripheral to the educational work taking place in schools. These examples highlight a tendency to view equality and diversity work as just one of many issues on which the school has to work. By constructing equality issues as a number of smaller problems that can be measured and solved relatively easily, for example by having a good plan or dealing with reported incidents of harassment, the wider implications of equality and diversity work, such as power, privilege and the implications of representations in educational material, are not taken into consideration. Rather, the focus is on 'ticking the boxes' for the planned audit.

In all the schools studied, the equality and diversity issues prioritized were based on staff assumptions about what the students needed. For example, it was assumed that unaccompanied minors studying at 'South' school needed to learn about sexual consent and religious freedom (which tended to be defined as freedom *from* religion), but not about everyday racism; and that students in 'Centre' school were subjected to heteronormativity rather than class structures. Of course, that is not to say that gender does not play a role in the lives of unaccompanied minors, nor that heteronormativity is less important than class in any context; rather, what is considered to be a problem requiring time and effort relates to relationships of power in the lived spaces where both social positions as well as staff's understanding of them are central. Inequality is understood as a matter of problematic norms and values held by those in subordinated positions, rather than a matter of relations of power. This understanding is also familiar in everyday descriptions of young people of colour in general, unaccompanied minors specifically, and working-class neighbourhoods.

Furthermore, while schools have a compensatory assignment and are required to work against discrimination, it is mainly work against harassment and insulting behaviour (*kränkande behandling*) that is highlighted as equality and diversity work. Similarly to hooks' argument above, this can be seen as a way of focusing on the experiences of white, middle-class, heterosexual, secular (etc.) students, and on the individual's right to an education free from discrimination and harassment, rather than equality at a societal level, thus making such issues peripheral to understanding what problems need to be addressed. The focus on individual incidents requires little, if any, commitment to dismantling systems of privilege and power.

The Marginalization of Equality Work

The various equality and diversity teams discussed urgent cases and issues relating to individual or groups of students. Much less time was spent discussing how equality and diversity issues should be implemented in teaching and other everyday interactions with students. In several interviews, it became clear that many of the schools' employees had difficulty defining what equality and diversity work was, on both conceptual and practical levels. It was often described in terms of core values, school culture, student health and wellbeing, student democracy, insulting behaviour, equal treatment or rights, bullying or harassment, or there was simply an implied consensus on what 'these issues' were. How diversity and equality work was both conceptualized and practised was clearly linked with 'insulting behaviour' rather than discrimination. This indicates that such work was seen as something that should correct (students') behaviour toward each other, rather than dismantling structures of inequality, power and privilege.

Of course, this relates to blurred distinctions in school organizations' goals and vision documents and in laws and regulations at different organizational levels, focusing on what the school should teach each student at an individual level. However, it is also indicative of how the concepts of equality and diversity are emptied of political content and reduced to individualized responsibilities for conduct, values and experience (Foucault 1977). In our material, school staff found it hard to give examples of how equality and diversity work was integrated into other areas of their work. In one example, a school principal was asked to describe how equality work was conducted in the classroom:

> They do have class councils, I they have... gosh, this is hard! Well they always have kind of a, ehm... evaluate the day... like an evaluation at the end of the day. What has happened? What worked well? So, that is one way... to evaluate, reflect together with the students. What will we take with us for tomorrow? And like that, I think it is really important work. Ehm... they have a lot of stuff... like... over the different levels [school levels], games... with each other, I mean like collaboration exercises and... ehm... I am really bewildered by this question! I think they do so much, they always have a reason for it (School principal).

Some teachers also found it difficult to work with the schools' social and civil mission in general, and preferred to focus on pedagogical issues, which they saw as separate from equality and diversity work. This was explained as a lack of knowledge or courage of convictions on what knowledge was important to convey to the students, but also as a matter of priorities. Even when there were ambitions and knowledge to put equality and diversity work at the centre of teaching, it was brushed aside, as visualized in a quote by a teacher whom both the students and the principal at the school regarded as devoted, who was also an expert on the norm-critical perspective:

> But sometimes it feels like, maybe, that – and I think that is quite typical for a lot of schools – that it happens that way, that you think that you're done. Like three years ago, I did workshops on norm-critical pedagogics, and after that it became a bit 'too much' according to some. There was resistance. From some more than others. And then you thought 'Let's back off a little. I think we're done with this', but then there are new staff, and they have never ever heard it. And it's not like we take it up and do it again, so to speak. We did an attempt at a drive last year, that we, during conference time[1] should give equality work as many time slots as other parts, like language development and there were different things. But it's like, yes, there was a will, but then in practice it was still 'well, now this other thing needs to be done', like that. At the end of the day, sometimes we tend to get stuck in this thing with support structures and incident reports, which is really important, but I mean… but that this… because what I work a lot with is the promotional work or exactly what is supposed to happen in class like all the time, so that we eventually won't have to kind of write incident reports. That's the goal of course, but… yeah, and that's where it sometimes feels like there isn't really time (Teacher and key actor).

It seems fair to say that equality and diversity work was not a priority in any of the schools, although they fulfilled their requirements. These examples show how the unequal balance of power is re-established when threatened (Acker 2006; Abrahamsson 2009). When a school invested time and money in a workshop to educate all staff, the work was considered 'too much', and promotional work was further downplayed by teachers when new staff were employed. Although allowing firebrands to put time and effort into specific courses for other staff members might be considered a way to bring the issue to the centre of attention, it clearly allowed other members of staff to underachieve (Ahmed 2012). In an interview with an equality team, the challenge of integration was discussed:

> And you have to start somewhere, and make priorities, what should we talk about now? We have a limited time where everyone can

meet. What should be do with that time? Is it the pedagogical discussion or is it the discussion around equal treatment? I think it is difficult, because my experience is that when we talk about equal treatment, we talk about the self-evident stuff and these simple things, like where everyone knows exactly what opinion you're supposed to have, everyone knows what you should think, what I should say in this context and in a teacher meeting, in front of grown people … But I don't think it can be transferred to those situations when you're dealing with students and parents, who… who are actually, in effect, who are mad as hell because their child comes home and has been called a slut, and stuff like that (Member of Equality team).

Discussions taking place in the teams did not always help in the everyday work of dealing with discrimination, abuse and harassment. Furthermore the organization of everyday work made it difficult for staff to go outside the given structure, not least when the workload forced them to prioritize some issues over others:

To fill in an incident report and support structure work entails a lot of administrative work. So I'm a bit concerned that you might choose not to. You think "it's too much hassle. (Member of Equality team).

These examples show the importance of organizational factors and working conditions for the success of equality and diversity work. Teachers' time is divided into smaller parts in which school managers set the priorities (see also Acker 2006). Although schools are obliged to conduct equality and diversity work, and teachers and other staff members claim to think it is important, they still struggle to find the time and resources, as other activities are prioritized. Focusing on work that goes against the governmentality of specific teams responsible for specific tasks, measurable results on specific indicators, and boxes that can be ticked is seen as a waste of time (at best). This shows that elements of equality and diversity work that are not urgent, for example being linked with obvious harassment or bullying, are difficult for staff to define, but also for them to find ways to integrate into their everyday work. Work focusing on changing power relations or critiquing norms and values that dominate the school culture often have to take a back seat in favour of work that is more important for school evaluations and results. No strategies to conduct equality work outside the school's organizational structures were mentioned in our interviews (see also Dovemark 2010; Beach and Dovemark 2011).

Turning to the content of the work, gender was clearly a prioritized inequality regime in all the schools studied (see Keisu 2014), and was often talked about in terms of liberal feminism, for example gender neutrality, rights, and the amount of attention given to boys and girls respectively:

> IP: Being a Swedish teacher, I always stress both male and female authors, and in Swedish we work a lot on how to use the language, pronouns like he/she/one, trying to have a gender-neutral language, things like that. A lot of that is in the teaching, is always done… That girls and boys should have the same opportunity to speak, as much as the other should. You try to think about that all the time as well. But then, we haven't worked on it more actively, like with a big project. We have not done that.
>
> IP2: But that is also a kind of work that is always done – informing them about what their rights are (School principals).

In all the schools, when connections were drawn between dimensions of power, such as race and gender, these were linked with gender relations among immigrant students:

> Equality is not about, like… I also feel that it is related to… […] now that we have more asylum-seeking students, I mean, there are cultural clashes, really clear ones in some cases. In part it's related to views on women and men, I mean, views on… who is in authority and not authority. In those cases, you have to rethink every single lesson you have with them. I teach them in social studies… we have quite hard fights sometimes, because I'm a woman. And then I also feel that equality is also about this thing about, I mean – if you consider those quote unquote 'Swedish students' – partly related to guys and girls and who takes up more space in class, and there I have to realize that I, personally, a lot of the time give more time to the guys than the girls (Equality committee).

Despite associating Other cultures with gender inequality (see e.g. De los Reyes and Mulinari 2005), and positioning the teacher as subordinated despite her class position in relation to her students owing to her subordinated gender (see e.g. Martinsson, Griffin, and Nygren. 2016), there was clearly a view that inequality between 'Swedish' students could not be tackled through confrontation and discussions ('fights'). While this worked for students seeking asylum, gender inequality among 'Swedish' students was the teacher's responsibility.

The following quote exemplifies how the informants argued why gender equality had to be prioritized and the school needed a team working specifically on gender issues:

> But actually the students themselves say that, they think the teachers need to get more fair in their treatment between boys and girls. So

gender... that's why I said that as long as... because some teachers feel that 'why can't the gender team be a part of the equality team? It's pretty much the same.' Mmm, what we do in the gender team, of course they are related, like when we arrange... gender days and activities, lectures, and stuff... but it has to be a separate group and a specific activity that only looks at issues regarding boys and girls. Because as long as the biggest issues are about just this, we have really a lot to work with, because otherwise these issues will drown in the other stuff we do. And they'll have to accept that for as long as I am principal here (School principal).

Although we are seeing a backlash against gender equality and diversity work in many countries, discussing gender issues is (still?) relatively uncontroversial in Swedish schools. One explanation for this is the historically strong position of gender in relation to other equality issues in Swedish policy (De los Reyes and Mulinari 2005). As illustrated in the previous quotes, gender is constructed in a binary way that marginalizes trans-experiences. It is also reduced to relations between the sexes, rather than relations based on masculinity/femininity, for example. Interestingly, 80% of the participants in this study (80 individuals) were women, most of whom were white and middle-aged. Therefore, it is unsurprising that gender was the inequality they felt most comfortable talking about, as it allowed them not to speak from a position of power, regardless of their organizational position (see also hooks 2000). Furthermore, as gender is one of few background variables asked about in surveys, it is also the inequality on which most data are available. Other inequalities, such as class, disability, sexual orientation, gender identity and religion, were mentioned only a few times in the interviews, often in response to explicit questions by the interviewers. Some schools had had theme days regarding LGBTQI+ issues, but even there, issues of heteronormativity and transphobia were not at the centre of equality and diversity work.

Margin and Centre in Equality and Diversity Work: The Inequality of Inequalities

In the schools in this study, equality and diversity work is described as autonomous from the organizations' societal context. This makes it possible to imagine, and (in theory) achieve, an organization that, despite systematic inequalities in society at large, manages to eliminate discrimination and inequality all together. The organization is perceived and organized as a closed system in which measuring inequality levels tends to be central. Focusing on attitudes and behaviour among those with least power (students) and how to fix the problem by supplying information and knowledge, not least through women's representation, also indicates that the importance of the school structure and culture itself, and the wider organizational context of the educational system, are marginalized. The work becomes a matter of tweaking the system rather than changing it. It also becomes an issue that can be dealt with within the school's existing culture and structure, thus not questioning the inequality regimes that make equality work necessary in the first place (Ahmed 2012). Furthermore, different forms of discrimination and harassment are lumped together under the heading of 'insulting treatment'. This means that insulting someone's ugly shoes is constructed as just as bad as harassment linked to centuries of violent abuse.

What follows from this is that students are described as the objects of intervention, although teachers and other staff describe organizational factors and their own lack of knowledge when explaining why not more work is done. This contradiction can be understood as a consequence of the relationship between the adult in power and the child/adolescent in a more peripheral position in the organizations' inequality regimes. While it is the teachers' job to transfer knowledge and information, this clearly becomes a way to avoid dealing with organizational factors, both at the school level and in the educational system as a whole. It is also clear that students do not participate in deciding which inequality problems need to be prioritized and how.

Furthermore, inequality is talked about in terms of extraordinary events. Although it is, of course, necessary to prevent and take action against openly racist, homophobic and sexist comments and actions, the everyday reproduction of inequality regimes remains at the periphery of attention (Essed 1991). Discrimination thus becomes an issue primarily for those subjected to it: girls/women, people of colour, LGBTQI+ students, etc. This means that everyday racism, sexism, etc. are allowed to remain out of sight and out of mind for those with most power and responsibility to destabilize them (Schmauch 2006). This may also explain what types of discrimination are centred and which are peripheralized in the work that does take place. In 'North' school, for example, ethnicity was discussed in relation to immigrant students, although ethnicity and race have long been central to (internal colonial) relations in the area. As Kobayashi and Peake (2000) argue, this tends to conceal the fact that the group in power is part of the power relation and, we argue, therefore part of the problem to be dealt with in equality and diversity work. When equality and diversity work is organized in such a way as to contribute to the normalization of privilege, it is unlikely to destabilize the status quo in a way that makes equality possible.

Equality work is located, both discursively and physically, in peripheral organizational spaces, such as by downplaying its importance and controlling what time and space are used to discuss the issues. Thus, the logic of NPM makes certain ways of organizing equality and diversity work seem more reasonable than others, limiting the range of possible action. Although systematic and continuous evaluation of the state of equality in schools, as measured for example in student surveys, might be considered an effective way to ensure that effort is concentrated where it has impact, we argue that it also tends to downplay the reproduction of inequality to one issue among many others that teachers and other staff are expected to handle. The bureaucratic way of organizing staff time by allocating time for specific tasks, such as conference time as mentioned above, makes efforts to find new, context-sensitive ways of organizing difficult. Defining priorities through pre-given definitions of problems in student surveys and reports of incidents that have already taken place leaves little room to address other problems. While work to meet schools' required social objectives may also take place outside the realm of equality and diversity work, the results of this study indicate a gap between the importance given to the work in policy documents and on the ground. The focus on inequality as something taking place elsewhere (in locker rooms, school hallways) or in other organizational settings (special theme days, special working groups of staff) tends to make issues of equality peripheral to the everyday educational practice of teaching. Thus, the political possibilities of social objectives in school tend to be downplayed or, in Ahmed's (2012) term, non-performed. Responsibility is placed on individual teachers and school principals, who find it difficult to find the time to think outside the boxes they are expected to tick for audit purposes. Although this is to some extent a matter of the priorities set by staff, school principals and other officials within the educational system, the present organization of equality work also enables it not to be prioritized.

Note

1 Conference time is time that teachers and other staff have available for meetings, etc. What should be done during this time is decided by the school principals, for example what topics need to be discussed, what needs to be planned (besides the teaching of the individual teacher).

References

Abrahamsson, Lena. 2009. *Att återställa ordningen [Restoring the order]*. Umeå, Sweden: Boréa.

Acker, Joan. 2006. "Inequality regimes: gender, class, and race in organizations". *Gender and Society* 20(4): 441–464.

Ahlbäck Öberg, Shirin and Sten Widmalm. 2016. "Att göra rätt även när ingen ser på" [Doing the right thing even when no one is looking]. *Statsvetenskaplig Tidskrift* 118(1), 7–17.

Ahmed, Sara. 2006. "The non-performativity of anti-racism." *Meridians* 7(1), 104–126.

Ahmed, Sara. 2012. *On being included: racism and diversity in institutional life.* London: Duke University Press.

Ahmed, Sara. 2019. "A complaint biography". *Biography* 42(3), 514–523.

Bacchi, Carol. 2010. *Foucault, policy and rule: challenging the problem-solving paradigm.* Aalborg, Denmark: Institut for Historie, Internationale Studier og Samfundsforhold, Aalborg Universitet.

Bacchi, Carol. 2012. "Introducing the 'what's the problem represented to be?' approach." In *Engaging with Carol Bacchi: strategic interventions and exchanges*, eds. Angelique Bletsas and Christine Beasley, 21–24. Adelaide, Australia: University of Adelaide Press.

Banks, James A. 1989. "Approaches to multicultural curriculum reform." *Trotter Review* 3(3), 17–19.

Banks, James A. 2013. "The construction and historical development of multicultural education, 1962–2012." *Theory into Practice* 52(S1), 73–82.

Beach, Dennis and Marianne Dovemark. 2011. "Twelve years of upper-secondary education in Sweden: the beginnings of a neo-liberal policy hegemony?" *Educational Review* 63(3), 313–327.

Bunar, Nihad. 2011. "Multicultural urban schools in Sweden and their communities: social predicaments, the power of stigma, and relational dilemmas." *Urban Education* 46(2), 141–164.

Crenshaw, Kimberlé W. 1988. "Race, reform, and retrenchment: transformation and legitimation in antidiscrimination law." *Harvard Law Review* 101(7), 1331–1387.

Dahl, Hanne Marie. 2009. "New public management, care and struggles about recognition." *Critical Social Policy* 29(4), 634–654.

De los Reyes, Paulina and Diana Mulinari. 2005. *Intersektionalitet: kritiska reflektioner över (o)jämlikhetens landskap [Intersectionality: critical reflections on the landscape of (in)equality].* Malmö, Sweden: Liber.

Dovemark, Marianne. 2010. "Teachers' collective actions, alliances and resistance within neo-liberal ideas of education: the example of the individual programme." *European Educational Research Journal* 9(2), 232–244.

Essed, Philomena. 1991. *Understanding everyday racism: An interdisciplinary theory.* London: Sage.

Foucault, Michel. 1977. *Discipline and punish: the birth of the prison.* New York, NY: Random House.

Foucault, Michel. 1982. "The subject and power." *Critical Inquiry* 8(4), 777–795.

Giritli-Nygren, Katarina and Ulrika Schmauch. 2012. "Picturing inclusive places in segregated spaces: a participatory photo project conducted by migrant women in Sweden." *Gender, Place and Culture* 19(5), 600–614.

Holvino, Evangelina. 2010. "Intersections: the simultaneity of race, gender and class in organization studies." *Gender, Work and Organization* 17(3), 248–277.

hooks, bell. 2000. *Feminist theory: from margin to center.* London: Pluto Press.

Kantola, Johanna and Emanuela Lobardo. 2017. "Feminist political analysis: exploring strengths, hegemonies and limitations." *Feminist Theory* 18(3), 1323–1341.

Keisu, Britt-Inger. 2014. "Om två råd blir ett" [If two committees are to become one]. In *Att bryta innanförskapet: kritiska perspektiv på jämställdhet och mångfald i akademin, [Challenge the privileged: critical perspective on gender equality and diversity in academia]*, ed. Kerstin Sandell, 144–169. Göteborg, Sweden: Makadam Förlag.

Keisu, Britt-Inger. 2018. "Sammanvävda praktiker? en studie av likabehandlingsarbete och vetenskapligt förhållningssätt i grundskolan" [Interwoven practices? a study of equality and diversity work and the scientific approach in compulsory schools]. In *Att leda skolor med stöd i forskning: exempel, analyser och utmaningar [Leading schools with support in research: case, analysis and challenges]*, eds. Niclas Rönnström and Olof Johansson, 417–447. Stockholm, Sweden: Natur och Kultur.

Keisu, Britt-Inger and Björn Ahlström. 2020. "The silent voices: pupil participation for gender equality and diversity." *Educational Research* 62(1), 1–17.

Keisu, Britt-Inger and Maria Carbin. 2014. "Administrators or critical cynics? a study of gender equality workers in Swedish higher education." *NORA – Nordic Journal of Feminist and Gender Research* 22(3), 204–218.

Kobayashi, Audrey and Linda Peake. 2000. "Racism out of place: thoughts on whiteness & antiracist geography in the new millennium." *Annals of the Association of American Geographers* 90(2), 392–403.

Kühn, Manfred. 2015. "Peripheralization: theoretical concepts explaining socio-spatial inequalities." *European Planning Studies* 23(2), 367–378.

Kühn, Manfred and Matthias Bernt. 2013. "Peripheralization and power." In *Peripheralization: the making of spatial dependencies and social injustice*, eds. Andrea Fischer-Tahir and Matthias Naumann, 302–317. Wiesbaden, Germany: Springer.

Kumashiro, Kevin K. 2000. "Toward a theory of anti-oppressive education." *Review of Educational Research* 70(1), 25–53.

Ladson-Billings, Gloria. 1994. "What we can learn from multicultural education research." *Educational Leadership* 51(8), 22–26.

Lefebvre, Henri. 1991. *The production of space*. Oxford: Basil Blackwell.

León Rosales, René. 2010. *Vid framtidens hitersta gräns: om maskulina elevpositioner i en multietnisk skola [At the hither side of the future: masculine pupil positions in a multiethnic school]*. Stockholm, Sweden: Botkyrka, Mångkulturellt Centrum.

Lundin, Mattias and Ann-Christin Torpsten. 2018. "The 'flawless' school and the problematic actors: research on policy documents to counteract discrimination and degrading treatment in schools in Sweden." *European Journal of Education* 53(4), 574–585.

Martinsson, Lena, Gabrielle Griffin and Katarina Giritli Nygren. 2016. *Challenging the myth of gender equality in Sweden*. Bristol: Policy Press.

Mudimbé, Valentin Y. 1988. *The invention of Africa: gnosis, philosophy, and the order of knowledge*. Bloomington, IN: Indiana University Press.

Öhrn, Elisabet. 2011. "Class and ethnicity at work: segregation and conflict in a Swedish secondary school." *Education Inquiry* 2(2), 345–357.

Power, Michael. 1999. *The audit society: rituals of verification*. Oxford: Oxford University Press.

Rodriguez, Jenny K., Evangelina Holvino, Joyce K. Fletcher and Stella M. Nkomo. 2016. "The theory and praxis of intersectionality in work and organisations: where do we go from here?" *Gender, Work and Organization* 23(3), 201–222.

Said, Edward W. 1978. *Orientalism*, 1st edn. New York, NY: Pantheon Books

Schmauch, Ulrika. 2006. *Den osynliga vardagsrasismens realitet [The reality of invisible everyday racism]*. Umeå, Sweden: Umeå University.

Schmauch, Ulrika and Katarina Giritli-Nygren. 2014. "The hidden boundaries of everyday places: migrant women, *homeplace* and the spatial practices of a small Swedish town." *ACME: An International E-Journal for Critical Geographies* 13(2), 372– 339.

SFS. 2008. Diskrimineringslag [The Discrimination Act], 2008:567 *Svensk författningssamling [Swedish codes of statutes]*. Stockholm, Sweden: Granskningskansliet.

SFS. 2010. Skollagen [The school law], 2010:800. *Svensk författningssamling [Swedish codes of statutes]*. Stockholm, Sweden: Granskningskansliet.

Skjeie, Hege and Trude Langvasbråten. 2009. "Intersectionality in practice? anti-discrimination reforms in Norway." *International Feminist Journal of Politics* 11(4), 513–529.

Skolverket. 2011. *Läroplan för gymnasieskolan [Curriculum for upper secondary school]*. Stockholm, Sweden: Utbildningsdepartementet.

Strathern, Marilyn. 1997. "Improving ratings: audit in the British university system." *European Review* 5(3), 305–321.

Thedvall, Renita. 2015. "Managing preschool the Lean way: evaluating work processes by numbers and colours." *Social Anthropology* 23(1), 42–52.

Tyler, Melissa and Laurie Cohen. 2010. "Spaces that matter: gender performativity and organizational space." *Organization Studies* 31(2), 175–198.

12 Freedom of Choice and Gender Equality in Swedish Home-Based Elderly Care

Annette Thörnquist

Introduction

In Sweden, as in many other countries, gender equality must be integrated into all policy areas and regular operations. As this gender mainstreaming strategy was launched in the mid-1990s – during a time of public-sector deregulation, marketization and retrenchments – it has also been linked with economic objectives (Callerstig and Lindholm 2011; Callerstig 2014; Jacquot 2010).[1] The Swedish Act on System of Choice in the Public Sector (LOV) provides an example of such interlinked economic and gender-equality policy objectives. The Act, which came into force in 2009, aimed to regulate and promote the exposure of primary healthcare and social care and services to private competition through customer/user choice. Choice in this sense means that users of tax-financed welfare services are entitled to choose between the public service provider and external providers authorized by the public principal. This reform, which was highly prioritized by the centre-right coalition government in office between the general elections of 2006 and 2014, would not only foster freedom of choice for the users, but also create a market for female entrepreneurs. While the regions (formerly county councils) have been obliged to operate LOV in primary healthcare since 2010, the municipalities can use the reform voluntarily in social care and services for the elderly and for people with functional impairments, as an alternative to competitive bidding under the Act on Public Procurement (LOU).[2] In July 2020, 160 of the 290 municipalities in Sweden had introduced LOV. In 157 of these municipalities, the reform was being applied to home-based elderly care, which is the municipal sector in which the reform has predominantly been implemented (SALAR 2020). The present chapter focuses on this sector.

Aim and Theoretical Approach

The aim of this chapter is to discuss the relationship between the economic and gender equality objectives in the freedom of choice reform.

The questions asked are: 1) what was the normative conception of gender equality implied in the reform; and 2) how have the gender equality objective been realized in home-based elderly care? The analysis is based on an *intersectional approach* in combination with a *centre–periphery perspective*. In addition, I use *precarious employment* as a multidimensional analytical concept. Theoretically, the purpose is to illustrate the benefit of integrating these three perspectives.

The *intersectional perspective* helps to reveal and explain how social structures, normative processes and patterns of behaviour create inequalities based on gender, as well as on class, ethnicity, age and other social categorizations. This approach does not question the benefit of using social categories analytically, but helps to contextualize the relevance of these categorizations and accentuate their interconnection (Lykke 2003; de los Reyes and Mulinari, 2005; McCall 2005; Acker 2012). In this chapter, the intersectional perspective helps to identify and interpret the normative conception of gender equality implied in the LOV reform, as well as the meaning of diversity. Like the notions of gender equality and gender mainstreaming, the meaning of diversity may also vary, depending on how it is communicated, and whether it is linked with other purposes (de los Reyes 2001; Walby 2005; Ahmed 2007). I also use the intersectional perspective for a critical discussion of the social implications of the reform in working life.

The second analytical perspective is the *centre–periphery divide*. Nyhlén and Giritli Nygren (2015) and Giritli Nygren and Nyhlén (2017) use this perspective in their analyses of the implementation of the national Swedish elderly care policy in rural areas. I relate to their research, and I also use the centre–periphery metaphor to illustrate distinguishing practices in the labour market, such as segregation and segmentation (Deakin 2013).

Regarding the notion of *precarious employment*, I use Lewchuk et al.'s (2003: 23) definition: 'a cumulative combination of atypical employment contracts, limited social benefits, poor statutory entitlements, job insecurity, short tenure and low wages'. However, I prefer to add another factor, namely a poor working environment. The cumulative aspect lies in the fact that these factors are interlinked and mutually reinforcing. This multi-dimensional definition corresponds well with the intersectional perspective, which also stresses the importance of multidimensional and cumulative processes.

The connection between these three perspectives appears even in a brief presentation of the character of the Swedish labour market in elderly care, which is segregated by gender and increasingly also by ethnicity, especially in metropolitan areas. In elderly care, 91% of auxiliary nurses are women (Statistics Sweden 2020). In a survey of workers in the Swedish Municipal Workers' Union (*Kommunal*) in 2012 (Wondmeneh 2013), foreign-born workers accounted for 24% in elderly care. In the county council of Stockholm, however, the proportion was twice as high. The study also showed that the share of fixed-term and hourly employment was considerably higher among foreign-born workers than among Swedish-born workers. In contrast, Giertz and Jönson's (2018) study based on the same dataset reveals no significant differences between immigrants and Swedish-born workers in how they perceived their working conditions. What is certain, however, is that non-unionized workers, who were not represented in these surveys, are more at risk of precarious employment. In the public sector in 2019, union density among foreign-born blue-collar workers was 65%, compared with 75% among Swedish-born workers. In addition, the general decline in union density during the period 2006–2019 was much higher (26 percentage points compared with 13 points) for the two categories (Kjellberg 2020: 51–53).

Material and Methodology

This chapter draws on an analysis of preparatory works[3] for the LOV reform, and especially the report from the government-appointed investigation behind the legislative proposal (Swedish Government 2008a), including the government's directive for this investigation (Swedish Government 2007), comment letters on the report and the government bill (Swedish Government 2008b). I also refer to relevant research in this field, including my previous studies published in Swedish (Thörnquist 2013, 2014). The former study, which concerned the consequences of LOV in working life, comprised 15 in-depth interviews with social partners, municipal officials and private providers in three municipalities that had introduced LOV into home-based elderly care in 2009. Analysis of the development up to 2020 is based on official statistics, reports and other documents from government agencies, municipalities and the social partners. In addition, I carried out five follow-up interviews in the summer of 2019 with representatives of *Kommunal* at the national and local level, with the Swedish Association of Local Authorities and Regions (SALAR), and with the local authority in one municipality featured in my 2013 study. In this municipality, where many small and medium-large actors contracted under LOV have provided domestic services to the elderly for the last ten years, there have been problems with security fraud and 'unhealthy competition', i.e. competition based on poor working conditions.

The Wider Social Context of LOV: Background

The transformation of the Swedish public sector in recent decades reflects the neoliberal trend in Western welfare states following the economic stagnation of the 1970s and early 1980s (Hood 1995; Koch 2006;

Almqvist 2006). In Sweden, this trend gained ground in the late 1980s and had a strong impact on the political agenda during the deep financial crisis of 1991–1994, when the then centre-right coalition government introduced a supply-side economic policy and an extensive deregulation and marketization policy. This also meant cuts to economic and personnel resources in the welfare sector. A new Local Government Act introduced in the summer of 1991, when the previous social democratic government was still in office, entitled municipalities and county councils to separate their roles as purchasers and providers, with the aim of improving economic efficiency and control. The purchaser-supplier split[4] became the main organizational prerequisite for the introduction of market-oriented solutions in line with New Public Management (NPM), including management by objectives, unbundling, outsourcing and privatization (Kastberg and Siverbo 2008; Erlandsson et al. 2013).

Through a comprehensive reform launched in 1992, the municipalities were given the overall responsibility for long-term care of elderly and disabled, including nursing homes previously run by the county councils. The municipalities were also obliged to provide various forms of more 'home-like' housing for service and care of elderly and disabled in need of special care and support.[5] After the Social Democratic Party returned to power in the autumn of 1994, the structural transformation continued, albeit at a slower space. The growing proportion of elderly in society helped push ahead structural and organizational changes in the elderly care sector. Residential care was to be used mainly for the oldest and most fragile individuals. This placed increasing pressure on home-based elderly care, and made work in this sector more complex and demanding (Trydegård 2003; Szebehely 2011).

In the 1990s, competitive bidding under LOU was the most commonly used method to expose the elderly care sector to private competition, whereas freedom of choice models developed more slowly until the mid-2000s. Unlike in disability care, customer choice in elderly care was not generally propelled by the users themselves, but was mainly an ideological reform relating to political priorities (Blomqvist 2004; Edebalk and Svensson 2005; Szebehely 2011). In October 2018, private providers accounted for 23% of the hours performed in home-based elderly care (SALAR 2019: 56).

A public monopoly exposed to private competition is referred to as a *quasi-market,* i.e. a tax-financed market in which both public and private actors compete (Bartlett and Le Grand, 1993; Le Grand 2007, 2009; Kastberg 2005). The public principal decides the rules and conditions for providers to follow and has ultimate responsibility for the system. Municipalities using LOV in home-based elderly care, for example, must treat their own and external providers on the same terms. As free-market forces do not operate, competition is based on quality rather than price. Local governments pay providers by the hour, and the compensation system is generally based either on the time that personnel spend with the users ('performed time') or the time approved by the care administrator for each user ('approved time'). Performed time has been the dominating system, but today approved time is equally common.[6] In principle, the fixed hourly compensation must cover all the provider's costs, such as labour costs, travel between users, time for planning, documentation, staff meetings, supervision and health and safety work. Potential providers under LOV can apply for authorization continuously, and all providers that meet local governments' formal requirements have access to the market, which aims to guarantee a diversity of providers, including small actors (SALAR 2019; Vårdföretagarna 2019). By contrast, public procurement through competitive bidding has often resulted in a few large providers dominating the market (Swedish Government 2008a; Sundin and Tillmar 2010; Vadelius 2015).

The Rhetoric of Gender Equality and Diversity in LOV

What then can be said about the normative conception of gender equality implied in the freedom of choice reform? The government-appointed investigation that preceded the government bill stated that:

> Since a majority of staff in health and social care are women, those who work in the municipalities and county councils that decide to apply the reform will be given a completely new opportunity to start business in a sector in which they have previously been employees.
>
> (Swedish Government 2008a: 275)[7]

The traditional division of labour between men and women in the strongly gendered health and welfare sector was expected to be a good breeding ground for female entrepreneurship. Thus, the gender equality policy implied in the reform seems to have been based on a perception that health and social care work is and will remain a female domain. The ambition was to foster female entrepreneurship by opening up the tax-financed welfare market to a diversity of providers, including small (female) actors. As entrepreneurs, women would be able to use the skills and competences they had gained as employees in the welfare sector (Swedish Government 2007; Swedish Government 2008a: 262; Swedish Government 2008b: 18f., 131ff.). By becoming a provider of elderly care, for example, female workers could change their employment status and career opportunities. In addition, employed workers would benefit indirectly from the reform, as a diversity of employers competing for labour was supposed to be an incentive for good working conditions, and would make it more attractive to work in this sector (Swedish Government 2008a: 346: Swedish Government 2008b: 18f).

Thus, the notions of gender equality and diversity were defined *in terms of the market* and were strongly interlinked with economic and neoliberal values, such as marketization, competition and entrepreneurship. This conception of gender equality relates to the notion of *neoliberal normativity* (Brown 2008), which highlights the influence of neoliberalism on the understanding of gender-equality. In line with Brown, Martinsson (2014: 250) underlines that in the neoliberal understanding of gender equality, the position of workers (employees) tend to be marginalized, along with expectations of the development of an 'entrepreneurial middle class'. The government bill did not problematize the gender imbalance in the welfare sector, nor did it discuss whether and how the reform might have an impact on this imbalance. Moreover, nothing was said about other power structures that might affect women's position in this labour market, nor how these structures relate to gender. This illustrates the need to widen the perspective on gender mainstreaming policies and practices to include an intersectional perspective, and thus also a power relations approach (see also Verloo 2006; Callerstig 2011; Olsson 2014; Martinsson 2014).

Regarding how the market was supposed to work in practice, the idea was that competition based on quality would replace the role of market forces in regulating the balance between demand and supply. Providers who did not meet the municipalities' quality standards and/or customers' requirements for quality would be unable to maintain their hold on the market (Swedish Government 2008b: 134). In the legislative proposal, the government touched on the fact that there might be conflict between the objectives of high quality and diversity. Municipalities should therefore design quality standards that even small companies could meet, in accordance with the principle of 'proportionality' in the EU's directive on public procurement.[8] The government underlined that 'a prerequisite for many women who are interested in setting up their own business is that they are given the opportunity to start small businesses' (Swedish Government 2008b: 62).[9] It added, however, that this policy must not challenge established labour standards. Another factor mentioned was providers' tax-funded compensation. If the hourly pay rate was too low, employers might avoid signing collective agreements (Swedish Government 2008b: 81). At the same time, the government emphasized that differences in employment security and working conditions might distort competition. For example, some municipalities entitled their elderlycare employees to full-time employment. Moreover, collective agreements might vary between private and public providers (Swedish Government 2008b: 62).

The trade unions *Kommunal* and the Swedish Association of Health Professionals (*Vårdförbundet*), and several other organizations that considered the proposed legislation, claimed that municipalities should include collective agreements in their requirements on the providers in order to prevent unfair competition and social dumping. Referring to the European Court of Justice's (ECJ's) judgement in the German Rüffert case, the government determined that this would be incompatible with EU regulations on public procurement, and the principles of free movement of services, non-discrimination and equal opportunities for all actors operating within the Single Market.[10] However, municipalities could refer to single demands laid down in collective agreements, as long as these complied with EU law (Swedish Government 2008b: 77f.). Traditionally, the EU has prioritized freedom of movement of services and labour over social protection. This was evident in the ECJ's judgement in the Rüffert case, as well as in the Viking, Laval and Luxembourg cases. As Moses (2011: 825) emphasises, the ECJ 'too often sees variance in national standards as an obstacle to free mobility'. Indeed, member states' dependence on EU case law implies a centre–periphery divide, which has promoted the neoliberal trend as well.

In summary, the understanding of gender equality in the reform proposal for LOV was highly influenced by neoliberal ideas (see also Thörnquist 2014; Andersson and Kvist 2015). Gender equality was to be realized by promoting female entrepreneurship – or to relate to the discussion on neoliberal normativity – by fostering the development of an 'entrepreneurial middle class', which in practice might imply marginalization of employed workers.

The Reality of Work

At this background, it is important to ask how the gender policy objectives implied in the LOV reform – to foster female entrepreneurship in the welfare sector, and indirectly also improve the working conditions of employees through increased competition – have been realized in home-based elderly care.

LOV and Female Entrepreneurship

In Sweden, entrepreneurship is less common among women than among men, and there has only been a slow increase in the proportion of female entrepreneurs, from 25% in 1980 to 33% in 2019 (Statistics Sweden 2019; Braunerhjelm et al. 2019: 37–41). In healthcare and social services, however, female entrepreneurs dominate numerically, and the share of female operative business managers is high, especially in elderly care (almost 71% in 2014) (Statistics Sweden 2019; Ekonomifakta 2016).

Can we then say that the freedom of choice reform has had the intended effects on female entrepreneurship? According to a 2012 survey of 183 companies in home-based elderly care by the Swedish Agency for Economic and Regional Growth (*Tillväxtverket*) together with the Swedish Agency for Growth Policy Analysis (*Tillväxtanalys*), women accounted for 63% of the operative business managers in owner-managed companies. In a similar survey, *Tillväxtverket* had found that women owned or managed all of the investigated companies established after 2009. The agencies estimated that LOV, together with a reform to tax relief introduced in 2007 for customers buying domestic services had contributed to female dominance. A majority of the external providers of domestic services contracted under LOV provide 'additional services', which the users can buy (Tillväxtverket 2012: 15; Swedish Government 2014: 184). More recent statistics from the *Tillväxtanalys* indicate that the number of start-up enterprises in home-based elderly care increased significantly after 2009, and that women owned or managed most of these companies. Since 2015, however, the trend has turned downward, reflecting the general trend in start-ups.[11] According to a recent report on Sweden by the Global Entrepreneurship Monitor (GEM), the main reason behind a negative trend in the total entrepreneurial activities in early stages (TEA) since 2013 is a decrease in female entrepreneurship. The report suggests that intense political debate about profit making in the tax-financed welfare sector has contributed to this development (Braunerhjelm et al. 2019).

Statistics from SALAR (2020) indicate that entrepreneurs' interest in entering the customer choice market has declined in recent years.[12] In the summer of 2020, over 30 of the 160 municipalities that had introduced LOV had, in fact, no authorized external providers. Moreover, an increasing number of municipalities have decided to curtail their use of the reform (from three municipalities in 2015 to 16 in 2020). According to SALAR, as well as the Association of Private Care Providers, the main reasons are lack of interest from both providers and users, political changes in local governments, and reports from trade unions and municipalities on unfair competition and fraud in the customer choice market (SALAR 2019; Vårdföretagarna 2019). Several of the municipalities that had dismantled LOV or had no external providers by October 2019 were situated in rural areas, or in other sparsely populated areas such as former industrial regions. Although the hourly compensation rate for providers of home-based elderly care is higher than in urban areas, mainly due to higher travelling costs, most providers prefer urban areas. At the same time as interest in entering the LOV market has declined, some municipalities situated in the region of Stockholm and in some densely populated municipalities in Scania (Skåne) in southern Sweden only have external providers (SALAR 2019). Hence, implementation of the freedom of choice reform in home-based elderly care reflects a centre–periphery divide. The reform appears to have been designed with urban and other densely populated areas in mind. This can be seen as another example of the problem of applying a national, urban-based elderly care policy to a rural context, as Nyhlén and Giritli Nygren (2015) and Giritli Nygren and Nyhlén (2017) have discussed.

The centre–periphery perspective also helps to illuminate how the market structure in elderly care may impact on implementation of the freedom of choice reform, including the possibilities for female entrepreneurs to enter the market. In terms of turnover, number of employees and hours performed, big actors such as municipal providers and large private care companies (often linked with international venture companies) dominate the welfare market in most municipalities (Szebehely 2011; Erlandsson et al. 2013; Vadelius 2015). This structure may impede realization of the gender policy aim to open up the public market to small female actors. An early local case study examining the effects of LOV on women indicated a tendency toward market peripheralization of female providers to less attractive rural areas, and also a trend toward masculinization in elderly care (Sundin and Tillmar 2010). Reports also indicate that it may be difficult for users to make active choices (Swedish Government 2014: 191; see also Meinow et al. 2011; Fotaki 2011; Andersson and Kvist 2015). In this case, too, large and well-known actors have a competitive advantage.

Labour Market Segmentation and Peripheralization

Looking back at the ten-year period that has elapsed since the freedom of choice reform was introduced, the centre–periphery perspective can be used to illustrate another phenomenon, namely the risk of labour market segmentation. This risk becomes even more evident through an intersectional approach and the multidimensional concept of precarious employment.

Many providers of home-based elderly care operating under LOV, especially small actors providing domestic services – the sector with the lowest entry barriers – use subsidized labour. The Swedish Public Employment Service provides considerable wage subsidies to employers in order to stimulate employment of long-term unemployed people and those facing particular difficulties in the labour market, such as newly-arrived immigrants. This means that the state may cover 50–100% of wage costs up to a certain wage level and for a specific period (Kornerud et al. 2018). Subsidized employment may well help to counteract unemployment (Forslund 2018); however, it may also cause market disturbances such as over-supply, increasing the risk of 'unhealthy competition'. This, in turn, generates social dumping and increases the risk of labour market segmentation and peripheralization on the basis of class, gender and ethnicity. In practice, it seems that labour market policy measures based on generous wage subventions tend to transfer the problem of subsidy-dependence from workers to employers.

Many hard-working small and medium-sized providers of home care and services for the elderly have established themselves successfully in the customer choice market. The vast majority of providers operating in this sector follow the rules and regulations of the labour market. Yet unhealthy competition and social dumping have caused considerable problems for serious actors in this market, as well as for the authorities, trade unions and workers, and ultimately users (Vårdföretagarna 2019; SALAR 2019).

The freedom of choice system presupposes a certain degree of over-supply in order to guarantee a diversity of providers to choose between. As there is no free price formation to regulate the balance between de-mand and supply, competition based on quality is, as already mentioned, supposed to play this role. However, the regulatory impact of quality competition has been limited, and in contrast to the intentions of the reform, competition has not always fostered quality. A contributory factor is the possibility for employers to obtain state-subsidized em-ployment. Although the Public Employment Service must consult the trade unions before a jobseeker starts subsidized employment at a workplace, the system has often been abused (Thörnquist 2013; Frödin and Kjellberg 2019; Johansson 2019).[13]

Because tough competition prevails in highly over-supplied areas, having a collective agreement may easily be regarded as a competitive disadvantage. Some providers may sign a collective agreement and pay their workers as stipulated, but may simultaneously extend their working hours beyond the paid time. This practice, which can be de-scribed as 'false collective agreements', is also found in other industries, such as construction, transport and cleaning, and often relates to the exploitation of labour migrants (Thörnquist 2013, 2015).

Competition on the basis of poor working conditions in the customer choice market for home-based elderly care has been clearest in the Stockholm region and in larger towns in other parts of the country. The municipality in my earlier study, which was followed up for this chapter, provides an example.[14] In 2009, the local government introduced LOV into domestic services for the elderly, while care and nursing remained within the public domain. By the end of 2012, around 30 external LOV providers were competing in the regional city, but fewer than 25% of them had collective agreements. According to the regional trade union representative in the local branch of *Kommunal*, with the job of sup-porting workers in the private companies specifically, the employers' main argument for not signing collective agreements was that the hourly compensation they received from the local government was too low and did not cover all costs. In several of these companies, there were serious problems with precarious employment and working conditions. The regional union representative believed that many employers system-atically used subsidized labour, and most of these workers were women and immigrants. In some cases neither the employer nor the employees were fully familiar with the rules and regulations of the Swedish labour market.

The workers were generally employed and paid by the hour, and in practice many lacked regular wages and working hours. The regional union representative had found single cases in which the workers were paid cash-in-hand, while their employers put part of the wage subsidy in their own pockets. Other problems concerned working alone without any kind of worker protection or support. As some employers either were unaware of or ignored their legal obligations, for example to pay social fees, several workers had no social insurance either. There was also a drift into the 'grey zone' between employment and self-employment. For example, employers sometimes required their employees to use their own cars and pay traveling costs when working, presumably because they could not invoice the municipality separately for such costs. The regional trade union representative had also met employees who had to use their own work equipment, such as cleaning devices and detergents. In fact, the employers were arbitrarily treating these employees as if they were self-employed. In a regular employment contract, the employer is responsible for all costs incurred in carrying out the work. Otherwise, employees have to pay for working (Thörnquist 2013, 2015).

Competition on the basis of poor employment and working conditions means that serious entrepreneurs run the risk of being out-competed, which particularly affects small actors with tight profit margins. Competition on these terms is both 'destructive' in classical economic terms and 'degenerative' (Behling and Harvey 2016), as it undermines skills and competence, and ultimately the quality of the services performed. Although such problems are unintended consequences of the freedom of choice reform, they of course make it difficult to realize the gender equality objectives implied in the reform – to increase the possibilities for female entrepreneurs to operate small enterprises in the tax-financed welfare market, and to improve the working conditions of employed workers. According to the current regional union representative in office since 2016, the situation improved in the latter part of the 2010s. The proportion of providers with collective agreements had increased to around 50% out of some 20 providers by the end of 2018. However, some employees were still required to pay travel costs, and the intense use of subsidized labour remained a problem. For example, employers sometimes ignored the fact that workers on subsidized wages may have reduced working capacity.[15]

The work situation described above is a good illustration of the multidimensional and cumulative character of precarious employment, as defined by Lewchuk et al. (2003) but also taking into consideration the work environment factor that I prefer to add to this definition. The situation shows how precarious employment relates to class, gender and ethnicity, as well as to functional capacity. It also illuminates how competition on the basis of precarious employment and poor working conditions creates considerable potential for labour market segmentation and peripheralization, especially as this practice may benefit from tax-financed subventions.

In addition, the example related above shows that, in practice, it may be difficult to combine the objectives of diversity and quality implied in the LOV reform. In many cases, it seems that the local governments have prioritized a diversity of providers over quality, especially during the first years after the reform was introduced. Moreover, the local governments long preferred not to include aspects of employment and working conditions in the quality requirements in the tender documents. The main arguments were that such requirements are not compatible with EU law, and that the Swedish labour market model implies that social partners must handle labour market issues on their own. Some municipalities included formulations such as 'conditions consistent with collective agreements'.[16] Nevertheless, even in these municipalities there were sometimes problems with providers competing with poor working conditions, affecting women and immigrants in particular. This illustrates the need for stricter control of the enforcement of regulations.[17]

In recent years, many municipalities, including the one described above, have included stricter labour law demands based on collective agreements in the tender documents, and they have also reinforced control of the providers.[18] In this process, municipalities have also cancelled contracts due to irregularities, such as social security fraud and manipulation of the registration of time performed.[19] The red-green Swedish Government in office since 2014 has launched several initiatives to forestall unhealthy competition in various industries. For example, since January 2019, all providers of home-based elderly care must apply for permission at the state Health and Social Care Inspectorate (IVO). However, structural risks for precarious work inherent in the freedom of choice system must also be taken into account.

Structural Risks for Precarious Work

Looking at how the freedom of choice system is organized in home care for the elderly, certain obvious structural risks for precarious employment are inherent in the system. In contrast to providers contracted under LOU, actors competing in a market regulated by LOV have no given customer base or production volume when signing a contract with the municipality. Instead they must seek to win and retain customers, who also have a right to change their choices at short notice. Small providers are more vulnerable to loss of customers than big actors with many users and more diversified production. An unstable customer base incentivizes employers to use temporary employment, such as employment by the hour and on-call jobs, as well as part-time employment, including daily schedules with unpaid hours between two shifts, which employers use to save labour costs.[20] The fact that the LOV system is strongly customer-oriented also puts pressure on employees to be flexible and willing to 'give a little bit extra' in order help recruit and retain customers, and thus also safeguard their own jobs. This may blur the borders between formal and informal work tasks.

Another inherent risk for precarious work relates to municipalities' compensation for providers, both the level of compensation and the system used. The hourly compensation to the providers has often been regarded as too low in the eyes of both the providers and the trade unions. A compensation system based on 'performed time' implies an incentive for providers to increase the time that personnel spend with users, as this is time that they can invoice. Accordingly, employers are also incentivized to reduce the time set aside for travelling between customers, as well as for planning, supervision, work safety and other staff welfare activities. Moreover, this compensation system is highly dependent on digitalized time-management systems for planning and documentation, which also means increased control of the workers. My previous research indicates that such a compensation system generates stress, informal work and self-exploitation among workers, who often work through lunch breaks and during unpaid time so as not to let down those they care for (Thörnquist 2013, 2014).

A third structural risk implied in the freedom of choice system relates to the fact that competition is based on quality rather than price. Therefore, providers need to find a niche to use as a competitive advantage. According to the legislative proposal behind LOV, a diversity of providers seeking to profile themselves in the market would not only secure users' freedom of choice, but would also provide incentives for efficiency and innovation (Swedish Government 2008b: 134). Providers performing care and nursing to elderly and disabled generally refer to their medical, psychological or physiotherapeutic expertise, whereas those who only provide domestic services must find other niches. The most common profile is based on languages and culture (see also Swedish Government 2014: 82ff; SALAR 2019).

Providers of elderly care with broad language competence undoubtedly have an important function in a multicultural society. At the same time, there is a risk that both users and workers may be stereotyped on the basis of ethnicity and culture. Thus, using language, culture or ethnicity as a competitive advantage may also result in social segregation and labour market segmentation. For example, studies identify a conception in society that 'immigrants', especially women, are particularly suitable for work in elderly care (Sörensdotter 2008; Torres 2010; Thörnquist 2013, 2014; Storm 2018). This suggests that people from countries outside Western welfare states are stereotyped, and it also implies a centre–periphery perspective. Stereotypical conceptions of people on the grounds of ethnicity, culture, gender, and implicitly also class, are easy to maintain and reproduce in a freedom of choice system, as such social categorizations are used as a competitive advantage, and thus become commodified.

In many cases, providers with only a few registered employees declare in their advertising that they cover a dozen languages, and that they can increase the supply 'if needed'. According to interviews with trade union representatives in 2012/2013 and 2019, additional personnel with a specific language skill were often employed on on-call schedules, and sometimes even engaged on a purely informal basis. In such cases, workers are at high risk of being pushed to the periphery of the labour market, where working conditions are difficult for unions and authorities to control.

To return to the question of how the gender policy objectives implied in the LOV reform have been realized in home-based elderly care, the reform has undoubtedly expanded the market for female entrepreneurship, even though entrepreneurship in this quasi-market may imply both obstacles and risks, especially for small actors. However, as far as this study can tell, it is hard to see that increasing competition between a diversity of providers in the welfare market would improve the working conditions of employees, and make work in home-based elderly care more attractive.

Conclusions

In this chapter, I have argued that the gender equality objective in the Swedish Act on System of Choice in the Public Sector (LOV) launched in 2009, was strongly influenced by neoliberal ideas (see also Thörnquist 2014; Andersson and Kvist 2015). The study, which focused on home-based elderly care, centred around two overarching questions concerning 1) the normative conception of gender equality implied in the reform, and 2) how the gender policy objectives have been realized in home care for the elderly. The analysis was based on an intersectional approach, combined with a centre–periphery perspective and a multidimensional definition of precarious employment. The intersectional perspective helped reveal and interpret the relationship between the economic and gender equality objectives of the reform. Gender equality was to be realized through female entrepreneurship. A central argument for this policy was the traditionally strong female dominance in the health and welfare sector. This meant that the centre-right government behind the reform proposal did not question the traditional gender imbalance in this sector. The aim was rather to increase the proportion of female entrepreneurs, i.e. to give employed workers the opportunity to change their employment status. Marketization, entrepreneurship and increasing competition between a diversity of providers in the tax-financed welfare market were values expected to foster quality and economic efficiency, as well as gender equality and good working conditions. This normative conception of gender equality implied a problematic relationship between the economic and social objectives in the reform. I highlighted this problem by referring to Brown's (2008) and Martinsson (2014) discussions of how a *neoliberal normativity* has come to impact on understanding of gender equality, which also means that gender equality tends to apply more to the development of an 'entrepreneurial middle class' than to the position of employed workers. In fact, the position of employees might even be marginalized.

Hence, this chapter also illustrates and emphasizes that the meaning of gender equality and diversity in gender mainstreaming policies and practices needs to be problematized, contextualized and clearly defined, especially when used for normative purposes as in the planning and introduction of new reforms. As several other researchers have underlined, it is therefore also important to widen the perspective on gender equality to include an intersectional approach, which takes account of the relevance of other power structures, such as structures based on class and ethnicity, and how they may interact with gender in working life (de los Reyes 2001; Walby 2005: Verloo 2006; Callerstig 2014).

Analysis of the implementation of the reform in home-based elderly care illustrates the relationship between the economic and social objectives in more concrete terms. The freedom of choice reform has made it easier for small entrepreneurs to enter the tax-financed market for home-based elderly care and services, and a majority of the entrepreneurs and operative managers in this market are women. In this sense, the reform has achieved its objective of promoting female entrepreneurship. At the same time, competition from large providers, different prerequisites for implementing the reform in urban and rural areas, and the structural risks for precarious employment inherent in the freedom of choice system create challenges for small actors in this market, as well as for their employees. The structural risks relate primarily to the design and logic of the compensation system the municipalities use to pay providers, especially if it is based on 'performed time'. Tight financial frames and the constant struggle to recruit and retain customers may also generate job strain and informal relations in working life.

Low entry barriers to the customer choice market in home-based elderly care, especially in the sector of domestic services, have made it difficult to realize the hope that competition between a diversity of service providers would benefit the working conditions of employed workers. In city areas, where most providers prefer to operate, harsh competition due to oversupply, fuelled by generous wage subsidies from the state, have in many cases resulted in unhealthy competition based on precarious employment and working conditions, i.e. social dumping. Overall, it is difficult to see a strong connection between competition and quality in the freedom of choice market, which was a vital argument for the reform. In fact, problems with unserious actors and unhealthy competition have been found mainly in areas with the most intense competition.

The need for niches to be used for competitive advantage, which is central to the customer choice market, may well generate innovative solutions and promote quality. However, when based on language and culture, for example, which is the most common niche and is undoubtedly very important in elderly care, it may also create distinctive practices founded on stereotypical categorizations of both users and workers. The fact that workers on subsidized wages, including many women and immigrants, are used as cheap labour raises the risk of labour market segmentation and peripheralization.

Even though the empirical basis for this study is limited, it interesting to note that the analysis of the implications of the reform in working life corresponds well with observation that if the gender equality policy is reduced to promote the development of an 'entrepreneurial middle class', the position of employees tends to be marginalized (Martinsson 2014). However, as the examples from home-based elderly care also shows, entrepreneurship in a quasi-market may imply considerable obstacles and risks for small providers as well.

Notes

1 Gender mainstreaming as a main strategy for gender equality work was adopted by the United Nations in 1995, closely followed by the European Union (EU). Sweden had laid down the strategy in law in 1994 (Swedish Government 1994). Even before that, gender equality was a right recognized in Swedish law.
2 LOV originally applied to the legal areas of the Act on Health Care Services, the Act on Social Services (SOL) and the Act on Support and Services to Certain Persons with Disabilities (LSS). For a while, the Public Employment Service was obliged to use LOV when engaging external actors to introduce newly arrived immigrants into the labour market, and can still use LOV in other areas of its work. Since 2013, authorities can also use LOV when purchasing electronic identification services.
3 In Swedish *förarbeten.*
4 In Swedish *beställar-utförare modellen, BUM.*
5 In Swedish *särskilda boendeformer.*
6 Information by e-mail from SALAR, 22 June 2020.
7 Author's translation.
8 Directive 2004/18/EC.
9 Author's translation.
10 C-346/06 (Rüffert).
11 Information by e-mail from the *Tillväxtanalys,* 24 June 2019.
12 Interview with official at SALAR, August 2019.
13 Interview with regional trade union representative, *Kommunal,* August 2019.
14 These examples are taken from Thörnquist (2013).
15 Interview with regional trade union representative, *Kommunal,* July 2019.
16 Based on a review of tender documents published on the municipalities' homepages.
17 Interview with municipal official (head of elderly care), June 2019; interview

with official at SALAR, August 2019; interview with ombudsman, *Kommunal*, June 2019.
18 According to the revised LOU (2016:11, Chapter 16), authorities may, and sometimes must, impose labour law demands in public procurement, based on collective agreements or ILO's core conventions, 'if needed'. This revision relates to the 'new' EU directive on public procurement, Directive 2014/24/EU. There is no corresponding formulation in LOV, but according to the National Agency for Public Procurement (*Upphandlingsmyndigheten*), it is possible to impose such demands in the application of LOV.
19 Interview with municipal official (head of elderly care), June 2019; interview with ombudsman, *Kommunal*, June 2019; interview with regional trade union reresentative, *Kommunal*, July 2019.
20 In Swedish *delade turer*.

References

Acker, Joan. 2012. "Gendered organisations and intersectionality: problems and possibilities." *Equality, Diversity and Inclusion* 31(3), 214–224.
Ahmed, Sarah. 2007. "The language of diversity." *Ethnic and Racial Studies* 30(2), 235–256.
Almqvist, Roland. 2006. *New Public Management: om konkurrensutsättning, kontrakt och kontroll [New Public Management: on competition, contract and control]*. Stockholm, Sweden: Liber AB, Almega and Nutek.
Andersson, Katarina, and Elin Kvist. 2015. "The neoliberal turn and the marketization of care: the transformation of eldercare in Sweden". *European Journal of Women's Studies*, 22(3), 274 –287. 10.1177/1350506814544912.
Bartlett, Will and Julian Le Grand. 1993. "The theory of quasi-markets." In *Quasi-markets and social policy*, eds. Julian Le Grand and Will Bartlett, 13–34. London: Palgrave Macmillan.
Behling, Felix., & Mark Harvey (2015). The evolution offalse self-employment in the British construction industry: a neo-Polanyianaccount of labour market formation. *Work, Employment & Society* 29(6), 969–988.
Blomqvist, Paula. 2004. "The choice revolution: privatization of Swedish welfare services in the 1990s." *Social Policy & Administration* 38(2), 139–155.
Braunerhjelm, Pontus, Carin Holmquist, Marcus Larsson, Martin Svensson and Per Thulin. 2019. *Entreprenörskap i Sverige: Nationell GEM-rapport 2019 [Entrepreneurship in Sweden: National GEM report 2019]*. Örebro, Sweden: GEM and Entreprenörskapsforum. Available at: https://entreprenorskapsforum.se/wp-content/uploads/2019/06/GEM2019_Nationell_rapport_web.pdf.
Brown, Wendy. 2008. *Att vinna framtiden åter: texter om makt och frihet i senmoderniteten [Winning the future again: texts on power and freedom in late modernity]*. Stockholm, Sweden: Atlas.
Callerstig, Anne-Charlott. 2014. *Making equality work: ambiguities, conflicts and change agents in the implementation of equality policies in public sector organisations*. Linköping, Sweden: Diss, Linköping University.
Callerstig, Anne-Charlott and Kristina Lindholm. 2011. "Det motsägelsefulla

arbetet med jämställdhetsintegrering" [Contradictory work on gender main-streaming]. *Tidskrift för Genusvetenskap 2–3*, 78–96.

de los Reyes, Paulina. 2001. *Mångfald och differentiering: diskurs, olikhet och normbildning inom svensk forskning och samhällsdebatt [Diversity and differentiation: discourse, inequality and norm formation in Swedish research and public debate]*. Stockholm, Sweden: Arbetslivsinstitutet.

de Los los Reyes, Paulina and Mulinari, Diana. 2005. *Intersektionalitet: kritiska reflektioner över (o)jämlikhetens landskap [Intersectionality: critical reflections on the landscape of (in)equality]*. Malmö, Sweden: Liber.

Deakin, Simon. 2013. *Addressing labour market segmentation: the role of labour-law*. ILO Working Papers No. 52, Geneva, Switzerland: International Labour Organization.

Edebalk, Per Gunnar and Marianne Svensson. 2005. *Kundval för äldre och funktionshindrade i Norden: konsumentperspektivet [Customer choice for the elderly and disabled in Nordic countries: the consumer perspective]*. Copenhagen, Denmark: Nordiska Ministerrådet.

Ekonomifakta. 2016. "Glastak byts ut mot vinsttak." [Glass ceiling replaced by profit ceiling]. *Ekonomifakta*, 9 September. Available at: https://www.ekonomifakta.se/Artiklar/2016/september/glastak-byts-ut-mot-vinsttak/.

Erlandsson, Sara, Palle Storm, Anneli Stranz, Marta Szebehely and Gun-Britt Trydegård. 2013. "Marketisation trends in Swedish eldercare: competition, choice and calls for stricter regulation." In *Marketisation in Nordic eldercare: a research report on legislation, oversight, extent and consequences*, eds. Gabrielle Meager and Marta Szebehely, 23–84. Stockholm, Sweden: Department of Social Work, Stockholm University.

Forslund, Anders. (2018). *Subventionerade anställningar: avvägningar och empirisk evidens [Subsidized employment: balances and empirical evidence]*, Report No. 2018:14. Uppsala, Sweden: IFAU.

Fotaki, Marianna. 2011. "Towards developing new partnerships in public services: users as consumers, citizens and/or co-producers in health and social care in England and Sweden." *Public Administration 89*(3), 933–955.

Frödin, Olle and Anders Kjellberg. 2019. *Anställningsbidragens roll i handeln: En jämförelse med branscherna hotell- och restaurang, städ och bemanning [The role of employment grants in retailing: A comparison with the hotel and restaurant, cleaning and staffing industries]*. Stockholm, Sweden: Handelsrådet.

Giertz, Anders and Håkan Jönson. 2018. "Har invandrare som arbetar inom äldreomsorgen en besvärligare arbetssituation än sina svenskfödda kollegor?" [Do immigrants who work in elderly care have a more difficult work situation than their Swedish-born colleagues?] *Socialvetenskaplig Tidskrift 2018*(1), 1–22.

Giritli Nygren, Katarina and Sarah Nyhlén. 2017. "Mapping the ruling relations of work in rural eldercare intersections of gender, digitalization and the centre–periphery divide." *Journal of Rural Studies 54*, 337–343.

Hood, Christopher. 1995. "The 'new public management' in the 1980s: Variations on a theme." *Accounting, Organizations and Society 20*(2/3), 93–109.

Jacquot, Sophie. 2010. "The paradox of gender mainstreaming: unanticipated effects of new modes of governance in the gender equality domain." *West European Politics* 33(1), 118–135.

Johansson, Ylva. 2019. "Regeringen vill stoppa missbruket av subventionerade anställningar" [Government wants to stop abuse of subsidized employment]. *Aftonbladet*, 28 June.

Kastberg, Gustaf. 2005. *Kundvalsmodeller: en studie av marknadsskapare och skapade marknader i kommuner och landsting [Customer choice models: a study of market creators and created markets in municipalities and county councils].* Diss. Göteborg, Sweden: Göteborgs Universitet, Förvaltningshögskolan.

Kastberg, Gustaf and Sven Siverbo. 2008. "The impossible split? a study of the creation of a market actor." *International Advances in Economic Research* 14(1), 65–75.

Kjellberg, Anders. (2020). *Den Svenska modellen i en oviss tid. Fack, arbetsgivare och kollektivavtal på en föränderlig arbetsmarknad. [The Swedish Model in an uncertain time. Trade unions, employers and collective agreements in a changing labour market].* Stockholm: Arena Idé.

Koch, Max. 2006. *Roads to post-Fordism: labour markets and social structures in Europe.* Farnham: Ashgate Publishing Company.

Kornerud, Staffan, Andreas Mångs and Henrik Olsson. 2018. *Subventionerade anställningar: En översikt [Subsidized employment: An overview].* Stockholm, Sweden: Arbetsförmedlingen.

Le Grand, Julian. 2007. *The other invisible hand: delivering public services through choice and competition.* Princeton, NJ: Princeton University Press.

Le Grand, Julian. 2009. "Choice and competition in publicly funded health care." *Health Economics, Policy and Law* 4(4), 479–488.

Lewchuk, Wayne, Alice de Wolff, Andy King and Michael Polanyi. 2003. "From job strain to employment strain: health effects of precarious employment." *Just Labour*, 3, 23–35.

Lykke, Nina. 2003. "Intersektionalitet: ett användbart begrepp för genusforskningen" [Intersectionality: a useful concept for gender research]. *Kvinnovetenskaplig Tidskrift 1*, 47–56.

Martinsson, Lena. 2014. "Intersektionell normkritik: om jämnställdhet, arbetsliv och omvandlingar av makt" [Intersectional norm criticism: equality, working life and transformations of power]. In *Inte bara jämställdhet: intersektionella perspektiv på hinder och möjligheter i arbetslivet [Not just gender equality: intersectional perspectives on obstacles and opportunities in working life],* ed. Paulina de los Reyes, 247–272. Stockholm, Sweden: Fritzes.

McCall, Leslie. 2005. "The complexity of intersectionality." *Journal of Women in Culture and Society* 30(3), 1771–1800.

Meinow, Bettina, Marti Parker and Mats Thorslund. 2011. "Consumers of eldercare in Sweden: the semblance of choice." *Social Science and Medicine* 73(9), 1285–1289.

Moses, Jonathon W. 2011. "Is constitutional symmetry enough? social models and market integration in the US and Europe." *Journal of Common Market Studies* 49(4), 823–843.

Nyhlén, Sarah and Katarina Giritli Nygren. 2015. "The 'home care principle' in everyday making of eldercare policy in rural Sweden." *Policy and Politics* 44(3), 427–439.

Olsson, Annika. 2014. "Arbetslivets villkorade jämställdhet: varför jämställdhetsarbete och intersektionalitet hör ihop" [Working life's conditional equality: why equality work and intersectionality are connected]. In *Inte bara jämställdhet: intersektionella perspektiv på hinder och möjligheter i arbetslivet [Not just gender equality: intersectional perspectives on obstacles and opportunities in working life]*, ed. Paulina de los Reyes, 87–107. Stockholm, Sweden: Fritzes.

SALAR. 2019. *Köp av verksamhet 2019: kommuner, landsting och regioner 2006–2018 [Procurement 2019: municipalities, county councils and regions 2006–2007]*. Stockholm, Sweden: Sveriges Kommuner och Landsting.

SALAR. 2020. "Valfrihetssystem i kommuner 2020: beslutsläget i införandet av LOV" [System of choice in municipalities 2020: decision situation on the introduction of LOV]. *Sveriges Kommuner och Landsting*, 3 July. Avilable at: https://skr.se/demokratiledningstyrning/driftformervalfrihet/valfrihetssystem ochersattningsmodeller/socialomsorg/valfrihetssystemikommunerbeslutslaget2020. 33705.html.

Statistics Sweden. 2019. "Entreprenörskap och företagande" [Entrepreneurship and business]. *SCB*, 17 December. Available at: https://www.scb.se/hitta-statistik/ statistik-efter-amne/levnadsforhallanden/jamstalldhet/jamstalldhetsstatistik/pong/ tabell-och-diagram/fordjupningar/entreprenorskap-och-foretagande/.

Statistics Sweden. 2020. "Undersköterska är Sveriges vanligaste yrke." [Auxiliary nurse is the most common occupation in Sweden]. *SCB*, 5 March. Available at: https://www.scb.se/hitta-statistik/statistik-efter-amne/arbetsmarknad/sysselsattning-forvarvsarbete-och-arbetstider/yrkesregistret-med-yrkesstatistik/pong/statistiknyhet/ yrkesregistret-med-yrkesstatistik-20182/.

Storm, Palle. 2018. *"Betydelsen av kön och hudfärg i äldreboendets vardag under olika organisatoriska villkor." [The meaning of gender and skin-color in the everyday life of nursing homes: The impact of organizational conditions]*. Diss. Stockholm: Institutionen för socialt arbete, Stockholms universitet.

Sundin, Elisabeth and Malin Tillmar. 2010. "Masculinisation of the public sector: local-level studies of public sector outsourcing in elder care." *International Journal of Gender and Entrepreneurship* 2(1), 49–67.

Swedish Government. 1994. Government Bill 1993/94:147. *Jämställdhetspolitiken: delad makt – delat ansvar [Gender equality policy: shared power – shared responsibility]*. Stockholm, Sweden: Swedish Government.

Swedish Government. 2007. Committee Directive 2007:38. *Fritt val inom äldre- och handikappomsorgen [Free choice in the care of the elderly and the disabled]*. Stockholm, Sweden: Swedish Government. Swedish Government. 2008

Swedish Government 2008a. SOU 2008:15. *LOV att välja – lag om valfrihetssystem. [Right to choose – act on freedom of choice systems]*. Stockholm: Fritzes.

Swedish Government. 2008b. Government Bill 2008/09:29. *Lag om valfrihetssystem [Act on freedom of choice system]*. Stockholm: Swedish Government.

Swedish Government 2014. SOU 2014:2. *Framtidens valfrihetssystem inom socialtjänsten. [Future of freedom of choice system in social services]*. Stockholm: Fritzes.

Sörensdotter, Renita. 2008. *Omsorgsarbete i omvandling: genus, klass och etnicitet inom hemtjänsten [Care work in transformation: gender, class and ethnicity in home care]*. Diss. Göteborg, Sweden: Makadam Förlag.

Szebehely, Marta. 2011. "Insatser för äldre och funktionshindrade i privat regi" [Interventions for the elderly and disabled in private direction]. In *Konkurrensens konsekvenser: vad händer med svensk välfärd? [The consequences of competition: what happens to Swedish welfare?]*, ed. Laura Hartman, 215–258, Stockholm, Sweden: SNS Förlag.

Thörnquist, Annette. 2013. "Mångfaldens marknad och arbetets villkor: om följder av kundval (LOV) i hemtjänsten" [Diversity markets and working conditions: on the consequences of customer choice (LOV) in home-based elderly care]. *Arbetsliv i Omvandling* 2013:2. Lund: Work, Technology & Social Change (WTS), Lund University. Available at: https://journals.lub.lu.se/aio/issue/view/2425.

Thörnquist, Annette. 2014. "Mångfaldens retorik och arbetets praktik: konkurrensutsättning och jämställdhet i hemtjänsten" [The rethoric of diversity and the reality of work: exposure to competition and gender equality in home-based elderly care]. In *Inte bara jämställdhet: Intersektionella perspektiv på hinder och möjligheter i arbetslivet [Not just gender equality: Intersectional perspectives on obstacles and opportunities in working life]*, ed. Paulina de los Reyes, 115–144. Stockholm: Fritzes.

Thörnquist, Annette. 2015. "False self-employment and other precarious forms of employment in the 'grey area' of the labour market." *International Journal of Comparative Labour Law and Industrial Relations* 31(4), 411–429.

Tillväxtverket. 2012. *Företag som arbetar med hemtjänst 2012: Mångfald och villkor i valfrihetssystem [Companies working with home care service 2012: Diversity and conditions in freedom of choice systems]*. Stockholm, Sweden: Tillväxtverket.

Torres, Sandra. 2010. "Invandrarskap och tvärkulturella omsorgsmöten." [Ethnic Otherness and cross-cultural interaction in elderly care]. In *Omsorg och mångfald [Social care and diversity]* ed. Stina Johansson 67–88. Malmö: Gleerups.

Trydegård, Gun-Britt. 2003. "Swedish Care Reforms in the 1990s: a first evaluation of their consequences for the elderly People." *Revue française des affairs sociales* 4, 443–460.

Vadelius, Elin. 2015. *"Paradoxernas marknad: en studie om företagande i hemtjänsten" [Paradoxes of the market: a study of private enterprise in the home care sector]*. Karlstad, Sweden: Diss. Karlstad University Studies 2015:38, Institutionen för sociala och psykologiska studier.

Vårdföretagarna. 2019. *10 år med LOV: En historisk reform i behov av förnyelse [10 years of LOV: a historical reform in need of renewal]*. Stockholm, Sweden: Vårdföretagarna, Almega.

Verloo, Mieke. 2006. "Multiple inequalities, intersectionality and the European Union." *European Journal of Women's Studies* 13(3), 211–228.

Walby, Sylvia. 2005. "Gender mainstreaming: productive tensions in theory and practice." *Social Politics* 12(3), 321–343.

Wondmeneh, Yeshiwork. 2013. *Mångfald i äldreomsorgen: om anställningsvillkor för utlandsfödda medlemmar i Kommunal [Diversity in the elderly: employment conditions for foreign-born members in Municipal 2013]*. Stockholm, Sweden: Kommunal.

13 How Do People Become Others to Be Used? Processes of Peripheralization in Swedish Unemployment Politics

Paula Mulinari

According to Leslie McCall intersectionality, 'is the most important theoretical contribution that women's studies, in conjunction with related fields, have made so far' (2005: 117). For the field of labour research, the concept of intersectionality has in many ways transformed how labour and work is understood and explored. My reading of intersectionality is inspired by intersectional analyses of labour. In this tradition, intersectionality combines macroeconomic, political and social relations, as well as race, nation and classification systems (Davis 1981; Crenshaw 1989; Anthias, Cain and Yuval-Davis 1992; Mohanty 2003; Acker 2005) that structure inequalities, with diverse collective and individual identities. The strength of a materialistic-inspired understanding of intersectionality lies in its ability to illuminate both regular patterns of inequality, and the variability and heterogeneity through which these are lived and resisted. In this article intersectionality is used as a tool to explore how 'the other' becomes labour to be used. According to Sara Ahmed,

> Capitalism is how 'the others' become labour to be used, or useless; how others become usable is how others become expendable; how others become expendable is how others become killable. Capitalism is how 'the others' become those who have to be welcomed to be at all … Capitalism is identity politics: how the few become the universe/universal; it is how the universal is handy because it makes others into the hands, helping hands, those who have to help reproduce the very system that reproduces their own subordination, or risk becoming unhandy hands, who are grasping at something that is not theirs (Ahmed 2015).

Marxist Feminist, postcolonial and anti-racist labour scholars have adopted various theoretical, methodological and epistemological viewpoints to study as Ahmed writes, how others become labour to be used. They have not only studied it (and struggled against it), but also expanded and deepened our understanding of what capitalism is, how it works, and how it is resisted. Inspired by feminist intersectional analyses of labour, in this chapter I explore how unemployment politics in a municipality forms racialized women, as a specific labour force to be used.

In her study of femonationalism, Farris (2017) argues that migrant women form part of the labour supply, as a regular army of reproductive labour that produces other labour and maintains lives.[1] According to Farris (2017: 188), gender scholars have made central contributions in analysing the colonial discourses embedded in this configuration, but less research has been conducted on the question of whether migrant women play a specific political-economic role as labour. Her theoretical perspective moves beyond focusing on the discursive construction of migrant women, to analysing what category of workers migrant women are created to be. Several other feminist and migration scholars have explored these links (e.g. Anderson and Shutes 2014; Williams 2014), creating a productive point of departure for exploring what form of labour supply migrant women are shaped to be in this specific conjecture of capitalism, and how police, regulations, dominant representations and laws produce and reinforce these processes. Inspired by these authors, in this chapter I explore how temporal organization towards racialized unemployed women within the unemployment complex[2] drives toward care and precarious work, but precarious at the periphery of the Swedish labour market.

The chapter has two aims. First, it explores dominant discourses around the figure of the 'foreign-born unemployed woman' through analysis of governmental and municipal documents. Second, it examines how this dominant representation shapes a labour force that is trained to be flexible, patient and disposable though various forms of temporal regulation. The chapter is based on interviews with 30 unemployed women between the ages of 25 and 54 who had all experienced migration from the Global South. Within the unemployment complex, the women I interviewed are defined as belonging to the category of 'unemployed woman with a foreign background' [*kvinnor med utlänskbackgrud*]. I use the term 'racialized woman' to convey that the processes analysed are processes of gendered racialization whereby, through governmental and municipal practices and categorizations, women are created as a specific labour force. This means that they are subjected to specific forms of time-labour organization, shaping their position in the labour market.

Under the Gaze of Unemployment

In Under Western Eyes: Feminist Scholarship and Colonial Discourses Chandra Talpade Mohanty (1986) identifies three strategic moves that:

produce the image of an 'average third world woman'. This average third world woman leads an essentially truncated life based on her feminine gender (read: sexually constrained) and being 'third world' (read: ignorant, poor, uneducated, tradition-bound, domestic, family-oriented, victimized, etc.). This, I suggest, is in contrast to the (implicit) self-representation of Western women as educated, modern, as having control over their own bodies and sexualities, and the freedom to make their own decisions (Mohanty 1986: 337).

While much has happened since Mohanty wrote her pioneering article, the representations identified in her article persist. For instance, Farris (2017) shows that the portrayal of Muslim women as victims, in need of Western white rescue, is a central discourse that normalizes and legitimizes their exploitation as reproductive labour. In contrast to Muslim men, she argues, Muslim women are presented as victims for whom, if properly assimilated, a space can be made in Western societies, and this space is often in reproductive work.

Inspired by Mohanty, I explore two temporal and spatial strategic moves applied in the discourse around 'unemployed foreign-born women' which create them as a specific 'other' to be used in the Swedish labour market. The first is fixing the woman in time and space, and the second is identifying paid work as an activity that enables entry into the current time line, and hence gender equality. The goal of 'establishing' foreign-born women in the labour market is highly prioritized by the state and central labour market actors. Unemployment among "forigen born woman" is described as both a problem for the women themselves, and a challenge to gender equality in Sweden. This group is defined by the national unemployment office as being 'far from the labour markets', and various projects have been set up to get the women 'closer' to these markets.

Intersectionality-inspired analyses of unemployment policies have explored how the category of 'migrants' is produced and reproduced within the 'unemployment complex' (Vesterberg 2015; Larsson 2015; McGlinn 2018). In his study of unemployment programmes financed by the European Social Fund (ESF), Vesterberg (2015) shows how labour market activities aim to ensure that participants emerge as employable subjects, by transforming them from 'migrants' into being identified as a 'Swedish' female labour force. In a similar study of several similar projects, Vesterberg and Dahlstedt (2018) show how the 'employable citizen' is created as the opposite of the racialized other. Migrant women, they assert, are represented as victims of their own cultures and traditions, and their unemployment is understood as being a consequence of these factors. According to Larsson (2015), 'cultural difference' is used as a hegemonic explanation for unemployment among migrant women by professionals in both national and local-state job-placement subvention institutions. The idea that 'foreign-born unemployed women' are culturally different is legitimized largely through the geographical metaphor of the woman being fixed in different time and space dimensions. According to Mohanty (1986), the first move in constructing the 'average third-world woman' is to fix her in time and space. In Sweden, 'foreign-born unemployed women' are described as being fixed in a bygone age. Announcing the investment of 135 million SEK to 'facilitate access to paid work for foreign-born women', Minister of Finance Magdalena Anderson stated:

> The big difference between foreign- and domestic-born women in the labour market is not acceptable. There are still women in Sweden who are waiting to make the journey that so many others did in the '50s, '60s and '70s, a journey toward freedom and autonomy (Swedish Government, 2017b, Author's translation).

In her analysis of parenting courses for 'foreign-born' women in Holland, Van den Berg (2016) analyses how space and time are central concepts in the 'legitimation of policy interventions into citizens' private lives'. Foreign-born citizens, she argues, are depicted as 'lagging behind', and hence the parenting courses are described as practices that will move women towards the centre. According to the author, space–time metaphors are central to the processes of "othering" migrant woman. Ann McClintock (1995) explores what she conceptualizes as *anachronistic space*, where a geographical difference across space is figured as a historical difference across time. As she argues:

> Within this trope, the agency of women, the colonized and the industrial working class are disavowed and projected onto anachronistic space: prehistoric, atavistic and irrational, inherently out of place in the historical time of modernity. According to the colonial version of this trope, imperial progress across the space of empire is figured as a journey backward in time to an anachronistic moment of prehistory. By extension, the return journey to Europe is seen as rehearsing the evolutionary logic of historical progress, forward and upward to the apogee of the Enlightenment in the European metropolis (McClintock 1995: 40).

According to McClintock, this trope, the idea that people need imperial progress to move forward, is central to the urban surveillance of women and the working class. In relation to Swedish unemployment policies, the idea of *anachronistic space*, of the woman being fixed in another time dimension, creates a space for legitimizing forms of control over the woman's time and mobility. The woman can thereby be forced into precarious labour while appearing to be 'helped' into gender equality and modernity. The idea of the woman being far from the labour market also hides the fact that when women enter paid work, they often end up in the most precarious work. A paradox emerges: while 'unemployed foreign-born women' are defined as being from the periphery they are at the same time through various political interventions, in many ways they are forced into the periphery of the labour market in terms of working conditions in referring to 'foreign-born women' as lagging 'behind' in time and space, labour market activation is depicted as a means of moving toward the future, toward so-called Swedish values of democracy and gender equality. The question of whether the labour market is too far from people is never posed. It is understood as a neutral place at the centre of Swedish society, toward which people must constantly strive.

If the first strategic move is to place the figure of the 'unemployed foreign-born woman' as peripheral to the labour market and in need of control to move forward, the second is to represent this as a move toward gender equality. The idea of paid work as a means to achieve gender equality has been central to the Swedish labour and women's movements (Carbin, Overud and Kvist 2017). The higher unemployment rate of 'foreign-born women' is therefore defined not only as a problem for them, but also as a threat to the national economy:

> If foreign-born women participate in the labour market in the same manner as domestic-born women, the GDP level is expected to be 1.5% higher, unemployment levels one per cent lower and public finances would be strengthened by approximately 37 billion SEK (Swedish Government, 2017b, Author's translation).

As 'foreign-born women' are represented as being in need of labour market 'salvation' in order to be free and gender-equal, labour market activities are portrayed as a form of 'rescue' work. The idea of 'rescue' plays a significant role in the creation of what Farris (2017) calls a regular army of reproductive labour, as it legitimizes the creation of a group of employees for whom labour market participation is represented as an act of liberation. The notion that the municipality and the whole Swedish nation is helping 'foreign-born women' to gain power and autonomy also places greater institutional demands on them to participate in these integration/labour market projects. An interesting paradox emerges, which is perhaps rather an ideological move that legitimizes gender-, race- and class-divided labour markets. On the one hand, care work is represented as a salvation for racialized women (from their cultures, their men, and even their laziness); on the other hand, we know that care work lies at the periphery of the labour market in terms of salaries, workers' influence, working hours, and so forth. Ideologically constructing reproductive labour as a means of salvation also reproduces the idea that care work is something that women do because they want or need to do so, rather than something on which society as a whole depends and should therefore be organized around. Therefore, I would argue, representing 'foreign-born women' as fixed in time and in need of salvation affects not only them, but all people engaged in care work, legitimizing and treating such work as peripheral.

Researchers argue that 'foreign-born women' in the unemployment complex are often depicted as victims (McGlinn 2018). I would argue that we are witnessing a trend toward a representation not only as victims of their cultures, but also as *villains* who relay and take advantage of the Swedish welfare state, without contributing to its sustenance. If women in the first move are identified as being fixed in a pre-modern space and time, in the second move they are identified as being fixed in their homes.

Just before the Social Democratic Party congress in 2017, an article appeared with the headline 'Newly arrived women cannot be locked in their homes' (Andersson and Lövfen, 2017). The party proposed several solutions to the 'problem', among the measures implemented, those especially targeting racialized women included restrictions on parental benefits, and a requirement to continue to study Swedish even while on parental leave, whereas parents studying other subjects have a right to take parental leave. The aim of this policy, they argued is to 'clarify the individual's responsibility for the knowledge needed to get into work' (Social Democratic Party 2018b). The right to parental leave was also restricted for parents who come to Sweden with children, in order the government argued, for the woman to more rapidly enter the labour market (Social Democratic Party 2018a). Commenting on the investment of 141 SEK for the establishment of 'foreign-born women', Johansson declared: 'The previous government introduced the right to paid work for new arrivals, we have added an obligation to participate' (Svensen 2018). In relation to racializing unemployed women, demands are often articulated as concerns for their gender equality, their children's well-being and promotion of national policy on gender equality; hence, the removal of social rights is presented as a feminist intervention. In defence of the proposed reduced days of parental leave for migrant parents, the Minister of Social Security declared: 'For our part, it is primarily an important gender equality reform. It's about shortening the time for foreign-born women to enter the labour market' (Aftonblandet 2017, Author's translation).

'Foreign-born women' are represented as victims of the patriarchal cultures in which they are locked up, but at the same time as exploiting the social system based on gender equality. Hence, some interventions are designed to restrict racialized women's ability to use the services and provisions gained by the feminist movement, such as day-care and parental leave, as it is implied that 'forigen born women' are trapped by these. The idea that unemployed racialized women need to be rescued first from their cultural heritage, defined by their geographical peripherality, and then from their homes is legitimized though a gender-equality rhetoric. For some, mothers' right to be at home is understood as a threat to their gender equality rather than as a right. In effect, reduced rights are presented as a feminist concern for unemployed women.

In this section, I have identified two strategic temporal and spatial moves within the unemployment complex in relation to racialized unemployed women, which create them as a specific category of workers, in terms of being fixed in time and space, as well as having too much time and being in need of rescuing from their homes. While these discourses are not new, they commonly appear on websites propagating ethno-nationalist ideas, where gender equality is defined as a central Swedish cultural value threated by migrants, restricting welfare and citizens' rights, with a constant focus on welfare as a cost. In the next section, I explore how these moves affect everyday experiences in the unemployment complex in relation to temporal control of the unemployed.

Waiting by Writing CVs

Waiting is a central experience of being unemployed shared by many people in Sweden today, including those awaiting asylum decisions (Khosravi 2018; Sager 2011), social security, financial aid and healthcare (IVO 2019; Kaluza 2018). According to Pierre Bourdieu (2000), waiting is one way in which the effects of power are experienced. Sociologist Javier Auyero (2012), who explores experiences of waiting by the urban poor in Argentina through an ethnographic study of waiting rooms, suggests that waiting is a 'temporal process in and through which political subordination is reproduced' (Auyero 2012: 2), and that the urban poor learn to be *patients of the state* though the process of waiting: 'To put it bluntly, everyday political domination is what happens when nothing apparently happens, when people just wait' (Auyero 2012: 19). Several studies focus on the coercive aspect of controlling the unemployed by regulating their time and the places where they are allowed to be (Paulsen 2015). In analyses of unemployment policies, waiting is often explored in terms of their effect rather than their purpose. However, how the power to make others wait is acted on and organized has not been theoretically explored.

I argue that the experience of waiting, through the asylum process and then within the unemployment complex, is a central aspect of the shaping of the labour force. Specifically, it embodies the experience of uncertainty and arbitrariness by being highly flexible to the demands of the state, municipalities and employers. The unemployed women whom I met shared similar waiting stories. They all spoke about 'waiting for a long time', and often used terms such as 'waiting a lot' and 'always waiting'. Hana described her waiting as being caught in the unemployment complex with no pathway toward a paid job or education:

> I came to Sweden ten years ago. And I have not been given any possibilities of working or studying. I was at the unemployment agency, and nothing happened in ten years. I applied for job, job, job, and nothing. Always waiting ... for the next course, next practice, next meeting.

I asked her what she did during this ten-year period, and she answered, shrugging her shoulders: 'I waited; I went back and forth, applied for new jobs, went to new courses, got a new social worker and a new job coach, telling them everything all over again, started again, wrote more CVs; I just waited.'

Waiting within the unemployment complex is not the same as doing nothing. On the contrary, while waiting, the unemployed go to meetings and attend courses on how to write and send their CVs. For the women I interviewed, the experience of waiting was also linked to the experience of repetition, with no progress or hope, for instance when sending CVs to employers. This repetition was also linked to the emotional labour needed when constantly meeting new municipal officials, who often asked them the same questions and forced them to re-tell their life stories and ambitions.

Writing a 'good' CV was a central activity in the municipal un-employment complex where I carried out my fieldwork. People attended CV-writing courses, and a good CV was said to increase the chances of getting a job. This focus on the CV reflects the idea that unemployment is an individual problem that can be resolved individually if only one be-comes more employable.

I interpret the endless updating and changing of the layout of CVs, even though most professionals in the municipality know that sending CVs will not lead to paid employment, as a form of symbolic (racist) violence. This aims to regulate unemployed racialized women's time and create a labour force socialized to accept irrational rules and meaningless tasks. In other words, the waiting aims to subordinate their selves, abilities and skills, creating docile subjects trained to accept the rules and wait.

As argued earlier, the experience of waiting was not new to these women, many of whom had been waiting for several years in the Swedish asylum process, or were still awaiting decisions in re-lation to their friends and families. Leila had long experience of waiting:

> I waited two years to get a residence permit, then two years for establishment, and then six months here, and then for financial aid, and then one month here, and then back again; three years of unemployment within the municipality.

Critical scholars of migration have explored the experience of waiting as a central element of the migration regime (Djampour 2018). Uncertainty and instability are key characteristics of asylum and immigration detention systems (Griffiths 2014) and, according to De Genova (2002), are a central feature of the condition of 'deportability'. Griffiths (2014: 1992) argues that time 'is a metaphor by which deportable migrants experience and describe the instability and powerlessness of the immigration system', and that 'temporal uncertainty and discord mark points of tension within the system'. Analysing time, she argues, illuminates the sources and experiential qualities of this insecurity. While I do not argue that refugees awaiting deportation or decisions on asylum are in the same situation as the unemployed women whom I interviewed, this nevertheless illuminates continuity in the practices of waiting, whereby the state and other actors control people in various ways by making them wait. Many of these women had waited for asylum decisions before entering the unemployment complex. They exemplify Auyero's (2012) concept of patients of the state, in that the state had already trained them to be patient and to wait through the migration process. My material raises the question of whether the practice of waiting in relation to the state not only creates patients of the state, as Auyero argues, but also shapes the labour supply that the state creates, with extensive experience of *waiting* and *uncertainty*, two central aspects of precarious employment. The experience of waiting, often for a long time, also orientates the women toward care work, as this kind of work is often more readily available to them. The process of waiting therefore deepens gender segregation in the Swedish labour market, placing racialized women in the most precarious employment.

Care Work and Caring for Work

Several programmes and projects in the municipality target the category of 'foreign-born unemployed women'. At both national and local levels, many of these programmes focus on becoming some kind of care worker. Gender researchers have explored how migration, care and employment regimes intersect in ways that correlate with the needs of Western welfare states, particularly in the reproductive sector (Williams 2014). In the context of the crisis of care, Farris (2017) argues that migrant women are often forced into care work. In Sweden, this crisis is partly addressed by suggesting that 'foreign-born women' can play a central role in the labour force of the public care sector. Hence, many projects and programmes are directed in various ways toward supplying care work.

A couple of months into my project, 30 women (out of 150 who had applied for the programme) were selected by the municipality to participate in a project funded by the ESF. The project was directed toward 'unemployed foreign-born women' who were 'far from the labour market'. For a period of three years, the 30 women participating in the project would study Swedish and healthcare in order to become assistant nurses. In parallel with their studies, they would also work in the healthcare system two days a week. The women selected were content and proud to have been chosen, first because the project provided them with a professional education, and second because it gave them financial stability with a monthly income, which meant that they did not need to depend on social welfare. As Emma said:

> Now everything is different. I promise you, if I had not had the possibility of entering this project, I would be unemployed forever. Now I know [that] when I am finished, after these three years, it will not be like it has been all these times, 'Oh, sorry, the position has been taken'; it will be, they will say, 'When do you want to begin to work?'

In contrast to many other projects and programmes in which the women had engaged, this one provided a monthly salary, and set expectations of what would happen in three years' time (or at least, that was what they, I and the project leaders believed at that time). There is enormous demand for assistant nurses in the Swedish labour market, and knowing that their studies would provide them with a paid job and enable them to receive a 'real' salary gave the women a sense of control over their futures.

Getting a job was important for all the women to whom I talked: 'It will take three years, but in the end I will have work. I will not be dependent on anyone, not the social services; I will have my own money, and it will be my money because I will work.' There was hope in how the women expressed themselves. Zeynep spoke about her plans to become a nurse after the project:

> I want to become a nurse. If someone had said to me that I could, like, be a nurse two years ago, I would have laughed. But to be here, to get paid, we do not work for free as usual; we are paid. And that creates an enormous feeling of being free, even though what they pay us is not much higher than the financial aid. I do not need to be in contact with them. I just get a normal salary. Well, not a normal one, but I do not care.

Working without being paid is a common experience among the unemployed in Sweden. Through various state policies and social programmes, they often work for periods during which the state pays the employers, with no guarantee that they will stay in the organizations or be recruited in the future (Paulsen 2015). Many of the women had had similar experiences of working for short periods and being paid differently from formal workers, without ever gaining permanent employment:

> The jobs I had before were all temporary; they were all in different programs, or some hours here and some hours there. I want to work, so I have to struggle; it is hard, you know, but it will become easier. It is not easy, it is not easy to get a job, it is not easy to come from another country, another language, but we struggle. And if I struggle, I know I will get a job. A job is a totally different thing.

This project was different, as it provided the participants with a professional degree that they knew might lead to paid work. While the women were glad to participate in the project (because they were paid and because they would get a job in the end), some had not originally wanted to do care work. Anya had entered the programme after being denied validation of her university degree in tourism:

> Did I have any experience of this? No. I was two years in establishing, and after that [I went] to [the] course in Hermosa [a private study organization]. And when they asked me, 'do you want to work in care?', and I was like, 'what is that? Working with [the] elderly? Noooo, that is not me. I want to continue with my studies in tourism.' I have studied tourism, and I know four languages: Arabic, English, French and Swedish. They said my education was not valid here. So I have lost five years of my life. It is not that I do not like the project, but it was not what I wanted to do. But here I am; at least I will get a job.

Despite not initially being interested in care work, many women had entered the programme for lack of other opportunities. For instance, Marwa had an economics diploma and loved numbers:

> I never thought of this, but it is better than sitting at home and waiting. But it would have been better if they could have helped me with my diploma in economics. I really like numbers and computers and Excel; that is what I want to work with and what I have been studying before. But this is better than sitting at home. I want to work, I want to do something in Sweden, and I do not want to get

financial aid from the municipality. I want my kids to know that I have a job, I want them to know that I have struggled, I want to influence society. Perhaps in the end I will go for studies in economics, but for now, for a while, I will work. I have an economics degree from my home country but I cannot use it, they said. I sent them my diplomas and everything, but they said no, it could not be translated, so I could not go to the university. And then I wanted to work, and they said no. They have stolen four years of my life.

Both Marwa and Anya had previously studied at university, and Hana, another of the women, had a degree in biology. An important aspect of the temporal and spatial control of the women was that no time other than 'Swedish time' was valued in their working records. Previous experience of work and education, as well as their lives in places other than Sweden, were often ignored. Both Marwa and Anya used the concept of *stealing* to explain why they had ended up on the programme (which they liked). I read this as referring to the rejection and denial of any experience, skill or knowledge gathered before entering Sweden. It appeared that experience and knowledge could only be obtained in Sweden. The appropriation of time (through denial of skills and through the women's socialization in waiting) created a space in which care work became the only possible and even desirable option.

The story might have ended here, with the women becoming care workers. However, once again they found themselves in a situation of uncertainty and arbitrariness. The experience of being robbed of their time was repeated when, with half a year remaining until the end of the programme, the participants were 'informed' that perhaps they would not be able to become assistant nurses, but only care nurses, because there was no money left in the project to pay them.

Stealing Time as an Organizational Practice

As discussed in the previous section, Marwa and Anya talked about the time they had invested in education having been stolen. I read the *stealing* of time as both neglect of previous temporal investments and experience, as previously discussed, and as practices in which the participants' time was systematically undervalued (Khosravi 2018). After being informed that perhaps they would not become assistant nurses after all, Nasira said:

They have taken three years of my life. If I had known that I would not become an assistant nurse, I would have chosen another path. I chose this because they said it was nearly guaranteed that we would get permanent employment. I did not want to become an assistant nurse, but I wanted paid employment, secure employment, and they said that this was it. And now here we are. Again, we do not know what will happen; again, we have to wait.

There is huge inequality of accountability within the unemployment complex. While for two-and-a-half years the women were held to account for every hour that they were absent, and had to justify every decision, the municipality was not required to explain or account for any decision, and when it did explain, often blamed factors beyond its control, such as the ESF, the budget and politicians. While in many ways this was true (the municipality has little control over state finances), the women were faced with an organization that had the unequal and enormous privilege of being able to change its decisions without being held accountable. They also encountered a situation in which their lives and challenges could seldom be used to explain being unable to meet all the demands placed on them.

According to Auyero (2012), since welfare clients have limited options, they cannot complain, partly because they would be punished if they did, but also because there would be no one to whom to complain. People who wait become patients of the state, and also learn to have patience, and therefore, according to Auyero, seldom engage in any collective resistance. However, the women enrolled on the project did complain. Over a period of two years the women had been paid, which had given them autonomy from the municipality. This was similar to the experience of the women on Swedish for Immigrants courses explored by Giritli-Nygren and Schmauch (2012), for whom the 'segregated' classroom was a location of belonging and collectivity, where for the first time in the unemployment complex they felt at 'home'. This sense of autonomy and collectivity was used by the women whom I interviewed to question the logic of the decision. Indeed, Hana questioned not only the decision, but the entire logic of the organization:

> I am insulted. First, they say in half a year, and then in the next half a year. They do not stand by their word. We are supposed to struggle, and then they do not stand by what they have promised. Now they say it will be in April, perhaps tomorrow in December. We struggle, but do they?

The women, who had been led to believe that they were dealing with a rational bureaucracy, made the contradictory claim that, in their case, the organization was rather unorganized, with no strategic plan and relatively chaotic. According to Nasira:

> It is chaos. First, they say you would be an assistant nurse, and then, no, you will only be a care assistant. This is chaos. I have been studying for something for two years, and now they say I will become something that takes ten weeks to become.

During the two-and-a-half-year period, the women had been told over and over again about the importance of being on time, of delivering, of doing serious and effective work and of standing by their word, yet the same standards did not apply to the municipality. A key paradox is the temporal inequality of accountability. While the women were ordered to be on time, to give their time and to learn the time, the municipality's regulations, principals and goals could be changed without providing any information and with no discussion with the people whom the changes affected.

In her analyses of how organizations handle sexual harassment complaints, Sara Ahmed uses the concept of *strategic inefficiency* to explore how organizations allow complaints to be delayed or lost: 'inefficiency is not just about the failure of things to work properly but can be how things are working... I had wondered about the *work* of inefficiency before; how inefficiency could be understood as an achievement' (Ahmed 2018). In the unemployment complex, there seems to be *strategic unaccountability*, where the organization demands the time of the unemployed, yet is in no way accountable for its own time and decisions, allowing little (if any) room for the unemployed to demand any pay-off for all the time they have given the organization. There is an organizational temporal paradox in which the unemployed women are required to subordinate and give themselves wholly to the organization, while the organization itself may be unpredictable, dis-organized and impatient when it suits it. The women in the projects I followed formed a collective, changing their position from patients of the state to workers claiming their rights. These women demanded answers and a meeting with those responsible. They were never given that opportunity, and their anger was identified as a serious problem higher up in the organization. They were defined as being ungrateful, angry, unable to understand the economic structure of the munici-pality, and so forth. These reactions reflect, I would argue, the muni-cipality's unpreparedness for the collective reaction through which the participants went from being patients of the state to workers de-manding their fundamental right to be paid for what they had done, and for the hours they had they spent on education to be valued. This lack of temporal predictability was a permanent aspect of the organi-zation's practice toward the unemployed racialized women, making their time a disposable commodity of others, and hence also making them disposable and replaceable subjects.

Concluding Remarks

If Capitalism, as Ahmed argues, is how 'the others' become labour to be used or useless, in this chapter I have explored an aspect of this *how* process in the unemployment complex in Sweden. How are racialized women in the unemployment complex created as disposable others to be used? I have argued that the unemployment complex, though various temporal forms of control, such as waiting and devaluing the women's time, shapes a flexible, patient and disposable labour force orientated toward care work, who experience high uncertainty and arbitrariness.

In the first section of the chapter, I identified two central temporal and spatial moves in the representation of 'unemployed foreign-born women'. The first is that the women are fixed in time and space, in a peripheral place on another time line. The second is that they are fixed in their homes, with an infinite amount of time that needs controlling otherwise they risk becoming villains robbing the Swedish welfare state of its gender equality. 'Unemployed foreign-born women' are represented as both victims of their cultures, and also as villains robbing the achievements of the gender-equal welfare state. Paid work is defined as the solution, or rather as the women's salvation. Through paid work, they can get onto the right (Swedish) time line, as well as achieving gender equality. The discourse of rights is often legitimized though a feminist rhetoric of saving women from gender oppression. The women are at first described as being 'far' from the labour market, at its periphery, but at the same time, though the unemployment complex, they are directed toward the periphery of the labour market in terms of working conditions and salaries. This paradoxical discourse – of women being fixed in time yet having no time limits – influences the forms of labour supply created by the municipality, which views migrant women as a flexible and disposable labour force whose time and mobility are highly controlled.

Temporal control has been explored in the chapter in three ways. First, people within the unemployment complex (and often previously in the migration complex) wait for a long time to gain any form of lasting employment. This waiting should be understood not as an effect of an inefficient organization, but rather as an organizational practice of power, whereby people learn to be patient, flexible and often more willing to take jobs that they perhaps did not originally want to do. Waiting is also linked to the second aspect of temporal organization within the unemployment complex, the devaluation of previous education and life experiences. Several of the women I interviewed had other dreams and had invested considerable time in education before entering Sweden in order to achieve those dreams. However, their education and aspirations were not valid in Sweden, forcing them into care work, as this option was in high demand and at least provided paid employment. Some of the women expressed this as a stealing of time, which I interpret as a concept embracing the rejection and denial of experience, skills and knowledge gained before entering Sweden. The stealing of time is linked to the idea that, before entering Sweden, the women had been fixed in places and times where no knowledge had been produced that was valued in modern and gender-equal Sweden. The stealing of time is also interrelated with shaping a labour force on the basis of placing less value on their time, the content and frequency of which is shaped by the interests and desires of others. The third central temporal aspect of the unemployment complex in relation to unemployed racialized women is what Sara Ahmed calls *strategic un-accountability*. Here, the unemployed are held accountable for all they do (or do not do), while the organization can change its rules and plans without being held accountable. The women are thus forced not only to be patient, but also to bear the uncertainty and arbitrariness of the organization.

These different forms of temporal and spatial control combined, I argue, shape a labour force that is flexible, with long experience of uncertainty and the unpredictably changing rules of the game. The 'others' become labour to be used through a racialized and gendered unemployment complex directing them toward the margins of the labour market, while rhetorically claiming that the margins are a symbol of gender equality. This also legitimizes an unequal gender, class and racialized labour market, in which working-class women's care work is underpaid, understaffed and precarious, becoming the periphery from which, at the political and organizational levels, they are arguably seeking to move away.

If capitalism is how "others" become labour to be used, or rendered useless, expendable and killable as Ahmed argues, forms of temporal and spatial control and organization are a central aspect though which by those processes are done. The spacial and temporal control of workforce, is essential to global capitalism. For me an intersectional analyses, is not only a theoretical point of departure, but a commitment to social stuggles that in different ways resist those inequalities. It locates woman's work, at the centre of the analyses, and from their explores both the economical, political and social structures that shape capitalism today, as well as exploring how people live and resist those structures.

Notes

1 There is broad feminist debate on the question of reproductive labour and social reproduction (e.g. Ferguson et al. 2016; Federici 2018). In this article, reproductive labour refers to labour that in some way produces labour or maintains life.

2 By the 'unemployment complex', I mean all actors somehow involved in unemployment politics, such as the municipality, the social security agency, the national unemployment agency, and private and civil society actors. Many of the woman interviewed were in contact with several different actors.

References

Acker, Joan. 2005. *Class questions: feminist answers*. Lanham, MD: Rowman & Littlefield.

Aftonblandet. 2017. *"Begränsad föräldrapeng för invandrare"* [Limited parental allowance for immigrants]. March 17. https://www.aftonbladet.se/nyheter/a/0a0wG/begransad-foraldrapeng-for-invandrare (retrieved March 2012)

Ahmed, Sara. 2015. "It is not the time for a party." *feministkilljoys [website]*, 13 May. Available at: https://feministkilljoys.com/2015/05/13/it-is-not-the-time-for-a-party/.

Ahmed, Sara. 2018. "Strategic inefficiency." *feministkilljoys [website]*, 20 December. Available at: https://feministkilljoys.com/2018/12/20/strategic-inefficiency/.

Anderson, Bridget and Isabel Shutes. 2014. *Migration and care labour: theory, policy and politics*. London: Palgrave Macmillan.

Andersson, Magdalen and Stefan Lövfen. 2017. "Nyanlända kvinnor får inte fastan i hemmet" [Newly arrived women cannot be locked in their homes]. *Aftonblandet*, 22 February. Available at: https://www.aftonbladet.se/debatt/a/j5aXb/nyanlanda-kvinnor-far-inte-fastna-i-hemmet.

Anthias, Floya, Harriet Cain and Nira Yuval-Davis. 1992. *Racialized boundaries: race, nation, gender, colour and class and the anti-racist struggle*. London: Routledge.

Auyero, Javier. 2012. *Patients of the state: the politics of waiting in Argentina*. Durham, NC: Duke University Press.

Bourdieu, Pierre. 2000. *Pascalian meditations*. Stanford, CA: Stanford University Press.

Carbin, Maria, Johanna Overud and Elin Kvist. 2017. *Feminism som lönearbete: om den svenska arbetslinjen och kvinnors frigörelse [Feminism as wage labour: the Swedish work line and women's liberation]*. Stockholm, Sweden: Leopard Förlag.

Crenshaw, Kimberlé. 1989. "Demarginalizing the intersection of race and sex: a black feminist critique of antidiscrimination doctrine." *University of Chicago Legal Forum 89*(1), 139–167.

Dahlstedt, Magnus and Philip Lalander. 2018. *Manifest: för ett socialt arbete i tiden [Manifest: for social work in time]*. Lund, Sweden: Stundentlitteratur.

Davis, Angela. 1981. *Women, race & class*. London: Woman's Press.

De Genova, Nicholas. 2002. "Migrant 'illegality' and deportability in everyday life." *Annual Review of Anthropology 31*, 419–447.

Djampour, Pouran. 2018. *"Borders crossing bodies: the stories of eight youth with experience of migrating."* PhD thesis, Malmö, Sweden: Malmö University.

Farris, Sara. 2017. *In the name of women's rights: the rise of femonationalism.* Durham, NC: Duke University Press.

Federici, Silva. 2018. *El patriarcado del salario: criticas feministas al Marxismo [The patriarchy of wages: feminist criticisms of Marxism].* Madrid, Spain: Traficantes de Sueños.

Ferguson, Susan, Genevieve LeBaron, Angela Dimitrakaki and Sara R. Farris. 2016. "Introduction." *Historical Materialism 24*(2), 25–37.

Giritli-Nygren, Katarina and Ulrika Schmauch. 2012. "Picturing inclusive places in segregated spaces: a participatory photo project conducted by migrant women in Sweden." *Gender, Place and Culture: A Journal of Feminist Geography 19*(5), 600–614.

Griffiths, Melanie. 2014. "Out of time: the temporal uncertainties of refused asylum seekers and immigration detainees." *Journal of Ethnic and Migration Studies 40*(12), 1991–2009.

Holmqvist, Anette and Pär Karlsson. 2018. "S lovar hårdare språkkrav på bidragstagare" [S promises stricter language requirements for contributors]. *Aftonbladet*, 14 March. Available at: https://www.aftonbladet.se/nyheter/samhalle/a/vmzJM4/s-lovar-hardare-sprakkrav-pa-bidragstagare.

IVO. 2019. "Lång väntan på socialtjänst-insatser får konsekvenser för både individ och kommun" [The long wait for social services has consequences for both the individual and the municipality]. *Inspektionen för Vård och Omsorg [website]*, 17 May. Available at: https://www.ivo.se/publicerat-material/nyheter/nyheter-2019/lang-vantan-pa-socialtjanstinsatser-far-konsekvenser-for-bade-individ-och-kommun/.

Kaluza, Johan. 2018. *"Sjukskrivnas arbetsbörda: arbetande medborgare möter en kundorienterad byråkrati" [Sick leave workload: working citizens face a customer-oriented bureaucracy].* PhD thesis, Karlstad, Sweden: Karlstads Universitet.

Karlsson, Pär. 2017. "Vi har inte gjort saker tillräckligt bra" [We haven't done things well enough]. *Aftonbladet*, 29 November. Available at: https://www.aftonbladet.se/nyheter/samhalle/a/8wwevw/ylva-johansson-vi-har-inte-gjort-saker-tillrackligt-bra.

Khosravi, Shahram. 2018. "Stolen time." *Radical Philosophy 2*(3), 38-41. Available at: https://www.radicalphilosophy.com/article/stolen-time.

Larsson, Jenni. 2015. *"The market of integration and labour: how gender equality, labour and other "Swedish" phenomena are constructed by employment service officials and private actors."* PhD thesis, Linköping, Sweden: Linköping University.

LO. 2017. *Anställningsformer och arbetstider [Forms of employment and working hours].* Stockholm, Sweden: Landsorganisationen i Sverige.

Malmö Stad. 2016. *ESF application, Diarienummer 2016/00465.* Malmö, Sweden: Malmö Stad.

McCall, L. (2005) "The complexity of intersectionality." *Signs: Journal of Women in Culture and Society 30*(3), 1771–1800.

McClintock, Ann. 1995. *Imperial leather: race, gender, and sexuality in the colonial contest.* New York, NY:Routledge.

McGlinn, Malin. 2018. *"Translating neoliberalism: the European Social Fund and the governing of unemployment and social exclusion in Malmö, Sweden."* PhD thesis, Malmö, Sweden: Malmö University.

Mohanty, Chandra. 1986. "Under Western eyes: feminist scholarship and colonial discourses." *Boundary* 2(12/13), 333–358.

Mohanty, Chandra. 2003. *Feminism without borders: decolonizing theory, practicing solidarity.* Durham, NC: Duke University Press.

Olsson, Lova. 2017. "Nyanlända ska lära sig svenska värderingar" [Newcomers should learn Swedish values]. *Sveriges Radio*, 12 December. Available at: https://sverigesradio.se/sida/artikel.aspx?programid=83&artikel=6841123.

Paulsen, Roland. 2015. *Vi bara lyder: En berättelse om Arbetsförmedlingen [We just read: A story about the Employment Service].* Stockholm, Sweden: Atlas.

Persson, Maria. 2017. "Välfärdslöftet 20 mijarder till kommunerna" [Welfare promise of 20 billion to the municipalities]. *Aktuellt i Politiken*, 5 July. Available at: https://aip.nu/2017/07/05/valfardsloftet-20-miljarder-extra-till-kommunerna/.

Sager, Maja. 2011. *"Everyday clandestinity: experiences on the margins of citizenship and migration policies."* PhD thesis, Lund, Sweden: Lunds Universitet.

Social Democratic Party. 2018a. "Extratjänster" [Extra services]. Available at: https://www.socialdemokraterna.se/var-politik/a-till-o/extratjanster/.

Social Democratic Party. 2018b. "Faster integration: everyone that can work should work – regardless of who you are." Available at: https://www.socialdemokraterna.se/engagera-dig/integration/.

Svensen, Love. 2018. "Spring budget: the government is investing in foreign-born women." *Dagens Arena*, 12 April. Available at: http://www.dagensarena.se/innehall/varbudgeten-regeringen-satsar-pa-utrikesfodda-kvinnor/.

Swedish Government. 2017a. "500 miljoner till kommuner och landsting som särskilt bidrar till att minska arbetslösheten" [SEK 500 million to municipalities and county councils especially to help reduce unemployment]. Press release. Available at: https://www.regeringen.se/pressmeddelanden/2017/06/500-miljoner-till-kommuner-och-landsting-som-sarskilt-bidrar-till-att-minska-arbetslosheten/.

Swedish Government. 2017b. "Regeringen vill att fler utrikes födda kvinnor ska komma i arbete" [The government wants more foreign-born women to come to work]. Press release. Available at: http://www.regeringen.se/pressmeddelanden/2017/09/regeringen-vill-att-fler-utrikes-fodda-kvinnor-ska-komma-i-arbete/.

Swedish Government. 2018. "Uppdrag att förbättra nätverk och kontakter på arbetsmarknaden för utrikes födda kvinnor" [Mission to improve networks and contacts in the labour market for foreign-born women]. Press release. Available at: https://www.regeringen.se/4948a5/contentassets/5902ae60335a4aa99db41-ce2c0f7b266/n18-01430.pdf.

Van den Berg, Marguerite. 2016. "'Activating' those that 'lag behind': space-time politics in Dutch parenting training for migrants." *Patterns of Prejudice* 50(1), 21–37.

Vesterberg, Victor. 2015. "Learning to be Swedish: governing migrants in labour-market projects." *Studies in Continuing Education* 37(3), 302–316.

Vesterberg, Victor and Magnus Dahlstedt. 2018. "Portrait of authority: a critical interrogation of the ideology of job and career coaching." *Pedagogy, Culture and Society* 13(4), 1–15.

Williams, Fiona. 2014. "Making connections across the transnational political economy of care." In *Migration and care labour: theory, policy and politics*, eds. Bridget Anderson and Isabel Shutes, 11–30. London: Palgrave Macmillan.

14 Thinking through Intersectionality at Work

A Feminist-and-Labour Geographer's Approach

Kristina Zampoukos

Introduction

Orlando (Woolf 1928) is the story of a handsome young nobleman who, while serving as ambassador in Constantinople, transforms into a woman. Orlando lives through centuries and spaces, from the reign of Elizabeth I to the reign of King Charles II in England, and as the story ends finds her-himself caught up in nineteenth-century life. As such, *Orlando* quite aptly illustrates the idea of identities as complex, historically variable and spatially contingent (McDowell 2008a; Valentine 2007), yet also reminds us of barriers to our freedom and how these may be transgressed.

Woolf's portrait of an individual's stream of consciousness, dwelling on being, self and identity, appeared more intuitive and true to me than many academic contributions I had read on the subject. As this experience happened to coincide with the invitation to write a chapter for the present collection, I decided to let Orlando serve as both my case and my companion in my endeavour to 'think through intersectionality at work':

> For she had a great variety of selves to call upon, far more than we have been able to find room for, since a biography is considered complete if it merely accounts for six or seven selves, whereas a person may well have several thousand (Woolf 1928: 217–218).

The above quote is taken from near the end of the final chapter, where the main character calls her Self, only to realize that there is no One Self, only many past and present Selves. As with Orlando, workers' identities are at once particular, complex and fluid. In spite of this, labour is assiduously compartmentalized, differentiated and remunerated along the axes of age, skin colour, gender, nationality and skills (Orzeck 2007), and workers become associated with (and disassociated from) certain occupations, work tasks and spaces of work through a series of stereotyping practices (Harvey 2000; McDowell 2009). The task of this chapter is threefold. First, I provide a review of leading feminist and labour geographers' writings on intersectionality and intersectional analysis, in order to think through how space and time matter. Second, I demonstrate how intersectionality is imbued with cartographic reason (Olsson 2007), as evidenced, for instance, by the very concept of 'intersection', as well as by the selection and limitation of categories to include (Brown 2012). The latter may be inevitable, but it is disturbing given that part of the agenda for intersectional analysis is to move away from fixed categories and essentialism. Third, I discuss the possibility that, although the analysis rests on the intersection of social categories and power relations, it may fall short in portraying the multidimensional, evolving Self because, like Orlando, workers' identities may evolve over the course of life, for instance as a result of their occupational and/or geographical mobility, or of restructuring that may cause unemployment and/or lead people to find jobs in new sectors of the economy. Finally, I propose an understanding of people as both being and becoming, as relational stories-so-far and as progressive biographies in evolving time-space (Zampoukos 2018; Massey 2005; Pred 1981). Thus, I engage with intersectionality first and foremost as a theoretical construct, since my primary objective is to understand the world, not to change it. Admittedly though, and as proposed by Gibson-Graham (2008: 615), I align myself with the idea that 'to change our understanding *is* to change the world'.

In what follows, I briefly explain some key concepts and my use of these, specifically the terms *category*, *identity* and *self*. First, I view these concepts as reflecting different layers when it comes to deciding *who we are*. In much of the literature, category/ies and identity/ies are used interchangeably. In my understanding, however, the term 'category' corresponds with the magic wand with which – abracadabra – we simultaneously make identity/difference. So for instance, when we speak of 'centre', we also imply 'periphery'. Categories make us believe that the world consists of detectable and durable entities as well as *id*entities. Like words, categories are likely to be social in character (otherwise they make little sense). The second term, 'identity', is used both to identify someone, and also to identify *with*, i.e. identity is used from an outsider's as well as insider's perspective, broadly denoting group belonging. In any of these cases, categories are utilized to bring attention to certain identities. By contrast, being one *Self* is always deeply personal, very much resembling Orlando's experience. Thus, the Self is tied to the shifting and rambling thoughts, feelings, desires, and so forth that relentlessly traverse our inner landscapes. The Self is not easily identified from the outside (nor from the inside, as demonstrated by Orlando); it is not to be captured by simple categories; it is constantly moving between one and the many, between past, present and future, speaking to itself, of itself, with a multitude of voices, consistent in all its inconsistency.

Some Methodological Considerations

Before reviewing the literature, I wish to share a few methodological considerations with the reader. First of all, in order to find literature themed around feminist and labour geographers' writings on intersectionality, an initial search was conducted in August 2019 using Google Scholar with the search words *Intersectionality* AND *Geography* AND *Labour*. This preliminary search resulted in 19,500 hits. A more fine-grained search was conducted in September 2019 using SCOPUS. The same search words were applied, resulting in 12 publications, of which six were deemed relevant to this chapter. In a second round (also conducted with SCOPUS), I used the search words *Intersectionality* AND *Work* AND *Geography*, producing 40 hits. Of these 40 publications, only seven were judged to match the requirements regarding the feminist and labour geography approach. Articles and chapters authored by sociologists were not included in the sample of publications, nor did I include more than one publication from authors with a quite extensive publication record, such as Linda McDowell and Peter Hopkins. I tried to select articles published in highly-ranked journals, since these have greater impact in terms of citations. Another important restriction was that only publications published since 2000 were included.

Ultimately, this chapter is based on close inspection of no more than nine articles published between 2007 and 2018. However, the number of publications addressing adjacent topics, such as complex and relational identities, difference, diversity, inequalities, bodies, and so forth is much larger. Hence, this chapter does not provide an exhaustive account of everything relating to intersectionality. Rather, to make the task manageable, only articles specifically using the term 'intersectionality', and only those deemed to be of relevance to FEMINIST and labour geography or to LABOUR and feminist geography, are included. Indeed, as pointed out by Mollett and Faria (2018), explicit use of the term 'intersectionality' is rare among geographers, and consequently affected the number of publications selected for this chapter.

Aside from delimiting the task in terms of what readings to include, there was also the issue of how to organize and present the material. Depending on how we present our material, different meanings appear. In the end, I decided to go with a thematic order and presentation. One recurrent theme relates to intersectional perspectives on migration and the lives and wellbeing of migrant workforces. This theme was touched on by four articles. Clearly, it could have made up a section in its own right. However, I chose to group the reviewed articles under three main themes: the pioneering work of the 'grand old ladies' and leading scholars in feminist and/or labour geography; anxieties and concerns of an intradisciplinary nature (two sections); and new directions in the use of intersectional analysis by feminist and labour geographers. Rather than focusing on the subject of each study (such as migrant workforces), my ambition is to portray some of the debates and currents in intersectional thinking in feminist-and-labour geography.

Space and Time Matters – Matters of Space and Time

Pioneering Work: Intersectional Bio(geo)graphies and Complex Migrant Identities

First in this review is an article by Gill Valentine (2007), who gives a substantive and pedagogical illustration of how feminist geographers can contribute to theorization of intersectionality in the wider social sciences. She begins by observing that early attempts to think about how more or less stable categories intersect were imbued with the language of geometry and mathematics. Later, an intensified focus on becoming and doing emerged, not least owing to the work of Judith Butler (1990). Understanding the intersection of identities as the 'coming together, of contingencies and discontinuities, clashes and neutralizations, in which positions, identities, and differences are made and unmade, claimed and rejected' (Valentine 2007: 14) also accredits agency to individuals, thus tending to avoid the determinism associated with fixed and stable categories of identity. Despite advances in theorizing intersectionality, social sciences have paid scant attention to how space influences processes of subject formation, Valentine remarks. She then turns to her case study and a biographical account of Jeanette, a white, middle-aged and D/deaf woman.

Jeanette's narrative is presented as six 'stories' to highlight 'the specific identification/disidentifications that emerge for Jeanette in particular spatial and temporal moments' (Valentine 2007: 15). Through these stories, Valentine convincingly demonstrates that Jeanette understands her identity differently depending on the socio-spatial contexts of which she is part, and that space and identities are co-implicated. Based on her findings, she argues that the identity of a particular space, be that home, school, workplace or a community space, is (re)produced through the presence and practices of the groups that occupy and dominate these spaces. For instance, in the case of Jeanette, the Deaf club is produced as Deaf, heterosexual and white, while the office workplace is construed as a hearing, masculinist space. At the end of the article, Valentine (2007: 19) touches on the old question of structure/agency in concluding that:

> existing theorization of the concept of intersectionality overemphasizes the abilities of individuals to actively produce their own lives and underestimates how the ability to enact some identities or realities rather than others is highly contingent on the power-laden spaces in and through which our experiences are lived.

A year later, and partly in response to Valentine, another prominent feminist geographer, Linda McDowell (2008a), addressed the issue of intersectionality in relation to migrant workers and labour-market segmentation. Whereas Valentine centres on context and on particular sites (home, school, Deaf club, etc.), McDowell takes a scalar and to some extent networked perspective. In particular, she perceives difference as the outcome of practices operating at and across different spatial scales. In essence, McDowell advocates an approach to studying global movements of labour that combines the analytical lenses of political economy and institutional practices.

Similarly to Valentine, McDowell begins with an account of intersectionality and its definitions, dwelling on the notions of 'anti-categorical', 'inter-categorical' and 'intra-categorical' complexity invented by McCall (2005). She continues by discussing, in turn, gendered and racialized identities and class practices, paying specific attention to how a 'move from there to here' (McDowell 2008a: 502) may alter identities. At the end of the article, she returns to concepts introduced by McCall, and specifically the issue of methodology and *how* to study intersectionality, suggesting (in contrast to Valentine) that the many case studies conducted hitherto should be complemented by complex statistical analyses in line with McCall's. However, McDowell concludes that, irrespective of whether researchers deploy an 'intra-categorical approach' or profess to inter-categorical complexity, the conclusions on complexity seem similar. In this respect she agrees with Valentine: different dimensions of identity formation and inequalities interact in certain ways because of context.

The final part of McDowell's paper reveals a scalar and networked conceptualization of space, as illustrated by the following quote:

> To understand the position of new economic migrants in London's labour market, for example, necessitates an analysis at multiple scales of the connections between global economic restructuring and the consequences for global divisions of labour, international flows of capital and labour, the consequences of spatial dislocation for millions of migrant labour, of class position, gender divisions and skin colour (and how these are reconstructed through migration), of racialized and national stereotypes, as well as of cultural assumptions and everyday practices in the workplace and the exclusive construction of citizenship that creates a division between the deserving and the undeserving migrant (McDowell 2008a: 504–505).

In summary, both Valentine and McDowell seem to agree that identities vary with context, whether this is perceived as a networked space where multiple practices intersect, or as a place more in line with the cultural geographies tradition, here represented by Valentine. Time is present in two different ways: in terms of the biography of a person, where certain aspects of identity are accentuated in specific sites-and-moments in a person's life; and in terms of the processual understanding inherent in 'migration' (from there to here) and 'practice'. In what follows, I delve into a concern that appears to be intra-disciplinary in nature, namely the issue of class in relation to other identities.

Intra-disciplinary Concerns I: Labour Geography Meets Complex Identities

Embracing intersectionality seems to be somewhat of a challenge for labour geographers since, for Marxian labour geographers in particular, class (i.e. labour as opposed to capital), together with wage relations and the formal workplace, have served as the locus of interest (Rutherford 2010). Marxist concepts of class and work have been challenged by feminist and post-structural researchers (for a detailed discussion, see Gibson-Graham, Resnick and Wolff 2001: 1–21), criticizing labour geography for clinging on to class as the sole relevant social category, and privileging paid labour. Nevertheless, scholars such as Tod Rutherford (2010) and Linda McDowell (2008b) express concern that the emphasis on difference and diversity, and the (partial) neglect of commonalities that exist across differences relating to locality, gender and lived experience, may in fact be counterproductive to workers' interests. For instance, Rutherford (2010: 774) observes that although post-structural perspectives have added new and meaningful insights into the differentiated nature of labour, the workplace and class, the 'increasing attention to identity and diverse economies should not come at the expense of the continued critical role of the formal work-place and the wage-relation'.

Rutherford gives an account of the evolution of labour geography, from its early developments in the 1960s and 1970s under the influence of Marxism, into a sub-discipline acknowledging the active participation of workers in the production of capitalist economic geographies. While unions used to play a significant role in labour geography as the primary source of worker agency, the attention has now shifted toward 'inter-sectionality strategies beyond the workplace with highly diverse work-forces in local communities' (Rutherford 2010: 770). Furthermore, current trends in working life, such as individualization and fragmentation, have contributed to the shift away from the workplace, wage relations and class. Difference and firm strategies of fragmentation are always present, Rutherford continues, but because work is by necessity a collective endeavour, there is always also the possibility of common worker identity and resistance. Thus, he concludes, seeking 'commonality in difference' remains critical for labour geographers.

The issue of class and how it interrelates with other identities is also addressed by Alison Stenning (2008), who starts with the observation that class appears to have resurfaced as a central issue in current debates on neoliberalization, transnationalism and empire, amongst others, whilst at the same time 'the engagement with class can be abstract, even ungrounded, and often hidden within discussions of power, inequality and difference' (Stenning 2008: 9). She then discusses the rise of 'new working-class studies' and the associated demand to reinvigorate the study and representation of working-class lives, cultures and politics.

In this line of thought, working classness is perceived as a dynamic and relational category, showing obvious similarities with the intersectional approach. Besides emphasizing an intersectional 'take' on working-class studies within geography, Stenning (2008: 10) also declares that '[w]orking classness is placed', meaning that, in accordance with dialectical thinking, it is performed and constructed within communities, as well as shaping these spaces. Stenning states that it is within communities, whether local or not so local, that the spatial practices of work and life intersect:

> Practices ... enacted within homes, workplaces, communities and the myriad other spaces of everyday life reflect the articulation of gender, generation and race ... and the employment of resources, economic, social, cultural ... in the negotiation of economic, political and social lives (Stenning 2008: 10).

These complex negotiations are emblematic of the study of working-class geographies.

Innovative work by feminist and development geographers has encouraged labour geographers to extend their appreciation of the geographies of work beyond the workplace, to contest conventional definitions of work, and to perceive workers not solely as workers but also as parents, partners, consumers, activists, and so forth. Yet working-class geographies remain important, Stenning (2008: 11) argues, because class relations are remade every day, all over the world, and the 'processes of neoliberalisation and globalisation are lived, negotiated and transgressed by working class people'. Whilst postcolonial and feminist critiques have brought voices from particular spaces to the forefront, less attention has been given to bringing voices from the margins to the centre, such as deindustrialized communities in Europe and the US (for a recent example, see McDowell and Bonner-Thompson 2019).

Labour geographers have obviously been influenced by feminist and post-structuralist ideas, but without abandoning the sub-discipline's fundamentals. Furthermore, seeking 'commonality in difference', as emphasized by Rutherford, is an important strategy for unions under global stress. However, interference by feminist geographers has clearly 'disrupted' the common-sense understanding of the boundaries of the sub-discipline among labour geographers. Spatiality and temporality, in this context, are therefore best understood in terms of the (contested) core of the sub-discipline and its shifting boundaries over time. Following this excursion into labour geography, I now turn to another intra-disciplinary concern, revolving mainly around intersections and how to produce a 'proper' intersectional analysis.

Intra-disciplinary Concerns II: Intersectional Anxieties

In Michael Brown's (2012) thematic progress report on *Gender and sexuality: Intersectional anxieties*, he outlines the connections between geographies of sexualities and other identities, and more specifically how these intersections have been practised in the literature. In so doing, he addresses a number of 'anxieties' in what he recognizes as 'the classical spirit of queer geography: to question all assumptions and theoretical moves, no matter how seemingly progressive or radical' (Brown 2012: 541). In line with Valentine (2007) and McDowell (2008a), Brown starts by discussing the term 'intersectionality' and the attention paid to the spatial dimension, for instance through the now widespread use of the 'crossroads' metaphor first introduced by Crenshaw (1991).[1] In fact, one of the 'anxieties' pointed out by Brown relates directly to this metaphor. Many geographers reject this image, he claims, on the grounds that it presumes an empirical or conceptual separation of race and sexuality.[2] Ironically, this separation has an essentializing effect, yet also implies an additive understanding of oppression (see also McCall 2005).

Brown continues by identifying an unevenness in geographies of sexualities regarding which identities and structures of oppression are addressed. Some categories, such as gender and race, clearly receive far more attention than other categories, such as sexuality and (dis)ability, or sexuality and religion. Brown then points to ongoing debates over 'just *which* identities we choose to intersect with sexualities' (Brown 2012: 544), as well as the *number* of intersections that must be considered to fulfil the requirements of 'proper' intersectional analysis. Methodological and theoretical justifications of the selection and delimitation of intersections to contemplate and examine are largely missing, he claims. In his opinion, responding to questions like these is particularly pertinent to intellectual and academic communities' adhering to anti-essentializing, anti-hierarchical philosophies, and even more so if combined with the belief that present-absences in texts are of methodological significance.

In a more recent progress report, Peter Hopkins (2017) pays specific attention to the use of intersectionality in social geography. He suggests that geographers need 'to pay more attention to the origins of intersectionality in black feminism and not only cite the work of white women and men', a statement rooted in a fear of geography always being a 'white, racist, colonialist, masculinist discipline' (Hopkins 2017: 3). Hopkins then maps intersectionality as part of social geography research, and identifies at least three areas where intersectionality and geography might fruitfully combine: ethnic residential segregation and the city, migration and translocal positionality, and embodiment and belonging.

Brown raises important questions about methodological and theoretical justifications for choices by researchers confessing to intersectional analysis. There is also a geography in the choices we make – a geography of cartographic reason (Olsson 2007). Evidently, not just the discipline but even the identities (including the bodies) of researchers engaged in intersectional analysis are matters for discussion.

The next section presents 'new directions' in the application of an intersectional approach by feminist (and) labour geographers. In part, these developments can be viewed as responses to Hopkins' call for diversity, at least in terms of geographies. Thus, we visit, in turn, Nepal, the United Arab Emirates and Canada to gain glimpses of some recent advances in geographers' intersectional thinking.

New Directions: Material-Symbolic Understandings and Intersectional Rhythmanalysis

Andrea Nightingale's (2011) groundbreaking article in *Geoforum* advanced intersectional theory by demonstrating how the embodied performance of gender, caste and other aspects of social difference collapse the distinction between the material and the symbolic. Anchored within feminist political ecology, Nightingale adopts the perspective that the material side of human existence plays an important role in producing subjectivities. Her agenda is to explore 'how material environments extend from and into the body with profound implications for social difference, space and ecologies' (Nightingale 2011: 153). For this, she draws on extensive ethnographic fieldwork carried out in Nepal.

Nightingale argues that feminist theory centred on the performance of gender tends to emphasize the discursive and symbolic dimension at the expense of material aspects. She continues by observing that although intersectional theory has been taken up by many anthropologists working in the field of feminist political ecology, it has thus far received little recognition from geographers. She expands this critique by pointing to the scant attention paid to materiality, even in work by feminist geographers such as Valentine (2007) mentioned earlier: '[S]pace is defined only by the social activities that occur within it: married partnership, work, or support session' (Nightingale 2011: 155).

Nightingale explains that in the nascent field of feminist political ecology, social difference is understood as emergent and produced out of seemingly mundane, everyday spatial practices. She then proceeds to discuss her findings and theoretical insights from Nepal. First, she highlights the importance of purity and pollution as a key basis for social difference in Nepal, and how ritual purity is maintained through a variety of everyday spatial and bodily practices. She then accounts for these practices, starting with menstruating Hindu women in the Nepalese Mugu district, and the restrictions placed on them owing to norms relating to purity/impurity. Not only are women kept separated spatially and socially during their menstruation or following their pregnancy, but they are also prevented from carrying out 'normal' tasks associated with 'womanhood', such as preparing food, collecting water and performing agricultural work. Thus, while 'polluted', women's bodies represent a risk to the social and ecological environment: crops will not yield properly if 'impure' women harvest them.

According to Nightingale, not only do biological substances emanating from the body define women as 'polluted', but material and ecological substances *rubbing off* on bodies may also act to underline social difference. For instance, engaging in agro-forestry work makes a person dirty in the literal sense, but dirt also underlines social (caste) hierarchies in terms of purity/impurity. As observed by Nightingale, it is obviously easier to keep clean if one does not have to engage in manual, dirty work. In this sense, class relations, cleanliness, power and status are intertwined.

Meanwhile, Michelle Buckley (2014: 339) presents three 'interventions' in the theorization of urbanization, one of which is relevant to intersectional thinking, namely 'the building process as a key locus of intersectional politics'. Drawing on feminist migration and postcolonial urban scholarship, this article revolves around construction labour markets in Dubai in the United Arab Emirates, which hosts many migrant construction workers from countries such as India, Bangladesh and Pakistan. Middle-Eastern cities have hitherto played a peripheral role in Western-dominated theorization of urbanization, and whereas migration theory tends to treat cities merely as containers for migrants' work and lives, Buckley's mission is to demonstrate migrants' significance as agents in the political economy and in the production of contemporary urban landscapes. Specifically, she claims that focusing on the 'migrant dimensions of construction labor markets disaggregates the urban landscape into an array of productive moments with geographies that extend well beyond the material and political borders of the city' (Buckley 2014: 344). David Harvey's (1985) conceptualization of commodity relations in the city serves as a point of departure: before material components of the built environment can be used for production and/or consumption, they are produced as commodities themselves. In the case of Dubai, the city has literally grown through the hands of hundreds of thousands of migrant construction workers, many of whom are subjected to conditions of forced labour.

Regarding the 'intersectional politics' involved, Buckley notes that the presence of such a large migrant workforce posed a dilemma, since the city was primarily designed to attract affluent foreign residents and tourists. This prompted the state to adopt a host of segregationist policies aimed at keeping tourists and low-wage builders apart, including the establishment of labour camps on the urban outskirts, and policing efforts to discourage migrant construction workers from visiting tourist spaces.

Contractors' and labour-sending consulates' hiring practices were based not only on assessments of skills and work experience, but also on stereotyped depictions of workers from certain regions and countries as being more suitable than others, particularly considering the 'city-state's agenda of becoming an affluent enclave of consumer urbanism' (Buckley 2014: 342). Hence, workers of certain national origins were portrayed as being more 'calm' and easy to manage, 'built' to cope with the Dubai climate and physically demanding construction work, and not 'prone' to promiscuity or 'ogling women in public'. Although construction sites are typically coded as masculine, their gendered nature seems to have escaped the notice of urban researchers. These observations lead Buckley to move beyond class relations to consider the broader politics of subjectivity sustaining material urbanization. Drawing on the work of Linda McDowell, she suggests:

> The point of attending to questions about the politics of ethnicity and race, citizenship, class, or gender is not to map how such social axes are simply attributes attached to particular bodies participating in the urbanization process, but to illuminate how the material production of urban built environments can depend on the parallel production of complex inequalities and intersecting forms of social difference (Buckley 2014: 342).

In a recent article, Emily Reid-Musson (2018: 881) argues that the framework offered by what she terms 'intersectional rhythmanalysis' is useful for conceptualizing the 'braiding together of rhythms, social categories of difference, and power on non-essentialist bases'. Reid-Musson combines French sociologist, Henri Lefebvre's (2004) writings on everyday life and rhythmanalysis with those of intersectional feminist thinkers such as Butler (1990) and Crenshaw (1991) in devising the concept of intersectional rhythmanalysis, which she discusses in relation to migration, mobilities and labour. Her overall argument is that control over rhythms is integral to the reproduction of labour migration regimes and to the social differences that underpin migration regimes. Rhythmanalysis, she writes, is both relational and interscalar, and does not privilege time over space, but rather integrates the two. According to Reid-Musson, Lefebvre studied the everyday life of the street from his window, using all his embodied sensory capacities to understand the social realities revealed by daily life rhythms.

Drawing on Lefebvre, Reid Musson argues that inequalities and oppressions are not static, but are made and remade through spatio-temporal arrangements such as rhythms. Rhythms impact on migrant workers' lives at many interconnected scales, for example through guest worker programmes that determine the longevity of work permits, through agricultural cycles and through work schedules. Hence, migrants coming to Canada through the Seasonal Agricultural Worker Program follow the annual rhythms of both the programme and the agricultural sector, while at weekly and daily levels they are subjected to the rhythms of work schedules. Working long hours and lacking means of transport, migrants may live very restricted lives with regard to free time and access to leisure spaces. However, in comparing men and women, Reid-Musson finds that female migrants face even more severe restrictions in terms of mobility and access to spaces beyond the realm of work:

> migrant women are not only monitored by men but can be dependent on them outside of work in order to circulate and gain access to services and social spaces like church or simply going out for coffee. Migrant women are much less visible in public spaces relative to men (Reid-Musson 2018: 892).

She proposes several avenues for advancing the framework of 'intersectional rhythmanalysis'. One is continued exploration of embodiment and rhythms without essentializing and naturalizing the body. Another revolves around migrant workers and how spatio-temporal rhythms relate to labour agency, identity and negotiation in migration processes.

To summarize this section, I find that Nightingale's approach to social difference lies at the heart of geography, as she unpacks with considerable delicacy how the material and symbolic, ecologies and sociologies, collapse into each other. She provides a highly persuasive case for understanding intersectionality as going beyond the meeting of social categories, and social difference as more than unjust geographies. Buckley, for her part, contributes to theorization of urbanization by successfully combining theories on the production of built environments with evidence of a migrant workforce serving as a central means of production, while simultaneously being marginalized discursively and with regard to their mobility and residency in the same environment. Nightingale and Buckley both seem preoccupied with linking social and material space together, whereas Reid-Musson is more concerned with thinking space and time together, hence her interest in rhythmanalysis. Her proposition, based on the work of Lefebvre, offers an interesting philosophical path for geographers, not least since the spatiotemporal rhythms in which we engage, or are subjected to, may be more or less constraining and/or enabling.

The Cartographic Reason of Intersectional Thinking

As observed in the methodological section, many geographers seem to prefer concepts other than intersectionality to denote and analyse the coming together of various dimensions of people's identities. Nevertheless, there is a widespread perception that space plays an active role in the process of identity formation. Table 14.1 provides an overview of both explicit and implicit understandings of space and time conveyed in the articles under scrutiny here. However, it is not always clear how intersectionality combines theoretically and/or empirically with space. The most concrete and straightforward examples seem to be found in Valentine's and Nightingale's contributions, possibly because of their empirical underpinning. Moreover, both Valentine and Reid-Musson are explicit about the temporal dimension. Valentine refers to a person's biography and specific moments in a person's life when certain aspects of identity are brought to the fore while others recede. Reid-Musson presents the idea of intersectional rhythmanalysis, making the point that '[s]ocial differences and social oppressions ... are made and remade through spatio-temporal arrangements like rhythms' (Reid-Musson 2018: 885).

Clearly, there are intra-disciplinary concerns relating to inter-sectionality, as manifested by the commonality–difference debate among labour geographers and feminist geographers, and discussion between feminist and post-colonial geographers regarding representation. However, what seems to be largely missing is a more thorough theori-zation of intersectionality, spatiotemporality and agency, a topic to which I shortly return. In what follows, though, I shall explain how and why I consider intersectionality to be imbued with cartographic reason. To do so, I must think back to my time as a PhD student. Among my professors at the Department of Social and Economic Geography at Uppsala University was Gunnar Olsson, who repeatedly suggested that language is inherently spatial, and that geography emanates from the human activity of wor(l)ding. In Olsson's own words, it is through the practice of naming that 'undifferentiated chaos is turned into differ-entiated cosmos' (Olsson 2007: 17). He also claims that our thinking is structured geometrically, and that we navigate the unknown with the help of invisible maps. Thus, professor Olsson was – and still is – pre-occupied with mapping cartographic reason and, perhaps even more importantly, critiquing it (2007).

Language gives us a clue. Fix-points of time and place, including the positions of then and now, the hierarchical coordinates of below and above, con-junctions and pre-positions, help us to make sense and create

Table 14.1 Spatial and temporal focus and/or ontology according to the themes identified

Main theme	Author	Spatial focus and/or ontology	Temporal focus and/or ontology
Intersectional bio (geo)graphies and complex migrant identities	Valentine (2007)	Space as context	Biographies and 'moments'
	McDowell (2008a)	Space as scale; networked space; space (as difference) produced by practices	Practices (evolving over time)
Labour geography meets complex identities	Stenning (2008)	Dialectical thinking: people shape communities – communities shape people's lives	Processes and practices
	Rutherford (2010)	Formal workplace as a site of local and translocal capital–labour relations and struggle	Development of labour geography as a subdiscipline
Intersectional anxieties	Brown (2012)	Language and philosophy of science as representational spaces	–
	Hopkins (2017)	A decolonized, diversity-sensitive discipline	Heritage of the discipline
		Residential areas, cities, translocal positions, the body	
Material-symbolic understandings and intersectional rhythmanalysis	Nightingale (2011)	Relational perspective centring on the interrelatedness of identity and ecology, symbolic and material	Identities not fixed but rather '*dynamic* results of contested practices'
	Buckley (2014)	The city; political economy and socio-spatial power relations underpinning the production of urban space	–

(*Continued*)

Table 14.1 (Continued)

Main theme	Author	Spatial focus and/or ontology	Temporal focus and/or ontology
	Reid-Musson (2018)	Space as interscalar and inter-connected rhythms experienced by the migrant worker	Intersectional *rythm*analysis – daily, weekly, annual rhythms

order out of messy reality. Yet every attempt to grasp the world with words is destined to be incomplete, since there are no perfect translations, nor perfect representations. Therefore, the strength of cartographic reason 'lies less in in its ability to tell the truth and more in its power to convince' (Olsson, 2007: 10). Imagination makes it possible to believe in a relationship between map and territory.

Obviously, my objective in this chapter is far more modest than that of Olsson. Nevertheless, there is at least a small connection because, as observed by Valentine (2007) and Brown (2012), amongst others, the term 'intersectionality' is intrinsically bound up with geography through its association with geometry. The term 'inter-section' essentially presupposes the existence of identifiable entities that coincide with and relate to each other. And for an entity to become identified (as an 'id-entity'), we must engage in the game of naming (Olsson 2007) and in making difference. The act of naming and sorting, in turn, inevitably involves the use of fixed, essentialist categories (otherwise they would neither be categories, nor meaningful). Furthermore, intersectional analysis (like any other analysis) implies the selection and de*limitation* of what categories or dimensions of people's identities to include. Thus, even though the meeting of id-entities may evoke specific positions, intersectionality rests on the inescapable practice of naming, delimiting and comparing (and thus of doing identity and difference).

A Feminist-and-Labour Geographer's Approach: Grappling with the Many Voices of the Self

As I have argued elsewhere (Zampoukos 2018; Zampoukos et al. 2018), thinking about people in terms of both being and becoming, as relational stories-so-far and as progressive biographies in evolving time-space, entails a shift in focus from social categories to the processes involved, yet it is also conducive to understanding how agency, space and time are intertwined. Thinking of space as in the *making* (Massey 2005) is now common among geographers, but the same philosophy may of course apply to human beings. People both embody and are embedded in diverse social and spatial relations, and these locations are far from static, but are produced in and through context – in and through social space and time. As we proceed toward 'the tip of an always advancing now line' (Pred 1981: 1), we simultaneously connect the dots between our present existence and past experiences. Imaginations of the future (space) influence how we cope with the present (space), yet the present (space) also determines to some extent how we imagine and act in relation to the future. These dimensions are incorporated in the agency of individual workers creating their own progressive biographies (Zampoukos et al. 2018).

At this point, I think of my interview with Bahar and her story, which she told me almost ten years ago and to which I keep returning (Zampoukos and Ioannides 2015; Zampoukos 2018). Bahar was a middle-class schoolgirl who fled the Khomeini regime with her parents and siblings, and after many years of repeated break-ups arrived in Sweden. By that time she was already a married woman and mother of two. On arrival in Sweden, Bahar took care of the children, while her husband eventually found a job as a taxi driver. Caring for the children and doing most of the unpaid housework left very little time and energy to learn the new language. As the children grew older, and having divorced from her husband, Bahar started to work her way into the Swedish labour market, and at the time of our interview was employed as a waitress on a regular contract. At the end of the interview, she made a remark about her life in retrospect, and expressed a wish that her children would be better off. Clearly, her hope for the future was strongly associated with her children.

I think of this story as an illustration of context or of 'situation' as *both* enabling *and* constraining, partly in response to Valentine's (2007) critique that there is a tendency in existing theorization to overemphasize individuals' abilities to actively produce their own lives. It seems to me that the pendulum has now swung the other way, entailing an emphasis on constraints, while ignoring the possibility that context and structure may be both constraining and enabling at the same time (Giddens 1984), and also disregarding the idea that everyone has agency, even though relative and relational in character. Bahar's story reveals a journey that involves both the crossing of borders, and movement across social boundaries over the course of time (middle-class Iranian citizen, refugee, asylum seeker, Swedish citizen, unmarried, married, divorced, daughter, woman, wife, mother, housewife, employed, working class, etc.). These are all easily detected and, I imagine, together make up the multitude of voices constituting her Self.

It is my contention that, after some introspection, we find that we are all just like Orlando. We are all built up of this multitude of voices, and that is why I want to end this chapter by proposing that researchers with an interest in subjectivity formation and intersectional analysis should delve into the inner process of identity making. Such a path might prove truly revolutionary, as it would enable intersectional analysis not only to combine the language of being with a language of becoming (Wilson 2017; Gibson-Graham et al. 2001), but also to connect observations of identities and differently positioned subjects with knowledge of the inner processes of the multitudinous Self. Social categories and identities may be useful as instruments of power, but the Self is powerful beyond these categories, not least since we have a remarkable capacity to vary our Selves in imagination.

Notes

1 Crenshaw was allegedly the first to adopt the analogy of 'road junctions where violent accidents repeatedly occur without being reported' (Valentine 2007: 12).
2 Crenshaw (1991: 1244) speaks of intersectionality as a 'provisional concept' and recognizes that it 'does engage dominant assumptions that race and gender are essentially separate categories'. By tracing the categories to their intersections, she hoped to produce a methodology that would disrupt the tendency to see race and gender as exclusive and separable. Whatever her original intention, it seems plausible that Crenshaw was experiencing what many authors encounter, namely that once our words are 'out there' they start to live a life of their own. In other words, there is a gulf between intention and interpretation. Therefore, debate over the meaning and use of 'intersectionality' is sure to continue.

References

Brown, Michael. 2012. "Gender and sexuality I: intersectional anxieties." *Progress in Human Geography* 36(4), 541–550.

Buckley, Michelle. 2014. "On the work of urbanization: migration, construction labor, and the commodity moment." *Annals of the Association of American Geographers* 104(2), 338–347.

Butler, Judith. 1990. *Gender trouble: feminism and the subversion of identity.* New York, NY: Routledge.

Crenshaw, Kimberlé. 1991. "Mapping the margins: intersectionality, identity politics, and violence against women of color." *Stanford Law Review 43*, 1241–1299.

Gibson-Graham, Julie Katherine. 2008. "Diverse economies: performative practices for 'other worlds'." *Progress in Human Geography* 32(5), 613–632.

Gibson-Graham, Julie Katherine, Stephen Resnick and Richard Wolff, Eds. 2001. *Re/presenting class: essays in postmodern Marxism.* Durham, NC: Duke University Press.

Giddens, Anthony. 1984. *The constitution of society.* Cambridge: Polity Press.

Harvey, David. 1985. *The urbanization of capital: studies in the history and theory of capitalist urbanization.* Baltimore, MD: John Hopkins University Press.

Harvey, David. 2000. *Spaces of hope.* Edinburgh: Edinburgh University Press.

Hopkins, Peter. 2017. "Social geography I: intersectionality." *Progress in Human Geography 43*(5), 937–947.

Lefebvre, Henri. 2004. *Rhythmanalysis: space, time and everyday life*, trans. Stuart Elden and Gerald Moore. London: Continuum.

Massey, Doreen. 2005. *For space.* Thousand Oaks, CA: Sage.

McCall, Leslie. 2005. "The complexity of intersectionality." *Signs: Journal of Women in Culture and Society 30*(3), 1771–1800.

McDowell, Linda. 2008a. "Thinking through work: complex inequalities, constructions of difference and trans-national migrants." *Progress in Human Geography 32*(4), 491–507.

McDowell, Linda. 2008b. "Thinking through class and gender in the context of working class studies." *Antipode 40*(1), 20–24.

McDowell, Linda. 2009. *Working bodies: interactive service employment and workplace identities.* Hoboken, NJ: John Wiley & Sons.

McDowell, Linda and Carl Bonner-Thompson. 2019. *"The other side of coastal towns: young men's precarious lives on the margins of England."* Environment and Planning A: Economy and Space 52(5), 916–932. https://doi.org/10.1177/0308518X19887968.

Mollett, Sharlene and Caroline Faria. 2018. "The spatialities of intersectional thinking: fashioning feminist geographic futures." *Gender, Place and Culture 25*(4), 565–577.

Nightingale, Andrea J. 2011. "Bounding difference: intersectionality and the material production of gender, caste, class and environment in Nepal." *Geoforum 42*(2), 153–162.

Olsson, Gunnar. 2007. *Abysmal: a critique of cartographic reason.* Chicago, IL: University of Chicago Press.

Orzeck, Reecia. 2007. "What does not kill you: historical materialism and the body." *Environment and Planning D: Society and Space 25*(3), 496–514.

Pred, Allan. 1981. "Social reproduction and the time-geography of everyday life." *Geografiska Annaler, Series B: Human Geography 63*(1), 5–22.

Reid-Musson, Emily. 2018. "Intersectional rhythmanalysis: power, rhythm, and everyday life." *Progress in Human Geography 42*(6), 881–897.

Rutherford, Tod. 2010. "De/re-centring work and class? a review and critique of labour geography." *Geography Compass 4*(7), 768–777.

Stenning, Alison. 2008. "For working class geographies." *Antipode 40*(1), 9–14.

Valentine, Gill. 2007. "Theorizing and researching intersectionality: a challenge for feminist geography." *The Professional Geographer 59*(1), 10–21.

Wilson, Helen F. 2017. "On geography and encounter: bodies, borders, and difference." *Progress in Human Geography 41*(4), 451–471.

Woolf, Virginia. 1928 2016. *Orlando.* London: Penguin.

Zampoukos, Kristina. 2018. "Hospitality workers and the relational spaces of labor (im)mobility." *Tourism Geographies 20*(1), 49–66.

Zampoukos, Kristina and Dimitri Ioannides. 2015. "Making difference within the hotel: labour mobility and the internationalisation of reproductive work." In *A hospitable world? organising work and workers in hotels and tourist resorts*, eds. David Jordhus-Lier and Anders Underthun, 29–44. London: Routledge.

Zampoukos, Kristina, Hege Merete Knutsen, Maiken Bjerga Kiil and Gunilla Olofsdotter. 2018. "Mobile with an agency: negotiating the spatiotemporalities of the temp migrant worker." *Geoforum 93*, 40–47.

About the Editors

Angelika Sjöstedt is an Associate professor in Gender Studies at Mid Sweden University, Sweden. She has published articles, book chapters, co-edited books and editorials concerning intersectional studies of work life and gender equality policy as well as studies of rural morality and rural resilience including centre and periphery relations. Her work often aims at linking feminist and critical theory with research fields more rarely addressed with such perspectives.

Katarina Giritli Nygren is Professor of Sociology at Mid Sweden University. Her current research addresses different forms of governance relationships with a focus on spatial processes of inclusion and exclusion in terms of gender, class, and ethnicity in different contexts. In her most recent research, she argues for feminist and intersectional analyses of the shifting governmentalities of neoliberal welfare states to elucidate the movement from a welfare to a punitive state with an increased focus on risks and national security. She is currently involved in research projects on rural refugee reception, critical sustainability studies and a rethinking of the Swedish gender equality model.

Marianna Fotaki is Professor of business ethics at the University of Warwick Business School and holds a PhD from the London School of Economics and Political Science. Marianna was an Edmond J. Safra Network Fellow (2014–2015) at Harvard University). She has published over 70 articles, book chapters and books on gender, inequalities, and the marketization of public services. The recent books include *Gender and the Organization. Women at Work in the 21st Century* (Routledge, 2018 co-authored with Nancy Harding), *Diversity, Affect and Embodiment in Organizing* (Palgrave 2019, co-edited with Alison Pullen). Marianna currently works on whistleblowing (funded by the ESRC and British Academy/Leverhulme Trust), solidarity responses to crisis and refugee arrivals in Greece.

About the Contributors

Ayşe Serdar is an assistant professor at Istanbul Technical University, Department of Humanities and Social Sciences. She received her PhD from Binghamton University, Department of Sociology in 2009. She was a visiting researcher at Mid Sweden University in 2019. Her research interests include nationalism, ethnicity and social movements.

Hara Kouki is an adjunct Lecturer at the University of Crete and at the Hellenic Open University. Trained as a historian at the University of Athens, she completed her PhD at Birkbeck College (University of London) and has worked as a research fellow at the European University Institute (Florence), at Newcastle University and at the Geography dpt. at Durham University. In her research, Hara traces the ways communities, inequalities and collective action take shape and interrelate in different contexts and periods of time.

Emelie Larsson is a PhD candidate in Sociology at the Department of humanities and social sciences and Forum for gender studies at Mid Sweden University. Her research focuses on healthcare restructuring, risk, gender and place.

Camila Esguerra Muelle (ORCID 0000-0002-6600-0324) is a honorary researcher for the Interdisciplinary Group on Gender Studies at the National University of Colombia and Full Professor at the District University of Bogotá. Postdoctorate in Gender and Development from the University of Los Andes, Colombia; with a Postdoctoral stay at the Universitat Pomepeu Fabra, Spain. Doctor in Humanities from the Carlos III University of Madrid, Spain (Cum Laude mention). Master in Gender and Ethnicity from the Utrecht University, The Netherlands, Erasmus Mundus fellow. Anthropologist from the National University of Colombia, degree thesis with a meritorious mention. Her main lines of research, addressed from the intersectional and heterarchical perspectives, are: migrations and global care chains; corporalities, sexualities and micropolitics; sexualities, politics and policies, visual and artistic studies.

Kristina Johansson (ORCID 0000-0002-3865-796X) is a Senior Lecturer in Human Work Science at the Department of Business Administration, Technology and Social Science at Luleå University of Technology, Sweden.

Her research focuses on gender structures and notions at work and in organisations.

Lisa Ringblom (ORCID 0000-0002-4060-2327) is a Postdoctoral Researcher at the Centre for Work Life and Evaluation Studies at Malmö University, Sweden but conducted the majority of work on the chapter in this book during her time as a doctoral candidate in Human Work Science at Luleå University of Technology, Sweden. Her research interest includes, but are not limited to work, male-dominated organisations, gender and gender equality.

Annette Thörnquist PhD, is Associate Professor of History educated at Uppsala University. Her main research interests are in industrial relations, employment relationships, occupational health and safety and labour migration, with a focus on trends and developments in recent decades. She has worked as senior researcher at the Swedish National Institute for Working Life, Stockholm University, Uppsala University, Linköping University, and at Forschungsinstitut für Arbeit, Technik und Kultur, Tübingen (F.A.T.K.), where she currently is an associated researcher. She has had several expert assignments for the European Commission, DG for Employment, Social Affairs and Inclusion, and she has published, e.g. in the Nordic Journal of Working Life Studies, Labour History, European Journal of Industrial Relations and International Journal of Comparative Labour Law and Industrial Relations.

Paula Mulinari is an Associate professor of Social work at the Department of social Work at Malmö University.

Ulrika Schmauch, Ph.D., is a lecturer at the department of Sociology at Umeå University. Her research is on social inequality in relation to race, place, and gender from an intersectional perspective.

Britt-Inger Keisu, Ph.D., is an Associate professor, Department of Sociology at Umeå University. Her theoretical interest intersects gender-organization and leadership theory.

Björn Ahlström, Ph.D., works at the Centre for Principal Development at Umeå University. His main research interests focus the social and civic objectives of schools and organizational theory.

Kristina Zampoukos (ORCID 0000-0001-6176-3595)) is a Senior Lecturer in Human Geography at the Department of Economics, Geography, Law and Tourism, Mid-Sweden University. Her research interests include feminist and labour geographies, in particular theorizations of the working body; socio-spatial divisions of labour; intersectionality; labour (im)mobilities and worker agency.

Lisa Ridzén is a Ph.D. Student in Sociology, Mid Sweden University. Her research focuses on men and masculinity. By focusing on life stories and the constitution of vulnerability and care among rural northern men, she critically investigates the intersections of gender and place.

Nandi Vanqa-Mgijima Nandi Vanqa-Mgijima is 50 year old and a feminist activist who has in her adult life been engaged in social justice activism at school and in the world of work. I was born from a poor working class family and raised by a divorcee woman in the township Guguletu, Cape Town in South Africa. Vanqa-Mgijima worked for a number of organisations in Cape Town including but not limited to, the Women On Farms Project a feminist organisation; the International Research & Information Group (ILRIG), a support service organisation, as a feminist researcher-educator, and currently she is working for the Casual Workers Advice Office, in Johannesburg as a project leader women worker organizer Co-ordinator. Research focus areas are new empirical material on the working and living conditions of working class women; the gendered nature of the labour market; feminisation of formal and informal labour; and how women are organizing differently. Research and political education interests are to develop understanding the gendered nature of globalisation - around areas of poor and working class women; employment patterns including social reproductive labour; delivery of social basis services; feminist organizing alternatives. In 2010 Vanqa-Mgijima was registered with the University of the Western Cape's Social Law Project for an Mphil, admitted based on the recognition of prior learning. It was not possible to complete this programme due to a host of complexities of being a black woman from working class communities, where the majority is still faced with realities of reproductive labour due to among other things the withdrawal of state to provide basic services, as neo-liberal policies dictate. Some of the previous research articles include Organizing on the Streets: A study of Reclaimers in the Streets of Cape Town by Koni Benson and Nandi Vanqa-Mgijima, 2010; Organizing for Empowerment in Exploited, Undervalued and Essential: Domestic Workers and the Realisation of their Rights, 2010 and written extensively ILRIG new articles around gender and feminism, Social Insecurities ilrigsa.org.za/category/news. This work is dedicate this to my parents Pam & Stan Vanqa-Mgjima, my two sons Lungisa; Bulumko and Leonard Gentle former Director at ILRIG.

Ambreen Tour Ben-Shmuel is a doctoral student in Sociology at the Hebrew University in Jerusalem and a research fellow at the Harry S. Truman Research Institute for the Advancement of Peace. She has spent over a decade working for and researching grassroots and advocacy organizations in Israel and Palestine focusing on multicultural and cross-border peace training, facilitation, and project management. She has also contributed to numerous writing, podcasting, training, and speaking initiatives to work toward more equitable gender representation in educational, religious, and peace organizations. Her most recent area of research focuses on intersectionality and cross-border environmental cooperation.

Manar Faraj is from a refugee camp in Bethlehem, Palestine. She is a doctoral candidate at the Friedrich Schiller University of Jena. Faraj holds a bachelor's degree in Global Trade from High Point University in the United States and a master's degree in Peace and Reconciliation from Coventry University in the United Kingdom. She has studied peace methods and conflict transformation in a number of international settings, including Rwanda, and she also obtained a Conflict Transformation Certificate from the School of International Training in Vermont. Throughout her career, she has lectured, managed programs, and implemented conflict-intervention projects in a number of different countries, also working as a facilitator, project manager, evaluator and consultant in peace and conflict initiatives. Faraj has a number of academic publications focusing on women, refugees, and conflict.

JosAnn Cutajar is an Associate Professor of Gender and Sexualities at the Faculty of Social Wellbeing at the University of Malta. Cutajar is an activist at community and policy level. She has been the coordinator of the Consultative Council for Women's Rights since 2017. The remit of this council is to advise the Ministry for Justice, Equality and Governance on what kind of women's issues to tackle and how. As an administrator of the Malta Trust Foundation, she is involved in two community projects, mainly Y-Assist which offers housing to single mothers, and Programm Tbissima, a community centre in a socially deprived area. In November 2020 she was assigned the role of co-chair of the Gender Equality and Sexual Diversity Committee at the University of Malta. The main remit of this committee to is to create and ensure the implementation of a gender equality and inclusive strategy for the higher education entity in question.

Index